An Educational Guide
to the
National Park System

by
CAROL SMALLWOOD

The Scarecrow Press, Inc.
Metuchen, N.J., & London
1989

British Library Cataloguing-in-Publication data available

Library of Congress Cataloging-in-Publication Data

Smallwood, Carol, 1939-
    An educational guide to the national park system / by
Carol Smallwood.
        p.   cm.
    Includes index.
    ISBN 0-8108-2137-0
    1. National parks and reserves--United States--Guide-
books. 2. National parks and reserves--United States--
Bibliography. 3. National parks and reserves--United
States--Study and teaching. 4. Subject headings--
National parks and reserves. I. Title.
E160.S63   1989   88-21639
016.363.6'8'0973--dc19

To Gordon Turner

News Editor, <u>Cheboygan Daily Tribune</u>

CONTENTS

MISSION CHURCHES

MOUNTAINS

NATIVE AMERICAN CULTURE

NATIONAL BRIDGES

PARKWAYS

PERFORMING ARTS

PRESIDENTS

RAILROADS

RECREATION

REVOLUTIONARY PERIOD

ROCK FORMATIONS

VOLCANOES

WAR OF 1812

WESTERN EXPANSION

WILDERNESS

WOMEN

WORLD WAR II AND VIETNAMESE CONFLICT

INTRODUCTION

The U.S. Department of the Interior has responsibility for most of our nationally owned public lands and natural resources. It encourages the best use of land and water, protects fish and wildlife, preserves the environmental and cultural values of the national parks and historical places, and provides outdoor recreation. It assesses energy and mineral resources and works to assure that development is in the best interest of the country. It also has a major responsibility for American Indian reservations and island territories under U.S. administration. An Educational Guide to the National Park System deals with the National Park Service, a bureau of the U.S. Department of the Interior.

In 1872 Congress established Yellowstone National Park and began a worldwide national park movement. In 1916 Congress established the National Park Service: "The Service thus established shall promote and regulate the use of the federal areas known as national parks, monuments and reservations ... by such means and measures as conform to the fundamental purpose of the said parks, monuments and reservations, which purpose is to conserve the scenery and the national and historic objects and the wild life therein and to provide for the enjoyment of the same in such manner and by such means as will leave them unimpaired for the enjoyment of future generations."

In 1933, an Executive Order transferred national monuments and military sites from the Forest Service and War Department to the National Park Service. In 1970 the General Authorities Act stated "that the National Park System, which began with the establishment of Yellowstone National Park in 1872, has since grown to include superlative natural, historic, and recreational areas in every region ... and that it is the purpose of this act to include all such areas in the system...."

National Park additions now are generally made through acts of Congress but the President has authority, under the Antiquities Act of 1906, to proclaim national monuments on lands that are under federal rule. Congress usually asks the Secretary of the Interior for recommendations on proposed park additions. The Secretary is guided by the National Park System Advisory Board made up of private citizens.

Affiliated areas included in this guide comprise properties that preserve significant facilities outside the national park system. Some have been recognized by acts of Congress while others have been designated National Historic Sites by the Secretary of the Interior. They draw technical or financial aid from the National Park Service.

Wild and Scenic Rivers System provides access to free-flowing streams for public use and enjoyment. Those that are units of The National Park Service are included in An Educational Guide to the National Park System, while the rest are omitted even if they received planning aid from the National Park Service because it was judged they would have less interest for educators. They are included in the classification listing with addresses, however.

National Trails System Act provides for establishing trails and is administered by the National Park Service. This Guide includes trails that have National Park Service addresses. Names and addresses for those not appearing in the Guide are found in the last section of the classification listing.

Facilities are included in this guide only if found in the most recent The National Parks Index produced by the Office of Public Affairs and the Division of Publications, National Park Service. This Guide is based on materials received from National Park Service facilities. An Educational Guide to the National Park System may be used in various ways. It may be used as a reference book for information on how many acres a facility has, features, when it was established and the like. It may be used as a source for materials as sales lists are included as well as audiovisual lists. It may be used as a directory for information on facilities by State, telephone numbers, type of facility, and related park findings. It may be an organizational aid with its suggested curriculum areas and Sears subject headings.

Books, maps, and a wide variety of material are usually on sale at on-site locations. Many features listed in the Guide are seasonal or limited in operation during winter months, so it is well to inquire about weather conditions which differ year to year and access roads may be closed. It is necessary in many facilities to make reservations for groups. Fees are not included; they change rapidly and are usually minimal. Inquire about fee waivers for educational use of a facility. Programs and materials may have been added or changed since this Guide was compiled.

Park facility materials give students a sense of relevancy and continuing history. For example, material about the Lewis and Clark Trail makes history come alive with current photos and maps. Material from the home of Eugene O'Neill gives added interest to his dramatic works. Audiovisual lists and sales lists offer a variety of educational material usually not found elsewhere. A few examples of sales items are: prairie seed mix, nose flutes, coal tar soap, Henry

Wadsworth Longfellow notecards featuring his poems with pictures, "gold" nuggets, sourdough bread starter packet, mini-planisphere, and a teacher's guide on Lincoln. Such materials as State maps, local museum guides, historic State sites' information, are included in this guide when sent from the facility if materials provided sufficient educational interest.

Features of facilities were selected with educational purposes in mind. Such activities as hunting, fishing, photography are not included. There is a wide variety of material available from facilities. Some issue complete teaching packets, audiovisual lists, bibliographies, student visiting guides, sales lists and other printed materials, while others offer a basic brochure.

Materials on one person may be gathered together. For example, for Lincoln's birthday, materials from the various facilities featuring Lincoln: Abraham Lincoln Birthplace, Lincoln Boyhood National Monument, Lincoln Home National Historic Site, Lincoln Memorial, Ford's Theatre National Historic Site. Bulletin Board displays featuring facilities of a State during observance of that State's week would be another idea. For example, Michigan Week, which is annually observed in May, could feature displays from Sleeping Bear Dunes National Lakeshore, or Isle Royale National Park; the following year could feature Pictured Rocks National Lakeshore, etc.

The 328 facilities are grouped under 47 subject headings, by major emphasis of the facility, in categories from "Architecture" to "World War II and Vietnamese Conflict."

Entries are arranged by: name, type of facility, address, telephone, acreage, year authorized or established, location, purpose, features of interest, visitor accommodations, free print material, Bibliography, Sales List, Audiovisual List, Sales/Audiovisual List, suggested curriculum application, suggested Sears subject heading. (Those sections underlined appear when there is such material.)

In assigning suggested curriculum application and Sears subject headings it is hoped that a general application was achieved. Selection was limited by my own experience and application will be based on each librarian's or teacher's need.

Audiovisuals are defined as materials requiring hardware, such as a film projector. Some examples of audiovisual titles are: "Cold Water Can Kill," "George Washington Birthplace," and "Life of a Tree." Request lists for complete postage/handling information for sales and audiovisuals. Some examples of books for sale are American Folk Toys, Around the Shores of Lake Superior, and A Field Guide to Birds Coloring Book. Sears subject headings are included for librarians. Suggested curriculum use is based on the main purpose of the facility, services, and materials.

Curriculum Suggestions:

(STATE THAT APPLIES)--STATE AND LOCAL STUDIES
AGRICULTURE--FARMING ISSUES
AMERICAN HISTORY--PAST EVENTS IN UNITED STATES
ARCHEOLOGY--EXCAVATIONS, RUINS OF PREHISTORIC CULTURES
ART--ARCHITECTURE, ARTS AND CRAFTS, SCULPTURE
BLACK STUDIES--FAMOUS BLACK PEOPLE, BLACK ISSUES
CLOTHING--CLOTHES AS PERIOD PIECES
ENGLISH--LITERATURE, JOURNALISM
ENVIRONMENTAL EDUCATION--CONSERVATION, LAND USE
GEOGRAPHY--PHYSICAL FEATURES OF THE UNITED STATES
GEOLOGY--FOSSILS, CAVES, VOLCANOES, ROCKS
GOVERNMENT--AMERICAN PRESIDENTS
INDUSTRIAL ARTS--IRON MAKING
NATIVE AMERICAN STUDIES--AMERICAN INDIAN ISSUES
NATURAL HISTORY--BIRDS, PLANTS, ANIMALS
PERFORMING ARTS--DANCE, THEATER, MUSIC
RECREATION--HIKING, SKIING, FIRST AID, WATER SPORTS
SCIENCE--PHYSICAL SCIENCE
SOCIAL STUDIES--COMMUNITY LIVING, BRIDGES, TRANSPORTATION
WOMEN'S STUDIES--FAMOUS WOMEN, WOMEN'S ISSUES

Suggested subject headings were based on what was perceived
as the main subject emphasis. Some of the most commonly used
Sears subject headings are:

(STATE THAT APPLIES)--DESCRIPTION AND TRAVEL--GUIDES
AMERICA--EXPLORATION
ARCHITECTURE--CONSERVATION AND RESTORATION
BLACKS--BIOGRAPHY
CAVES
FORTIFICATION
FOSSILS
FRONTIER AND PIONEER LIFE
GEOLOGY--U.S.
GLACIERS
INDIANS OF NORTH AMERICA--HISTORY
ISLANDS
LAKES
MOUNTAINS
NATIONAL PARKS AND PRESERVES--U.S.
NATURAL HISTORY--(STATE THAT APPLIES)
OUTDOOR RECREATION
OVERLAND JOURNEYS TO THE PACIFIC (U.S.)
PRESIDENTS--U.S.
PUBLIC LANDS--(STATE THAT APPLIES)
RIVERS
TREES--U.S.
U.S.--DESCRIPTION AND TRAVEL--GUIDES

U.S.--GEOGRAPHY
U.S.--HISTORY--CIVIL WAR, 1861-1865
U.S.--HISTORY--COLONIAL PERIOD, 1600-1775
U.S.--HISTORY--REVOLUTION, 1775-1783
VOLCANOES
WILDERNESS AREAS
WOMEN--U.S.

Some facilities have Spanish or French language publications with information about respective heritages that French/Spanish teachers would find helpful. For example, a pamphlet included in Saint Croix Island International Historic Site on page 59 is printed in French/English about French colonization of Maine.

In the back matter, facilities are grouped by type, such as National Historical Park. Facilities are grouped by the State they use as a mailing address. Facilities are alphabetically arranged by facility name in the Index.

Addresses for entries in the Guide as well as those few that do not appear in the Guide are included in the State grouping. In the few cases that a facility was not included as a Guide entry, it means that one of the following reasons applies: the facility has limited or no federal facilities, the facility was not yet open to the public when the Guide was compiled, no response was received, or it did not have materials educators would commonly use. Addresses are mailing addresses--in most cases also the location, but in a few cases the location is different and is indicated in the "Location" section.

I would like to acknowledge the support and patience of my 17-year-old daughter, Ann, and my 19-year-old son, Mike, in this project. I wish to thank Martin Cohen, Professor Emeritus, School of Librarianship, Western Michigan University, for inspiring appreciation of government publications, and Randal L. Smith, proofreader.

GLOSSARY

The sites within the National Park System provide great variety. Sites usually offer a visitor center where you may see films and exhibits and obtain answers to your questions.

National Battlefield Park: Area associated with American military history.

National Battlefield Site: Area associated with American military history.

National Historic Sites: The name most commonly used by Congress in authorizing the addition of such areas to the National Park System.

National Historical Park: Usually areas of greater physical extent and complexity than National Historic Sites.

National Lakeshores: Preserves while providing recreation. Can be established on any natural freshwater lake.

National Memorial: Most often used for areas that are primarily commemorative.

National Military Park: Area associated with American military history.

National Monument: Preserves at least one nationally important resource and is usually smaller than a National Park and lacks diversity.

National Park: Covers a large area and variety of resources; includes enough water or land to ensure adequate protection of the resources.

National Parkways: Ribbons of lands by roadways that allow driving through scenic areas.

National Preserves: Protects certain resources.

National Recreation Areas: Lands and waters set aside for recreational use.

National Scenic Trails: Usually long-distance footpaths passing through places of natural beauty.

National Seashores: Preserves natural value while providing recreation.

Performing Arts: Sites primarily for the performing arts.

ARCHITECTURE

- FREDERICK LAW OLMSTED
National Historic Site. 99 Warren Street. Brookline, MA 02146.
(617) 566-1689. 1.75 acres. 1979. Eastern Massachusetts, 4 miles
from downtown Boston, off Route 9.

Home and work place of "The Father of Landscape Architecture in
America." On-site tours, walking tours of Olmsted-designed landscapes. Over 63,000 photographs and 150,000 drawings and plans
are at the site. Slide program. Group programs require advance
reservations. Inquire about special orientation programs to student
and adult groups. Food and lodging in greater Boston area.

Free Print Material:
  "Frederick Law Olmsted National Historic Site." 4-fold. Life
    and career of Olmsted, collection and legacy of the landscape
    architect.
  "Group Leader Information." 1 page. What the site offers in its
    continuing activities schedule, types of tours and programs.

Sales List:
  "Mail Order List." 3 pages. Books, post cards, workbook,
    papers. Title, description, price. Mail order form, ordering
    directions, purpose of the Eastern National Park and Monu-
    ment Association. Includes materials designed for young
    readers.
  Post Card: "Fairsted." 1894 photograph of Flo's Brookline
    residence (NPS Archive). $.10.

Suggested Curriculum Application:
  ART
  MASSACHUSETTS STATE AND LOCAL STUDIES

Suggested Sears Subject Heading:
  ARCHITECTURE, AMERICAN
  LANDSCAPE ARCHITECTURE
  MASSACHUSETTS--DESCRIPTION AND TRAVEL--GUIDES
  MASSACHUSETTS--PUBLIC LANDS
  OLMSTED, FREDERICK LAW, 1822-1903
  U.S.--DESCRIPTION AND TRAVEL--GUIDES

- HAMPTON

National Historic Site.   535 Hampton Lane, Towson, MD   21204.
(301) 823-7054.   59.44 acres.   1948.   Northcentral Maryland, Accessible from I-695 by exits 27 and 28 north.

Large and ornate mansion built 1783-90, with historic outbuildings,
gardens, trees.   For over 150 years Hampton belonged to the Ridgely
family.   Guided house tours, summer grounds and garden tours, exhibits, seasonal programs.   Advance notice for groups are requested
and special tours may be arranged in advance.   Tearoom serves
luncheon, gift shop, picnicking.   Food and lodging in Towson.

Free Print Material:

"Exterior Tour and On-site Activities."   11 pages.   Descriptions,
sketches of buildings, grounds and their evolution through six
generations of Ridgely family occupancy.

"Gardens and Grounds."   16-fold.   History and development of
the mansion and grounds, narrative walking tour.   Photos,
sketch, maps.   Hours of grounds and mansion, how to get to
Hampton.

"Hampton."   18 pages.   Ridgely family history, development and
preservation of "Hampton."   Sketches, photos.

"Interior Tours and On-site Activities."   5 pages.   Energy comparison chart of farm life 1790's-1865 and present-day life,
questions about the great hall, music room, and other rooms,
follow-up questions, energy requirements yesterday and today.

"Leaf Identification--Teacher's Guide."   4 pages.   Student activity suggestions, 3 pages of leaf sketches.

"National Park Service Travel Tips."   8-fold.   What the National
Park System offers, selecting park areas to visit, making
reservations and other visitor information.

"National Parks of the United States Guide and Map."   30-fold.
Guide to facilities arranged by state.   Maps.   Name, address,
telephone of regional offices of the National Park Service.

"Post Visit Material."   10 pages.   Evaluation of Hampton field
trip, post activities, crossword puzzles, word search, creative
writing suggestions, sketch.

"Pre-visit Material."   5 pages.   Area history, vocabulary enrich-
ment, suggested pre-visit activity.

"Teachers' Guide."   8 pages.   Pre-visit manual for grades 7-12.
Includes such information as what to expect from a visit,
general instructions for a visit, tours and other information.
Sketches.

"A Walking Tour of Hampton's Grounds."   10 pages.   To acquaint
the visitor with some of the more distinguished plantings at
Hampton, along with descriptions of the buildings seen along
the garden walk and driveways.   People involved with the development of the gardens.   Sketches.

Audiovisual List:

Information about a slide/tape program for classroom use is included in "Pre-visit Material" described above.

Suggested Curriculum Application:
ART
AMERICAN HISTORY
MARYLAND STATE AND LOCAL STUDIES

Suggested Sears Subject Heading:
ARCHITECTURE--CONSERVATION AND RESTORATION
LANDSCAPE GARDENING
MARYLAND--DESCRIPTION AND TRAVEL--GUIDES
MARYLAND--HISTORY
MARYLAND--PUBLIC LANDS
U.S.--DESCRIPTION AND TRAVEL--GUIDES

- OLD POST OFFICE TOWER
c/o National Capital Parks--Central. 900 Ohio Drive, S.W., Washington, D.C. 20242. (202) 523-5691. The tower is part of a larger building. 1983. Nancy Hanks Center, corner of 12th and Pennsylvania Avenue, N.W., Washington, D.C.

315-foot clock tower, second tallest only to the Washington Monument in Washington. Part of Post Office building constructed in 1899, the tower hosts 10 large congress bells. Tours provide scenic vista of Washington, view of the congress bells, rangers provide information on the tower's history. Inquire if the observation deck is open as when this was being compiled it was being repaired and tours were only being provided to the bell level. Due to the small elevators, ten visitors are accommodated at a time. The first two floors have many restaurants and shops. Food and lodging in Washington, D.C.

Free Print Material:
"Nancy Hanks Center: The Old Post Office." 8-fold. The efforts to save the Old Post Office building, photos, Cooperative Use Act of 1976, accomplishments of Nancy Hanks, sketches, current public use.
"Old Post Office Tower." 8-fold. Construction and use of the Old Post Office building, the use of the congress bells (that range in weight from 581 to 2953 pounds), photos, contributions of Nancy Hanks, efforts to save the Old Post Office, chronology of events beginning with 1890 when the site was selected and congressional committee drafted the bill for purchase.

Suggested Curriculum Application:
DISTRICT OF COLUMBIA LOCAL STUDIES
GOVERNMENT

Suggested Sears Subject Heading:
ARCHITECTURE--CONSERVATION AND RESTORATION
BELLS

DISTRICT OF COLUMBIA--DESCRIPTION AND TRAVEL--GUIDES
DISTRICT OF COLUMBIA--PUBLIC LANDS
U.S.--DESCRIPTION AND TRAVEL--GUIDES
WASHINGTON, DC--HISTORIC BUILDINGS, ETC.
WASHINGTON, DC--HISTORY

- TOURO SYNAGOGUE
National Historic Site. 85 Touro Street, Newport, RI 02840.
(401) 847-4794. 0.23 acres. 1946. Eastern Rhode Island.

Colonial religious architecture, still used as a place of worship.
Tours at certain times of the synagogue. Old burial ground in which
many men who were important in the development of the synagogue
are buried. Check ahead about when synagogue is open to visitors.
Food and lodging in Newport.

Free Print Material:
"Touro Synagogue." 12-fold. Sketches, photos, map, history of
the small synagogue and background on the architect, Peter
Harrison.

Suggested Curriculum Application:
AMERICAN HISTORY
RHODE ISLAND STATE AND LOCAL STUDIES

Suggested Sears Subject Heading:
ARCHITECTURE--CONSERVATION AND RESTORATION
RHODE ISLAND--DESCRIPTION AND TRAVEL--GUIDES
SYNAGOGUES
U.S.--DESCRIPTION AND TRAVEL--GUIDES

- VANDERBILT MANSION
National Historic Site. 249 Albany Post Road, Bellfield Headquarters,
Hyde Park, NY 12538. (914) 229-9115. 211.65 acres. 1940.
Eastern New York, 6 miles north of Poughkeepsie, on U.S. 9. North
of the village of Hyde Park in the Hudson Valley.

Example of a Hudson Valley home built by 19th-century millionaires.
The 54-room mansion was built by Frederick W. Vanderbilt, Cor-
nelius Vanderbilt's grandson. Tour of the mansion and grounds,
exhibits, audiovisual program, scenic views of the Hudson and surrounding countryside. Visitor center. Food and lodging nearby.

Free Print Material:
"Vanderbilt Mansion." 16-fold. Location, hours, administration,
photos, floor plans, tour guide to the mansion.

Suggested Curriculum Application:
AMERICAN HISTORY

ART
NEW YORK STATE AND LOCAL STUDIES

Suggested Sears Subject Heading:
ARCHITECTURE--CONSERVATION AND RESTORATION
MILLIONAIRES
NEW YORK--DESCRIPTION AND TRAVEL--GUIDES
NEW YORK--PUBLIC LANDS
U.S.--DESCRIPTION AND TRAVEL--GUIDES

AUTHORS

- CARL SANDBURG HOME
National Historic Site. P.O. Box 395, Flat Rock, NC 28731.
(704) 693-4178. 263.52 acres. 1968. Southern North Carolina,
26 miles south of Asheville, off of U.S. 25.

Farm home for the last 22 years of Carl Sandburg: poet, newspaperman, biographer, autobiographer, fiction writer, folk singer. Exhibits, guided tour, self-guided tour of the grounds, farm animals,
gardens, barns and various buildings, programs. Visitor center,
picnicking. Food and lodging in Hendersonville.

Free Print Material:
"Carl Sandburg Home." 8-fold. Photos, map, grounds tour,
biographical sketch, visitor information.
"A Guide for Young Readers from the Carl Sandburg Collection
Development Project." 8-fold. Carl Sandburg the poet, the
newspaperman, biographer, autobiographer, fiction writer,
folk singer. Description and activities. List of books by
Sandburg. (Teachers may reproduce the guide for classroom
use.)
"Parks for America." 16-fold. Photos, sketches, description
of the variety of areas within the National Park System,
history, development.

Bibliography:
Included in "A Guide for Young Readers from the Carl Sandburg
Collection Development Project." Grouped by: Sandburg cen-
tennial publications, adult books, children's books.

Sales/Audiovisual List:
"Eastern National Park and Monument Association Mail Order
Catalog." 4 pages. Arranged by: hardbacks, paperbacks,
cassettes, records, related items. Ordering information, aims
of the association. Title, author, unit price, with blanks for

indicating quantity and price.
"Abraham Lincoln." 1 vol. edition, Carl Sandburg, $39.95.

Suggested Curriculum Application:
ENGLISH
NORTH CAROLINA STATE AND LOCAL STUDIES

Suggested Sears Subject Heading:
AMERICAN LITERATURE
NORTH CAROLINA--DESCRIPTION AND TRAVEL--GUIDES
NORTH CAROLINA--PUBLIC LANDS
SANDBURG, CARL, 1878-1967
U.S.--DESCRIPTION AND TRAVEL--GUIDES

* EDGAR ALLAN POE
National Historic Site. c/o Independence National Historical Park.
313 Walnut Street, Philadelphia, PA 19106. (215) 597-8780. 0.52
acres. 1978. Eastern Pennsylvania, 532 North Seventh Street, six
blocks north of Market St., in Philadelphia.

Home of Edgar Allan Poe, the well-known poet, critic, author,
and editor, during 1843-44. House tours, exhibits, audiovisual
program, garden. Groups should make arrangements in advance.
Visitor center, picnicking. Food and lodging in Philadelphia.

Free Print Material:
  "Chronology of Edgar Allan Poe." 1 page. Dates, events in his
    life, selected works, beginning with his birth in 1809 to his
    death in 1849.
  "Edgar Allan Poe." 8-fold. Biographical Sketch, photos, visitor
    information, the importance and influence of Poe, descriptions
    and photos of other sites honoring Poe.

Bibliography:
  "Reference Books." 1 page. Author, title, place of publication,
    publisher, date of recommended books for further information
    or research about Edgar Allan Poe.

Sales/Audiovisual List:
  "Sales Items--Mail Order." 3 pages. Grouped by: Edgar Allan
    Poe's works, works by Poe designed for children, three il-
    lustrated classics by Poe, biography and criticism, related
    subjects, cassette tapes, Poe's contemporaries framing post
    cards, Poe's Philadelphia framing post cards, National Park
    Service. Also includes documents, replica of the "The Black
    Cat," Poe cachet-postal cancelled on the 100th anniversary of
    his death, Poe post cards. Ordering instructions.
  "Complete Poetry and Selected Criticism of Poe." Ed. A. Tate.
    New York: New American Library, 1981. $7.95.

Suggested Curriculum Application:
ENGLISH
PENNSYLVANIA STATE AND LOCAL STUDIES

Suggested Sears Subject Heading:
AMERICAN LITERATURE
AUTHORS, AMERICAN
PENNSYLVANIA--DESCRIPTION AND TRAVEL--GUIDES
PENNSYLVANIA--PUBLIC LANDS
POE, EDGAR ALLAN, 1809-1849
U.S.--DESCRIPTION AND TRAVEL--GUIDES

• EUGENE O'NEILL
National Historic Site. 4202 Alhambra Avenue, Martinez, CA 94553.
(415) 838-0249. 13.19 acres. 1976. Western California, 26 miles
east of downtown San Francisco, on the west side of Danville, from
Interstate 680.

Built for Eugene O'Neill, Tao house was the playwright's home 1937-
1944. Visits are by reservation only. Guided tours of Tao house,
self-guiding tours of the grounds. The park has a volunteer in the
park program, a slide show and a speaker available upon request.
The site is available for special activities, such as meetings, upon
approval from the park superintendent. Visitor center. Only public access permitted is by a van and tours are by reservation by
calling the telephone previously listed. Food and lodging in San
Francisco.

Free Print Material:
"Eugene O'Neill." 8-fold. Description of Tao house, biographical
sketch, quotations from "Lazarus Laughed" and "Long Day's
Journey into Night," photos, visitor information.
"Homes of Eugene O'Neill." 3 pages. Date, name, location of
various places of O'Neill's residence.
"Visitor Information." 2 pages. Location, access, hours of operation, programs offered, safety concerns, special activities,
size and facilities, map.

Bibliography:
"Check-list of Works and Dates Important to the Study of Eugene
O'Neill." 3 pages. Arranged by: works by Eugene O'Neill
(title, place of publication, date), works about Eugene O'Neill
(author, title, place of publication, date). Includes unpub-
lished works available on microfilm or Xerox copies in the
Bancroft Library of the University of California.

Sales List:
"Sales List." 2 pages. Title, price. Includes books, calendar,
brochure, post cards, stamps, booklet.
"Ah, Wilderness." $4.75.

Suggested Curriculum Application:
ENGLISH
CALIFORNIA STATE AND LOCAL STUDIES

Suggested Sears Subject Heading:
AMERICAN LITERATURE
CALIFORNIA--DESCRIPTION AND TRAVEL--GUIDES
CALIFORNIA--PUBLIC LANDS
DRAMATISTS, AMERICAN
O'NEILL, EUGENE, 1888-1953
U.S.--DESCRIPTION AND TRAVEL--GUIDES

• LONGFELLOW
National Historic Site. 105 Brattle St., Cambridge, MA 92138.
(617) 876-4491. 1.98 acres. 1972. Eastern Massachusetts.

The poet, Henry Wadsworth Longfellow lived here from 1837 to 1882.
The house, built in 1759, was Washington's headquarters during
1775-76. Tours through the house and grounds. Call about group
tours. Summer classical musical concert series and poetry readings.
Contact the park ranger about school programs. School groups may
eat their lunch in the garden. Meals and lodging in Cambridge and
greater Boston area.

Free Print Material:
"Educational Programs." 1 page. Descriptions of programs that
    are adaptable in terms of length, curriculum needs, suitability
    for age groups.
"Henry W. Longfellow." 12-fold. "Longfellow's friends, family
    life. Photos, map.
"Longfellow Garden Concert Series." 4 pages. Quotations by
    Longfellow concerning music, music he enjoyed, history of
    Longfellow's house.
"Longfellow's Garden." 3-fold. Sketches and names of various
    flowers and plants. Words of his favorite quote appearing on
    his garden sundial, garden layout.
"Significance." 3 pages. Why the home of Longfellow is impor-
    tant, history, themes to consider, visitor tips.

Sales/Audiovisual List:
"Sales Items Available at the Longfellow National Historic Site
    Cambridge, Massachusetts." 6 pages. Grouped by: poetry
    publications; versefolders; other publications; post cards;
    children's books and other items. Order form.
"Henry Wadsworth Longfellow--Selected Poems"--with illustrations.
    Peter Pauper Press, Hardcover, 63 pages, 25 poems--includes
    "Psalm of Life," "Children's Hour," "The Fire of Driftwood,"
    $4.95.

Suggested Curriculum Application:
ENGLISH
MASSACHUSETTS STATE AND LOCAL STUDIES

Suggested Sears Subject Heading:
AMERICAN LITERATURE
MASSACHUSETTS--DESCRIPTION AND TRAVEL--GUIDES
MASSACHUSETTS--PUBLIC LANDS
POETS, AMERICAN
U.S.--DESCRIPTION AND TRAVEL--GUIDES

BLACKS

- BOOKER T. WASHINGTON
National Monument. Route 1, Box 195, Hardy, VA 24101. (703)
721-2094. 223.92 acres. 1956. Central Virginia, 20 miles southeast
of Roanoke, 16 miles northwest of Rocky Mount on VA 122N.

Preserve Washington's birthplace and boyhood home. Recreate
plantation life. Demonstrations, farm animals and crops and other
plantation recreations, trails, education and cultural center, group
tours, program information, exhibits, slide program. Inquire about
available educational services. Visitor center, picnic area. Campgrounds nearby. Meals and lodging in Bedford, Roanoke and Rocky
Mount.

Free Print Material:
  "Booker T. Washington." 20-fold. What the monument has to
    offer, biographical background, sketches, map.
  "Booker T. Washington National Monument, Hardy, Virginia."
    2 pages. Location, description, visitor facilities, other ser-
    vices.

Sales/Audiovisual List:
  "ENP&MA [Eastern National Parks & Monument Assn.] Price List."
    2 pages. Items arranged alphabetically by title. Includes
    books, puzzles, records, stamps, coloring books, maps, post-
    cards and other items.
  "Audubon Wildflower Field Guide." $13.50.
  "Free-loan Film Information." 1 page. Description of available
    films, booking and user information.
  "What's a Heaven For?" (1966). 16mm. Color/sound. 17 min.
    This film depicts the life and accomplishments of Booker T.
    Washington. Featured are: his beginnings as a slave born
    in 1856; the difficulties he faced in obtaining an education;
    his founding of Tuskegee Institute; his becoming the most in-
    fluential black man of his time.

Suggested Curriculum Application:
  AMERICAN HISTORY
  BLACK STUDIES
  VIRGINIA STATE AND LOCAL STUDIES

Suggested Sears Subject Heading:
  ARCHITECTURE--CONSERVATION AND RESTORATION
  BLACKS--BIOGRAPHY
  U.S.--DESCRIPTION AND TRAVEL--GUIDES
  VIRGINIA--DESCRIPTION AND TRAVEL--GUIDES
  VIRGINIA--PUBLIC LANDS
  WASHINGTON, BOOKER T., 1856-1915

• BOSTON AFRICAN AMERICAN
National Historic Site. 46 Joy St., Boston, MA 02114. (617)
742-5415. 1980. Eastern Massachusetts. Visitor center is at 15
State Street about a 15-minute walk from the African Meeting House
on Beacon Hill, Boston.

Preserve pre-Civil War Black historic structures and properties of
outstanding national significance. Twelve are private residences
not open to the public but may be viewed from the outside aided by
trail markers. There are two public buildings and one public structure. African Meeting House, George Middleton House, Charles
Street Meeting House, Smith Court Residences, Abiel Smith School,
John J. Smith House, 54th Regiment Memorial, Phillips School, Lewis
and Harriet Hayden House, Coburn's Gaming House. Self-guided
walk along the Black Heritage Trail has trail markers, historical and
cultural traveling exhibits, ranger talks, film, concerts, conferences.
Visitor center. Food and lodging in Boston.

Free Print Material:
  "Black Heritage Trail." 12 pages. Photos, chart, map. Descrip-
      tion of the Black Heritage Trail that is a walking tour explor-
      ing the history of Boston's 19th-century black community, a
      neighborhood now called the North Slope of Beacon Hill.
  "Boston African American National Historic Site." 6-fold. Des-
      cription, list of Black Heritage Trail attractions.
  "The North Star." 8 pages. Sketches, map, prepaid page for
      comments to clip and mail, restoration plans. A planning bul-
      letin to make people aware of the site and plans, to involve
      people, to keep people informed about upcoming activities.

Bibliography:
  "Collection of Afro-American Literature." 15 pages. Issued since
      1971 by Suffolk University and the Museum of Afro-American
      History and in 1981 the newly established Boston African
      American National Historic Site joined the project. This is a
      list of acquisitions published annually. It is arranged by
      Library of Congress call numbers, beginning with reference

works and followed by works according to subject and author.
McDonnell, Robert W. "The Papers of W.E.B. Du Bois: 1803
(1877-1963) 1979." Sanford, NC: Microfilming Corporation of
America. REF E 185.97 .D73 A3 X, 1980 Guide.

Sales List:
Description of a bibliography for sale is included in "Collection of
Afro-American Literature" described above.

Suggested Curriculum Application:
AMERICAN HISTORY
BLACK STUDIES
MASSACHUSETTS STATE AND LOCAL STUDIES

Suggested Sears Subject Heading:
ARCHITECTURE--CONSERVATION AND RESTORATION
BLACKS--BOSTON
MASSACHUSETTS--BUILDINGS
MASSACHUSETTS--DESCRIPTION AND TRAVEL--GUIDES
MASSACHUSETTS--PUBLIC LANDS
U.S.--DESCRIPTION AND TRAVEL--GUIDES

• FREDERICK DOUGLASS HOME
National Capital Parks--East. 1900 Anacostia Drive S.E., Washing-
ton, D.C. 20020. (202) 426-5960. 8.08 acres. 1962. District of
Columbia, 1411 W. Street S.E., in Washington, D.C.

Preserve Cedar Hill, restored home of 19th-century black orator,
writer, abolitionist, antislavery editor. Exhibits, sales area, audiovisual program, guided home tours through the restored home and
furnishings. Visitor center. Food and lodging in D.C. area.

Free Print Material:
"Frederick Douglass Home." 8-fold. Chronology, photos, accomplishments and life, sketches.

Bibliography:
"Reading About Frederick Douglass, A Selection." 1 page.
Grouped by: his own works, books about him, for children.
Title, place of publication, publishers, date, grade level for
children's books.
"Narrative of the Life of Frederick Douglass." Boston, 1845;
reprinted with Quarles, Benjamin, ed. Cambridge: Harvard
University Press, 1960.

Suggested Curriculum Application:
AMERICAN HISTORY
BLACK STUDIES
DISTRICT OF COLUMBIA STATE AND LOCAL STUDIES

Suggested Sears Subject Heading:
ABOLITIONISTS
BLACKS--BIOGRAPHY
DISTRICT OF COLUMBIA--GUIDES
DISTRICT OF COLUMBIA--PUBLIC LANDS
DOUGLASS, FREDERICK, 1818-1895
SLAVERY IN THE U.S.
U.S.--DESCRIPTION AND TRAVEL--GUIDES

- GEORGE WASHINGTON CARVER
National Monument. Diamond, MO 64840. (417) 325-4151. 210
acres. 1943. Southwestern Missouri, three miles from Diamond,
Interstate 44 is nine miles north of Diamond.

Site of birthplace, home, landmarks of the famous black scientist,
Carver as a child. Carver family graves, springs and pond, grove
of trees, self-guiding trail, birthplace cabin, museum, film, statue.
Some weekends offer special film series and historical tours. Ranger-
guided tours for groups upon 4-6 weeks advance notification.
Visitor center, picnicking area. Food and lodging in Diamond,
Joplin.

Free Print Material:
"George Washington Carver." 8-fold. Biographical material and
features of the national monument. Photos follow Carver's
career, map of Carver's birthplace and nearby area.
"George Washington Carver National Monument Map." 1 page.
Map shows main roads leading to Diamond and the location of
the monument to Carver. Information on museum and Carver
film.
"George Washington Carver National Monument." 1 page. Location, description, hours, reservations and other visitor information.
"George Washington Carver National Monument Planning and Information Packet." 16 pages. Autobiographical and biographical information, list of by-products from peanuts and list of
products made from sweet potatoes by Carver, bulletins by
Carver, planning information for educators.

Bibliography:
Number, date, title of "Bulletins by George Washington Carver"
appears in "George Washington Carver National Monument
Planning and Information Packet" described above.

Sales/Audiovisual List:
Included in "George Washington Carver National Monument Planning and Information Packet" described in the previous entry,
on pages 13-14. Publications and souvenirs listed include
books, postcards, T-shirts, "Carver: Man of Vision" VHS
video tape, prairie seeds, stationery, a Carver poster and

speech. Order form.
"Carver of Tuskegee" by Ethel Edwards. $2.75.

Suggested Curriculum Application:
    AGRICULTURE
    AMERICAN HISTORY
    BLACK STUDIES
    MISSOURI STATE AND LOCAL STUDIES

Suggested Sears Subject Heading:
    AGRICULTURE--RESEARCH
    BLACKS--BIOGRAPHY
    CARVER, GEORGE WASHINGTON, 1864-1943
    MISSOURI--DESCRIPTION AND TRAVEL--GUIDES
    MISSOURI--PUBLIC LANDS
    U.S.--DESCRIPTION AND TRAVEL--GUIDES

• MARTIN LUTHER KING, JR.
National Historic Site. 522 Auburn Avenue, N.E., Atlanta, GA
30312. (Limited Federal Facilities). 23.16 acres. 1980. Central
Georgia.

Birthplace, church, grave of Dr. Martin Luther King, Jr.
Ebenezer Baptist Church, Martin Luther King, Jr. birth home,
Freedom Hall complex includes King's gravesite. Visitor center
planning is underway. Food and lodging in Atlanta.

Free Print Material:
    "Litter-ally Speaking...." 2 pages. Litter and what it costs
       Americans.
    "Martin Luther King, Jr." 16-fold. Photos, sketches, map.
       Landmarks and sites, the life and dream of Martin Luther King,
       Jr., various quotations by King.
    "The National Parks and the Bicentennial of the United States
       Constitution." 12-fold. The making of the Constitution,
       national park sites connected with America's experiment in self-
       government, photos.

Suggested Curriculum Application:
    AMERICAN HISTORY
    BLACK STUDIES
    GEORGIA STATE AND LOCAL STUDIES

Suggested Sears Subject Heading:
    BLACKS--CIVIL RIGHTS
    GEORGIA--DESCRIPTION AND TRAVEL--GUIDES
    GEORGIA--PUBLIC LANDS
    KING, MARTIN LUTHER, 1929-1968
    U.S.--DESCRIPTION AND TRAVEL--GUIDES

- TUSKEGEE INSTITUTE

National Historic Site. P.O. Drawer 10, Tuskegee Institute, AL
36088. (205) 727-3200. 74.39 acres. 1977. Central Alabama, near
the city of Tuskegee, on State Route 126.

Commemorate Booker T. Washington's work. Includes Washington's
home, museum, college. Guided tours of The Oaks, home of Booker
T. Washington. George Washington Carver Museum. Self-guiding
tours of historic campus district, audiovisuals, antebellum mansion,
nature trail. Visitor center. Camping within 15 miles. Food and
lodging on the campus during regular academic times and in the city
of Tuskegee.

Free Print Material:
   "George Washington Carver Museum." 2 pages. Contributions of
      Carver and description of the museum and contents.
   "The Oaks--Home of Booker T. Washington." 2 pages. Bio-
      graphical information, description of The Oaks.
   "Tuskegee Institute." 16-fold. Visitor information, map, photos,
      background on Washington, Carver and the Institute.

Sales List:
   "Eastern National Park & Monument Association." 2 pages. Items
      arranged under: history, children's, other.
   "Booker T. Washington: the making of a black leader, 1856-1901."
      $19.95 hardcover.

Audiovisual List:
   "Audiovisual Materials Available for Loan." 3 pages. Description
      of 16 films and slide programs.
   "Greenhouse"--11 minutes, color, 1973. Purpose: to develop a
      respect for the feelings, rights and property of others, and
      build a sense of responsibility for one's actions. This film
      ties nicely into Dr. Carver's love of plants and the greenhouse
      that he had at the Carver Museum.

Suggested Curriculum Application:
   ALABAMA STATE AND LOCAL STUDIES
   AMERICAN HISTORY
   BLACK STUDIES
   SCIENCE

Suggested Sears Subject Heading:
   ALABAMA--DESCRIPTION AND TRAVEL
   ALABAMA--HISTORY
   ALABAMA--PUBLIC LANDS
   BLACKS
   CARVER, GEORGE WASHINGTON, 1864-1943
   COLLEGES AND UNIVERSITIES
   TUSKEGEE INSTITUTE
   U.S.--DESCRIPTION AND TRAVEL--GUIDES
   WASHINGTON, BOOKER T., 1859-1915

CANALS

- C & O CANAL
National Historical Park. P.O. Box 4, Sharpsburg, MD 21782.
(301) 739-4200. 20,781 acres. 1971. Maryland, District of Columbia, West Virginia. Along the route of the 184-mile canal along the Potomac River between Washington, D.C. and Cumberland, MD.

Follows the route of the canal that was built between 1828 and 1850, the waterway to the West. Hiking, conducted walks, canal and towpath, programs, bicycling, boating. Visitor center, camping, picnicking. Food available at stores along various access roads. Food and lodging nearby.

Free Print Material:
"Calendar of Events." 1 page. Dates, hours, events.
"Chesapeake & Ohio Canal." 32-fold. History of canal construction, recreation today for the visitor along the canal, map, photos.
"Geology and Engineering, Chesapeake and Ohio Canal Spring Gap to Cumberland." 5 pages. Geological study, chart, bibliography.
"Great Falls Tavern." 2 pages. History of the tavern which became the park's main visitor center.
"Teacher Aids." 18 pages. History, canal operation, boats, mules. Pre-visit activities, puzzles, sketches.
"Visitor Information." 18 pages. Packet is designed to answer any questions about the various activities in the park.

Sales List:
"Publications." 1 page. Grouped by: trail guides, miscellaneous. Ordering information. Boy Scouts of America, "184 Miles of Adventures, Hiker's Guide to the C&O Canal, 1977." Cost: $1.75. (Contains brief historical highlights of the entire canal.)

Suggested Curriculum Application:
DISTRICT OF COLUMBIA STATE AND LOCAL STUDIES
MARYLAND STATE AND LOCAL STUDIES
SOCIAL STUDIES
WEST VIRGINIA STATE AND LOCAL STUDIES

Suggested Sears Subject Heading:
C & O CANAL
CANALS
DISTRICT OF COLUMBIA--PUBLIC LANDS
DISTRICT OF COLUMBIA--DESCRIPTION AND TRAVEL--GUIDES
MARYLAND--DESCRIPTION AND TRAVEL--GUIDES

MARYLAND--PUBLIC LANDS
U.S.--DESCRIPTION AND TRAVEL--GUIDES
WEST VIRGINIA--DESCRIPTION AND TRAVEL--GUIDES
WEST VIRGINIA--PUBLIC LANDS

• ILLINOIS AND MICHIGAN CANAL
National Heritage Corridor. c/o Midwest Region, National Park
Service, 1709 Jackson St., Omaha, NE 68102. (402) 221-3472.
1984. From Chicago southwest to LaSalle/Peru. One hundred mile
area along the Desplaines and Illinois rivers.

Follow the Illinois and Michigan Canal begun in 1836 to complete the
link between Lake Michigan and the Mississippi, connecting natural
areas, historic and archaeological sites, industrial and engineering
structures. In the planning stages.

Free Print Material:
    "Illinois and Michigan Friends of the Canal." 2 pages. Heritage,
    history of the canal. The Illinois and Michigan Canal corridor
    plan calling for a partnership between federal, state and county
    agencies and the private sector. Membership blank for the
    friends of the Illinois and Michigan Canal National Heritage Cor-
    ridor.

Suggested Curriculum Application:
    AMERICAN HISTORY
    ILLINOIS STATE AND LOCAL STUDIES
    SOCIAL STUDIES

Suggested Sears Subject Heading:
    CANALS
    ILLINOIS--DESCRIPTION AND TRAVEL--GUIDES
    ILLINOIS--PUBLIC LANDS
    ILLINOIS AND MICHIGAN CANAL
    U.S.--DESCRIPTION AND TRAVEL--GUIDES

CANYONS

• BIGHORN CANYON
National Recreation Area. P.O. Box 458, Fort Smith, MT 59035.
(406) 666-2412. 120,277.86 acres. 1966. Southern Montana,
northern Wyoming. Access to the south end of the park is by U.S.
310 from Billings, MT or U.S. 14A from Sheridan, WY. From
Hardin, MT, take Mont. 313 to get to the north end of the park.

Bighorn Lake extends 71 miles, including 47 miles through Bighorn Canyon. The lake is formed by the Yellowtail Dam on the Bighorn River. Boating, water skiing, auto tape tour, scuba and skin diving, film, exhibits, wildlife, Bad Pass trail, Devil Canyon over-look, guided tours through the visitor center's solar heating system and Mason-Lovell Ranch site, Yellowtail Dam powerplant tours, evening campfire programs, special events, nature trail, swimming, hiking. Inquire about various ranger-led activities, special demon-strations and naturalist-guided programs. Visitor centers, picnick-ing, campgrounds, marina, boat launch and boat ramps, ranger sta-tions, snack bar. Food and lodging in Lowell, WY, Hardin, MT, Fort Smith, MT.

Free Print Material:
"Bighorn Canyon." 12-fold. Maps, diagrams, photos. Descrip-tion of features, boating tips, accommodations, historic use of the land. Time table from 1492 to 1968.
"Bighorn Canyon National Recreation Area." 2 pages. Camping and accommodations that are available.
"Bighorn Canyon Vacation Planner." 2 pages. Camping, boating, interpretive activities, weather and other visitor information.
"Canyon Echoes." 4 pages. Newspaper format. Visitor guide to Bighorn Canyon National Recreation Area. Photos, calendar of events, maps, ranger-led activities.
"Golden Eagle, Golden Age, Golden Access Passports." 10-fold. Federal recreation fee program described for people under 62, 62 and older, for blind and disabled persons.
"Montana Highway Map." 24-fold. Points of interest, mileage table, index, map, attractions of various sections of the state, photos.
"Yellowtail." 10-fold. Description of the Yellowtail Unit located on the Bighorn River. Powerplant, irrigation, water, recrea-tion, fish and wildlife. Photos, map. Physical data of the dam and reservoir.

Suggested Curriculum Application:
MONTANA STATE AND LOCAL STUDIES
RECREATION
WYOMING STATE AND LOCAL STUDIES

Suggested Sears Subject Heading:
BIGHORN LAKE
DAMS
LAKES
MONTANA--DESCRIPTION AND TRAVEL--GUIDES
MONTANA--PUBLIC LANDS
OUTDOOR RECREATION
U.S.--DESCRIPTION AND TRAVEL--GUIDES
WYOMING--DESCRIPTION AND TRAVEL--GUIDES
WYOMING--PUBLIC LANDS
YELLOWTAIL DAM

- BLACK CANYON OF THE GUNNISON
National Monument. P.O. Box 1648, Montrose, CO 81402.
(303) 240-6522. 20,762.70 acres. 1933. Central Colorado, on Colo.
347, 15 miles from Montrose, CO.

Carved by the Gunnison River, with 12 miles of deepest gorge making unique geological features in the wilderness. Deep, narrow
canyon's dark walls of schist and gneiss that are in heavy shadows
most of the day, unspoiled wild river, scenic overlooks, variety of
wildlife and birds, exhibits, trails of varying length. Visitor center, campground on each rim, light lunches sold in the summer.
Food and lodging in Montrose.

Free Print Material:
> "Black Canyon of the Gunnison." 16-fold. Features, history,
> activities, maps, chart, park regulations and safety and other
> visitor tips.
> "Canyon Plants." 18 pages. First part covers the more con-
> spicuous flowering plants of the Black Canyon that are ob-
> served along the side of the road and overlooks. The second
> section contains a listing of all plants identified within Black
> Canyon listed by scientific family name, with genus and species
> name and common name.
> "Canyon Geology." 26 pages. First part gives an overview of the
> geologic story of Black Canyon. The second gives a descrip-
> tive road trip along the south rim scenic drive. Sketches,
> geologic time scale, geologic sections.
> "Inner Canyon Routes Description." 2 pages. Description with
> descent, ascent, river access, vertical drop, miles, campsites
> for: Tomichi, Gunnison, Warner points on the south rim;
> S.O.B. Draw, Long Draw, Slide Draw on north rim.
> "Vicinity Map." 2 pages. State map and close-up map.

Suggested Curriculum Application:
> COLORADO STATE AND LOCAL STUDIES
> GEOGRAPHY
> GEOLOGY

Suggested Sears Subject Heading:
> COLORADO--DESCRIPTION AND TRAVEL--GUIDES
> COLORADO--PUBLIC LANDS
> GEOLOGY--U.S.
> U.S.--DESCRIPTION AND TRAVEL--GUIDES

- GRAND CANYON
National Park. P.O. Box 129, Grand Canyon, AZ 86023.
(602) 638-9304. 1,218,375.24 acres. 1919. Northern Arizona, in
three separate areas.

Preserve the world-famous Grand Canyon with nearby uplands.

Erosion has exposed a great variety of formations illustrating long periods of time. Yavapai Museum, Tusayan Museum, trails along the rims and into the canyon, river trips, hiking, ranger programs, mule trips. Visitor center, ranger stations. Grand Canyon Village has lodging, food, service station, medical clinic, pet kennel, post office, tent and trailer campgrounds and other services. Reservations for lodging, campgrounds and mule trips should be made as far in advance as possible.

Free Print Material:

"Accommodations and Services." 8-fold. Name, location, visitor information. Arranged by location such as North Rim or South Rim and includes such services as kennels, banks, lodges, car rental services, air transportation.

"Campground Reservations." 10-fold. Reservation procedures in person, by mail, fees, cancellation and other information. Names of campgrounds, facilities, location and special information.

"Grand Canyon Climates." 4 pages. Description of climates for the inner canyon, North Rim, South Rim. Charts on temperatures, precipitation.

"Grand Canyon National Park Lodges." 10-fold. Description, location, photos, rates of various lodges.

"Grand Canyon National Park South and North Rim Village." 2 pages. Maps and visitor information.

"Grand Canyon Official Map and Guide." 2 pages folded. History, features, safety tips, activities, maps.

"Grand Canyon's Young Adventurer." 8 pages. Activities for children. Stories, games, quizzes, drawings.

"Hiking at Bright Angel and Kaibab Trails." 8-fold. How to obtain backpacking permits and reservations, medical tips, seasonal tips and distances. Map and trail descriptions.

Sales/Audiovisual List:

"Publications." 4 pages. Materials arranged under: books, for children, Grand Canyon Natural History Association maps, United States Geological Survey Maps, other publications available through GCNHA. Information about the Grand Canyon Natural History Association.

"Along the Rim" by Nancy Loving. 52-page book containing a brief history of South Rim development, discussion of plant life, wildlife and guide to points along East and West Rim drives from desert view to Hermits Rest. 56 full-color and black-and-white photographs, four maps, two double-page full-color panoramas with landmark keys. $2.95.

Suggested Curriculum Application:

ARIZONA STATE AND LOCAL STUDIES
GEOGRAPHY
GEOLOGY

Suggested Sears Subject Heading:
    ARIZONA--DESCRIPTION AND TRAVEL
    ARIZONA--PUBLIC LANDS
    GEOLOGY--U.S.
    GRAND CANYON NATIONAL PARK
    NATIONAL PARKS AND RESERVES--U.S.
    U.S.--DESCRIPTION AND TRAVEL--GUIDES
    U.S.--GEOGRAPHY

CAVES

- CARLSBAD CAVERNS

National Park. 3225 National Parks Highway, Carlsbad, NM 88220.
(505) 785-2322. 46,755.33 acres. National Monument, 1923;
National Park, 1930. 20 miles from Carlsbad in southern New
Mexico, on U.S. 62-180. 150 miles east of El Paso, TX.

Preserve around 70 caves. Carlsbad, the largest, has one room
with a floor area equal to 15 football fields and tall enough for the
U.S. Capitol building in one corner. Orientation services, exhibits,
cavern tours, guided tours, elevator trips, bat flight programs,
lantern trips, nature trails, scenic drives, hiking and backpacking.
Visitor center, kennel service, restaurant, picnicking, gift shop,
nursery. Food and lodging, campgrounds and trailer parks nearby.
White's City is 7 miles and Carlsbad is 20 miles from the caverns.

Free Print Material:
    "Access Guide." 2 pages. Accommodations above ground and
        in cave, map.
    "Area Information." 2 pages. Accommodations in Carlsbad and
        White's City. List of motels, campgrounds, points of interest,
        map.
    "The Bat Flight." 2 pages. Bat flight program, best flights,
        return flights, bat flight breakfast (held annually in mid-
        August sponsored by park employees to encourage visitors
        to watch the bats as they return to the cavern at dawn),
        safety tips, additional reading list on bats.
    "Carlsbad Caverns." 24-fold. Maps, photos, block diagram,
        geology, bats, development and use by man, wildlife, pre-
        cautions, what to see and do, climate, accommodations.
    "Carlsbad Caverns: Silent Chambers, Timeless Beauty." 36
        pages. Issued by the Carlsbad Caverns Natural History
        Association, many full page photos, description, history and
        development of the park. Some photos are those of early
        visitors in the 1920's. Includes geological diagrams.
    "Cavern Information." 2 pages. Various tours, hours, fees,

services, photography, wheelchairs, bat flights, map and other visitor information.

"Guadalupe Journal." 8 pages. Newspaper format guide to the Carlsbad-Guadalupe Mountains area of New Mexico and Texas published by the Carlsbad Caverns Natural History Association. What to see and do, articles, photos, schedules, map.

"New Cave--A Guided Lantern Trip Through an Undeveloped Cave." 1 page. How to get there (23 miles from park visitor center), tour schedule, reservations, equipment, fees, map.

Bibliography:
A reading list is included in "The Bat Flight" described above.

Sales/Audiovisual List:
"Carlsbad Caverns." 6-fold. Grouped by: books, caves, children, geology, maps, posters, postcards, slides. Order form and mail order instructions. Under the children category appears coloring books, books, field guides.

"American Indian Food and Lore." Carolyn Niethammer. 191 pages. $10.95.

Suggested Curriculum Application:
GEOGRAPHY
GEOLOGY
NEW MEXICO STATE AND LOCAL STUDIES

Suggested Sears Subject Heading:
BATS
CARLSBAD CAVERNS NATIONAL PARK
CAVES
GEOLOGY--U.S.
NATIONAL PARKS AND RESERVES--U.S.
NEW MEXICO--DESCRIPTION AND TRAVEL--GUIDES
NEW MEXICO--PUBLIC LANDS
U.S.--DESCRIPTION AND TRAVEL--GUIDES

• JEWEL CAVE
National Monument. P.O. Box 351, Custer, SD 57730. (605) 673-2288. 1,273.51 acres. 1908. Western South Dakota, on U.S. 16, 13 miles west of Custer.

Limestone Caverns with a series of chambers connected by narrow passages, many side galleries and calcite crystal encrustations. Underground cave tours. Visitor center, picnicking. Food and lodging in Custer, SD and Newcastle, WY and other outlying communities. Campgrounds are near these towns, such as Custer State Park.

Free Print Material:
"Bats and Their Conservation." 6-fold. Commercial, scientific,

ecological values of bats, threats to bat survival, endangered
U.S. bats, photos.
"Jewel Cave." 16-fold. Geology, administration, accommodations
and facilities, underground tours, map, photos.

Sales/Audiovisual List:

"Wind Cave/Jewel Cave Natural History Association Sales List."
6-fold. Grouped by: books, coloring books, guides, prints,
postcards, maps, slides, stickers, order form and ordering information, membership form and association aims, photo. Title,
number of pages, price of publications. Other items have title,
size and composition of sets.
"Badlands." Ruth Kirk. 32 page. $2.75.

Suggested Curriculum Application:

GEOGRAPHY
GEOLOGY
SCIENCE
SOUTH DAKOTA STATE AND LOCAL STUDIES

Suggested Sears Subject Heading:

BATS
CAVES
GEOLOGY--U.S.
JEWEL CAVE NATIONAL MONUMENT
NATURAL MONUMENTS--U.S.
SOUTH DAKOTA--DESCRIPTION AND TRAVEL--GUIDES
SOUTH DAKOTA--PUBLIC LANDS
U.S.--DESCRIPTION AND TRAVEL--GUIDES
U.S.--GEOGRAPHY

• LEHMAN CAVES

National Monument. Baker, NV 89311. (702) 234-7331. 640 acres.
Eastern Nevada, 5 miles west of Baker, near the Nevada-Utah
boundary at terminus of State Highway 488.

Tunnels, galleries with stalactites and stalagmites. The caves were
discovered by a local rancher in 1885. Cave tours. Spelunking
tours (minimum age is 14), are also given to learn about caving.
Evening programs, exhibits, film, hiking and riding trails. Spelunking tour requires completed reservation form prior to intended tour
date and those 14-17 years old need the signed consent of respon-
sible adult. Request form far in advance. Visitor center, picnicking, concessioner sells food and souvenirs. Campgrounds nearby.
Food and lodging in Baker.

Free Print Material:

"Lehman Caves." 6-fold. Description, history, geology, maps,
photo, visitor information.
"Lehman Caves National Monument, Nevada." 6-fold. Cave tour
schedules, evening programs, sketch, maps, weather, visitor

facilities.

"Spelunking Tour Information." 2 pages. Description and tour
regulations. Required equipment, optional but recommended
equipment.

"Wheeler Peak Scenic Area." 8-fold. Description of the area,
how to obtain visitor maps for Humboldt National Forest.
Photos, map. Chart of general information, facilities, activities and attractions. The caves are surrounded by the national
forest and lie on the east side of Mt. Wheeler.

Suggested Curriculum Application:
GEOLOGY
GEOGRAPHY
NEVADA STATE AND LOCAL STUDIES

Suggested Sears Subject Heading:
CAVES
GEOLOGY--U.S.
NATURAL MONUMENTS
NEVADA--DESCRIPTION AND TRAVEL--GUIDES
NEVADA--PUBLIC LANDS
U.S.--DESCRIPTION AND TRAVEL--GUIDES
U.S.--GEOGRAPHY

• MAMMOTH CAVE
National Park. Mammoth Cave, KY 42259. (502) 758-2328.
52,394.94 acres. 1941. Central Kentucky, 3 miles south of
Hodgenville on U.S. 31E and KY 61.

Preserve series of underground passages with limestone gypsum,
travertine formations, deep pits and high domes, underground
river. Cave trips, surface activities, river cruising, self-guiding
nature trails. School groups should inquire about tours. Visitor
center, Mammoth Cave hotel, Lodge and cottages are available.
Accommodations are also available in nearby communities. The
service center has a post office, service station, coin-operated
laundry, showers, supplies. Camping and picnicking are available
as well as dining room and coffee shop.

Free Print Material:
"General Description of Cave Forming Processes." 1 page. Information on cave passageways, stalactites, stalagmites,
columns, draperies, domes and pits.

"Mammoth Cave." 16-fold. Visitor tips, photos, maps, history,
services available.

"Mammoth Cave Blindfish." 1 page. Habits of the blindfish that
were discovered in Echo River.

"Mammoth Cave National Park Kentucky." 10-fold. Information
about cave trips, services, pet kennels, campgrounds, lodge,
hotel, cottages, gift and craft shops and other services.

"Scenic Boat Ride at Mammoth Cave National Park." 2 pages.

Information about the boat and ride. Photo, schedule and rates.
"A Visitor's Introduction to Mammoth Cave National Park." 9 pages. History of the cave, physiography and hydrology, maps, features, bibliography.

Suggested Curriculum Application:
GEOGRAPHY
GEOLOGY
KENTUCKY STATE AND LOCAL STUDIES

Suggested Sears Subject Heading:
CAVES
GEOLOGY--U.S.
KENTUCKY--DESCRIPTION AND TRAVEL--GUIDES
KENTUCKY--PUBLIC LANDS
MAMMOTH CAVE NATIONAL PARK
NATIONAL PARKS AND RESERVES--U.S.
U.S.--DESCRIPTION AND TRAVEL--GUIDES
U.S.--GEOGRAPHY

- OREGON CAVES
National Monument. 19000 Caves Highway, Cave Junction, OR 97523. (503) 592-2100. 487.98 acres. 1909. Southwest Oregon, 20 miles east of Cave Junction on OR Route 46.

Limestone cave passages with intricate flowstone formations, in the virgin forest of Siskiyou Mountains. Cave tours, hiking trails, big tree (1,200-1,500-year-old Douglas fir tree), Inspiration Point on cliff nature trail, interpretive talks, talks by park rangers. Wildlife and birds with checklists of the park's birds, animals and plants being available upon request at park headquarters. Park information booth, ranger station, gift shop, snack bar, child care service, church services, food and lodging. Campgrounds nearby. Food and lodging in Cave Junction.

Free Print Material:
"General Information." 2 pages. Hours, tour ticket prices, when to visit, activities, regulations and other visitor information.
"Oregon Caves." 14-fold. Geology, photos, maps, bird and wildlife, cave tour information and regulations.

Sales/Audiovisual List:
"Oregon Caves National Monument Crater Lake Nature History Association Sales Items." 1 page. Books, map, slide sets. Maps include coloring maps, topographic, tour route map and others. Books include those for young readers. Title, author, price included for publications. Title, number or size of other items.
"Animals of the Northwest." (Children's book), Fran Hubbard. $2.00.

Suggested Curriculum Application:
GEOGRAPHY
GEOLOGY
NATURAL HISTORY
OREGON STATE AND LOCAL STUDIES

Suggested Sears Subject Heading:
CAVES
GEOLOGY--U.S.
OREGON--DESCRIPTION AND TRAVEL--GUIDES
OREGON--PUBLIC LANDS
U.S.--DESCRIPTION AND TRAVEL--GUIDES
U.S.--GEOGRAPHY

- RUSSELL CAVE

National Monument. Route 1, Box 175, Bridgeport, AL 35740.
(205) 495-2672. 310.45 acres. 1961. Northeast Alabama, 8 miles
west of Bridgeport. U.S. Route 72 at Bridgeport, Jackson County
roads 91 and 75.

Archeological site with 8,000-9,000 years of Indian life. Museum,
audiovisual programs, nature trail, Indian garden, hiking trail,
horse trail, demonstrations, exhibit in the archeological excavation
in the cave. Inquire about guided tours and other services. Wild
cave exploration by permit from unit manager. Visitor center, lunch
area. Campgrounds nearby. Food and lodging in South Pittsburg,
TN, and Stevenson, AL.

Free Print Material:
"Eight Thousand Year Record of Man's Life." 8-fold. Archaeological exploration, human use, Indian life during different
periods. Sketch.
"A Geological Report of the Russell Cave System in Alabama."
5 pages. When the cave began, drainage, water, surrounding
caves, composition of rock.
"Indian Garden." 4-fold. Description of common agricultural
crops planted at Russell Cave by 1000 A.D. Sketch.
"List of Trees, Land Mass, Vines, Wildflowers, Animals, Birds."
1 page. Longest list appears under the wildflowers heading,
the shortest list under the land mass heading.
"Plant List." 1 page. Botanical name and common name lists.
"Russell Cave." 16-fold. Photos, map. Description of Mis-
sissippian Period, Woodland Period and Archaic Period with
photo of arrowpoint and spearpoints, importance of the cave,
Indian life. Chronology from 10,000 B.C. to 1300 A.D.

Sales/Audiovisual List:
"Russell Cave Sales Items." 3 pages. Publications, reproductions,
post cards, slides, coloring books, maps and other items.
Title, price.
"Russell Cave Points." Reproduction. $4.20.

Suggested Curriculum Application:
ALABAMA STATE AND LOCAL STUDIES
AMERICAN HISTORY
ARCHEOLOGY
NATIVE AMERICAN STUDIES

Suggested Sears Subject Heading:
ALABAMA--DESCRIPTION AND TRAVEL--GUIDES
ALABAMA--HISTORY
ALABAMA--PUBLIC LANDS
CAVE DWELLERS
CAVES
EXCAVATIONS (ARCHEOLOGY)
INDIANS OF NORTH AMERICA--HISTORY
MAN, PREHISTORIC
U.S.--DESCRIPTION AND TRAVEL--GUIDES

• TIMPANOGOS CAVE
National Monument. RR 3, Box 200, American Fork, UT 84003.
(801) 756-5238. 250 acres. 1922. Central Utah, roads from Salt
Lake City (35 miles), Provo (20 miles), Herber City/Provo Canyon.

Preserve three interconnected highly decorated limestone caves.
Cave trail, nature walk tour, exhibits, slide program. Various
types of cave tours such as candlelight, flashlight, geology,
photography, historic. The cave has water-created formations that
grow regardless of gravity. Visitor center, snack bar, picnic area.
Campgrounds in adjacent Uinta National Forest. Food and lodging in
Salt Lake City and Provo.

Free Print Material:
"Planning Your Visit." 8-fold. Tour information, cave operating
season, safety and visitor information, map, sketch.
"Special Tours." 8-fold. Types of tours that are available,
schedules, sketches.
"Timpanogos Cave." 12-fold. How the cave was formed, maps,
visitor and safety tips, cave description and administration.

Audiovisual List:
"Film Catalog." 1 page. List of films and filmstrips. Number,
title. 1. "For All to Enjoy."

Suggested Curriculum Application:
GEOGRAPHY
GEOLOGY
SCIENCE
UTAH STATE AND LOCAL STUDIES

Suggested Sears Subject Heading:
CAVES
GEOLOGY--U.S.

U.S.--DESCRIPTION AND TRAVEL--GUIDES
U.S.--GEOGRAPHY
UTAH--DESCRIPTION AND TRAVEL--GUIDES
UTAH--PUBLIC LANDS

• WIND CAVE
National Park. Hot Springs, SD 57747. (605) 745-4699.
28,292.08 acres. 1903. Western South Dakota. The visitor center
is off U.S. 385, 11 miles north of Hot Springs.

Preserve 37 miles of 60,000 million-year-old scenic limestone cavern
passageways that have boxwork and calcite crystal formations. The
surface is a mix of prairie and ponderosa pine containing abundant
wildlife. Evening campfire programs, wildlife, varied cave tours,
self-guiding nature trails, exhibits. Inquire about group reservations by mail or calling (605) 745-4600. Picnicking, visitor center,
campground. Food, lodging, supplies and services are available
in Hot Springs and in Custer.

Free Print Material:
    "Check-List of Birds and Mammals of Wind Cave National Park."
        1 page. Grouped by: insectivores; bats; carnivores; rodents;
        hares and rabbits; approximate number in park; grebes;
        herons; geese and ducks; vultures, hawks and falcons; galli-
        naceous birds; cranes and rails; and others.
    "Wind Cave." 12-fold. Early exploration, wildlife, touring the
        cave, visitor tips, touring the park. Maps, photos.
    "Wind Cave National Park Schedule." 1 page. When tours are
        available, hours of the visitor center, what kind of shoes to
        wear, cave temperature.
    "Wind Cave Park Information." 2 pages. Facilities, activities,
        description, wildlife, tours and reservations. Photos.
    "Wind Cave Wildlife." 4 pages. Habits of prairie dogs, prong-
        horn antelope, American bison, mule deer, American elk,
        coyote. Wildlife checklist with sketches, scorecard.

Sales/Audiovisual List:
    "Sales List." 6-fold. Sales items grouped by: books; coloring
        books; guides; prints, postcards, maps; slides; stickers.
        Order form with ordering information; membership form for the
        Windcave/Jewel Cave Natural History Association. Photo.
        Title, author, pages, price of books.
    "Badlands." Ruth Kirk, 32 pages, $2.75.

Suggested Curriculum Application:
    GEOGRAPHY
    GEOLOGY
    SOUTH DAKOTA STATE AND LOCAL STUDIES

Suggested Sears Subject Heading:
    CAVES

GEOLOGY--U.S.
NATIONAL PARKS AND RESERVES--U.S.
SOUTH DAKOTA--DESCRIPTION AND TRAVEL--GUIDES
SOUTH DAKOTA--PUBLIC LANDS
U.S.--DESCRIPTION AND TRAVEL--GUIDES
U.S.--GEOGRAPHY
WIND CAVE NATIONAL PARK

CIVIL WAR

• ANDERSONVILLE
National Historic Site. Rt. 1, Box 85, Andersonville, GA 31711.
(912) 924-0343. 475.72 acres. 1970. Central Georgia, 50 miles south
of Macon, on Georgia Highway 49, 1/2 mile from Andersonville.

Confederate military prison site, national cemetery commemorates
American war prisoners from the Revolutionary to Vietnam wars.
During its 14 months of existence, more than 45,000 Union soldiers
were kept here and 12,000 died here. Tour of Andersonville prison
site and National Cemetery, self-guided tour, free tape recorded
tour, talks, special events such as candlelight tours and dramatiza-
tions, slide programs, card catalog, museums. A personalized tour
may be arranged by calling ahead. Inquire about "Learn, Share,
and Enjoy" educational outreach program developed by the site staff
for students. A pre-visit packet for classroom use is available upon
request at no charge for a two-week period. Make reservations for
group tours. Visitor center, picnicking. Campground nearby.
Food in Andersonville, lodging in Americus, Montezuma.

Free Print Material:
  "Andersonville." 16-fold. Maps, photos, lithographs, description
    of Andersonville, prison life, changes of status until it was
    designated a National Historic Site, establishment and descrip-
    tion of Andersonville National Cemetery. The initial interments
    were the over 12,000 who died in the nearby prison camp.
  "Georgia's Andersonville Trail to Plains." 6-fold. Maps, photos.
    The Andersonville Trail is 75 miles of gardens, home of
    President Carter, antebellum homes, Andersonville National
    Historic Site and other highlights.
  "Learn, Share, Enjoy." 6-fold. What the site has to offer in
    educational/outreach programs for students. Photo, map.
  "The Story of Andersonville Prison and American Prisoners of
    War." 52 pages. A collection of educational activities, his-
    torical narratives and interesting facts developed for grades
    5-12 but may be adapted to other grade levels as well. Per-
    mission is granted for duplication of materials. Graphics,
    human interest stories, suggested activities, puzzles.

"Visit Andersonville Civil War Village." 6-fold. Description of Log Church, welcome station and museum, annual Andersonville Historic Fair, highlights of Andersonville Trail.

"Visiting Andersonville National Historic Site: A Guide for Bus and School Groups." 6-fold. Description of Andersonville Prison, how to get to Andersonville National Historic Site, lodging, camping, sketch, map, eating facilities, reservations, special events and other visitor information.

Sales/Audiovisual List:
Information about a slide and videotape available free of charge for offsite use is included in "Visiting Andersonville National Historic Site: A Guide for Bus and School Groups."

"Eastern National Park and Monument Association Andersonville National Historic Site Publications." 3 pages. Books, slide strips, post cards, prints. Title, author, price for books. Order blank, ordering information.

"Andersonville Prison." A reprint of articles that have appeared in "Civil War Times Illustrated." $1.75.

Bibliography:
One page in "The Story of Andersonville Prison and American Prisoners of War" described above. Arranged by: Civil War; Andersonville; POWs. Includes author, title, publisher, date.

Suggested Curriculum Application:
AMERICAN HISTORY
GEORGIA STATE AND LOCAL STUDIES

Suggested Sears Subject Heading:
ANDERSON NATIONAL CEMETERY
CEMETERIES
GEORGIA--DESCRIPTION AND TRAVEL--GUIDES
GEORGIA--PUBLIC LANDS
PRISONERS OF WAR
U.S.--DESCRIPTION AND TRAVEL--GUIDES
U.S.--HISTORY--CIVIL WAR, 1861-1865--PRISONERS AND
   PRISONS

• ANTIETAM
National Battlefield. P.O. Box 158, Sharpsburg, MD 21782. (301) 432-5124. 3,246.44 acres. 1890. Southern Maryland, one mile north of Sharpsburg, 10 miles south of Hagerstown along MD Highway 65.

Site of bloodiest day (over 23,000 casualties) in the civil war. Battle ended Confederacy's first invasion of the north in 1862. Site of Antietam (Sharpsburg) National Cemetery with 5,032 interments. Exhibits, audiovisuals, talks, oil paintings by eyewitness, bicycling, birdwatching, canoeing, interpretive programs, hiking, walks, demonstrations, driving tour of battlefield, national cemetery. Cassette-

tape tour is available for rent. Visitor center. Picnicking nearby.
Food and lodging in Sharpsburg, Hagerstown.

Free Print Material:
"Antietam." 8-fold. Account of the battle, touring the battlefield, visitor information. Chromolithograph, maps, photos.
"The Antietam (Mumma) Bible." 1 page. Leather-bound Bible
donated to the Mumma or Dunker Church in 1851, now displayed
in the museum of the visitor center at Antietam National Battlefield.
"Antietam National Battlefield Visitor Information." 5 pages.
Introduction, park location, audiovisual program, tours, account
of the battle, nearby national parks, overnight accommodations.
"Antietam National Cemetery." 7 pages. Beginning and administration, list of dignitaries and dates they visited the cemetery,
map, construction of "The Private Soldier" Monument, entrance
and lodge house, iron guns, rostrum, memorial or decoration
day, types of trees, sketches.
"Artillery at Antietam." 2 pages. Types of artillery displayed
north of the visitor center. Description of the limber, ammu-
nition chest, projectiles, and others. List of men commanding
the Confederate gun position north of the visitor center in the
early morning on the day of the battle. Number of Union and
Confederate cannons. References.
"Auto Tour of South Mountain Battle Gaps." 2 pages. Map, account of the Battle of South Mountain.
"Clara Barton at Antietam." 1 page. Clara Barton's work after
the Battle of Antietam as taken from a National Park Service
handbook, sketch.
"The Dunker Church." 9 pages. Who the German Baptist
Brethren of the Dunker Church were and their customs, significance of the church during the battle, reconstruction of
the church, the Dunker Church Bible. Sketches.
"Emancipation Proclamation." 2 pages. The proclamation was
read by Lincoln to his cabinet five days after the Federal victory at Antietam. Copy of the official version signed January
1, 1863.
"Lee's Lost Dispatch." 2 pages. Special orders, No. 191, September 9, 1862, headquarters army of northern Virginia.
"Lee's Maryland Campaign." 1 page. Battle of Sharpsburg,
casualties, national cemetery and soldiers buried there,
memorial bench.
"Lee's Proclamation to the People of Maryland." 1 page. September 8, 1862 from headquarters army of northern Virginia
near Fredericktown, MD.
"Soldier's Expressions." 9 pages. Quotations of privates,
lieutenants, army correspondent, resident of Shepherdstown
and others (from the North and South) about the battle.

Bibliography:
"Bibliography--Antietam." 2 pages. Includes title, author, place
of publication, date.

"Bibliography of Women in the Civil War." 2 pages. Arranged alphabetically by author. Includes author, title, publisher, place of publication, date.

Sales/Audiovisual List:
Inquire about films: "The Battle at Antietam Creek," "Mathew Brady," "Antietam Visit," "Clara Barton," available for short term loan.
"Parks and History Association Sales List." 6 pages. Arranged by: publications, calendars, films, maps, photographs, post cards, James Hope paintings, record albums, slide set, souvenirs, stamps, cassettes, games, VCR. Title, price. Publications include handbooks, sketchbooks, coloring books, paper dolls, guides, diaries, trivia quiz. Ordering directions.
"Abraham Lincoln." $1.75.

Suggested Curriculum Application:
AMERICAN HISTORY
MARYLAND STATE AND LOCAL STUDIES

Suggested Sears Subject Heading:
ANTIETAM, BATTLE OF (SHARPSBURG)
ANTIETAM (SHARPSBURG) NATIONAL CEMETERY
CEMETERIES
MARYLAND--DESCRIPTION AND TRAVEL--GUIDES
MARYLAND--PUBLIC LANDS
U.S.--DESCRIPTION AND TRAVEL--GUIDES
U.S.--HISTORY--CIVIL WAR, 1861-1865--CAMPAIGNS AND
    BATTLES

• APPOMATTOX COURT HOUSE
National Historical Park. P.O. Box 218, Appomattox, VA 24522. (804) 352-8987. 1,325.08 acres. 1930. Central Virginia, 3 miles northeast of Appomattox on VA 24 in south central Virginia.

Site of the surrender of Robert E. Lee, April 9, 1865. Restored and reconstructed buildings of McLean house, Meeks store, Woodson law office, Clover Hill tavern, courthouse, jail, Kelly house, Mariah Wright house, surrender triangle, Isbell house, Peers house. Museum, slide shows, living history program. Visitor center. Food and lodging in Appomattox. Picnic tables on either side of Route 24. Nearest campground is at Holiday Lake State Park.

Free Print Material:
"Appomattox Court House." 12-fold. What the park contains, Civil War background and the surrender, how the park was created, maps, photos.
"Appomattox Courthouse National Historical Park." 42 pages. Guide for teachers to assist in planning a trip and preparing students to visit the park. The material can be used before,

during and after the visit. Includes bibliography, maps,
sketches, statistics, chronology, questions, organization of
both armies, classroom activities, biographical sketches, reproduction of Lee's letter of surrender.
"Need More Virginia Travel Information?" 4-fold. Post card to
send for more information. Has lines to list your specific
interests or destinations after tearing 2-folds.

Bibliography:
"Appomattox Campaign Bibliography." 2 pages. Arranged by
author. Includes title, place of publication, publisher, date.
Includes works by historical societies, commercial publishers,
the U.S. War Department and others.

Sales/Audiovisual List:
"Publications for Sale at Appomattox Court House National Historical Park Through Eastern National Park and Monument
Association." 4 pages. Grouped by: publications, children's
books, Civil War Times Illustrated, individual post cards, slide
strips. Ordering information.
"A New Birth of Freedom." Hardbound. $22.50.

Suggested Curriculum Application:
AMERICAN HISTORY
VIRGINIA STATE AND LOCAL STUDIES

Suggested Sears Subject Heading:
ARCHITECTURE--CONSERVATION AND RESTORATION
VIRGINIA--BUILDINGS
VIRGINIA--DESCRIPTION AND TRAVEL--GUIDES
VIRGINIA--PUBLIC LANDS
U.S.--DESCRIPTION AND TRAVEL--GUIDES
U.S.--HISTORY--CIVIL WAR, 1861-1865

• ARLINGTON HOUSE
The Robert E. Lee Memorial. c/o George Washington Memorial
Parkway, Turkey Run Park, McLean, VA 22101. (703) 557-0613.
27.91 acres. 1925. Arlington, Virginia overlooking the Potomac
River and Washington, D.C. Access from Washington is by the
Memorial Bridge.

Memorial to General Lee, the house was built by the grandson of
Martha Washington by her first marriage and is associated with the
families of Washington, Custis, and Lee. Mansion tour. Servants'
quarters on the west circular drive, museum north of the mansion
contains memorabilia of the Custis and Lee families. Guided group
tours by appointment. Subway service is available from Washington
and Alexandria. Parking is available at the Arlington Cemetery
visitor center. (200 acres of Lee's property became the beginning of
Arlington National Cemetery.)

Free Print Material:
"Arlington House." 8-fold. Tour of Arlington House with first
and second floor maps, photos. A Lee chronology and narrative history.
"Robert E. Lee." 5 pages. Family history, Lee's career, quotations by Lee.

Suggested Curriculum Application:
AMERICAN HISTORY
VIRGINIA STATE AND LOCAL STUDIES

Suggested Sears Subject Heading:
ARCHITECTURE--CONSERVATION AND RESTORATION
ARLINGTON NATIONAL CEMETERY
CEMETERIES
LEE, ROBERT E., 1807-1870
VIRGINIA--DESCRIPTION AND TRAVEL--GUIDES
VIRGINIA--PUBLIC LANDS
U.S.--DESCRIPTION AND TRAVEL--GUIDES

• BRICES CROSS ROADS
National Battlefield Site. c/o Natchez Trace Parkway, R.R. 1,
NT-143, Tupelo, MS 38801. (601) 842-1572. 1 acre. 1929. North-
ern Mississippi, 6 miles west of Baldwyn on Miss. 370.

Civil War battle site of June 10, 1864. Much of the scene of the
battle is within view of the park, monuments and markers. There
are no facilities or personnel present, but park interpreters at the
Tupelo visitor center of the Natchez Trace Parkway are available to
answer questions. Food and lodging in Tupelo, Booneville.

Free Print Material:
"Brices Cross Roads, Mississippi." 2 pages. Account of the
contributions of black soldiers in the battle.
"Brices Cross Roads, Tupelo." 10-fold. Sketches, maps, ac-
counts of the Battle of Brices Cross Roads and the Battle of
Tupelo, visitor information.

Suggested Curriculum Application:
AMERICAN HISTORY
BLACK STUDIES
MISSISSIPPI STATE AND LOCAL STUDIES

Suggested Sears Subject Heading:
BRICES CROSS ROADS, BATTLE OF
MISSISSIPPI--DESCRIPTION AND TRAVEL--GUIDES
MISSISSIPPI--PUBLIC LANDS
U.S.--DESCRIPTION AND TRAVEL--GUIDES
U.S.--HISTORY--CIVIL WAR, 1861-1865--CAMPAIGNS AND
BATTLES

- CHICKAMAUGA AND CHATTANOOGA
National Military Park. P.O. Box 2128, Fort Oglethorpe, GA 30742.
(404) 866-9241. 8,102.54 acres. 1890. Northern Georgia and
southern Tennessee. Chickamauga Battlefield is 7 miles south of
Chattanooga on U.S. 27.

Preserve a number of Civil War separate areas such as: Chickamauga
Battlefield; Point Park and Lookout Mountain Battlefield; Orchard
Knob; Missionary Ridge contains a series of small units or reservations along its summit. The park was the first and largest national
military park and the one upon which the establishment and development of most other national military and historical parks was based.
Slide program, tours, talks, demonstrations, special events, Ochs
Museum and overlook, Garrity's battery, Corput's battery, Parrott
rifles, Cravens house, Bluff Trail, Orchard Knob Reservation,
Bragg Reservation, Ohio Reservation, Illinois Monument, Claude E.
and Zenada O. Fuller Collection of American Military Arms, Chickamauga Battlefield tour, Wilder Tower, Snodgrass Hill, Signal Point
Reservation and others. Most of the 1,400 monuments and historical
markers on the battlefields were planned and placed by participants
of the battles. Visitor centers, picnicking, ranger stations. Camping, food and lodging nearby.

Free Print Material:
    "Chickamauga and Chattanooga." 16-fold. Painting, maps,
        photos, military activities, what the park offers the visitor,
        history of the park's development.

Suggested Curriculum Application:
    AMERICAN HISTORY
    GEORGIA STATE AND LOCAL STUDIES
    TENNESSEE STATE AND LOCAL STUDIES

Suggested Sears Subject Heading:
    CHATTANOOGA, BATTLE OF
    CHICKAMAUGA, BATTLE OF
    GEORGIA--DESCRIPTION AND TRAVEL--GUIDES
    GEORGIA--PUBLIC LANDS
    LOOKOUT MOUNTAIN, BATTLE OF
    TENNESSEE--DESCRIPTION AND TRAVEL--GUIDES
    TENNESSEE--PUBLIC LANDS
    U.S.--DESCRIPTION AND TRAVEL--GUIDES
    U.S.--HISTORY--CIVIL WAR, 1861-1865--CAMPAIGNS AND
        BATTLES

- FORT DONELSON
National Military Park. P.O. Box F, Dover, TN 37058. (615)
232-5348. 536.66 acres. 1928. Northwestern part of middle Tennessee, about 75 miles northwest of Nashville. The park is located
on the west side of Dover, Tennessee on U.S. 79.

Site of the first major Union victory in the Civil War in 1862 that began the rise of Brigadier General Ulysses S. Grant. Remains of Fort Donelson, the war batteries, three miles of rifle pits, Dover Hotel where the surrender happened, Confederate monument, troop maneuvering land, Fort Donelson National Cemetery, slide program, museum, six-mile tour route of the fort and battlefield, nature trails, reproduction soldiers' cabins, demonstrations. Visitor center, picnicking, primitive campsite available only by prior arrangement to organized youth groups. Campgrounds 10 and 16 miles from the fort. Food and lodging in Dover, Clarksville.

Free Print Material:
"Fort Donelson Official Map and Guide." 8-fold. Maps, photos, painting, the Battle of Fort Donelson, narrative guide to the park.
"Visitor Information." 3 pages. Introduction, what to see and do, nearby attractions, accommodations, weather, and related visitor information. Names, addresses and telephones for more information.

Sales List:
"Eastern National Park and Monument Association Publications List." 2 pages. Title, cost. Includes post cards, prints, boy scout trail patch, tin whistles, national park calendar besides publications. Ordering instructions.
"Army of the Heartlands." $20.00

Suggested Curriculum Application:
AMERICAN HISTORY
TENNESSEE STATE AND LOCAL STUDIES

Suggested Sears Subject Heading:
CEMETERIES
FORT DONELSON, BATTLE OF
FORT DONELSON NATIONAL CEMETERY
TENNESSEE--DESCRIPTION AND TRAVEL--GUIDES
TENNESSEE--PUBLIC LANDS
U.S.--DESCRIPTION AND TRAVEL--GUIDES
U.S.--HISTORY--CIVIL WAR, 1861-1865--CAMPAIGNS AND
BATTLES

• FREDERICKSBURG AND SPOTSYLVANIA COUNTY BATTLEFIELDS MEMORIAL
National Military Park. P.O. Box 679, Fredericksburg, VA 22404. (703) 373-4461. 5,909.02 acres. 1927. Eastern Virginia, 60 miles from Washington, D.C., the Fredericksburg Battlefield visitor center is on 1013 Lafayette Boulevard, Fredericksburg. Another visitor center is at Chancellorsville, 10 miles west of Fredericksburg on Va. 3.

Parts of four major Civil War battlefields: Fredericksburg, Chancellorsville, The Wilderness, Spotsylvania Court House and three related sites. The 12-acre Fredericksburg National Cemetery near the park was transferred from the War Department in 1933. Museum, displays, exhibit shelters, talks, living history presentations, Old Salem Church, Stonewall Jackson Shrine, Fredericksburg National Cemetery, Chatham (large Georgian mansion), self-guiding walking and auto tours, hiking trail, interpretive trails, bicycling. Visitor centers, picnicking. Camp nearby. Food and lodging in Fredericksburg.

Free Print Material:

"The Battle of Spotsylvania Court House." 4 pages. Battle account between the North and South, map, trail.

"Bloody Angle Walking Tour." 4 pages. Narrative account by participants, the Battle of Spotsylvania, Map.

"Chatham." 4 pages. History of Georgian mansion and its use during the Civil War. Sketches, floorplans.

"Fredericksburg." 16-fold. Photos, illustrations, maps, battles at Fredericksburg, Chancellorsville, Wilderness, Spotsylvania Court House, visitor information.

"Fredericksburg Battlefield Sunken Road Walking Tour Guide." 4 pages. Account of the battle and what to see along the walking tour.

"Fredericksburg National Cemetery." 4 pages. Sketch, map, a walking tour. The cemetery was authorized in 1865.

"Fredericksburg, Virginia Visitor Guide." 40 pages. Accommodations, restaurants, campgrounds, area attractions, entertainment, map, calendar of events, photos, sketches.

"Hazel Grove." 4 pages. Sketches, accounts of the three day struggle, map.

"Jackson Shrine." 4 pages. Sketches, account of Thomas J. "Stonewall" Jackson's death in the building that became the shrine.

"Old Salem Church." 4 pages. Narrative tour and map. Narrative includes on the scene soldier accounts.

"Visitor Activities." 2 pages. Features of: Fredericksburg battlefield, Chancellorsville battlefield, Wilderness battlefield, Spotsylvania battlefield, Chatham, Old Salem Church, "Stonewall" Jackson Shrine.

Sales/Audiovisual List:

"Eastern National Park and Monument Association Catalog of Products/Publications Available from Fredericksburg Agency." 4 pages. Grouped by publications, children's publications, other products, items under "other products" category include: notecards, auto tape tours, video, 35mm slides, photographic prints and others. Title, price. Order form, ordering directions, aim of the Eastern National Park and Monument Association.

"A.P. Hill-Lee's Forgotten General." $13.95.

Suggested Curriculum Application:
AMERICAN HISTORY
VIRGINIA STATE AND LOCAL STUDIES

Suggested Sears Subject Heading:
CEMETERIES
CHANCELLORSVILLE, BATTLE OF
FREDERICKSBURG, BATTLE OF
FREDERICKSBURG NATIONAL CEMETERY
SPOTSYLVANIA, BATTLE OF
U.S.--DESCRIPTION AND TRAVEL--GUIDES
U.S.--HISTORY--CIVIL WAR, 1861-1865--CAMPAIGNS AND
   BATTLES
VIRGINIA--DESCRIPTION AND TRAVEL--GUIDES
VIRGINIA--PUBLIC LANDS
THE WILDERNESS, BATTLE OF

- GETTYSBURG
National Military Park. Gettysburg, PA 17325. (717) 334-1124.
3,865.11 acres. 1895. Southern Pennsylvania, near Gettysburg.
The visitor center is located on PA 134, near its intersection with
U.S. 15.

Site of a crucial July 1-3, 1863 Civil War battle, the Gettysburg
National Cemetery and Lincoln's Gettysburg Address. Electric map
program presents a graphic demonstration of the battle action
through the use of colored lights. The Cyclorama Center has the
painting of "Pickett's Charge" with a dramatic sound and light
program. Auto tour of the battlefield, displays, High Water Mark
Trail, Big Round Top Loop Trail, Billy Yank Trail, Rosensteel
Collection of Civil War Artifacts, Johnny Reb Trail, Gettysburg
National Cemetery, bike tours, bridle trail for horses. The east
cavalry battlefield site 3 miles east of Gettysburg on PA 116. Inquire about battlefield guides available for hire for car or bus
tours. Visitor center, picnicking. Camping only for organized
youth groups from mid-April to mid-October and may be reserved
by calling the number previously given, at extension 65. Food and
lodging at Gettysburg.

Free Print Material:
   "Gettysburg." 16-fold. Maps, photos, account of the three day
      battle, how to see the battlefield, narrative of auto tour stops.
      Description of the Gettysburg National Cemetery, Eisenhower
      National Historic Site, the Gettysburg Address.
   "Gettysburg Cyclorama--Electric Map." 4 pages. Descriptions of
      the 356 feet by 26 feet Gettysburg Cyclorama and the 750-
      square-foot map with over 600 colored lights. Both present
      programs for visitors. Illustrations, photo, map, schedule,
      fee, capacity for the cyclorama and electric map.
   "Visitor Information Sheet." 1 page. Description of tours, guides,
      camping, picnic area, hours, visitor center and other features.

Bibliography:
   "Bibliography, The American Civil War 1861-1865." 1 page.
      Grouped by: general, children's, novels. Author, title.
      The majority of books are in the general category.
   "Bibliography: The Battle of Gettysburg." 3 pages. A selective
      bibliography. Author, title, place of publication, publisher,
      date, annotation. Arranged alphabetically by author.

Sales/Audiovisual List:
   "Gettysburg National Military Park List of Sales Items." 4 pages.
      Arranged by: books; slides and tapes; post cards, prints,
      maps; miscellaneous items. Ordering information. Miscellane-
      ous items includes records, notepaper, puzzle, uniform sets.
      The list is a partial list of what is carried so you are asked
      to inquire if interested in specific items that may be available.
   "American Heritage Pictorial History of the Civil War" by Bruce
      Catton. $15.95. The epic struggle of the blue and grey with
      more than 800 illustrations.

Suggested Curriculum Application:
   AMERICAN HISTORY
   PENNSYLVANIA STATE AND LOCAL STUDIES

Suggested Sears Subject Heading:
   CEMETERIES
   GETTYSBURG, BATTLE OF
   GETTYSBURG NATIONAL CEMETERY
   PENNSYLVANIA--DESCRIPTION AND TRAVEL--GUIDES
   PENNSYLVANIA--PUBLIC LANDS
   U.S.--DESCRIPTION AND TRAVEL--GUIDES
   U.S.--HISTORY--CIVIL WAR, 1861-1865--CAMPAIGNS AND
      BATTLES

• HARPERS FERRY
National Historical Park. P.O. Box 65, Harpers Ferry, WV 25425.
(304) 535-6371. 2,238.37 acres. 1944. Eastern West Virginia, off
of Rt. 340, 66 miles from Washington, D.C. Visitor center is on
Shenandoah Street.

Preserve the area of John Brown's 1859 raid. Museum and other
buildings associated with John Brown's historic raid. Activities,
programs, walks. Visitor center. Food and lodging in Harpers
Ferry.

Free Print Material:
   "Activities." 1 page. Time and event of tours.
   "John Brown." 1 page. Chronology beginning with Brown's
      birth in 1800 in Connecticut to his execution in 1859 after
      being captured in the armory fire engine house.
   "Park Map." 1 page. Features of interest located and described.

"The Raid--1859." 1 page Events from July 3 with John Brown and sons Oliver and Owen and Jeremiah Anderson arrives in Harpers Ferry to his December 2 execution in Charles Town.

Sales/Audiovisual List:
"Harpers Ferry Historical Association National Park Videos Films and Books, Too." 4 pages. Videos grouped by: America's Treasures; Alaska: The Last Frontier; Man and Nature: A Delicate Balance; Along America's Shores; Indian Art and Culture; Westward Expansion; Civil War; Great Americans. Books grouped by: national park handbooks; general publications. Write for information about rental or purchase of films about historic and natural parks. Order form. The bookstore number is (304) 535-6371 Ext. 6330.
"National Parks: Our Treasured Lands." $29.95. Narrated by Wally Shirra, this film explores the diverse nature of our national parks--small and large, historic and natural, backcountry and urban. An excellent introduction to America's treasures. (1983, 28 minutes)

Suggested Curriculum Application:
AMERICAN HISTORY
WEST VIRGINIA STATE AND LOCAL STUDIES

Suggested Sears Subject Heading:
ABOLITIONISTS
BROWN, JOHN, 1800-1859
SLAVERY IN THE U.S.
U.S.--DESCRIPTION AND TRAVEL--GUIDES
WEST VIRGINIA--DESCRIPTION AND TRAVEL--GUIDES
WEST VIRGINIA--PUBLIC LANDS

• KENNESAW MOUNTAIN
National Battlefield Park. P.O. Box 1167, Marietta, GA 30061. (404) 427-4686. 2,884.38 acres. 1917. Northwestern Georgia, 3 miles north of Marietta, accessible from U.S. 41 and I-75.

Commemorate the engagements that took place between Union and Confederate forces during the Atlanta Campaign, June 20-July 2, 1864. Trails, buildings, historic objects, geologic specimens, earthworks, self-guiding auto tour, living history programs, observation overlook, wayside exhibits. Visitor center, park headquarters, picnicking. Food and lodging in Marietta, Smyrna, Atlanta.

Free Print Material:
"Atlanta's Museums and Historic Sites." 3 pages. Lists sites alphabetically, gives description, address, telephone.
"Historic Roswell." 2 pages. History and attractions, map of the city of Roswell located 20 miles north of Atlanta.
"Hotels and Motels in Cobb County." 1 page. Alphabetical listing includes name, address, telephone and number of rooms.

"Kennesaw Mountain." 8-fold. Maps, photos and background of the campaign for Atlanta and the battle of Kennesaw.

"Meet the General at Big Shanty Museum." 4 pages. Photos, map, information about the Andrews railroad raid.

"The Napoleon 12-Pounder." 2 pages. Description, illustrations of artillery used in the Civil War.

"Teacher's Handbook." 48 pages. Tips for class trip reservations, maps, history of Kennesaw Mountain, bibliography, addresses, quizzes, definitions, and other material.

"Southeast National Parks and National Forests." 18-fold. Names, addresses, telephone, description of various parks and forests in the Southeast. Map, photos.

"Where History is Alive!" 2 pages. Photos, map, description of the Atlanta Historical Society.

Sales/Audiovisual List:
"Kennesaw Mountain Historical Association Mail Order Price List." 4-fold. Purpose of sales, discounts.

"Historical Guide to Kennesaw Mt. and Marietta, GA." By Bowling C. Yates, 47 pages. $2.00.

Suggested Curriculum Application:
AMERICAN HISTORY
GEORGIA STATE AND LOCAL STUDIES

Suggested Sears Subject Heading:
GEORGIA--DESCRIPTION AND TRAVEL--GUIDES
GEORGIA--PUBLIC LANDS
KENNESAW MOUNTAIN, BATTLE OF
U.S.--DESCRIPTION AND TRAVEL--GUIDES
U.S.--HISTORY--CIVIL WAR, 1861-1865--CAMPAIGNS AND BATTLES

• MANASSAS
National Battlefield Park. Box 1830, Manassas, VA 22110.
(703) 754-7107. 4,513.39 acres. 1940. Northern Virginia, 26 miles southwest of Washington, D.C., near the intersection of I-66 and VA 234.

Site of the battles of First Manassas (First Bull Run), on July 21, 1861 and Second Manassas (Second Bull Run) on August 28-30, 1862. Museum, slide programs, one-mile self-guided walking tour with taped messages and interpretive signs of First Manassas Battlefield; a 12-mile driving tour of the Second Manassas Battlefield. A 1.4-mile loop walking trail at the Stone Bridge and a .6-mile walking trail at Sudley highlight other areas of the First Manassas Battlefield. Guided tours available on request. Visitor center, picnic area. Food and lodging in Manassas.

Free Print Material:
"Manassas." 16-fold. Accounts of the two battles, photos, illustration, maps, descriptive tour of both battlefields.

Sales/Audiovisual List:
"Book Guide and Price List." 3 pages. Grouped by: books,
audio and visual aids. Title, price. Includes magazines,
cassette, post card, maps, records, slide strips, stationery,
prints. Ordering information.
"Clara Barton Handbook." $5.50.

Suggested Curriculum Application:
AMERICAN HISTORY
VIRGINIA STATE AND LOCAL STUDIES

Suggested Sears Subject Heading:
FIRST MANASSAS, BATTLE OF (FIRST BULL RUN)
SECOND MANASSAS, BATTLE OF (SECOND BULL RUN)
U.S.--DESCRIPTION AND TRAVEL--GUIDES
U.S.--HISTORY--CIVIL WAR, 1861-1865--CAMPAIGNS AND
BATTLES
VIRGINIA--DESCRIPTION AND TRAVEL--GUIDES
VIRGINIA--PUBLIC LANDS

• PEA RIDGE
National Military Park. Pea Ridge, AR 72751. (501) 451-8122.
4,300.35 acres. 1956. Northern Arkansas, 98 miles north from
Fort Smith on U.S. 62.

One of the major Civil War battles west of the Mississippi, ending in
a Union victory in 1862 saving Missouri for the North. Self-guiding
auto tour of the battlefield, exhibits. Guided group tours can be
arranged. Visitor center, picnicking. Camping nearby. Food and
lodging in Rogers.

Free Print Material:
"Pea Ridge." 12-fold. Maps, sketch, account of the battle
March 7, 1862 and March 8, 1862. Visitor information.

Sales/Audiovisual List:
"Eastern National Park and Monument Association Price List."
5 pages. Books, cassettes, prints, slides, VHS, photographs,
reproductions, patches, and other items. Name of item, price.
"Abraham Lincoln-Fact Book." $2.95.

Suggested Curriculum Application:
AMERICAN HISTORY
ARKANSAS STATE AND LOCAL STUDIES

Suggested Sears Subject Heading:
    ARKANSAS--DESCRIPTION AND TRAVEL--GUIDES
    ARKANSAS--PUBLIC LANDS
    PEA RIDGE, BATTLE OF
    U.S.--DESCRIPTION AND TRAVEL--GUIDES
    U.S.--HISTORY--CIVIL WAR, 1861-1865--CAMPAIGNS AND
      BATTLES

• PETERSBURG
National Battlefield. P.O. Box 549, Petersburg, VA 23803.
(804) 733-2400. 2,735.38 acres. 1926. Central Virginia, Park
Visitor Center is off VA 36, east of Petersburg.

Site of Lee's last stand. The Union Army held a 10-month campaign
beginning June 9, 1864 to seize Petersburg, the center of the railroads supplying Richmond and Lee's army. Military maneuvers,
Petersburg National Battlefield Trail, various side trails, city point
unit, battlefield and Poplar Grove National Cemetery, various buildings still standing, presentations, programs. Visitor center.
Food and lodging in Petersburg.

Free Print Material:
    "City Point Unit." 16-fold. Grant's strategy, the siege of
      Petersburg, the strategic location (the junction of the James
      and Appomattox rivers) of City Point in war efforts. Photos,
      map.
    "Petersburg." 16-fold. Photos, maps, tour of the battlefield,
      history of the siege.
    "Petersburg National Battlefield National Recreation Trail." 8-
      fold. Trail tours, side trails, park regulations, park signifi-
      cance.
    "Petersburg, Virginia." 12-fold. History of Petersburg,
      historic sites, maps, photos.

Sales/Audiovisual List:
    "Eastern National Park and Monument Association Sale Publica-
      tions." 3 pages. Grouped by: books, children's books, in-
      dividual post cards, slide strips. Ordering information.
    "Adapt or Perish." $17.50. Hard bound.

Suggested Curriculum Application:
    AMERICAN HISTORY
    VIRGINIA STATE AND LOCAL STUDIES

Suggested Sears Subject Heading:
    CEMETERIES
    POPLAR GROVE NATIONAL CEMETERY
    U.S.--DESCRIPTION AND TRAVEL--GUIDES
    U.S.--HISTORY--CIVIL WAR, 1861-1865--CAMPAIGNS AND
      BATTLES

VIRGINIA--DESCRIPTION AND TRAVEL--GUIDES
VIRGINIA--PUBLIC LANDS

- RICHMOND
National Battlefield Park. 3215 East Broad Street, Richmond, VA
23223. (804) 226-1981. 771.41 acres. 1936. Eastern Virginia,
off I-95, headquarters at 3215 East Broad Street. A complete tour
of the park involves a 100-mile drive as the park consists of various separate units.

Commemorates several battles to capture Richmond during the Civil
War. Nine units in three counties and Chimborazo visitor center.
Park units include: Chickahominy Bluff, Beaver Dam Creek, Watt
House, Malvern Hill, Drewry's Bluff, Cold Harbor, Garthright
House, Fort Harrison and vicinity, Parker's Battery. Exhibits,
audiovisual program, living history programs, events, historical
markers, interpretive facilities, tape tour rentals, hiking trails,
self-guiding trails, ranger-conducted tours. Guides for organized
groups can be obtained by calling the park at least four weeks in
advance and tours are individualized to age group, interest and time
requirements. Visitor centers, picnicking. Food and lodging in
Richmond.

Free Print Material:
"Chimborazo Hospital." 4-fold. Construction and function of the
hospital, map, sketch, photo, hospital administration.
"Cold Harbor." 8-fold. Events of the battle, May 31, 1864-
June 12, 1864, map, sketch, touring the battlefield stops and
other visitor information.
"Fort Harrison." 8-fold. Description of fort tour, photos, map,
battle account and people involved in the fighting.
"Metropolitan Richmond." 24-fold. Photos, map, descriptions of:
museums, entertainment and sports, history, historic homes,
tours, government. Descriptions include name of the attraction, location, description, telephone number, map location.
"Richmond National Battlefield Park." 16-fold. Touring description of Richmond's battlefields, history, visitor information,
sketches, photos, maps.

Suggested Curriculum Application:
AMERICAN HISTORY
VIRGINIA STATE AND LOCAL STUDIES

Suggested Sears Subject Heading:
BEAVER DAM CREEK, BATTLE OF
COLD HARBOR, BATTLE OF
FORTIFICATION
GAINES MILL, BATTLE OF
MALVERN HILL, BATTLE OF
U.S.--DESCRIPTION AND TRAVEL--GUIDES

U.S.--HISTORY--CIVIL WAR, 1861-1865--CAMPAIGNS AND
BATTLES
VIRGINIA----DESCRIPTION AND TRAVEL--GUIDES
VIRGINIA--PUBLIC LANDS

- SHILOH

National Military Park. Shiloh, TN 38376. (901) 689-5275.
3,837.50 acres. 1894. Southern Tennessee, Highway 22, 50 miles
south of I-40 and 100 miles east of Memphis via Highway 57 and
Highway 64.

Site of 1862 battle that destroyed the south's chances for an early
win. Audiovisual exhibits, museum, self-guiding tour of battlefield,
ranger-led programs, auto tape tour. Inquire about group services.
National cemetery, Indian mounds adjoin the park. Visitor center,
picnicking. Campground nearby. Meals and lodging in Pickwick,
Savannah, Adamsville.

Free Print Material:
"General Information." 8-fold. Features, ranger activities, map,
sketch, accommodations.

Audiovisual List:
"Films Available." 1 page. Grouped by: Shiloh, bicentennial
subjects, environmental subjects.
"Shiloh: Portrait of a Battle."

Suggested Curriculum Application:
AMERICAN HISTORY
TENNESSEE STATE AND LOCAL STUDIES

Suggested Sears Subject Heading:
SHILOH, BATTLE OF
TENNESSEE--DESCRIPTION AND TRAVEL--GUIDES
TENNESSEE--PUBLIC LANDS
U.S.--DESCRIPTION AND TRAVEL--GUIDES
U.S.--HISTORY--CIVIL WAR, 1861-1865--CAMPAIGNS AND
BATTLES

- STONES RIVER NATIONAL BATTLEFIELD

Rt. 10, Box 495, Murfreesboro, TN 37130. (615) 893-9501.
(615) 893-9501. 330.86 acres. 1927. Central Tennessee, 30 miles
southeast of Nashville, one mile northwest of Murfreesboro off U.S.
Highway 41.

Site of December 31, 1862-January 2, 1863 Civil War battle. The
Union victory began an offensive which split the Confederacy,
paving the way for General Sherman's march to the sea. Living
history programs, self-guided tour by car, audiovisuals, one-hour

auto tape tour, hiking trails, national cemetery. Special programs and tours can be arranged for groups with advanced notice. Visitor center, picnicking. Campgrounds nearby. Food and lodging in Murfreesboro.

Free Print Material:
"For Your Safety." 8-fold. Tips about driving; poison plants, insects, snakes; not climbing on cannons and monuments and other tips. Sketches.
"Murfreesboro and Rutherford County." 14 pages. Map, points of interest. Photos and description of the Stones River National Battlefield is included along with other points of interest.
"Stones River." 10-fold. Tour stop guide to the battlefield, the struggle for middle Tennessee, battle events that resulted in an estimated 13,000 Union loss and 10,000 Confederate loss. Maps, photos. Visitor tips.
"Two and Five Mile Hiking Trail Guide." 8-fold. Sketches, map, description of 18 hiking stops. Five-mile trail traces battle events.

Sales/Audiovisual List:
"Eastern National Park and Monument Association Sales List." 2 pages. Grouped by: related to Stones River, general Civil War literature, other Civil War related items, record albums, post cards. Ordering information. Includes title and price of item--if a publication it includes the author.
"Stones River National Battlefield Auto Tape Tour." $3.25.

Suggested Curriculum Application:
AMERICAN HISTORY
TENNESSEE STATE AND LOCAL STUDIES

Suggested Sears Subject Heading:
CEMETERIES
STONES RIVER (MURFREESBORO) NATIONAL CEMETERY
STONES RIVER, BATTLE OF (MURFREESBORO)
TENNESSEE--DESCRIPTION AND TRAVEL--GUIDES
TENNESSEE--PUBLIC LANDS
U.S.--DESCRIPTION AND TRAVEL--GUIDES
U.S.--HISTORY--CIVIL WAR, 1861-1865--CAMPAIGNS AND
    BATTLES

• TUPELO
National Battlefield. c/o Natchez Trace Parkway, R.R. 1, NT-143, Tupelo, MS 38801. (601) 842-1572. 1 acre. 1929. Northeastern Mississippi, on Miss. 6, about 1 mile west of intersection with U.S. 45.

Site of July 13-14, 1864, Civil War battle. Tupelo National Battlefield Site is located near the place where the Confederate line was formed to attack the position of the North. Interpretive signs and markers. Park interpreters at the Tupelo visitor center can answer questions about the battle. Food and lodging in Tupelo.

Free Print Material:
 "Brices Cross, Roads, Tupelo." 10-fold. Sketches, maps, accounts of the Battle of Brices Cross Roads and the Battle of Tupelo, visitor information.
 "Tupelo, Mississippi." 1 page. Black soldiers and their contribution to the Battle of Tupelo near Harrisburg, Mississippi.

Suggested Curriculum Application:
 AMERICAN HISTORY
 BLACK STUDIES
 MISSISSIPPI STATE AND LOCAL STUDIES

Suggested Sears Subject Heading:
 MISSISSIPPI--DESCRIPTION AND TRAVEL--GUIDES
 MISSISSIPPI--PUBLIC LANDS
 TUPELO, BATTLE OF
 U.S.--DESCRIPTION AND TRAVEL--GUIDES
 U.S.--HISTORY--CIVIL WAR, 1861-1865--CAMPAIGNS AND
  BATTLES

• VICKSBURG
National Military Park. 3201 Clay Street, Vicksburg, MS 39180. (601) 636-0583. 1,619.70 acres. 1899. Western Mississippi, 1 mile off Interstate 20.

Maintain preserved fortifications of the 47-day Civil War siege of Vicksburg ending July 3, 1863. Victory gave the North control of the Mississippi River. Vicksburg National Cemetery was transferred from the War Department in 1933. Exhibits, audiovisual program. The 16-mile battlefield tour includes: Battery Degolyer, Shirley House, Third Louisiana Redan, Ranson's Gun Path, Stockade Redan Attack, Thayer's Approach, Battery Selfridge, Vicksburg National Cemetery, Fort Hill, Stockade Redan, Great Redoubt, Second Texas Lunette, Railroad Redoubt, Fort Garrott, Hovey's Approach. The Vicksburg National Cemetery, established in 1866, has about 17,000 Union soldiers, Confederates, veterans of the Spanish-American War, World Wars I and II and the Korean conflict. Inquire about special programs and activities. The U.S.S. Cairo Museum is near the cemetery. Visitor center. Food and lodging in Vicksburg.

Free Print Material:
 "Vicksburg." 12-fold. Photos, sketches, maps, description of main features of the battlefield tour and the gunboat Cairo.

Bibliography:
 "Vicksburg Bibliography." 2 pages. Books, firsthand accounts,

official reports, correspondence, handbooks, magazine. Grouped by: primary sources; naval operations; biography; Vicksburg; Vicksburg 1862, and Vicksburg Campaign, 1863; Vicksburg National Military Park. Includes author, title, place of publication, publisher, date for books.

Audiovisual List:
Inquire about the film "In Memory of Men" about the Vicksburg Campaign and its significance in the Civil War and the film about the sinking and salvage of a Union Civil War river gunboat, the U.S.S. Cairo. They are freely loaned to public schools.

Sales/Audiovisual List:
"Eastern National Park and Monument Association Sales List." 6 pages. Paperback and hardback books, films, prints, post cards, maps, cassettes, calendars, slides, reproductions, paper dolls and other items. Item number, item title, selling price, ordering information.
10194 "National Park Map and Guide." $.50.

Suggested Curriculum Application:
AMERICAN HISTORY
MISSISSIPPI STATE AND LOCAL STUDIES

Suggested Sears Subject Heading:
ARCHITECTURE--CONSERVATION AND RESTORATION
CEMETERIES
MISSISSIPPI--DESCRIPTION AND TRAVEL--GUIDES
MISSISSIPPI--PUBLIC LANDS
U.S.--DESCRIPTION AND TRAVEL--GUIDES
U.S.--HISTORY--CIVIL WAR, 1861-1865--CAMPAIGNS AND
    BATTLES
VICKSBURG, BATTLE OF
VICKSBURG NATIONAL CEMETERY

• WILSON'S CREEK
National Battlefield. Postal Drawer C, Republic, MO 65738. (417) 732-2662. 1,749.91 acres. 1960. Southwestern Missouri, 3 miles east of Republic and 10 miles southeast of Springfield, off U.S. 60.

Site of 1861 Civil War battle for control of Missouri. Film, fiber optic battle map program, Civil War research library, self-guiding battlefield tour, interpretive signs, foot trail departure points. Visitor center, picnicking. Food and lodging in Springfield.

Free Print Material:
"Educators' Study Guide to Wilson's Creek National Battlefield." 14 items in a folder. Maps, sketches, sales publication list, bibliography, battlefield foundation, battle information and others.

Bibliography:
> Part of the "Educators' Study Guide to Wilson's Creek National
> Battlefield" folder described above. Books, articles and other
> material about the Battle of Wilson's Creek; titles relating to
> Greene County in early formation.

Sales List:
> Part of the "Educators' Study Guide to Wilson's Creek National
> Battlefield" folder described above. Name and price and
> postage, order form.
> "Battle of Wilson's Creek" (170 pages, paperback). $3.95. .50
> postage.

Audiovisual List:
> Inquire about one 13-minute film on the battle that is available
> for free loan.

Suggested Curriculum Application:
> AMERICAN HISTORY
> MISSOURI STATE AND LOCAL STUDIES

Suggested Sears Subject Heading:
> MISSOURI--DESCRIPTION AND TRAVEL--GUIDES
> MISSOURI--HISTORY
> MISSOURI--PUBLIC LANDS
> U.S.--DESCRIPTION AND TRAVEL--GUIDES
> U.S.--HISTORY--CIVIL WAR, 1861-1865--CAMPAIGNS AND
>   BATTLES
> WILSON'S CREEK, BATTLE OF

COLONIZATION

- ARKANSAS POST

National Memorial. Route 1, Box 16, Gillet, AR 72055. (501)
548-2432. 389.18 acres. 1960. Eastern Arkansas, located on
Ark. 169, 7 miles south of Gillett by U.S. 165.

Site of the first permanent French settlement in the Lower Mississippi
Valley in 1686, memorial to various people who played a vital role in
the growth and development of the United States. Audiovisual program, trails, wildlife, historic walking tour, exhibits. Visitor center,
picnicking. Food and lodging in Gillett, Dumas.

Free Print Material:
> "Arkansas Post National Memorial, Arkansas." 16-fold. Map, il-
> lustrations, photos. History of: the French period, 1683-1765;

the Spanish regime, 1765-1800; Arkansas during the American Revolution, 1779-1783; Napoleonic France and the Louisiana Purchase, 1800-1803; a frontier settlement 1803-1865.

Suggested Curriculum Application:
AMERICAN HISTORY
ARKANSAS STATE AND LOCAL STUDIES

Suggested Sears Subject Heading:
ARKANSAS--DESCRIPTION AND TRAVEL--GUIDES
ARKANSAS--HISTORY
ARKANSAS--PUBLIC LANDS
COLONIZATION
LAND SETTLEMENT
U.S.--DESCRIPTION AND TRAVEL--GUIDES

• CASTILLO DE SAN MARCOS
National Monument. 1 Castillo Drive, St. Augustine, FL   32084. (904) 829-6506. 20.48 acres. 1924. Northeastern Florida.

Oldest masonry fort in continental United States, begun in 1672 by the Spanish to protect St. Augustine, the first permanent settlement by Europeans in the continental United States. Tours, interpretive ranger talks, living history programs, torchlight programs, displays, audio stations, markers. Inquire about a new pre-visit teacher packet (in progress at time of publication). Gift shop. Food and lodging in St. Augustine.

Free Print Material:
"Castillo De San Marcos." 14-fold. Chronology of the fort, photos, sketches, life of a private soldier, the history of St. Augustine, maps, French and English competition.

Sales/Audiovisual List:
Copies of photographs and slides are provided at cost upon request. Inquire about publication sales lists from: The Castillo Shop, P.O. Drawer M, St. Augustine, FL   32085.

Suggested Curriculum Application:
AMERICAN HISTORY
FLORIDA STATE AND LOCAL STUDIES

Suggested Sears Subject Heading:
AMERICA--EXPLORATION
COLONIZATION
FLORIDA--DESCRIPTION AND TRAVEL--GUIDES
FLORIDA--HISTORY
FLORIDA--PUBLIC LANDS
FORTIFICATION
LAND SETTLEMENT
U.S.--DESCRIPTION AND TRAVEL--GUIDES

• CHRISTIANSTED
National Historic Site. P.O. Box 160, Christiansted, St. Croix, VI
00820. (809) 773-1460. 27.15 acres. 1952. U.S. Virgin Islands.

Commemorates colonial development of Virgin Islands with 18th- and
19th-century colonial structures at former Danish West Indies capital
on St. Croix Island. The island was discovered by Columbus and
purchased from Denmark in 1917. Walking tour of restored buildings: Fort Christiansvaern, Old Danish Customs House, Scalehouse,
Government House, Danish West Indian and Guinea Company Warehouse, Steeple Building Museum. Visitor center. Food and lodging
in Christiansted.

Free Print Material:
    "Christiansted." 12-fold. History, photos, map, walking tour
        attractions.

Suggested Curriculum Application:
    AMERICAN HISTORY
    VIRGIN ISLANDS STATE AND LOCAL STUDIES

Suggested Sears Subject Heading:
    AMERICA--EXPLORATION
    ARCHITECTURE--CONSERVATION AND RESTORATION
    COLONIZATION
    LAND SETTLEMENT
    U.S.--DESCRIPTION AND TRAVEL--GUIDES
    VIRGIN ISLANDS--DESCRIPTION AND TRAVEL--GUIDES
    VIRGIN ISLANDS--PUBLIC LANDS

• FORT CAROLINE
National Memorial. 12713 Fort Caroline Road, Jacksonville, FL 32225.
(904) 641-7155. 138.39 acres. 1959. Northeast Florida, 10 miles
east of downtown Jacksonville, by Fla. 10.

Overlooks the location of the French 1564-65 attempt at settlement
within the current United States. Scale replica of fort, museum,
self-guiding trail. Picnicking. Food and lodging in Jacksonville.

Free Print Material:
    "Fort Caroline." 12-fold. Sketches, maps, engraving, establish-
        ment of the colony and conflict with Spain, visitor information.

Suggested Curriculum Application:
    AMERICAN HISTORY
    FLORIDA STATE AND LOCAL STUDIES

Suggested Sears Subject Heading:
    COLONIZATION
    FLORIDA--DESCRIPTION AND TRAVEL--GUIDES

FLORIDA--HISTORY
FLORIDA--PUBLIC LANDS
FORTIFICATION
U.S.--DESCRIPTION AND TRAVEL--GUIDES

• FORT MATANZAS
National Monument. c/o Castillo De San Marcos, National Monument,
1 Castillo Drive, St. Augustine, FL 32084. (904) 471-0116.
227.76 acres. 1924. Northeastern Florida, 14 miles south of
St. Augustine, by Fla. A1A on Anastasia Island. The monument is
on Rattlesnake Island where the fort is located and on Anastasia
Island where the visitor center is located.

Fort built 1740-42 by the Spanish to protect St. Augustine from the
British. Swimming and other water activities, tours, nature trail,
audio station. Visitor center, docks, ferry. Food and lodging in
St. Augustine.

Free Print Material:
    "Fort Matanzas." 12-fold. History, strategic location of Fort
    Matanzas, the Spanish-French struggle. Sketches, photo,
    map.

Suggested Curriculum Application:
    AMERICAN HISTORY
    FLORIDA STATE AND LOCAL STUDIES

Suggested Sears Subject Heading:
    ANASTASIA ISLAND
    COLONIZATION
    FLORIDA--DESCRIPTION AND TRAVEL--GUIDES
    FLORIDA--HISTORY
    FLORIDA--PUBLIC LANDS
    FORTIFICATION
    LAND SETTLEMENT
    RATTLESNAKE ISLAND
    U.S.--DESCRIPTION AND TRAVEL--GUIDES

• FORT RALEIGH
National Historic Site. c/o Cape Hatteras National Seashore, Route
1, Box 675, Manteo, NC 27954. (919) 473-5772. 157.27 acres.
1941. Eastern North Carolina, Roanoke Island, 3 miles north of
Manteo, on U.S. 64-264.

Site of the "Lost Colony," first English attempt to colonize the New
World in the 1580's. From this Roanoke Island site, 116 men, women
and children mysteriously disappeared. Sir Walter Raleigh was the
imaginative force behind the Roanoke colonies. Restored fort, exhibits, live drama, talks, film, Elizabethan gardens, Tudor gate

house, Thomas Hariot Nature Trail. Visitor center. Food and lodging in Mateo.

Free Print Material:
"Camping Information." 2 pages. Name of five campgrounds, reservations, fees, check-out time and other visitor information.
"Fort Raleigh." 12-fold. Colonizing efforts, maps, illustrations, England's sea efforts, relations with the Indians, what to see and do at the site.
"In the Park." 12 pages. Newspaper format. Visitor information about Fort Raleigh National Historic Site, Wright Brothers National Memorial, Cape Hatteras National Seashore. Photos, schedules of activities, articles, maps, sales list.

Sales/Audiovisual List:
Items for sale from the Eastern National Park and Monument Association included in "In the Park" described above. Items include: adult books, miscellaneous, children's books, slides, puzzle, posters, note cards, model kits. Purpose of the Eastern National Park and Monument Association, ordering directions.

Suggested Curriculum Application:
AMERICAN HISTORY
ARCHEOLOGY
NORTH CAROLINA STATE AND LOCAL STUDIES

Suggested Sears Subject Heading:
AMERICA--EXPLORATION
ARCHITECTURE--CONSERVATION AND RESTORATION
FORTIFICATION
HARIOT, THOMAS, 1560-1621
NORTH CAROLINA--DESCRIPTION AND TRAVEL--GUIDES
NORTH CAROLINA--HISTORY
NORTH CAROLINA--PUBLIC LANDS
RALEIGH, SIR WALTER, 1554-1618
ROANOKE ISLAND
U.S.--DESCRIPTION AND TRAVEL--GUIDES

• SAINT CROIX ISLAND
International Historic Site. c/o Acadia National Park, P.O. Box 177, Bar Harbor, ME 04609. (207) 288-3338. 35.39 acres. National Monument, 1949; International Historic Site, 1984. Eastern Maine, the entrance is 8 miles south of Calais, along U.S. 1.

Commemorate French settlement efforts. St. Croix Island National Monument is administered by the National Park Service in cooperation with the Canadian government. Walking, interpretive shelter on the mainland explains the historic significance of St. Croix, interpretive programs in summer. Picnicking. Food and lodging in Calais.

Free Print Material:
"Saint Croix Island." 16-fold. One side is printed in French,
the other in English. History of French colonization in Saint
Croix, named by the head of the expedition because nearby
two long coves meet with the river to form a cross. Historical
sketches, maps.

Suggested Curriculum Application:
AMERICAN HISTORY
MAINE STATE AND LOCAL STUDIES

Suggested Sears Subject Heading:
COLONIZATION
MAINE--DESCRIPTION AND TRAVEL--GUIDES
MAINE--PUBLIC LANDS
U.S.--DESCRIPTION AND TRAVEL--GUIDES

CONSERVATION

• BIG THICKET
National Preserve. P.O. Box 7408, Beaumont, TX 77706.
(409) 839-2689. 85,849.55 acres. 1974. Eastern Texas, separate
locations north of Beaumont. Information station on FM 420, 2.5
miles east of U.S. 69, 7 miles north of Kountze.

Preserve a varied biological diversity of life forms. Elements from
Southeastern swamps, Appalachians, Eastern forest, Central Plains,
Southwest deserts. Species of 85 trees, over 60 shrubs, about
1,000 flowering plants, abundant wildlife, nearly 300 kinds of
birds. Composed of 12 units or 8 tracts and 4 corridors of land.
Hiking and nature trails, naturalist activities. Preserve information
center, campgrounds. Lodging and food in Beaumont.

Free Print Material:
"Big Thicket." 24-fold. Features, attractions, history, sketches,
photos, maps. Visitor tips and information on using the
large map.
"Hiking Trails." 2 pages. Map, sketches, description of six
trails. Visitor tips, where to obtain more information.
"Naturalist Activities." 2 pages. Calendar and description of
events. How to make reservations or confirm schedules, addresses of nearby organizations, map.

Suggested Curriculum Application:
ENVIRONMENTAL EDUCATION
GEOGRAPHY

NATURAL HISTORY
TEXAS STATE AND LOCAL STUDIES

Suggested Sears Subject Heading:
CONSERVATION OF NATURAL RESOURCES
TEXAS--DESCRIPTION AND TRAVEL--GUIDES
TEXAS--PUBLIC LANDS
U.S.--DESCRIPTION AND TRAVEL--GUIDES

• JOHN MUIR
National Historic Site. 4202 Alhambra Avenue, Martinez, CA 94553.
(415) 228-8860. 8.90 acres. 1964. Western California, San Francisco Bay Area.

Commemorate Muir's championship of "Wilderness is a Necessity" with
his home and working orchard. Born in 1838, Muir believed that all
forms of life have significance and publicized widely the current
ecological and preservation viewpoint. Guided house tours, groups
should be arranged in advance for guided tours. Audiovisual shows,
lectures, fruit sampling in season. Visitor center, picnicking.
Food and lodging in Martinez.

Free Print Material:
"Chronology of Important Events in the Life of John Muir."
2 pages. Begins with 1838--Muir's birth in Scotland, includes
publications.
"John Muir." 8-fold. Muir's life and contributions to wilderness
preservation, map, photos.
"Map of John Muir National Historic Site." 1 page. Map shows
orchards, home, parking and other areas of visitor interest.
"Park Information Sheet." 1 page. Hours, facilities, fees, interpretive services, access, buses.
"A Safe Visit to John Muir National Historic Site." 2 pages.
Sketches, safety tips about bees, poison oak, ladders, rug
edges and other hazards. Map.

Suggested Curriculum Application:
CALIFORNIA STATE AND LOCAL STUDIES
ENVIRONMENTAL EDUCATION
SOCIAL STUDIES

Suggested Sears Subject Heading:
CALIFORNIA--DESCRIPTION AND TRAVEL--GUIDES
CALIFORNIA--PUBLIC LANDS
CONSERVATION OF NATURAL RESOURCES
MUIR, JOHN, 1838-1914
NATURE CONSERVATION
U.S.--DESCRIPTION AND TRAVEL--GUIDES
WILDERNESS AREAS

• PRINCE WILLIAM
Forest Park. P.O. Box 208, Triangle, VA 22172. (703) 221-7181.
18.571.55 acres. 1936. Northern Virginia about 20 miles north of
Fredericksburg and 20 miles south of the 496 beltway.

Reclaimed worn-out farmland used for recreation and wildlife.
Naturalist events, hiking trails, nature center, talks. Picnicking,
campgrounds, travel trailer village, group cabin camps and tents.

Free Print Material:
    "Application for Carter's Day Camp-Picnic Use Only." 2 pages.
        Description, instructions, application.
    "Application for Group Tent Camping in Turkey Run Ridge."
        2 pages. Application, instructions and description.
    "Cabin Camping Application." 1 page. Instructions and appli-
        cation.
    "Camping Guide--Oak Ridge Campground." 2 pages. Regulations,
        services, general information.
    "Camping Guide--Turkey Run Ridge Campground." 2 pages.
        General information for the user, map.
    "Naturalist Events." 8-fold. Schedule and description of various
        events, sketches, map.
    "Prince William Forest Park." 12-fold. Suggested activities,
        photos, safety regulations, history, map.
    "Travel Trailer Village." 4-fold. Services available, location,
        map, mileage from the village to various attractions, sketches,
        photo.

Sales/Audiovisual List:
    Films are only available for viewing at the nature center. They
        are shown upon request during the weekends and by appoint-
        ment during the week. For more information/list call
        (703) 221-2104.

Suggested Curriculum Application:
    ENVIRONMENTAL EDUCATION
    RECREATION
    VIRGINIA STATE AND LOCAL STUDIES

Suggested Sears Subject Heading:
    OUTDOOR RECREATION
    SOIL CONSERVATION
    U.S.--DESCRIPTION AND TRAVEL--GUIDES
    VIRGINIA--DESCRIPTION AND TRAVEL--GUIDES
    VIRGINIA--PUBLIC LANDS

DESERTS

- DEATH VALLEY

National Monument. Death Valley, CA 92328. (619) 786-2331.
2,067,727.68 acres. 1933. Eastern California, border of Nevada
and California, U.S. 395 passes west of Death Valley and connects
with Calif. 178 and 190 to the park. U.S. 95 passes east and connects with Nev. 267, 374, 373 to the park, I-15 passes southeast
and connects with Calif. 127.

Lowest point in the Western Hemisphere, large desert surrounded
by high mountains. Includes Scotty's Castle and other remains of
gold and borax mining activity. Harmony Borax Works Interpretive
Trail, Golden Canyon Interpretive Trail, Zabriskie Point, Artists
Drive, Historic Stovepipe Wells, Salt Creek Interpretive Trail, Hells
Gate, Scotty's Castle, Grapevine, Ubehebe Crater, Mesquite Spring,
Mosaic Canyon, Telescope Peak, Kilns, Devil's Golf Course, lowest
elevation point, Eagle Borax Works, Jubilee Pass, Ashford Mill Ruins,
Mahogany Flat, wildflowers. Programs, talks, tours of Scotty's
Castle, museums, ranger-conducted programs, self-guiding tours,
photography workshops, sketching strolls, hiking, horseback riding,
sightseeing tours. The monument is 1-1/2 times the size of Delaware
and has two national park bookstores. Visitor center, ranger stations, campgrounds, church services, food, gift shops, two resorts
provide lodging and other commercial services.

Free Print Material:

"Camping in Death Valley." 6-fold. Facilities, regulations, services.
"Death Valley." 24-fold. Photos, diagram, chart, maps. Visitor
information such as driving, park regulations, car trouble,
heat, what to see and do.
"Death Valley Visitor Guide." 8 pages. Newspaper format.
Articles, photos, sketches, activities, trivia quiz, visitor services, aims of Death Valley Natural History Association, membership application.
"Hot Weather Hints." 4-fold. Tips on surviving your summer
trip through Death Valley, sketches.
"Precipitation Records." 2 pages. Records go back to 1911.
72-year average annual precipitation and total precipitation,
monthly averages.
"Scotty's Castle." 4 pages. Life of Walter E. Scott (1872-1954),
the namesake of "Scotty's Castle." Sketch.
"Visitor Information Sheets." 11 pages. Historical restoration
project, ghost towns, cacti, fish, Ubehebe Crater, Racetrack
Valley, flora, hikes, endemic plants, Mosaic Canyon, animal
life, Indian culture and other information.

Sales List:
 Description of featured publication appears in "Death Valley
  Visitor Guide" described above.

Suggested Curriculum Application:
 AMERICAN HISTORY
 CALIFORNIA STATE AND LOCAL STUDIES
 GEOGRAPHY
 GEOLOGY
 NATURAL HISTORY

Suggested Sears Subject Heading:
 CALIFORNIA--DESCRIPTION AND TRAVEL--GUIDES
 CALIFORNIA--PUBLIC LANDS
 DESERTS
 GEOLOGY--U.S.
 NATURAL HISTORY--CALIFORNIA
 NATURAL HISTORY--NEVADA
 NATURAL MONUMENTS
 NEVADA--DESCRIPTION AND TRAVEL--GUIDES
 NEVADA--PUBLIC LANDS
 MINES AND MINERAL RESOURCES--U.S.
 U.S.--DESCRIPTION AND TRAVEL--GUIDES
 U.S.--GEOGRAPHY

• JOSHUA TREE
National Monument. 74485 National Monument Drive, Twentynine
Palms, CA 92277. (619) 367-7511. 559,954.50 acres. 1936.
Southern California, 140 miles east of Los Angeles, near Twentynine
Palms.

Preserve a unique portion of the California desert with a wide
variety of vegetation and animals, stand of Joshua trees. Key's
View, Hidden Valley, Jumbo Rocks, Split Rock, Cholla Cactus
Garden, nine nature trails, Joshua trees located in the central and
western portions of the monument, wildlife, Oasis of Mars, Barker
Dam, Ryan Mountain, Lost Horse Mine, Cottonwood Spring, Transition Zone, geology tour road, guided walks, Lost Palms Oasis,
Fortynine Palms Oasis, talks, programs. Visitor centers, campgrounds. Food and lodging in Joshua Tree, Twentynine Palms and
other nearby communities.

Free Print Material:
 "General Information." 2 pages. Description, attractions, facilities, visitor safety, campground elevations and other visitor
  tips, map with points of interest keyed and described.
 "Information for Campers." 1 page. Chart of campgrounds includes campground name, description, number of sites and
  elevation. Visitor tips.

Audiovisual List:
   "Movie List."   8 pages. Includes title, running length, annota-
      tion, if preparation is useful, recommended grade levels, type
      of film such as art, live action. Not arranged alphabetically
      or by subject.
   "Early Americans-1776," length: 30 minutes. This motion pic-
      ture about Americans west of the Appalachians in 1776 looks
      at settlements in New Mexico, Hawaii, and Alaska, as well as
      Spanish missions in California, giving a picture of life.

Sales/Audiovisual List:
   "Joshua Tree Natural History Association Sales Catalog." 6-fold.
      Grouped by: animals, archeology, deserts, flowers and
      plants, general, golden guides, history, other items for sale,
      pamphlets. Ordering information and statement of purpose of
      the association. Other items for sale include color slides,
      cloth patch, maps, prints, posters, post cards and other items.
      Sketch. Includes title, author, price for publications, title
      and price of others.
   "Amphibians of N. America," $6.95, Smith, H. M.

Suggested Curriculum Application:
   CALIFORNIA STATE AND LOCAL STUDIES
   GEOGRAPHY
   NATURAL HISTORY

Suggested Sears Subject Heading:
   CALIFORNIA--DESCRIPTION AND TRAVEL--GUIDES
   CALIFORNIA--PUBLIC LANDS
   DESERTS
   JOSHUA TREES
   NATURAL HISTORY--CALIFORNIA
   TREES--U.S.
   U.S.--DESCRIPTION AND TRAVEL--GUIDES

• ORGAN PIPE CACTUS
National Monument. Route 1, Box 100, Ajo, AZ 85321.
(602) 387-6849. 1,489.76 acres. 1937. Southern Arizona, junction
of Interstates 8 and 80, take State Route 85 south. Headquarters
located 40 miles south of Ajo.

Desert plants and animals unique to this country, traces of historic
trail, natural features in a portion of the Sonoran Desert. Nature
trails, mine trail, guided walks, talks, programs. Scenic drives:
The 21-mile Ajo Mountain Drive through the foothills of the Ajo
Mountains and the 53-mile Puerto Blanco Drive circles the Puerto
Blanco Mountains and various scenery. Visitor center, campground,
picnicking. Food and lodging in Ajo.

Free Print Material:
   "Campground Regulations."   2 pages. Quiet hours, camping

limits and other user information. Map of campground showing
numbers of site locations, pet areas, dump station and others.
"How to Survive Your Visit to Organ Pipe Cactus National Monument." 1 page. Tips on wildlife, plant life, hiking and backpacking, driving, sketches.
"Organ Pipe Cactus." 12-fold. Features, trails, camping, description of the desert landscape, maps. Illustration with identified wildlife and plants.

Sales/Audiovisual List:
Grouped by: publications; posters, slides, post cards and
miscellaneous. Slides section includes slide and cassette program. Miscellaneous includes notecards and map. Publications
are identified by title, author, weight, price. Directions for
ordering.
"A Field Guide to Birds Coloring Book," Peterson, Alden and
Sill, 8 ounces. $3.95.

Suggested Curriculum Application:
ARIZONA STATE AND LOCAL STUDIES
GEOGRAPHY
NATIONAL HISTORY

Suggested Sears Subject Heading:
ARIZONA--DESCRIPTION AND TRAVEL--GUIDES
ARIZONA--PUBLIC LANDS
CACTUS
DESERTS
NATURAL HISTORY--ARIZONA
U.S.--DESCRIPTION AND TRAVEL--GUIDES
U.S.--GEOGRAPHY

• SAGUARO
National Monument. Old Spanish Trail, Route 8, Box 695, Tucson,
AZ 85730. (602) 296-8576. 83,573.88 acres. 1933. Southeast Arizo-
na, the Rincon Mountain Unit visitor center is located on Old Spanish
Trail at Freeman Road, 2 miles from Tucson.

Protect the stand of giant saguaro cactus, some reaching 50 feet
and 200 years of age. Monument is in two desert sections: Rincon
Mountain Unit (62,499 acres), and Tucson Mountain Unit (21,154
acres). Scenic drive, hiking and nature trails, exhibits, overlooks,
cactus forest drive, naturalist walks, wildlife, wildflowers. Visitor
center, information center, picnic sites. Food and lodging in
Tucson.

Free Print Material:
"Saguaro." 16-fold. Features of the two mountain units, maps,
facilities, photos, chart, regulations, plant and wildlife, plant
community life and saguaro adaptations.

Sales/Audiovisual List:
  "Southwest Parks and Monuments Association List of Items Sold
    at Saguaro National Monument, Rincon Mountain Unit." 4
    pages. Coloring book, books, guides, prints, posters, slide
    strips, calendars, card-game, prints and other items. Title,
    price, poster size. Order information includes postage and
    handling costs.
  "American Indian Food and Lore" (100 recipes), by Niethammer.
    $10.95.

Suggested Curriculum Application:
  ARIZONA STATE AND LOCAL STUDIES
  GEOGRAPHY
  NATURAL HISTORY

Suggested Sears Subject Heading:
  ARIZONA--DESCRIPTION AND TRAVEL--GUIDES
  ARIZONA--PUBLIC LANDS
  CACTUS
  DESERTS
  NATURAL HISTORY--ARIZONA
  U.S.--DESCRIPTION AND TRAVEL--GUIDES
  U.S.--GEOGRAPHY

DUNES

• GREAT SAND DUNES
National Monument. Mosca, CO 81146. (303) 378-2312. 38,662.18
acres. 1932. Southern Colorado, U.S. 160 east from Alamosa, CO
to Colo. 150, in the San Luis Valley.

Preserve North America's tallest sand dunes, probably formed as
the last ice age ended. Ranger activities, exhibits, 4-wheel drive
tours, self-guiding trail, programs. Visitor center, picnic area,
campground.

Free Print Material:
  "Great Sand Dunes." 8-fold. Sketches, photos, maps, visitor
    tips, history, features, activities.
  "Great Sand Dunes Educators Guide." Various pages in first
    draft form. Inquire if interested. The material is designed
    for classroom use and includes fill-in-the blank and background
    materials.
  "List of Vesculer Plants." 12 pages. Scientific name, common
    name; arranged by families.
  "Mammals of the Great Sand Dunes National Monument and Vicinity."

2 pages. Common and scientific names of: have been sighted
or presence is likely, presence is possible but sighting unlikely, presence very unlikely.
"Mineral Composition of Sand." 2 pages. Components, percentage
values, how the dunes are made.
"Montville Trail Area." 8 pages. Map, sketches, to help the
visitor enjoy the features along the trail.
"Sand Sleuthing." 8-fold. Identifying animals by the tracks and
trails, sketches, making plaster casts.

Sales/Audiovisual List:
"Southwest Parks and Monuments Association Publications List."
2 pages. Grouped by: Great Sand Dunes/San Luis Valley,
history and culture, plants and animals, Colorado and Geology,
children, national parks, maps, miscellaneous. Slide sets are
included in miscellaneous. Order form and ordering directions.
"Great Sand Dunes, the Shape of the Wind." By Trimble-$1.90.
Spectacular photography and lively writing tell the story of
the dunes and their relationship to the San Luis Valley. It is
the best general information source to the area. Color photos.
32 pages.

Suggested Curriculum Application:
COLORADO STATE AND LOCAL STUDIES
GEOGRAPHY
GEOLOGY

Suggested Sears Subject Heading:
COLORADO--DESCRIPTION AND TRAVEL--GUIDES
COLORADO--PUBLIC LANDS
GEOLOGY, U.S.
SAND DUNES
U.S.--DESCRIPTION AND TRAVEL--GUIDES
U.S.--GEOGRAPHY

• INDIANA DUNES NATIONAL LAKESHORE
1100 N. Mineral Springs Road, Porter, IN 46304. (219) 926-7561.
12,869.65 acres. 1966. Northwest Indiana, on over three miles of
Lake Michigan's southern shore. The visitor center is 3 miles east
of Ind. 49 on U.S. 12 at Kemil Road.

Preserve dunes that rise as high as 180 feet above Lake Michigan's
southern shore, beaches, bogs, marshes, swamps, prairie remnants,
partially restored historic sites. Audiovisuals, swimming, Bailly
Homestead, Chellberg Farm, West Beach Area, dune climbing, hiking
trails, boating, horseback riding, cross-country skiing, snowshoeing,
guided trips, Mount Baldy, Miller Woods, Cowles Wetlands Area,
Pinhook Bog, special activities, guest lectures, films, festivals,
ranger-led hikes, Paul H. Douglas Center for Environmental Education. School groups may use the interpretive services by making

advance arrangements. Inquire about guided trips and special activities throughout the park or possibly at your school for preschool to graduate level students. Visitor center, ranger stations, campground, youth tent camping, concession and campground grocery, fast food and souvenirs, bathhouse, picnicking. Campgrounds nearby. Food and lodging in Michigan City.

Free Print Material:
"Indiana Dunes." 16-fold. Mapping glacial advances and a shrinking shoreline, plants, the Paul H. Douglas Center for Environmental Education, visitor information, how dunes are formed, photos, map.
"Paul Howard Douglas." 10-fold. Efforts of Senator Paul Douglas to preserve the dunes along with photos and other biographical sidelights.
"Singing Sands Almanac." 8 pages. Sketches, photos, map, list of activities, articles. Guide for visitors by the Friends of Indiana Dunes National Lakeshore.
"Teachers Guide." 20 pages. What is offered at the lakeshore, how to prepare for a field trip, scheduling a field trip, how to arange a ranger-conducted activity, photos, park map, program descriptions.
"Trail Map." 8-fold. Description of trails, regulations, activities and facilities. Maps, photo.

Audiovisual List:
"Film List." 8 pages. Alphabetically arranged by title. Title of film, running length, color, suitable age level, producer, date. Films available for on-site viewing. Two films available for loan are among those described.
"A Matter of Time." 28 minutes. Color. Upper Elementary-adult. Conservation Foundation, 1967. Reviews some past technologies of the planet and shows possible results of unrestricted industrial growth.

Sales/Audiovisual List:
"Publications available at the Indiana Dunes National Lakeshore." 2 pages. Arranged by: books, Indiana Dunes posters and prints, south shore prints, USGS topographic maps, slide strips. Title, author included with only the first title, price. Order blank, ordering directions.
"Indiana Dunes," by Waldron. $3.95.

Suggested Curriculum Application:
ENVIRONMENTAL EDUCATION
GEOGRAPHY
GEOLOGY
INDIANA STATE AND LOCAL STUDIES

Suggested Sears Subject Heading:
GEOLOGY--U.S.

INDIANA--DESCRIPTION AND TRAVEL--GUIDES
INDIANA--PUBLIC LANDS
SAND DUNES
U.S.--DESCRIPTION AND TRAVEL--GUIDES
U.S.--GEOGRAPHY

- SLEEPING BEAR DUNES
National Lakeshore. 400 Main Street, Frankfort, MI 49635.
(616) 352-9611. 71,021.14 acres. 1970. Northwestern lower peninsula
of Michigan, Lake Michigan shores, north of Frankfort on Mich. 22.

Large sand dunes, beaches, forests, lakes on Lake Michigan shoreline and two offshore islands. Exhibits, maritime museum, hiking
trails, canoeing, boating, birdwatching, swimming, slide program,
snowshoeing, cross-country ski trails. During summer: guided
walks, evening programs, scenic drive. South Manitou Island has
huge white cedar trees, lighthouse and other historic sites and has
a commercial motor tour and restaurant during the summer. North
Manitou Island has 15,000 acres of wilderness. Visitor centers,
ranger stations, picnicking, campgrounds. Ferry service and
cruises to the islands available, May through October. Food and
lodging in Frankfort, Glen Arbor, Honor, Beulah.

Free Print Material:
"Alligator Hill Cross Country Ski Trails." 6-fold. Description of
the three loops and a beginner spur, general cross-country
ski trail information, maps, sketches.
"Alligator Hill Hiking Trail." 6-fold. Description of the trail,
aerial photo, maps, general trail information.
"Climate of Sleeping Bear Dunes National Lakeshore." 2 pages.
General influences and local climatic conditions.
"Cultural Resources of Sleeping Bear Dunes National Lakeshore."
2 pages. Human use of the area and advance of progress.
"The Dunes Hiking Trail." 6-fold. Maps, sketch, the dunes
trail system, general trail information.
"Empire Bluff Cross Country Ski Trail." 6-fold. Description of
the 1.5 advanced trail, maps, sketches, general cross-country
ski trail information.
"Empire Bluff Self Guiding Hiking Trail." 8-fold. Trail description, geological background, description of the old farm and
beech-maple forest, old orchard, overlook. Sketches, photos,
map.
"Geology of Sleeping Bear Dunes National Lakeshore." 2 pages.
Effect of glacial advance 50,000 years ago, what happened
when the meltwaters flowed southward from the glacier front.
"Good Harbor Bay Cross Country Ski Trail." 6-fold. Description
of the beginner loop, general cross-country ski trail information,
maps, sketches.
"Historic Resources of Sleeping Bear Dunes National Lakeshore."
2 pages. Historic sites such as former towns, docks, sawmills,
lighthouses.

"North Manitou Island." 8-fold. Map, photos, description, visitor facilities, history.

"Old Indian Cross Country Ski Trail." 6-fold. Maps, sketches, description of Old Indian Trail, general cross-country ski trail information.

"Old Indian Hiking Trail." 6-fold. Description of the trail, general trail information, maps, sketches.

"Pierce Stocking Scenic Drive." 6-fold. Description, sketches, map of this seasonal drive.

"Platte Plains Cross Country Ski Trails." 6-fold. Description of platte plains trails, general cross-country ski trail information, maps, sketches.

"Platte Plains Hiking Trail." 6-fold. Description of the trail, general trail information, maps, sketches.

"Pyramid Point Hiking Trail." 6-fold. Maps, sketch, aerial photo, description of 2-1/2-mile trail.

"Ranger Programs." 6-fold. Description, schedule of programs.

"Shauger Hill Cross Country Ski Trails." 6-fold. Description of three trails, general cross-country ski trail information, maps, sketches.

"Shauger Hill Hiking Trail." 6-fold. Description of 2.4 trail, general trail information, maps, sketches.

"Sleeping Bear Dunes." 12-fold. Chippewa Indian legend about how the dunes got their name, photos, description of the dunes, how the dunes were formed, map, visitor information.

"The Story of the Sand Dunes." 10-fold. Geologic maps, the ice age, changing shorelines, dunes and how they are classified, plants, photos.

"South Manitou Island." 8-fold. Sketch, map, photos, the Chippewa Indian legend about how the island was created, description of the island, visitor facilities, special places to see.

"Vegetation of Sleeping Bear Dunes National Lakeshore." 2 pages. Plant succession description. Begins on Sandy Beach and ends in beech/maple forest inland.

"What To Do While the Scenic Drive is Closed." 24-fold. Photos, map, description of other areas of the park.

"Wildlife of Sleeping Bear Dunes National Lakeshore." 2 pages. Diverse wildlife populations are a reflection of the varied habitats that exist in the dunes.

"Windy Moraine Cross Country Ski Trail." 6-fold. Description of the single intermediate loop, general cross-country ski trail information, maps, sketches.

Sales/Audiovisual List:

"Catalog of Sales Items at Sleeping Bear Dunes National Lakeshore." 4 pages. Grouped by: South Manitou Island, children's books, geology, animals, history, miscellaneous. Miscellaneous includes guides, slides, post cards. Children's books include coloring books on Michigan, animals, birds, lumbering. Title, price. Ordering information, purpose of the Eastern National Park and

Monument Association.
"Isle of View." $4.25.

Suggested Curriculum Application:
MICHIGAN STATE AND LOCAL STUDIES
ENVIRONMENTAL EDUCATION
GEOGRAPHY
GEOLOGY
NATURAL HISTORY
RECREATION

Suggested Sears Subject Heading:
GEOLOGY--U.S.
ISLANDS
MICHIGAN--DESCRIPTION AND TRAVEL--GUIDES
MICHIGAN--PUBLIC LANDS
NATURAL HISTORY--MICHIGAN
NORTH MANITOU ISLAND
OUTDOOR RECREATION
SAND DUNES
SOUTH MANITOU ISLAND
U.S.--DESCRIPTION AND TRAVEL--GUIDES
U.S.--GEOGRAPHY

• WHITE SANDS
National Monument. P.O. Drawer 458, Alamogordo, NM 88310.
(505) 437-1058. 144,458.24 acres. 1933. Central New Mexico,
15 miles southwest of Alamogordo on U.S. 70/82.

Preserve the world's largest gypsum dunefield. 230 square miles
of brilliant, changing white dunes rising 60 feet high, walks, programs, auto caravans, self-guiding 16 mile round trip tour, displays.
Picnic areas, refreshments and souvenirs, visitor center, backcountry campsite. Camping in Lincoln National Forest, Oliver Lee
Memorial State Park and Aguirre Springs.

Free Print Material:
"Fee Waiver Regulations." 1 page. Regulations concerning any
group requesting a fee waiver for scientific or educational purposes.
"Hours of Operation." 1 page. Schedule for dunes drive, visitor
center and gift shop, full moon nights, Lake Lucero caravans,
entrance fee.
"Monthly Weather Conditions." 1 page. Average high, average
low, highest, lowest, average, precipitation for each month.
Other climatic facts.
"White Sands." 16-fold. Description of the heart of the sands
loop drive, map, regulations, safety tips. Photos, visitor
tips, geological history.

Bibliography:
"Selected Bibliography of Publications Relating to White Sands
National Monument and the Tularosa Basin, New Mexico."
9 pages. Arranged alphabetically by author. Date, title,
name, date and page/volume of periodical. Includes master's
theses, reports.

Audiovisual List:
"National Park Service Film Survey." 2 pages. Title, source,
date, film size, color or B & W, sound or silent, length,
nitrate or safety film, condition or comments.
"The Age of Alaska." Richter-McBride Production, unknown
date, 16mm, color, sound, 21 minutes, safety, excellent.

Suggested Curriculum Application:
GEOGRAPHY
GEOLOGY
NEW MEXICO STATE AND LOCAL STUDIES

Suggested Sears Subject Heading:
GEOLOGY--U.S.
NEW MEXICO--DESCRIPTION AND TRAVEL--GUIDES
NEW MEXICO--PUBLIC LANDS
SAND DUNES
U.S.--DESCRIPTION AND TRAVEL--GUIDES
U.S.--GEOGRAPHY

EXPLORATION

• CABRILLO
National Monument. P.O. Box 6670, San Diego, CA 92106.
(619) 293-5450. 143.94 acres. 1913. Southern California, at the
southern end of Point Loma at the end of Catalina Blvd (Route 209).

Tribute to Juan Rodríguez Cabrillo, Portuguese explorer who claimed
the west coast of the United States for Spain in 1542. Cabrillo
statue, Whale overlook, tidepool area, Old Point Loma Lighthouse,
interpretive exhibits, self-guided walks and lighthouse tours, audiovisual programs, hiking trail, exhibits. Visitor center. Food and
lodging in San Diego.

Free Print Material:
"Cabrillo." 16-fold. Maps, photos, illustrations. The age of
discovery, Cabrillo's voyage, features of interest such as the
annual gray whale migrations.
"School Guide." 17 pages. Guidelines for the safety and enjoy-

ment of visiting school groups. Includes pre-visit activities, on-site activity and post-site activities, questions and exercises. Sketches.

Bibliography:
A one-page reading list grouped by: general, Cabrillo, lighthouses, whales, tidepools is included in the "School Guide" described above.

Sales List:
"Cabrillo Historical Association Book List." 9 pages. Arranged alphabetically by title. Includes title, publisher, date.
"Afoot and Afield in San Diego County." Wilderness Press. $12.95.

Suggested Curriculum Application:
AMERICAN HISTORY
CALIFORNIA STATE AND LOCAL STUDIES

Suggested Sears Subject Heading:
AMERICA--EXPLORATION
CABRILLO, JUAN RODRIGUEZ, ?-1543
CALIFORNIA--DESCRIPTION AND TRAVEL--GUIDES
CALIFORNIA--HISTORY
CALIFORNIA--PUBLIC LANDS
EXPLORERS
U.S.--DESCRIPTION AND TRAVEL--GUIDES

• CORONADO
National Memorial. Rural Route 1, Box 126, Hereford, AZ 85615. (602) 366-5515. 4,750.47 acres. 1952. Southern Arizona, 22 miles south of Sierra Vista and 30 miles southwest of Bisbee off Route 92.

Commemorates first European exploration, in 1540-42, of the southwest, by Francisco Vasquez de Coronado. Hiking, exhibits, birds, plants, museum, Montezuma Pass, view of part of the route Coronado used. Annual festival, other cultural activities. Visitor center, picnicking. Amphitheater. Campground nearby. Food and lodging at Sierra Vista, Bisbee.

Free Print Material:
"Coronado." 8-fold. Maps, photos, visitor activities, safety regulations, weather. Illustration of volunteers leaving to join Coronado. Account of the Coronado expedition.
"Coronado Borderlands Festival." 1 page. Information about the annual spring festival. Sketch.
"General Information." 2 pages. Visitor interest information such as park regulations. General description and purpose of the memorial. Sketch.
"The National Parks and the Bicentennial of the United States

Constitution." 12-fold. Photos, connection between the be-
ginnings of our federal system and the National Park System.

Sales/Audiovisual List:
"Coronado National Memorial Book List." 1 page. Title, price
of books, maps, post cards, posters, game, stamps, VHS,
coloring book, calendar, checklists.
"Coronado Route Map." 0.75.

Suggested Curriculum Application:
AMERICAN HISTORY
ARIZONA STATE AND LOCAL STUDIES

Suggested Sears Subject Heading:
AMERICA--EXPLORATION
ARIZONA--DESCRIPTION AND TRAVEL--GUIDES
ARIZONA--HISTORY
ARIZONA--PUBLIC LANDS
CORONADO, FRANCISCO VASQUEZ DE, 1510-1554
U.S.--DESCRIPTION AND TRAVEL--GUIDES

• DE SOTO
National Memorial. 75th Street, NW, Bradenton, FL 33529.
(813) 792-0458. 26.84 acres. 1948. West central Florida, on
Tampa Bay, five miles west of Bradenton, off Star Route 64.

Commemorates Hernando de Soto's landing in Florida in 1539 and his
four-year expedition across the southeastern United States. Demonstrations, talks, nature trail, monument, Tabby House ruin, mangrove jungle, Camp Ucita, cove, De Soto Point, exhibits, audiovisual
program. Visitor center. Food and lodging in Bradenton.

Free Print Material:
"De Soto." 10-fold. De Soto's aims and expedition, map,
sketches, of his trips and the park. Features to see in the
park, map and safety tips.
"De Soto." (in Spanish) 5 pages. Description of De Soto and
his expedition, map, administration of the park.
"Litter-ally Speaking...." 2 pages. How much litter costs, tips
on keeping areas clean.
"Local Places of Interest." 1 page. Name, phone number,
features, hours, admission, directions. Includes such places
as the Manatee Village Historical Park, the Marie Selby Botanical Gardens and a variety of others.

Audiovisual List:
"Summaries of Movies at De Soto National Memorial." 2 pages.
title, audience, running length, annotation.
"Stream Environment." Good for all ages. 9 minutes. This film
is not narrated. It shows the evolution of a stream ... melting

snow ... gushing streams ... then how animal life depends on
it (deer eating grass, fish eating insects).

Sales/Audiovisual List:
"Sales List Relating to the History of Hernando De Soto and His
Expedition." 1 page. Historical publications. Title, author,
publisher, date, price. Inquire about a 22-minute video of
the De Soto expedition for $39.95 plus postage.
"Narratives of De Soto: In the Conquest of Florida." Translated
by Buckingham Smith. Palmetto Books, Gainesville, FL,
Kallman Publishing Co., Gainesville, FL. Copyright 1968.
$17.95.

Suggested Curriculum Application:
AMERICAN HISTORY
FLORIDA STATE AND LOCAL STUDIES

Suggested Sears Subject Heading:
AMERICA--EXPLORATION
DE SOTO, HERNANDO, 1500-1542
FLORIDA--DESCRIPTION AND TRAVEL--GUIDES
FLORIDA--HISTORY
FLORIDA--PUBLIC LANDS
U.S.--DESCRIPTION AND TRAVEL--GUIDES

● FATHER MARQUETTE
National Memorial. Parks Division, Michigan Department of Natural
Resources, P.O. Box 30028, Lansing, MI 48909. (906) 643-8620.
52 acres. 1975. Southeastern upper peninsula of Michigan, off of
U.S. 2, in Straits State Park near St. Ignace.

Pay tribute to the accomplishments of Father Jacques Marquette,
French priest and explorer. Founded Jesuit mission in St. Ignace,
buried in St. Ignace. Museum has interpretive exhibits highlighted
by artifacts and reproductions, film, memorial, amphitheater. Copy
of the explorer's journal in both the original French and in English
translation. Outdoor memorial overlooks the Straits of Mackinac.
Food and lodging in St. Ignace. Picnicking and interpretive center.

Free Print Material:
"Father Marquette National Memorial and Museum." 4-fold. Map,
photos, features, biographical information on Father Marquette.

Suggested Curriculum Application:
AMERICAN HISTORY
MICHIGAN STATE AND LOCAL STUDIES

Suggested Sears Subject Heading:
AMERICA--EXPLORATION
EXPLORERS

MARQUETTE, JACQUES, 1637-1675
MICHIGAN--DESCRIPTION AND TRAVEL--GUIDES
MICHIGAN--HISTORY
MICHIGAN--PUBLIC LANDS
U.S.--DESCRIPTION AND TRAVEL--GUIDES

- FORT CLATSOP
National Memorial. Route 3, Box 604-FC, Astoria, OR 97103.
(503) 861-2471. 125.20 acres. 1958. Northwest Oregon, 96 miles
northwest of Portland, 5 miles southwest of Astoria on U.S. 101.

Site of an encampment December 7, 1805-March 23, 1806 of the Lewis
and Clark Expedition after their 4,000-mile journey from the Mississippi River to the Pacific Ocean. The first American-built structure
on the Pacific slope was named after a friendly local Indian tribe.
Reconstruction of the fort site, exhibits, audiovisual programs,
costumed summer interpretations, self-guiding trails, canoe landing.
On-site ranger-conducted educational programs can be arranged for
school groups from September through May by contacting the park
at least two weeks in advance. Visitor center. Picnicking, campgrounds nearby. Food and lodging in Astoria and Warrenton.

Free Print Material:
"Fort Clatsop." 8-fold. Importance of the Lewis and Clark Expedition, why Fort Clatsop was built and how the expedition
spent their time there, photos, illustration.
"Fort Clatsop Information." 8-fold. Facilities and services,
ranger programs, exploring the site, safety tips, maps, illustration.
"Map with Today's Nomenclature and Expedition's Nomenclature."
1 page. Washington and Oregon area.
"School/Group Planning Guide." 6-fold. Description of ranger
programs, planning hints, what to see and do, safety tips,
film loans, hours and location, history of the fort. Maps,
illustration.

Audiovisual List:
A list of films for schools appears in "School/Group Planning
Guide" described above. It includes recommended grade level
and running time.

Sales/Audiovisual List:
"Fort Clatsop Historical Association Mail Order Price List." 8-
fold. Grouped by: general books on the expedition, the
journals of the expedition, for the Lewis and Clark aficionado,
photographic essays of the Lewis and Clark Trail, children's
books, Native Americans at the mouth of the Columbia River,
post cards and slides, medallions, prints, items for your possible bag, decorative items. Order blank, ordering information. Title, description, size, price. If publication, also
includes number of pages, if hard or soft cover and author.

"Gone West!" Magazine, Spring, 1983. Features articles on
Lewis and Clark at Fort Clatsop, the history of Fort Clatsop
National Memorial and Astoria. Softbound. 14 pages. $2.00.

Suggested Curriculum Application:
AMERICAN HISTORY
OREGON STATE AND LOCAL STUDIES

Suggested Sears Subject Heading:
EXPLORERS
FORTIFICATION
LEWIS AND CLARK EXPEDITION
NORTHWEST, PACIFIC
OREGON--DESCRIPTION AND TRAVEL--GUIDES
OREGON--PUBLIC LANDS
OVERLAND JOURNEYS TO THE PACIFIC (U.S.)
U.S.--DESCRIPTION AND TRAVEL--GUIDES
U.S.--EXPLORING EXPEDITIONS

• SAN JUAN
National Historic Site. P.O. Box 712, Old San Juan, PR 00902.
(809) 724-1974. 75.13 acres. 1949. Northern Puerto Rico.

Large masonry fortifications, oldest in the territorial limits of the
United States, begun in the sixteenth century to guard the harbor
and avenues to the New World. Spanish-built forts of El Morro,
San Cristobal, El Canuelo, and the city walls. Guided tours, slide
programs in English and Spanish. Food and lodging in San Juan.

Free Print Material:
"Official Transportation Map." Multi-folded map. Photos, map,
attractions.
"San Juan National Historic Site." 16-fold. Sketches, maps,
history, need for fortifications, in English and Spanish.
"Que Pasa." 98 pages. Official visitor guide to Puerto Rico,
photos, attractions, maps. In Spanish and English.

Suggested Curriculum Application:
AMERICAN HISTORY
PUERTO RICO LOCAL STUDIES
SPANISH

Suggested Sears Subject Heading:
AMERICA--EXPLORATION
FORTIFICATION
PUERTO RICO--DESCRIPTION AND TRAVEL--GUIDES
PUERTO RICO--PUBLIC LANDS
U.S.--DESCRIPTION AND TRAVEL--GUIDES

FORTIFICATIONS

• FORT FREDERICA
National Monument. Route 9, Box 286-C, St. Simons Island, GA
31522. (912) 638-3639. 216.35 acres. 1936. East coast of Georgia,
on St. Simons Island, 12 miles from Brunswick, GA. Brunswick-
St. Simons toll causeway connects with U.S. 17 at Brunswick.

British fort built in 1736-48 as a result of the competition with Spain
over current southeastern United States. Exhibits, self-guiding
tour of townsite and fort, audiovisuals, demonstrations. Inquire
about group visits to receive arrangement notification of tours, film
craft demonstrations, other activities. Visitor center. Picnicking
in Brunswick. Food and lodging in Brunswick and on St. Simons
Island.

Free Print Material:
"Fort Frederica National Monument." 12-fold. History of
Frederica, natural features, visitor information, tour map
and narrative of the town and fort.
"St. Simons Island, Sea Island." 16-fold. Maps, attractions,
history, map, photos.

Sales List:
"Fort Frederica Association Catalogue of Sales Items." 2 pages.
Title, pages, date, description, price. Publications include
coastal activities book and coloring book.
"A Guide to Georgia Coast" by the Georgia Conservancy, 199
pages, published in 1984. A guide to Cumberland Island,
Okefenokee Swamp, Suwanee River, and 45 other sites and
rivers on the Georgia coast, plus I-95 driving tours, trip
planning guide, and more. $9.95.

Audiovisual List:
Inquire about 25-minute visitor center film "This is Frederica"
that can be shipped in advance of school visits.

Suggested Curriculum Application:
AMERICAN HISTORY
GEORGIA STATE AND LOCAL STUDIES

Suggested Sears Subject Heading:
FORTIFICATION
GEORGIA--DESCRIPTION AND TRAVEL--GUIDES
GEORGIA--HISTORY
GEORGIA--PUBLIC LANDS
U.S.--DESCRIPTION AND TRAVEL--GUIDES
U.S.--HISTORY--COLONIAL PERIOD, 1600-1775

- FORT JEFFERSON

National Monument. c/o Everglades National Park, P.O. Box 279, Homestead, FL 33030. (305) 247-6211. 64,700 acres. 1935. Off the southern tip of Florida, about 70 miles west of Key West, lies seven coral reefs called Dry Tortugas. Named Las Tortugas (The Turtles) by Spanish explorer Ponce de Leon who discovered them in 1513, and later named Dry Tortugas because the islands contain no fresh water.

Fort Jefferson was built on the Dry Tortugas island group to protect navigation in the Gulf of Mexico and is the largest of American masonry 19th-century coastal forts. Served as a federal military prison during and after the Civil War. Self-guiding tour of the fort including the cell of Dr. Samuel Mudd, convicted of complicity in President Lincoln's assassination. Underwater nature trail, marine life, coral formations, slide program, swimming, snorkeling, bird refuge. Transportation to the fort is by private boat, commercial seaplane, chartered boat. For information contact the Chamber of Commerce located at: 3330 Overseas Highway, Marathon, FL 33052; Old Mallory Square, Key West, FL 33040; 1700 N. Tamiami Trail, Naples, FL 33940. All fresh water, fuel, food, and supplies must be brought with you. Picnicking, campground, public dock. Food and lodging in Key West.

Free Print Material:
>"Fort Jefferson." 16-fold. Maps, sketches, photos. Construction and functions of Fort Jefferson, marine and plant life, birdlife, visitor information.
>"Fort Jefferson National Monument Visitor Information." 2 pages. Camping, dock policy, access, buoy chart and other visitor information.
>"Pa-Hay-Okee." 8 pages. Newspaper format. Articles, photos, sketches, schedules and attractions of south Florida's national park areas.
>"Public Docking Policy-Fort Jefferson National Monument." 2 pages. Docking regulations, map, coordinates of boundary corners.

Suggested Curriculum Application:
>AMERICAN HISTORY
>FLORIDA STATE AND LOCAL STUDIES

Suggested Sears Subject Heading:
>FLORIDA--DESCRIPTION AND TRAVEL--GUIDES
>FLORIDA--PUBLIC LANDS
>FORTIFICATION
>MARINE RESOURCES
>PRISONS--U.S.
>U.S.--DESCRIPTION AND TRAVEL--GUIDES

- FORT NECESSITY
National Battlefield. The National Pike, Farmington, PA 15437.
(412) 329-5512. 902.80 acres. 1931. Southwestern Pennsylvania,
11 miles east of Uniontown, PA on U.S. 40.

Preserve and interpret George Washington's first battle in 1754,
marking the beginning of the French and Indian War. Mount
Washington Tavern, archeological exhibits, reconstructed fort,
guided tours, special events, slide program, hiking trail, cross-
country ski trails, Braddock's grave, Jumonville Glen. Visitor center, picnicking, campgrounds nearby. Food and lodging in Uniontown.

Free Print Material:
    "Fort Necessity." 2 pages. Purpose, what to do, hours, map.
        Location of Friendship Hill and Fort Necessity, administration.
    "Information Letter." 2 pages. Hours, description and purpose
        of Fort Necessity National Battlefield and Friendship Hill
        National Historic Site.
    "Jumonville Glen." 6-fold. Skirmish in May 1754 that was the
        first in a series of important war events. Maps, battle, Eng-
        lish and French colonial rivalry.
    "The Story of Mount Washington Tavern." 4 pages. Purpose,
        sketches, history of the great Turnpike or National Road that
        began 1811 in Cumberland and reached Wheeling in 1818.

Audiovisual List:
    "Films Available for Loan from Fort Necessity National Battlefield.
        7 pages. Most films are on early America. Title, annotation,
        running time, type of film, age group.
    "The Age of Alaska." This film outlines the "Four Systems" of
        national forests, wildlife refuges, parks, and wild and scenic
        rivers which have been recommended to the Congress by the
        Secretary of the Interior under terms of the Alaska Native
        Claims Settlement Act. It depicts.... Also inquire about a
        slide presentation with tape about George Washington and his
        role in the Battle of Fort Necessity and a soldier's knapsack
        program, which contains several common utensils and items
        used by soldiers of the time (availability can be limited).

Sales/Audiovisual List:
    "Eastern National Parks and Monument Association Sales List."
        7 pages. Grouped by: publications, illustrative materials,
        slides, reproductions. Illustrative material includes post cards,
        maps, crewel kit, notecards. Reproductions include musket
        balls, dice, lead pencil, paper cartridge, wooden spinning top.
        Trivia card game on national parks. Order sheet, ordering
        directions. For publications includes title, author, annotation,
        publisher, date, pages, type of cover, price. Most other
        items are annotated.
    "Advice to Officers." Sixth edition of a 1783 manual of humorous
        instructions. 134 pages, soft cover $2.50.

Suggested Curriculum Application:
AMERICAN HISTORY
PENNSYLVANIA STATE AND LOCAL STUDIES

Suggested Sears Subject Heading:
FORTIFICATION
FORT NECESSITY, BATTLE OF
PENNSYLVANIA--DESCRIPTION AND TRAVEL--GUIDES
PENNSYLVANIA--PUBLIC LANDS
U.S.--DESCRIPTION AND TRAVEL--GUIDES
U.S.--HISTORY--FRENCH AND INDIAN WAR, 1755-1763
WASHINGTON, GEORGE, 1732-1799

• FORT POINT
National Historic Site. P.O. Box 29333, Presidio of San Francisco,
CA 94129. (415) 556-1693. 29 acres. 1970. Western California,
beneath the Golden Gate Bridge at the foot of Lincoln Boulevard
and Long Avenue in the Presidio of San Francisco.

Preserve an example of a brick seacoast fort built in the 1800's to
protect harbors. Constructed during 1853-1861 to protect the Bay
of San Francisco, abandoned in 1886, used as a base of operations
for building the Golden Gate Bridge, used during World War II as
part of a submarine net. Tours, museums, exhibits, special events,
demonstrations in the loading and firing of a Civil War cannon.
Group tours should be arranged at least a week in advance. Overnight environmental living program allows a 4th- through 6th-grade
class to experience the life of a soldier during the 1860's for one
weeknight during the school year from 5 P.M. to 9 A.M. the next
morning; classroom preparation and teacher overnight workshop. A
daytime living history program for 4th- through 6th-grade classes
is also available from 10 A.M. to 4 P.M. Also inquire about the
schoolsite visit program suitable for all grades for schools within a
20-mile radius of Fort Point. Visitor center, picnic area. Food and
lodging nearby.

Free Print Material:
"Fort Point National Historic Site, California." 8-fold. Photos,
history in different periods, construction and architecture.
"Visitor Information." 3 pages. Visiting days and hours, facilities, programs available, location, museums and exhibits.

Suggested Curriculum Application:
AMERICAN HISTORY
CALIFORNIA STATE AND LOCAL STUDIES

Suggested Sears Subject Heading:
CALIFORNIA--DESCRIPTION AND TRAVEL--GUIDES
CALIFORNIA--HISTORY
CALIFORNIA--PUBLIC LANDS

FORTIFICATION
U.S.--DESCRIPTION AND TRAVEL--GUIDES

• FORT PULASKI
National Monument. Box 98, Tybee Island, GA 31328. (912) 786-
5787. 5,623.10 acres. 1924. Eastern Georgia, 13 miles east of
Savannah, off U.S. 80.

Preserve early nineteenth-century masonry fort, proven outmoded
when hit by cannon during the Civil War. Named for a Polish
general serving in the American Revolutionary army. Museum, interpretive programs and displays, fort and grounds self-guiding tour,
hiking, guided walks, talks. Visitor center, picnicking. Boat ramp
and campground nearby. Meals and lodging in Savannah area.

Free Print Material:
    "Fort Pulaski." 16-fold. Illustrations, maps, photos of the his-
        tory of the fort. Features, things to know.
    "Fort Pulaski Discovery Guide." 16 pages. Maps, sketches, nar-
        rative to help the visitor understand and enjoy visiting the
        fort. How the fort got its name, information about nearby
        Tybee Island.

Sales/Audiovisual List:
    "Fort Pulaski National Monument Sales Catalog." 5 pages.
        Grouped by books, audiovisual aids, theme-related souvenirs.
        Title, price. Order blank.
    "Across Five Aprils." $2.25.

Suggested Curriculum Application:
    AMERICAN HISTORY
    GEORGIA STATE AND LOCAL STUDIES

Suggested Sears Subject Heading:
    FORTIFICATION
    GEORGIA--DESCRIPTION AND TRAVEL--GUIDES
    GEORGIA--HISTORY
    GEORGIA--PUBLIC LANDS
    U.S.--DESCRIPTION AND TRAVEL--GUIDES

• FORT SCOTT
National Historic Site. Old Fort Boulevard, Fort Scott, KS 66701.
(316) 223-0310. 16.69 acres. 1979. Eastern Kansas, 6 miles west
of Larned, just north of Fort Scott on KS 156.

Preserve the restored and reconstructed building of Fort Scott to
recreate the American frontier. The restored frontier military fort
includes a post hospital, guardhouse, dragoon barracks, stables,
bakery, officer's quarters, powder magazine and master's storehouse.

Special weekend events and change of season celebrations. Audio-visual program, exhibits, guided tours, demonstrations, programs and special events. Visitor center, picnicking. Campground near-by. Food and lodging in Fort Scott.

Free Print Material:
   "Exploring the Tallgrass Prairie at Fort Scott National Historic
      Site." 6-fold. Types of grasses and wildflowers. The early
      explorer's reactions to this type of land. Sketches and
      descriptions. Maps.
   "Fort Scott." 4 pages. The policing of the frontier functions
      of the fort, how the fort was built, the fort's activity in the
      Mexican War, Civil War and other events. Photos, maps,
      illustrations of the fort and fort life.
   "Fort Scott National Historic Site Schedule of Activities." 2
      pages. Hours, dates and events of routine and special events
      for the current year.
   "Historic Fort Scott, Kansas Where History Lives!" 6-fold. At-
      tractions of the fort told by narrative and illustrated by
      photos.

Bibliography:
   "Bibliography--Fort Scott National Historic Site." 1 page. Author,
      title, publisher, date. Those intended for the general reader
      are indicated.

Sales/Audiovisual List:
   "SPMA Sales Items." 2 pages. Name of items and prices.
      Grouped by: books, post cards, historic post cards, hawk
      post cards, other. Other category includes coal tar soap,
      prints, cards, buttons, slide sets, notecards, prairie seed
      mix, sampler, cups. Item, price.
   "Amanda Moves West." $5.95.

Suggested Curriculum Application:
   AMERICAN HISTORY
   KANSAS STATE AND LOCAL STUDIES

Suggested Sears Subject Heading:
   ARCHITECTURE--CONSERVATION AND RESTORATION
   FORTIFICATION
   FRONTIER AND PIONEER LIFE
   KANSAS--DESCRIPTION AND TRAVEL--GUIDES
   KANSAS--PUBLIC LANDS
   U.S.--DESCRIPTION AND TRAVEL--GUIDES

• FORT SMITH
National Historic Site. P.O. Box 1406, Fort Smith, AR   72902.
(501) 783-3961. 73.36 acres. 1961. Western Arkansas, downtown
Fort Smith, on Rogers Avenue.

Preserves one of the first U.S. military posts in the territory of
Louisiana; contains the remains of two frontier military forts and a
federal court. Self-guiding tour of the fort. Second Fort Smith,
first Fort Smith, commissary storehouse, barracks-courthouse-jail,
gallows, initial point marker (reconstruction), second Fort Smith
flagpole. Inquire about group tours in advance. Visitor center.
Campground nearby. Food and lodging in Fort Smith.

Free Print Material:
> "Fort Smith." 8-fold. History and functions, photos, map,
> touring features, painting.
> "Fort Smith." 12-fold. Function and activities of Fort Smith
> during its frontier duties. Photos, map, sketch.
> "Fort Smith: A Visitors Guide." 16 pages. Lodging, restaurants,
> history, attractions, special events, lakes, rivers, streams,
> mountain scenery. Photos, map, fact page.
> "Take Pride in America." 8-fold. Campaign of national public
> awareness to take pride in the country's natural and cultural
> resources. Photos.
> "Western Arkansas Bonanza Land." 32 pages. A guide featuring
> lodging, restaurants, history, attractions, special events,
> lakes, rivers, streams, mountain scenery. Photos, calendar
> of events, maps, points of interest.

Sales List:
> "Sales List." 2 pages. Grouped by: Fort Smith and Judge
> Parker, the Old West, Native Americans and Indian removal,
> Indian policy, westward expansion, U.S. army in the West,
> Civil War, national parks, Arkansas, and Oklahoma, pictorial
> books, especially for children, etc. Order blank and ordering
> directions.
> "Fort Smith elevator (newspaper reprint). .30.

Suggested Curriculum Application:
> AMERICAN HISTORY
> ARKANSAS STATE AND LOCAL STUDIES

Suggested Sears Subject Heading:
> ARKANSAS--DESCRIPTION AND TRAVEL--GUIDES
> ARKANSAS--PUBLIC LANDS
> FRONTIER AND PIONEER LIFE
> FORTIFICATION
> U.S.--DESCRIPTION AND TRAVEL--GUIDES

• FORT SUMTER
National Monument. 1214 Middle Street, Sullivan's Island, SC
29482. (803) 883-3123. 189.32 acres. 1948. Eastern South Carolina. Fort Sumter is located in Charleston Harbor, Fort Moultrie is
on West Middle Street, Sullivan's Island 10 miles north of Charleston
off U.S. 17 and SC 703.

Fort Sumter is site of the first engagement of the Civil War, April 12, 1861. Fort Moultrie is the scene of American Revolutionary War victory June 28, 1776. Shows development of seacoast defense from 1776 to 1947. Site of Chief Osceola's grave. Groups should make reservations for guided tours. Fort Moultrie, Fort Sumter, interpretive talks, guided tours, museums, tour boats, audiovisuals. Visitor center. Food and lodging in Charleston.

Free Print Material:

"Daily Tours of Ft. Sumter and Charleston Harbor-Riverboat Rambler Excursions." 8-fold. Fort tours daily from municipal marina and Patriots Point, Riverboat Rambler excursions leaving from Patriots Point, starlight dinner cruises, schedules, Civil War action, map, photos, illustrations.

"Famous People at Fort Moultrie." 24 pages. Portrait and biographical information about such people as William Moultrie, Francis Marion, Chief Osceola, Edgar Allan Poe, General William T. Sherman, George C. Marshall. Also a list of some of the other famous people associated with fort Moultrie but not included with biographies.

"Fort Moultrie." 12-fold. Illustrations, photos. Uses of the fort in its 171-year history during the Revolutionary War, Civil War, World War I, World War II. Visitor information.

"Fort Sumter." 12-fold. Civil War action, map of Fort Sumter and Charleston Harbor, floorplan of Fort Sumter, description of walking tour.

"Fort Sumter National Monument." 2 pages. Description of Fort Moultrie, description of Fort Sumter. Sketch, map.

Suggested Curriculum Application:

AMERICAN HISTORY
SOUTH CAROLINA STATE AND LOCAL STUDIES

Suggested Sears Subject Heading:

FORTIFICATION
FORT MOULTRIE, BATTLE OF
SOUTH CAROLINA--DESCRIPTION AND TRAVEL--GUIDES
SOUTH CAROLINA--HISTORY
SOUTH CAROLINA--PUBLIC LANDS
U.S.--DESCRIPTION AND TRAVEL--GUIDES
U.S.--HISTORY--CIVIL WAR, 1861-1865--CAUSES
U.S.--HISTORY--REVOLUTION, 1775-1783--CAMPAIGN AND BATTLES

- FORT WASHINGTON PARK
National Capital Parks--East. 1900 Anacostia Drive, S.E., Washington, D.C. 20020. (301) 292-2112. 341 acres. 1930. Southern Maryland, on the Maryland side of the Potomac River, south on I-295 and east on I-495.

Preserve example of early 19th-century coastal defense, on the site of the earliest fort erected for the defense of the national capital begun in 1814. Museum, demonstrations, fort, park. Picnicking. Food and lodging in Washington, D.C.

Free Print Material:
    "Basic Information for Program Planning." 4 pages. Enabling legislation, National Park Service management policies and long-term management plans, current planning documents, selected bibliography of information sources.
    "Fort Washington." 8-fold. Purpose of the fort, repairs and alterations, service before and after the Civil War. Visitor information, photos.

Bibliography:
    Included in "Basic Information for Program Planning" described above. List includes some of the information sources used for interpretive programs. Includes: author, title, publisher, date.

Sales List:
    "Parks and History Association Alphabetic Title Listing by Site for Fort Washington Park." 4 pages. Arranged by item, title, author, category, price, on hand/on order. Includes souvenirs, books, maps, post cards.

Suggested Curriculum Application:
    AMERICAN HISTORY
    MARYLAND STATE AND LOCAL STUDIES

Suggested Sears Subject Heading:
    FORTIFICATION
    MARYLAND--DESCRIPTION AND TRAVEL--GUIDES
    MARYLAND--PUBLIC LANDS
    U.S.--DESCRIPTION AND TRAVEL--GUIDES
    U.S.--DEFENSES
    U.S.--HISTORY--WAR OF 1812

FOSSILS

• AGATE FOSSIL BEDS
National Monument. P.O. Box 427, Gering, NE 69341.
(308) 668-2211. 3,055.22 acres. 1965. Western Nebraska, 30 miles from Harrison, near Agate, off Nebr. 29.

Quarries containing Miocene mammal fossils. Fossil exhibits, self-guiding trail to area of exposed fossils. Food and lodging in Scottsbluff.

Free Print Material:
    "Agate Fossil Beds." 8-fold. Photos, illustration, map, geology
        of the site, ancient life, scientific excavations. Visitor infor-
        mation, administration.

Suggested Curriculum Application:
    GEOLOGY
    NEBRASKA STATE AND LOCAL STUDIES

Suggested Sears Subject Heading:
    FOSSILS
    GEOLOGY--U.S.
    NEBRASKA--DESCRIPTION AND TRAVEL--GUIDES
    NEBRASKA--PUBLIC LANDS
    U.S.--DESCRIPTION AND TRAVEL--GUIDES

• DINOSAUR
National Monument. Box 210, Dinosaur, CO   81610.   (303) 374-2216.
211,141.69 acres.   1915.   Northeast Utah, northwest Colorado.
Dinosaur quarry visitor center is 7 miles north of U.S. 40, Jensen,
UT.   Headquarters visitor center is on U.S. 40, 2 miles east of
Dinosaur, CO.

Bones of ten varieties of dinosaurs and fossils of sea creatures older
than dinosaurs preserved in rock.   Deep canyons made by Green and
Yampa rivers.   Hiking trails, overlooks, exhibits, split mountain,
petroglyphs, Red Rock Nature Trail, river float trips, display of
dinosaur fossils in quarry, slide program, Harpers Corner scenic
drive, Echo Park Road, Jones Hole, Gates of Lodore and Deerlodge
Park.   Boaters need permits and whitewater craft expertise.
Visitor centers, campgrounds, picnicking, ranger stations, shuttle-
bus.   Food and lodging in Vernal, UT and Rangely, CO.

Free Print Material:
    "Dinosaur." 16-fold. Photos, illustrations of various dinosaurs,
        map, features and visitor information of the park, geological
        survey.
    "Dinosaurland Northeastern Utah." 16 pages. Maps; attractions;
        natural history; accommodations and services arranged by city;
        national forests, parks and recreation areas.
    "Planning Your Visit." 2 pages. Facilities and services, recrea-
        tional activities, suggestions, camping chart, local area services
        chart, climate chart, picnic area locations.

Sales/Audiovisual List:
    "Dinosaur Nature Association Catalog of Sales Items." 6 pages.

Grouped by: Dinosaur National Monument (includes a resource packet for students and teachers), dinosaurs for adults, dinosaurs for children, dinosaur color and activity book for children, color slides, maps, charts and posters, post cards. Title, author, publisher, date, type of cover, price, weight. Order form, ordering directions, aims of the Dinosaur Nature Association.

"Dinosaur National Monument" (park map/general information) NPS/GPO, 1986, $.23, 1 oz.

Suggested Curriculum Application:
ARCHEOLOGY
COLORADO STATE AND LOCAL STUDIES
SCIENCE
UTAH STATE AND LOCAL STUDIES

Suggested Sears Subject Heading:
COLORADO--DESCRIPTION AND TRAVEL--GUIDES
COLORADO--PUBLIC LANDS
DINOSAURS
FOSSILS
U.S.--DESCRIPTION AND TRAVEL--GUIDES
UTAH--DESCRIPTION AND TRAVEL--GUIDES
UTAH--PUBLIC LANDS

• FLORISSANT FOSSIL BEDS
National Monument. Box 185, Florissant, CO 80816. (303) 748-3253. 5,998.09 acres. 1969. Central Colorado, 35 miles from Colorado Springs, on U.S. 24.

Large collection of fossil insects, fish, mammals, birds, and other remains of the Oligocene period along with standing petrified sequoia stumps. Over 1,100 species of insects and over 140 plants species are among the over 80,000 specimens dug up since the lakebed was discovered in 1874. Nature trail, view of Pike's Peak, Golden Eagles, self-guiding trails around fossil beds, natural history talks, evening programs, nature walks, children's programs, extended nature hikes, homestead tours, museum, petrified tree stumps, horseback riding, cross-country skiing. If you are bringing a large group, you are asked to notify the monument in advance. Visitor center, picnicking. Campgrounds nearby. Food and lodging in Woodland Park, Cripple Creek, Colorado Springs.

Free Print Material:
"Area Accommodations." 1 page. List of various communities and what facilities are available. Addresses of chambers of commerce.
"The Evolution of the Florissant Fossil Beds." 1 page. Events that shaped the making of fossils. Sketches.
"A Few Fossils of the Florissant Fossil Beds National Monument."

4 pages. Description and scientific/common names of verte-
brates, wasps, fossil flies, wolf spiders, dragon and damsel
flies, beetles found fossilized in the Florissant Fossil Beds.
Sketches.

"Florissant Fossil Beds." 6-fold. Map, sketches. The changing
earth and the story that fossils tell, finding the lakebed and
identifying specimens. Access to Florissant, visitor activities,
regulations.

"The Hornbek Homestead." 1 page. Description of the homestead
of Adaline Hornbek, what happened to the place until the
federal government bought the property. Restoration began
by the National Park Service in 1976.

"Newsletter." 2 pages. Activities, articles. Photos.

"What's the Weather Like?" 1 page. Description of the climate,
monthly chart for temperature and precipitation.

Sales/Audiovisual List:
"Rocky Mountain Nature Association Florissant Fossil Bed N.M."
3 pages. Alphabetical arrangement by title of book or by
category such as film, poster, slides. Includes stock number,
title, retail price. Most of the items are paperback and hardcover books. Includes maps, coloring books, and such books
as "Teaching Science Outdoor Environment."
150-702 "A Colorado History." $13.50.

Suggested Curriculum Application:
COLORADO STATE AND LOCAL STUDIES
GEOLOGY
SCIENCE

Suggested Sears Subject Heading:
COLORADO--DESCRIPTION AND TRAVEL--GUIDES
COLORADO--PUBLIC LANDS
FOSSILS
GEOLOGY--U.S.
U.S.--DESCRIPTION AND TRAVEL--GUIDES

● FOSSIL BUTTE
National Monument. Box 527, Kemmerer, WY 83101. (307) 877-3450.
8,198 acres. 1972. Western Wyoming near the Utah border, 10 miles
north of Kemmerer on U.S. 30, 422 miles from Denver.

Country's largest concentration of fossilized freshwater fish in about
60-million-year-old layers of shale. Well-preserved fossil insects,
snails, turtles, birds, bats and plant remains are also found in the
rock layers. Hiking trails, wildlife, exhibits, interpretive programs,
cross-country skiing, bicycling. Visitor center, picnicking. Camping
on surrounding Bureau of Land Management land. Food and lodging
in Kemmerer.

Free Print Material:
> "Fossil Butte." 6-fold. The process of fossilization, photos,
> types of fossils found at Fossil Butte, visitor information.
> "Visitor Information." 3 pages. Weather, elevation, accommoda-
> tions, wildlife, programs, addresses of the Nature and History
> Association and other visitor information.

Suggested Curriculum Application:
> GEOLOGY
> SCIENCE
> WYOMING STATE AND LOCAL STUDIES

Suggested Sears Subject Heading:
> FOSSILS
> GEOLOGY--U.S.
> WYOMING--DESCRIPTION AND TRAVEL--GUIDES
> WYOMING--PUBLIC LANDS
> U.S.--DESCRIPTION AND TRAVEL--GUIDES

- JOHN DAY

Fossil Beds National Monument. 420 West Main, John Day, OR
97845. (503) 575-0721. 14,011.90 acres. 1974. Central Oregon,
visitor center is near Dayville, 40 miles west of John Day.

Preserves one of the most complete fossil records of the story of
ancient life from the time dinosaurs disappeared to just before the
last ice age began. Streams and mountains, trails, overlooks,
wayside exhibits. Fossils and geologic evidence of ancient times
appear in the separated areas of Sheep Rock, Painted Hills, and
Clarno. Visitor center, picnicking. Lodging and food in nearby
communities. Local campgrounds.

Free Print Material:
> "The Fossil Record." 4 pages. Geological photos and articles,
> features of the monument, questions and answers.
> "John Day Fossil Beds." 12-fold. Illustrations and descriptions
> about what life was like 40, 30 and 25 million years ago.
> Geological background, park visitation information, maps,
> photo.

Sales List:
> List of titles, authors, prices and interpretive themes. 1 page.
> "Ancient Forests of Oregon." Ralph W. Chaney. $2.00.
> Climatology.

Suggested Curriculum Application:
> ARCHEOLOGY
> GEOGRAPHY
> GEOLOGY
> OREGON STATE AND LOCAL STUDIES

Suggested Sears Subject Heading:
  FOSSILS
  GEOLOGY-U.S.
  OREGON--DESCRIPTION AND TRAVEL--GUIDES
  OREGON--PUBLIC LANDS
  U.S.--DESCRIPTION AND TRAVEL--GUIDES
  U.S.--GEOGRAPHY

GEOGRAPHICALLY MULTI-FEATURED FACILITIES

• ACADIA
National Park. P.O. Box 177, Bar Harbor, ME 04609.
(207) 288-3338. 39,706.91 acres. 1916. Eastern Maine, 47 miles
southeast of Bangor, the only part of the park on the mainland is
reached by ME 186.

Preserve rugged coastal area of the highest elevation on the Eastern
Seaboard, mainland peninsula, cliffs. Mount Desert Island,
Schoodic Peninsula, Isle au Haut. Trails, naturalist programs, boat
trips, museums, nature center, swimming, winter activities, loop
road. Visitor center, ranger stations, campgrounds. Villages offer
lodging and restaurants.

Free Print Material:
  "Acadia National Park." 24-fold. Features to see, activities,
    history, maps, photos, visitor tips.
  "Acadia's Beaver Log." 4 pages. Schedule of naturalist activities,
    tips, informative articles for visitors.
  "Acadia Map." Folded map. Visitor information, maps of Acadia
    National Park, Isle au Haut, Schoodic Peninsula, Mount Desert
    Island.
  "Picture-taking in the Acadia National Park Area." 10-fold.
    Tips for taking pictures in this scenic area, photos, map.

Sales List:
  "Publications & Maps Available Through Eastern National Park &
    Monument Association." 3 pages. Grouped by publications,
    maps, miscellaneous. Order form.
  "Field Guide to Acadia National Park" by Russell Butcher.
    $6.95.

Audiovisual List:
  "Films Available for Loan." 2 pages. Description of film, reser-
    vation and mailing information.
  "A Force of Citizens," color, 14 minutes--the formation of the
    national army and the navy of the United States at the time

of the American Revolution is depicted in art work in this motion
picture.

Suggested Curriculum Application:
ENVIRONMENTAL EDUCATION
GEOGRAPHY
MAINE STATE AND LOCAL STUDIES

Suggested Sears Subject Heading:
ACADIA NATIONAL PARK
MAINE--DESCRIPTION AND TRAVEL--GUIDES
MAINE--PUBLIC LANDS
NATIONAL PARKS AND RESERVES--U.S.
NATURE PRESERVATION
U.S.--DESCRIPTION AND TRAVEL--GUIDES
U.S.--GEOGRAPHY

- BADLANDS
National Park. P.O. Box 6, Interior, SD   57750.   (605) 433-5361.
243,302.33 acres.   1929.   Western South Dakota, 28 miles southwest
of Kadoka, headquarters is 2 miles northeast of interior on Route
SH240.

Preserve the canyons and ridges, spires and knobs, fossils and
geological record, wildlife, shortgrass prairie. The area was called
"Bad Lands" to travel across by early French-Canadians.
Wayside exhibits, self-guiding trails, guided nature walks, programs,
animal fossils, prairie grasslands, exhibits, videotape, wildlife,
buttes. Visitor center, camping, cabins, food. Food and lodging
in nearby towns.

Free Print Material:
"Badlands." 16-fold. Geological history, photos, cultural history,
visitor information. Map, weather chart.
"The Big Badlander." 4 pages. Newspaper containing articles,
program information, features to enjoy, map and area guide,
safety and regulations.

Suggested Curriculum Application:
GEOGRAPHY
GEOLOGY
SOUTH DAKOTA STATE AND LOCAL STUDIES

Suggested Sears Subject Heading:
BADLANDS NATIONAL PARK
GEOLOGY--U.S.
NATIONAL PARKS AND RESERVES--U.S.
SOUTH DAKOTA--DESCRIPTION AND TRAVEL--GUIDES
SOUTH DAKOTA--PUBLIC LANDS
U.S.--DESCRIPTION AND TRAVEL--GUIDES
U.S.--GEOGRAPHY

- BIG BEND

National Park. Big Bend National Park, TX   79834.   (915) 477-2251.
741,118.40 acres. 1935. Southwestern Texas. The Rio Grande
forms the southern boundary of the park as well as the international
boundary between U.S. and Mexico.

Preserve scenic mountain, desert, and river area where a variety of
unusual geological formations are found. Guided horseback trips,
wildlife, river float trips, backcountry trails, guided nature walks,
naturalist programs, scenery. Headquarters building, camping,
food and lodging.

Free Print Material:
  "Big Bend Reptiles." 6-fold. Description, sketches of snakes,
    turtles, lizards.
  "Big Bend Birds." 6-fold. The great variety of birds, sketches,
    and where they can be seen within the park.
  "Big Bend Geology." 6-fold. Events of the Paleozoic, Mesozoic
    and other eras, map.
  "Big Bend History." 6-fold. Ecological background, prehistoric
    and historic eras, political efforts to establish the park, facts
    and figures, sketches.
  "Big Bend National Park." 10-fold. Features, services and ac-
    commodations, photos, maps.
  "Big Bend Wildflowers." 4-fold. Kinds of flowers, sketches,
    and where and when they bloom.
  "Wilderness Journeys." 10 pages. River trips in Colorado,
    Texas hill country and Big Bend country, Mexico. Photos,
    maps, trip fees and reservation form.

Sales List:
  "Big Bend Natural History Association Catalog of Sales Items."
    12-fold. Grouped by: guide books and maps, river guides,
    maps. Includes an index to 7.5' minute maps, order informa-
    tion and form.
  "Road Guide." $1.25. Describes points of interest visible from
    all paved and improved dirt roads in the park. 48 pages;
    black and white photographs.

Suggested Curriculum Application:
  GEOGRAPHY
  GEOLOGY
  RECREATION
  TEXAS STATE AND LOCAL STUDIES

Suggested Sears Subject Heading:
  BIG BEND NATIONAL PARK
  GEOLOGY-U.S.
  NATIONAL PARKS AND RESERVES--U.S.
  OUTDOOR RECREATION
  TEXAS--DESCRIPTION AND TRAVEL--GUIDES

TEXAS--PUBLIC LANDS
U.S.--DESCRIPTION AND TRAVEL--GUIDES
U.S.--GEOGRAPHY

- GATEWAY

National Recreation Area. Floyd Bennett Field, Bldg. #69, Brooklyn, NY 11234. (718) 338-4493. 26,310.93 acres. 1972. Southern New York, eastern New Jersey, four separate units. Sandy Hook, the New Jersey Unit, Rockaway Peninsula in New York is where Breezy Point is located, Staten Island Unit and Jamaica Bay Unit is in New York.

Provide beaches, marshes, islands, waters in the New York harbor area for recreational use. The Sandy Hook Unit in New Jersey provides beaches, plant and animal life, historic structures and the Sandy Hook Lighthouse thought to be the oldest (1764) operational light in the country. Jamaica Bay Wildlife Refuge, Breezy Point Tip, Fort Tilden, Riis Park, Floyd Bennett Field (New York's first municipal airport), Plumb Beach, Dead Horse Bay, Canarsie Pier, Sandy Hook, Miller Field, tours of Fort Hancock and natural areas, lifesaving demonstrations and presentations, puppet shows and lectures, Great Kills Park. Birdwatching, swimming, sports, hiking, bicycling, beach trails, discovery walks. Guided programs at North Channel, Dead Horse Bay and Plumb Beach to school classes during the spring and fall and to the general public during the summer. A summer crafts mobile, tours of Fort Tilden's dune areas, classes, programs, monarch butterfly walks, special events, films, workshops, Sandy Hook Museum. New York City educators may call the Gateway Environment Study Center at (718) 252-8285 and obtain current schedules of events for students as the center is a joint venture of the New York City Board of Education and Gateway National Recreation Area. Visitor centers, gateway ecology village campsite. Food and lodging nearby.

Free Print Material:
"Current Events at the Gateway Environmental Study Center."
4 pages. Teacher workshops, film series, activities, student visits, travel directions and map, registration form, sketches.
"Gateway." 24-fold. Photos, features to see, sketches, maps, how to get to gateway, visitor information and regulations, descriptions of Jamaica Bay, Breezy Point, Staten Island, Sandy Hook.
"Gateway Environmental Study Center." 8-fold. Map, sketches, formation and aims of the center, description of day visits, camping, networking, events.
"Gateway National Recreation Area Student Pages." 11 pages. Introduction to Gateway, puzzles, sketches, activities, maps for a student visit.
"Gateway Program Guide." 8-fold. Travel directions on getting to Gateway, information about Breezy Point, Floyd Bennett

Field, Jamaica Bay Wildlife Refuge, Sandy Hook, Staten Island. Seasonal programs grouped in such categories as: orientation, nature, film/lecture series, history, recreation, special events. Sketches.

Suggested Curriculum Application:
ENVIRONMENTAL EDUCATION
NATURAL HISTORY
NEW JERSEY STATE AND LOCAL STUDIES
NEW YORK STATE AND LOCAL STUDIES
RECREATION

Suggested Sears Subject Heading:
AIRPORTS
BIRDS--PROTECTION
JAMAICA BAY WILDLIFE REFUGE
LIGHTHOUSES
MARINE RESOURCES
NATURAL HISTORY--NEW JERSEY
NATURAL HISTORY--NEW YORK
NATURE CONSERVATION
NEW JERSEY--DESCRIPTION AND TRAVEL--GUIDES
NEW JERSEY--PUBLIC LANDS
NEW YORK--DESCRIPTION AND TRAVEL--GUIDES
NEW YORK--NATURAL HISTORY
NEW YORK--PUBLIC LANDS
OUTDOOR RECREATION
REFUGES
U.S.--DESCRIPTION AND TRAVEL--GUIDES
WILDLIFE--CONSERVATION

- GUADALUPE MOUNTAINS
National Park. 3225 National Parks Highway, Carlsbad, NM 88220. (915) 828-3385. 76,293.06 acres. 1966. Western Texas, 110 miles east of El Paso, TX, 55 miles southwest of Carlsbad, NM. on U.S. 62-180.

Largest exposed fossil reef on earth. Of permian limestone, the mountains rise from the desert. The park also has a large earth fault, the highest peak in Texas, unusual flora and fauna. Backpacking, campfire programs, conducted hikes, hiking trails, Frijole Historic Site, Butterfield State Station Historic Site, Williams Ranch Historic Site, scenic drive offers views of El Capitan, Guadalupe Peak and the eastern and western escarpments. Visitor center, campgrounds, picnicking. Food and lodging in Carlsbad, NM and White City, NM.

Free Print Material:
"Dog Canyon." 2 pages. Description, activities, regulations, map, phone numbers and address to obtain more information.

"Guadalupe Journal." 8 pages. Newspaper format. Guide to the
Carlsbad-Guadalupe mountains area in New Mexico and Texas
issued by the Carlsbad Caverns Natural History Association.
Articles, photos, map, schedules, fees, services.

"Guadalupe Mountains." 20-fold. Maps, photos, features, history,
wildlife, what to see and do, accommodations.

"The Guadalupes." 32 pages. Geology, features, history, development. Many large photos. Issued by the Carlsbad Caverns
Natural History Association.

"Hiking and Backpacking Information." 3 pages. Day hiking
tips, backpacker regulations, horse trips. A chart page of
temperatures and precipitation.

Suggested Curriculum Application:
GEOGRAPHY
GEOLOGY
RECREATION
TEXAS STATE AND LOCAL STUDIES

Suggested Sears Subject Heading:
FOSSILS
GEOLOGY, U.S.
GUADALUPE MOUNTAINS NATIONAL PARK
MOUNTAINS
NATIONAL PARKS AND RESERVES--U.S.
OUTDOOR RECREATION
TEXAS--DESCRIPTION AND TRAVEL--GUIDES
TEXAS--PUBLIC LANDS
U.S.--DESCRIPTION AND TRAVEL--GUIDES
U.S.--GEOGRAPHY

● HALEAKALA
National Park. P.O. Box 369, Makawao, HI 96768. (808) 572-9177.
28,655.25 acres. 1916. Southern part of the island of Maui, from
the summit of Mt. Haleakala down the southeast flank to the Kipahulu
coast near Hana.

Preserve Haleakala Crater, protect ecosystems and biotic species,
scenic pools and coast. Overlooks, swimming, exhibits, hiking trails,
ranger-guided walks and hikes, concessionaire-guided trips through
the crater. Visitor center, park headquarters, picnicking, campground, cabins (reserve at least 90 days in advance). Food and
lodging in Kula.

Free Print Material:
"Camping and Hiking." 8-fold. Visitor tips on backpacking such
as recommended footwear, clothing, equipment, food, packload,
camping regulations.

"Crater Cabin Information." 8-fold. Description of cabins,
facilities, what visitors must bring, access, reservations, rates
and other information. Reservation request form.

"Haleakala National Park." 14-fold. Photos, diagram, map. Activities, camping, the legend of Maui, visitor information, geological story of Haleakala Crater.

"Mileages and a Few Statistics." 1 page. Mileages of various roads, trails and other park features. Area of the crater, elevation of the summit of Red Hill and other statistics.

"'Ohe'o." 2 pages. Description of plant and forest life, pools, wildlife, history, visitor tips, map, photos.

"Safety Rules." 2 pages. How to protect the park and yourself by driving carefully, watching your children, not swimming alone, dressing properly, don't travel alone and keeping the park headquarters informed of your plans.

Suggested Curriculum Application:
 GEOGRAPHY
 GEOLOGY
 HAWAII STATE AND LOCAL STUDIES
 NATURAL HISTORY

Suggested Sears Subject Heading:
 HALEAKALA NATIONAL PARK
 HAWAII--DESCRIPTION AND TRAVEL--GUIDES
 HAWAII--PUBLIC LANDS
 NATIONAL PARKS AND RESERVES--U.S.
 NATURAL HISTORY--HAWAII
 NATURE PRESERVATION
 U.S.--DESCRIPTION AND TRAVEL--GUIDES
 VOLCANOES

• LAKE CLARK
National Park/Preserve. 701 C Street, Box 61, Anchorage, AK 99513. (907) 271-3751. National Park, 2,874,000 acres; National Preserve, 1,171.000 acres; wilderness area, 2,470,000 acres. 1980. Southern Alaska, a short flight from Anchorage, Kenai, Homer.

Preserves great geologic diversity such as jagged peaks, granite spires, active volcanoes, Lake Clark and other features. Cook Inlet coastal region, the Alaska-Aleutian mountain ranges, the western foothills and lakes, the interior lowlands, and the Lake-Clark-Kontrashibuna region. Access by chartered aircraft. You must possess good backcountry skills for wilderness survival. Write for a list of businesses licensed to operate in the area. In the park and preserve you are dependent on your own resources.

Free Print Material:
 "Alaska Float Trips Southwest Region." 18 pages. A partial copy for rivers in and adjacent to Lake Clark National Park and Preserve. Provides information to the recreating public.

 "Alaska National Parklands 3 Steps to Bear Safety." 8-fold. Safety tips to minimize chances of bear trouble.

"Commercial Use Operators for Lake Clark National Park/Preserve." 9 pages. Lists various business/commercial use operators licensed to provide services for the Lake Clark National Park and Preserve area. Most operators have been organized under: lodging, air taxi operators, and/or wilderness adventures.

"Lake Clark." 16-fold. Map, photos, visitor information such as weather, precautions, logistics, supplies. Surveys what Lake Clark has to offer.

"Minimum Impact Camping." 8-fold. Lists 14 techniques for good wilderness environmental camping.

"Natural and Cultural History of Lake Clark National Park & Preserve." 15 pages. Chart and tables. Cultural heritage, geology, climate, history, animals, vegetation types, earthquake occurrences.

"Public Use Regulations." 2 pages. Map and partial summary of public use and recreational regulations.

Bibliography:
"Books." 1 page. List of books and an article to learn more about the Lake Clark area. Includes title, date, publisher, place of publication for books. Author, title of article, magazine, volume, date, publisher for article.

Audiovisual/Sales List:
Please write to the following address for information on film rental or purchase and book sales lists: Parks and Forests Information Center, 2525 Gambell Street, Anchorage, AK 99503-2892. (907) 271-2643.

Suggested Curriculum Application:
ALASKA STATE AND LOCAL STUDIES
GEOGRAPHY
RECREATION

Suggested Sears Subject Heading:
ALASKA--DESCRIPTION AND TRAVEL--GUIDES
ALASKA--PUBLIC LANDS
LAKE CLARK NATIONAL PARK AND PRESERVE
NATIONAL PARKS AND RESERVES--U.S.
OUTDOOR RECREATION
U.S.--DESCRIPTION AND TRAVEL--GUIDES
WILDERNESS AREAS

• NORTH CASCADES
National Park. 800 State Street, Sedro Woolley, WA 98284. (206) 855-1331. 504,780.94 acres. 1968. Northern Washington, northeast of Seattle-Tacoma area, Interstate 5 and Wash. Rt. 20.

Preserve natural peaks, glaciers, lakes, streams, waterfalls, icefalls, forests, meadows, valleys. Hiking, mountain climbing, naturalist activities, scenic drives, charter plane tours, backcountry trails, horseback riding. Professional guide and packtrain services available, camping, food and lodging.

Free Print Material:
"Accommodations and Services." 2 pages. Name, address, some telephones for overnight accommodations, cabins for rent, boating services, ski tours, gift and photo shops, outdoor equipment shop, food service and groceries, transportation, float trips, alpine/backpacking/climbing.
"Main Trails and Backcountry Camp Areas." 24-fold. Map, sketches, backcountry rules, minimizing visitor impact on the environment, hypothermia.
"National Parks and National Forests in the Pacific Northwest." 24-fold. Photos, map. Charts of features and attractions for Oregon, Idaho, Washington. Addresses to obtain additional information. Background on the forest service, the National Park Service, fees and passports.
"North Cascades." 24-fold. Description of North Cascades National Park, Ross Lake National Recreation Area, Lake Chelan National Recreation Area, visitor information, photos, driving in the park area.
"Visitor Form Letter." 3 pages. Activities, backcountry permits, camping and other visitor information.

Suggested Curriculum Application:
GEOGRAPHY
RECREATION
WASHINGTON STATE AND LOCAL STUDIES

Suggested Sears Subject Heading:
NATIONAL PARKS AND RESERVES--U.S.
NATURE CONSERVATION
NORTH CASCADES NATIONAL PARK
OUTDOOR RECREATION
U.S.--DESCRIPTION AND TRAVEL--GUIDES
WASHINGTON----DESCRIPTION AND TRAVEL--GUIDES
WASHINGTON--PUBLIC LANDS
WILDERNESS AREAS

• OLYMPIC
National Park. 600 East Park Avenue, Port Angeles, WA 98362. (206) 452-4501 (north side); (206) 374-6925) (west side); (206) 877-5254 (east side). 914,576.46 acres. National Monument, 1909; National Park, 1933. Northwestern Washington, Highway 101 south on the ocean beach, 36 miles south of Forks, WA.

Mountain wilderness has the best remnant of Pacific Northwest rain forest, a mountainous core with active glaciers, and a wild scenic ocean shore. Fifty miles of ocean shore; hurricane ridge; wildlife;

Hoh, Queets, Quinault River scenic roads; trails; horseback riding; mountaineering; audiovisuals; exhibits; about 60 glaciers crowning Olympic peaks with the largest being on Mount Olympus at about 10 square miles; interpretive programs; swimming; nature walks. Visitor center, summer ranger stations, picnicking, amphitheater, campgrounds, cabins, lodges, trailer parks. Food and lodging nearby.

Free Print Material:
"Bird Check List." 6-fold. Name of various birds with indication if they are common, fairly common, uncommon, rare, hypothetical. Lines indicate when birds may be seen in winter, spring, summer, fall. Terms and abbreviations explained.
"Climate and Seasons of Olympic National Park." 2 pages. Survey of winter, spring, summer, fall. Precipitation averages in various areas.
"Facilities and Services." 2 pages. Hours and telephones, transportation services, concessioner accommodations, day use facilities.
"Glaciers." 2 pages. What glaciers are, how climate influences Olympic glaciers, access, movement, scientific study.
"Olympic National Park." 28-fold. Maps, photos, sketches, chart, features of interest to visitors, plantlife, geology, wildlife.
"Record Trees in Olympic National Park." 2 pages. List giving the size and location of Olympic's record trees. Includes circumference, height, spread, total points.
"Temperate Rain Forest of Olympic National Park." 2 pages. What makes a temperate rain forest, temperatures, common trees, animal life and other features.
"Wilderness Beach Hiking in Olympic National Park." 2 pages. Tips for users such as not building fires in driftwood piles, maximum group size and other items of interest to beach hiking visitors.

Sales List:
"Pacific Northwest National Parks and Forests Association Olympic National Park Branch Sales List." 2 pages. Grouped by: backpacking/hiking guides, geology, pictorial/travel guides, plants and animals, seashore books, maps. Title, author, annotation, pages, price. Order form, ordering instructions.
"Backpacking: One Step at a Time." Manning. $8.95. Informative handbook for all levels of hikers; cleverly illustrated with advice on techniques, equipment, and route finding, emphasis on wilderness ethic. 414 pages.

Suggested Curriculum Application:
GEOGRAPHY
GEOLOGY
NATURAL HISTORY
RECREATION
WASHINGTON STATE AND LOCAL STUDIES

Suggested Sears Subject Heading:
GLACIERS
MOUNTAINS
MOUNT OLYMPUS
NATIONAL PARKS AND RESERVES--U.S.
NATURAL HISTORY--WASHINGTON
OLYMPIC NATIONAL PARK
U.S.--DESCRIPTION AND TRAVEL--GUIDES
U.S.--GEOGRAPHY
WASHINGTON--DESCRIPTION AND TRAVEL--GUIDES
WASHINGTON--PUBLIC LANDS
WILDERNESS AREAS

• OZARK
National Scenic Riverways. P.O. Box 490, Van Buren, MO 63965.
(314) 323-4236. 80,788.34 acres. 1964. Southeastern Missouri,
175 miles south of St. Louis. Current River and Jacks Fort River
flows through Ozark Hills.

Preserve 134 miles of river flowing through notable features such
as large fresh-water springs and many caves through the Ozark
Hills. Caves, springs, wildlife, flowering plants, water sports,
overlooks, demonstrations. Camping, picnicking, food and lodging
along the way.

Free Print Material:
"Ozark Riverways." 16-fold. Maps and description to plan activities along the riverbanks or to choose the river section you
want to float.
"Ozark Riverways Information." 8-fold. Tips for camping, cold
and wet weather camping and canoeing, picnicking and camping
regulations.
"Ozark Riverways: National Scenic Riverways Missouri." 16-fold.
Description of the Ozark waterways, travel time table, things
to do and observe, list of flowering plants, mammals, fish,
birds, reptiles and amphibians, services chart, map, photos,
flow comparison of springs.
"Whitewater in an Open Canoe." 8-fold. Sketches, safety tips
for canoeing. Safety services and information available from
the Red Cross.

Suggested Curriculum Application:
GEOGRAPHY
MISSOURI STATE AND LOCAL STUDIES
RECREATION

Suggested Sears Subject Heading:
CANOES AND CANOEING
CURRENT RIVER
JACKS FORT RIVER

MISSOURI--DESCRIPTION AND TRAVEL--GUIDES
MISSOURI--PUBLIC LANDS
OUTDOOR RECREATION
RIVERS
U.S.--DESCRIPTION AND TRAVEL--GUIDES

- PINELANDS
National Reserve. c/o Mid-Atlantic Region, National Park Service,
143 S. Third Street, Philadelphia, PA 19106. (609) 292-2797.
1,100,000 acres. 1978. Southern New Jersey, portions of the
counties of Atlantic, Burlington, Camden, Cape May, Cumberland,
Gloucester, Ocean.

Undeveloped tract on the Eastern Seaboard noted for its water resources and dwarfed pines. The reserve concept involves close,
cooperative preservation efforts among federal, state, local governments, private owners. Limited public facilities, varied recreational
opportunities. For information about recreation, contact: New
Jersey Department of Environmental Protection, CN 402, Trenton,
NJ 08625, and the New Jersey Division of Travel and Tourism,
One West State Street, CN 826, Trenton, NJ 08625. For accommodations, check with the addresses given above.

Free Print Material:
"History of the Pinelands." 1 page. Begins with the period 170
to 200 million years ago when the Atlantic coastal plain began
to form.
"The Pinelands of New Jersey." 12-fold. Photos, map, highlights of the pinelands, comprehensive planning, the Pinelands
Commission.

Suggested Curriculum Application:
GEOGRAPHY
NEW JERSEY STATE AND LOCAL STUDIES

Suggested Sears Subject Heading:
NATURE CONSERVATION
NEW JERSEY--DESCRIPTION AND TRAVEL--GUIDES
NEW JERSEY--PUBLIC LANDS
U.S.--DESCRIPTION AND TRAVEL--GUIDES

- POINT REYES
National Seashore. Point Reyes, California 94956. (415) 663-1092.
71,046.07 acres. 1962. Westcentral California, about 35 miles north
of San Francisco, by Sir Francis Drake Boulevard from U.S. Highway
101 West to State Route 1.

Preserve peninsula of beaches, high white cliffs, lagoons, forested
ridges, wildlife. Displays, dioramas, film, trail follows a 0.7-mile

walk along the San Andreas Fault, woodpecker nature trail, Morgan horse ranch where horses are raised and trained for use in the national parks, a replica of a Coast Miwok Indian village, Limantour Beach, birdwatching, horseback riding, tidepools, Mount Vision overlook, beachcombing, swimming, Point Reyes Lighthouse, whale-, elk-, and sea lion-watching, bicycling, trail hiking, sculptured beach, Arch Rock. Visitor center, campgrounds, picnicking. Food and lodging at Inverness, Point Reyes and others nearby.

Free Print Material:
"Birdwatching at Point Reyes National Seashore." 1 page. What to look for and where.
"The California Gray Whale." 2 pages. Life cycle, activities of the whales.
"Checklist of Mammals." 3 pages. Common and scientific names arranged by orders.
"The Deer of Point Reyes National Seashore." 2 pages. Types and characteristics of deer.
"The Geology of Point Reyes Peninsula." 1 page. Description of four main topographic sections.
"The Harbor Seal." 1 page. Life cycle and habits.
"The Morgan Horse Ranch Point Reyes National Seashore." 2 pages. Origin, characteristics, training, why the Point Reyes National Seashore chose the Morgan horse for their ranch.
"Point Reyes." 16-fold. Visitor information, photos, geology, weather, map, safety precautions.
"Point Reyes Bird Observatory." 10-fold. Sketches, map, purpose, research, conservation, education, membership. The nonprofit organization is located at 4990 Shoreline Highway, Stinson Beach, CA 94970.
"Point Reyes Hostel." 4-fold. Location, accommodations suited to group use. Map, sketches.
"What to Do During Your Time at Point Reyes National Seashore." 1 page. Things to do for one hour, two hours, three hours, four hours, all day, two to three days.

Sales/Audiovisual List:
"Coastal Parks Association Publications." 2 pages. Grouped by: publications, maps, notecards, post cards, visual aids, posters, Erikson maps. Title and price. Visual aids includes cassette, stamps, bookmarkers and other items. Publications include coloring books, guides.
"American Wildflowers Coloring Book." $2.50.

Suggested Curriculum Application:
CALIFORNIA STATE AND LOCAL STUDIES
ENVIRONMENTAL EDUCATION
GEOGRAPHY
NATURAL HISTORY
SCIENCE

Suggested Sears Subject Heading:
   CALIFORNIA--DESCRIPTION AND TRAVEL--GUIDES
   CALIFORNIA--PUBLIC LANDS
   NATURAL HISTORY--CALIFORNIA
   U.S.--DESCRIPTION AND TRAVEL--GUIDES
   U.S.--GEOGRAPHY

• SEQUOIA AND KINGS CANYON
National Parks. Three Rivers, CA 93271. (209) 565-3341. Kings
Canyon, 461,636.20 acres. Sequoia, 402,487.83 acres. 1890.
Central California, accessible from the west by Visalia, Fresno and
Bakersfield, CA.

Protect giant sequoia, credited with being the largest living thing
in the world. Includes the highest mountain in the United States
outside of Alaska, Mount Whitney. The two parks contain a large
stretch of the Sierra crest and the Great Western Divide. 800 miles
of trails, glacial features, exhibits, winter sports, naturalist guided
walks, interpretive talks, more than 1,000 glacial lakes, Mount
Whitney, certain giant sequoia trees (estimated from 3000 to 2000
years old) called the General Sherman and the General Grant,
Valley of the Kings, wildlife, the Auto Log, Moro Rock, Tunnel Log,
meadows, Crystal Cave. Campgrounds, visitor centers, lodges,
cabins and motel-type rooms.

Free Print Material:
   "A Brief Account of the Wildlife of Sequoia and Kings Canyon
      National Parks." 2 pages. Brief review of the most outstand-
      ing kinds depending on the elevation, climate and habitat of
      the two parks.
   "A Brief History of Sequoia and Kings Canyon National Parks."
      2 pages. Description of the Native American era, exploration,
      early resource use, preservation, modernization, enlargement,
      recent times.
   "Fee Information." 2 pages. Entrance, campground, Crystal
      Cave tours, group campsites.
   "General Information-Sequoia and Kings Canyon National Parks."
      2 pages. Fees, services, and facilities for visitors.
   "General Sherman and General Grant--Giant Sequoias." 1 page.
      Statistics of the two trees such as estimated age, estimated
      weight of trunk, height above base, circumference at ground
      and other statistics. Discovery of the two trees, determining
      age.
   "Picture-taking in Sequoia and Kings Canyon National Parks."
      8-fold. Picture-taking spots, tips for each park. Camera-
      handling hints, descriptive photos.
   "Seeing the Giant Forest." 1 page. What to see and do, features
      such as trails, meadows, trees, logs in the giant forest of
      Sequoia National Park.
   "Sierran Weather." 1 page. Month by month statistics of the low

elevations and the middle elevations. Characteristics of the foothills; the Giant Forest/Grant Grove; 9,000 feet and above.

"Sequoia/Kings Canyon." 8-fold. Features and attractions of the parks. Maps, photos, sketches. Sequoia reproduction, size and age.

"Sequoia/Kings Canyon Map and Guide." 12-fold. Large general map, locator map, Mineral King map, Grant Grove map, Giant Forest map, Cedar Grove map. Description, activities and accommodations for the various sections.

Sales List:

"Books-Pamphlets and Maps About Sequoia and Kings Canyon National Parks and Devils Postpile National Monument." 8-fold. Grouped by: natural history, the giant sequoias, trees and flowers, miscellaneous, topographic maps, special maps, animal life, children's books, trail and general guides, national parks and conservation. Order form, ordering directions, purpose and membership of the Sequoia Natural History Association. Schools and libraries are granted discounts on those items published by the association. All paper covers except where noted.

"Sequoia-Kings Canyon" (Tweed). Story behind the scenery. Authoritative text--beautiful color illustrations. $4.50.

Suggested Curriculum Application:

CALIFORNIA STATE AND LOCAL STUDIES
GEOGRAPHY
NATURAL HISTORY
SCIENCE

Suggested Sears Subject Heading:

CALIFORNIA--DESCRIPTION AND TRAVEL--GUIDES
CALIFORNIA--PUBLIC LANDS
KINGS CANYON NATIONAL PARK
MOUNT WHITNEY
NATIONAL PARKS AND RESERVES--U.S.
NATURAL HISTORY--CALIFORNIA
SEQUOIA NATIONAL PARK
SEQUOIA
TREES--U.S.
U.S.--DESCRIPTION AND TRAVEL--GUIDES

● YOSEMITE

National Park. P.O. Box 577, Yosemite National Park, CA 95389. (209) 372-0265. 761,170.18 acres; 1,397.99 acres, El Portal Administrative Site; 677,600 acres, wilderness area. 1890. East central California, Hwy. 140, 120 East.

Groves of giant sequoias, mountains, lakes, waterfalls (including the nation's highest). Audiovisuals, Sierra sunrise program, cross-country ski tours, bicycling, valley floor tour, glacier point, snowshoeing tours, ranger walks, exhibits, horseback riding, Indian cultural museum, gallery camera walk, Yosemite field studies, Yosemite theater, tours, self-guiding auto tour, walk and hikes, mariposa grove, Wawona Pioneer Yosemite History Center, Crane Flat, Badger Pass. Inquire about Junior Snow Rangers for children. Field studies, children's hour, stroll with John Muir, special Christmas activities. To receive a catalog about classes that are offered call or write the Yosemite Association, P.O. Box 230, El Portal, CA 95318 at (209) 379-2646. The association offers winter ski tours and spring seminars. Visitor center. Shuttle bus offers free transportation to the visitor center and other parts of eastern Yosemite Valley, campgrounds, church services, service stations, kennels, babysitting, groceries, food service, gift shops, and other services. Food and lodging.

Free Print Material:

"Birds and Mammals of Yosemite National Park." 1 page. Life zones in the Yosemite with plant and animal indicators, such as the Upper Sonoran, Transition, and three others.

"Campgrounds for Use by Organized Groups." 2 pages. Group camping policy, food storage, description of various group camps.

"The Giant Sequoia." 2 pages. Size, age, habits. The trees occur in 75 groves on the west slopes of the Sierra Nevada. The mariposa grove in Yosemite contains the oldest known (2,700 years), and fifth largest sequoia.

"Ollenya Environmental Study Area Guide." 92 pages. Guide is aimed at upper levels of elementary school, but can be adapted for use with kindergarten through high school. It is designed in three phases: pre-site, on-site, and post-site. Activities, sketches, questions and discussion, teacher's notes. Covers plant life, wildlife, human history.

"Picture-Taking Spots and Tips." 12-fold. Photos, tips by Kodak. Yosemite and Kings Canyon/Sequoia National Parks.

"Weather in Yosemite National Park." 1 page. Elevation from 2,000 to 13,000 feet plays a major role in Yosemite weather. Four seasons, road conditions, chart of average precipitation and temperatures in Yosemite Valley.

"Yosemite Guide." 16 pages. Information about the Yosemite Association, membership form, visitor activities chart, park information, safety tips, photos, maps.

"Yosemite Black Bears and their Management." 1 page. Necessity of breaking bears' reliance upon human food sources.

"Yosemite National Park: A Brief History." 2 pages. Indian people lived in the area more than 2000 years ago, exploration and development of Yosemite. Number of visitors per year, planning under the Yosemite general management plan.

"Yosemite National Park Fact Sheet." 2 pages. Miles in trails, how many species of birds, how many campsites, average precipitation, size of park, landmark and waterfall feet and other statistics.

"Yosemite's Geology." 1 page. Origin of the Sierra Nevada.

Sales List:
"Catalogue of Publications from the Yosemite Association." 8-fold. Books, maps, trail guides. Grouped by: Yosemite National Park and the Sierra Nevada--general; National Parks--general; geology; weather; national history--general; natural history--animal life; national history--birds; natural history--general plant life; natural history--flowers; natural history--trees; history; for young people; trail and climbing guides; U.S. Geological Survey maps. Title, description, pages, price. Some books available in soft and hard covers. Photos. Map sketch index to topographic maps of Yosemite National Park. Order blank and ordering directions.

"Beautiful Yosemite National Park." Will. Full-color photographic album with brief descriptive text. 80 pages. $7.95.

Suggested Curriculum Application:
CALIFORNIA STATE AND LOCAL STUDIES
ENVIRONMENTAL EDUCATION
GEOGRAPHY
NATURAL HISTORY

Suggested Sears Subject Heading:
CALIFORNIA--DESCRIPTION AND TRAVEL--GUIDES
CALIFORNIA--PUBLIC LANDS
NATIONAL PARKS AND RESERVES--U.S.
NATURAL HISTORY--CALIFORNIA
SIERRA NEVADA MOUNTAINS
SEQUOIA
U.S.--DESCRIPTION AND TRAVEL--GUIDES
U.S.--GEOGRAPHY
WILDERNESS AREAS
YOSEMITE NATIONAL PARK

GEYSERS/HOT SPRINGS

• HOT SPRINGS
National Park. P.O. Box 1860, Hot Springs National Park, AR 71902. (501) 624-3383. 5,823.54 acres. 1921. Central Arkansas, southwest of Little Rock in the Zig Zag Mountains. Hot Springs is accessible by U.S. 270, 70 and Ark. 7.

Thermal springs bring people to soak in the naturally sterile water for relaxation or relief from injury or illness. People have used the springs for 10,000 years. Wooded trails, horseback riding, exhibits, slide program, interpretive programs such as bathhouse tours, conducted hikes, campfire talks, boating, scenic drives with overlooks. Bathhouses provide such services as tub and pool baths, shower, steam cabinet, hot and cold packs, whirlpool, massage, alcohol rub. Visitor center, campground, ranger stations. Food and lodging in Hot Springs.

Free Print Material:

"Blue-Green Algae." 1 page. Type of algae living in Hot Springs, tufa outcrops.

"A Brief Outline of the Geology of the Ouachitas Hot Springs National Park, Arkansas." 1 page. From Paleozoic times, perid of deposition, period of mountain-making forces and others.

"Display Springs." 1 page. Description of the two open springs that show the hot water bubbling to the surface from deep within the earth.

"Heat Exchanger." 1 page. Methods used to cool the hot springs down about 43 degrees for bathing purposes.

"Hot Springs." 12-fold. The development of Hot Springs into a popular spa, the mineral content of the thermal springs water, services, and things to do for the visitor. Illustration, maps, photos.

"Hot Springs Has It ... Diamond Lakes Country." 24-fold. Photos, map, list of accommodations, shopping guide, attractions, addresses and telephones for visitor information. "Diamond" Lakes include: Ouachita, Degray, Hamilton, Catherine, Greeson.

"Hot Springs Mountain Tower." 6-fold. History of the tower, location, rates, sights you see on the 216-foot tower. Illustrations, sketches, map, photos.

"Hot Springs Water." 1 page. Chemical analysis and radioactivity analysis.

"The Thermal Water Distribution System." 1 page. How the water from 45 of the hot springs is piped by gravity flow into the reservoir beneath park headquarters.

Audiovisual List:

"Bicentennial Films." 6 pages. Title, appropriate audience, running length, description.

"Americans 1776." All ages. 20 minutes. Descriptions of several people who helped shape our country's future, people uniting to form a new country.

Sales/Audiovisual List:

"Eastern National Parks and Monument Association Hot Springs National Park, Arkansas Sales List." 2 pages. Books, coloring books, slide strips, stamp books, stones, post cards, field guides, maps. Title, date (on most), over counter price,

member price, mailed price.
"150th Anniversary Stamp Cachet." $1.00, $.85, $1.20.

Suggested Curriculum Application:
    ARKANSAS STATE AND LOCAL STUDIES
    GEOGRAPHY
    GEOLOGY
    SCIENCE

Suggested Sears Subject Heading:
    ARKANSAS--DESCRIPTION AND TRAVEL--GUIDES
    ARKANSAS--PUBLIC LANDS
    GEOLOGY--U.S.
    HEALTH RESORTS, SPAS, ETC.
    HOT SPRINGS NATIONAL PARK
    NATIONAL PARKS AND RESERVES--U.S.
    U.S.--DESCRIPTION AND TRAVEL--GUIDES
    U.S.--GEOGRAPHY
    WATER

• YELLOWSTONE
National Park. P.O. Box 168, Yellowstone National Park, WY   82190.
(307) 344-7381. 2,219,822.70 acres. 1872. Northwestern Wyoming,
reached from the east by U.S. 20, 14, 16.

Thousands of geysers and hot springs make this the earth's greatest
geyser region which, with other scenic features, made this the first
national park. Old Faithful Geyser, Mammoth Hot Springs, wildlife,
Grand Canyon of the Yellowstone River, tour programs, scenic
coach excursions. Tours can be designed to meet visitors' needs,
variety of year-around activities. Concessioners' food services,
campgrounds, church services, general stores, lodging facilities and
others.

Free Print Material:
    "Information Papers on Wildlife, Geysers, Fossils, Vegetation."
        23 pages. Background on American antelope, mule deer, fossil
        forests and other natural history.
    "Visitor Information Yell-175." 17 pages. Climative summary,
        campgrounds, fees, history, and other visitor information.
    "Yellowstone." 16 pages. Many photos and narrative survey
        features of the park and includes park accommodations and
        activities.

Sales List:
    "Books, Maps and Pamphlets About Yellowstone National Park."
        2 pages. Grouped by: general, geology, plant life, animal
        life, history, posters and prints, maps, educational games,
        recommended for children, mail order form, ordering directions.
        Children's books have recommended age levels in some

annotations. Book entries include title, author, pages, description, price, and some indicate type of cover.

"Hamilton's Guide," Lystrup, 160-page guidebook to the grand loop tour of Yellowstone with current information on facilities and services. Color photos and maps. $3.95.

Suggested Curriculum Application:
GEOGRAPHY
GEOLOGY
IDAHO STATE AND LOCAL STUDIES
MONTANA STATE AND LOCAL STUDIES
WYOMING STATE AND LOCAL STUDIES

Suggested Sears Subject Heading:
GEOLOGY--U.S.
GEYSERS
IDAHO--DESCRIPTION AND TRAVEL--GUIDES
IDAHO--PUBLIC LANDS
MONTANA--DESCRIPTION AND TRAVEL--GUIDES
MONTANA--PUBLIC LANDS
NATIONAL PARKS AND RESERVES--U.S.
U.S.--DESCRIPTION AND TRAVEL--GUIDES
U.S.--GEOGRAPHY
WYOMING--DESCRIPTION AND TRAVEL--GUIDES
WYOMING--PUBLIC LANDS
YELLOWSTONE NATIONAL PARK

GLACIERS

• GLACIER

National Park. West Glacier, MT 59936. (406) 888-5441. 1,013,594.67 acres. 1910. Northwestern Montana, on U.S. 2 and 89.

Preserve peaks, about 50 glaciers, lakes and streams, variety of wildlife. Guided walks, programs, presentations, boating, hiking, and various outdoor activities, wilderness trails, glaciers, wildlife. Visitor centers, ranger stations, campgrounds, hotels, lodges, cabins.

Free Print Material:
"Backcountry Glacier National Park, MT." 24-fold. Background preparation for hikers, campers, climbers, and other outside activities. Map of 62 campgrounds, bear safety tips, backcountry regulations. Addresses to obtain detailed maps.
"Entrance and Camping Fees." 2 pages. Fee schedules, free

entrance requirements, camping fees. Weather table by month
gives average, maximum, minimum for temperature, precipitation, snowfall.

"Fatigue-Exhaustion." 6-fold. Tips on sustaining life in outdoor
activities. What to look out for in exhaustion, exposure,
stress.

"Glacier National Park Accommodations and Services." 2 pages.
Overnight accommodations, food service, boats, stores, showers
and others for within the park and outside the park.

"Golden Eagle Golden Age Golden Access Passports. 10-fold.
What these three congressionally authorized passes mean and
how they can help in enjoying federal parks and recreation
areas. Federal entrance fee areas, addresses of information
services.

"Is the Water Safe?" 8-fold. How to protect yourself when
drinking raw water.

"Waterton/Glacier." 24-fold. Features to see at the Waterton
Lakes National Park in Canada and Glacier National Park,
united as the Waterton/Glacier International Peace Park.
Photos of wildlife and scenery, map, visitor tips such as
driving in the parks, and safety considerations.

"You Are in Grizzly Country." 24-fold. Basic rules for personal
safety when visiting grizzly country.

Sales List:
"Glacier Natural History Association, Inc. Catalog of Publications."
2 pages. Grouped by: animals; birds; plants-trees-flowers;
general; special; maps; Native Americans; national geographic
books; art; geology; guides; mountaineering; young readers;
photographs; history; order form."

"Animal Friends of the Northwest." Hubbard. 1957. 32 pages.
Black and white. $1.70.

Suggested Curriculum Application:
GEOGRAPHY
MONTANA STATE AND LOCAL STUDIES

Suggested Sears Subject Heading:
GLACIER NATIONAL PARK
GLACIERS
MONTANA--DESCRIPTION AND TRAVEL--GUIDES
MONTANA--PUBLIC LANDS
NATIONAL PARKS AND RESERVES--U.S.
U.S.--DESCRIPTION AND TRAVEL--GUIDES
WILDERNESS AREAS

• GLACIER BAY
National Park/Preserve. Bartlett Cove, Gustavus, AK 99826.
(907) 697-2231. National Park, 3,225.197.95 acres; National
Preserve, 55,000 acres; wilderness area, 2,770,000 acres. National

Monument, 1925; National Park and Preserve, 1980; wilderness, 1980.
Southeast Alaska by boat or air. Boating distance from Juneau is
about 65 miles.

Great tidewater glaciers, plant communities from rocky terrain to
temperate rain forest, wide variety of animals. Guided hikes, films,
guided kayak trips, hiking trails, slide-illustrated evening talks,
exhibits, glaciers, wildlife, tour boat, boating. For lists of tours,
guides, accommodations inquire: Alaska Division of Tourism,
Pouch E, Juneau, AK 99811. Visitor center, food and lodging,
campground. Food and lodging in Juneau, Gustavus.

Free Print Material:
    "Glacier Bay." 24-fold. Tidewater glaciers, the world of whales,
        plants and animals, maps, access and services, photos, weather.
    "Glacier Bay Traveler Information." 2 pages. Activities such as
        hiking, kayaking, how to get to Glacier Bay, weather, cruise
        ships and other information.

Sales/Audiovisual List:
    "Alaska Natural History Association." 2 pages. Grouped by:
        general, visual aids, plants-animals, maps-nautical charts.
        Title, price, description, pages, type of cover for publica-
        tions. Visual aids includes a video and a slide set. Order
        blank and order instructions. Aims and membership of the
        Alaska History Association.
    "Glacier Bay National Park Service." $5.00. This 140-page
        national park handbook offers a good summary of the park's
        natural and human history and includes recent findings about
        tidewater glaciers. A section of how to see the park provides
        visitor access information. Full color. Paperback.

Suggested Curriculum Application:
    ALASKA STATE AND LOCAL STUDIES
    GEOGRAPHY
    GEOLOGY
    NATURAL HISTORY

Suggested Sears Subject Heading:
    ALASKA--DESCRIPTION AND TRAVEL--GUIDES
    ALASKA--PUBLIC LANDS
    GLACIER BAY NATIONAL PARK AND PRESERVE
    GLACIERS
    NATIONAL PARKS AND RESERVES--U.S.
    NATURAL HISTORY--ALASKA
    U.S.--DESCRIPTION AND TRAVEL--GUIDES
    U.S.--GEOGRAPHY
    WILDERNESS AREAS

• ICE AGE
National Scientific Reserve. Wisconsin Department of Natural Resources, Box 7921, Madison, WI 53707. (608) 266-2181.
32,500 acres. 1964. Wisconsin, nine separated units across Wisconsin from Lake Michigan to the Minnesota-Wisconsin border.
Interstate Unit is the most westerly located unit near the city of
St. Croix Falls, while Two Creeks Buried Forest Unit, 12 miles
north of Two Rivers, is the most easterly. Most of the operating
units are in southcentral Wisconsin.

Units are managed for wildlife management, recreation, scientific
study as the first national scientific reserve containing nationally
important features of continental glaciation. Individual units: Two
Creeks Buried Forest, Kettle Moraine, Campbellsport Drumlins,
Horicon Marsh, Cross Plains, Devil's Lake, Mill Bluff, Chippewa
Moraine, Interstate. At the time of compilation, the following units
were not yet in operation: Two Creeks Buried Forest, Campbellsport
Drumlins, Cross Plains, Chippewa Moraine. Naturalist programs,
exhibits, nature center, trails, nature study, scenic drive, swimming,
boating, hiking, cross-country skiing, wildlife. Glacial features
such as: drumlins, buried forest, kames, eskers, kettles interlobate
moraine, extinct glacial lake, subglacially formed gorge, erratics,
potholes, end moraines, sandstone buttes, and others. Interpretive
center, visitor center, campgrounds, trailside shelter, trailer dumping
stations, picnicking.

Free Print Material:
  "A Guide for the Mobility Impaired." 12-fold. Name, address,
    telephone, facilities, features of various parks and recreation
    areas, trails, forests. Senior citizen recreation cards, special
    permits, group fee waivers and other visitor information.
  "Hiking and Backpacking in Wisconsin State Parks and Forests."
    2 pages. Information about various parks and forests, ad-
    dresses for backpacking.
  "Horicon." 24-fold. Maps, photos, what to see and do in the
    Horicon Marsh Wildlife Area, a national ice age reserve unit.
    Seasonal attractions, hiking trails and other visitor information.
  "Ice Age National Scientific Reserve, Wisconsin." 24-fold. Il-
    lustrations show a scene ten to twelve thousand years ago and
    glaciers covering portions of North America. Definitions and
    photos of end moraines, erratics and other glacial features.
    Diagram showing what scientists think the landscape looked like
    as the great ice sheets were retreating. Geology, description
    of the reserve units, maps, visitor information.
  "Multiple Benefits from Forest Management." 16-fold. Natural
    beauty, wildlife, timber, watershed considerations, photos,
    specialized management practices.
  "Naturalist Program in Wisconsin State Parks and Forests." 7
    pages. Why naturalist programs are offered, what the pro-
    grams do, what programs are offered. Charts surveying:
    12-month programs, 3-month programs, occasional programs.

Suggested Curriculum Application:
GEOGRAPHY
GEOLOGY
WISCONSIN STATE AND LOCAL STUDIES

Suggested Sears Subject Heading:
GEOLOGY--U.S.
GLACIAL EPOCH
U.S.--DESCRIPTION AND TRAVEL--GUIDES
WISCONSIN--DESCRIPTION AND TRAVEL--GUIDES
WISCONSIN--PUBLIC LANDS

- KENAI FJORDS
National Park. P.O. Box 1727, Seward, AK 99664. (907) 224-3175.
670,000 acres. National Monument, 1978; National Park, 1980.
Southern Alaska, 20 miles south and west of Seward and 130 miles
south of Anchorage by Seward Highway.

Major ice cap in icefield wilderness, waterfalls in canyons, glaciers,
mountain valleys, coastline. Exhibit, slide program, naturalist-led
hikes to the glacier's base, campfire programs, all-day hikes to
Harding Icefield, special events, day-skiing or expeditions, nature
trails, flightseeing, kayak trips, boat charters, backpacking.
Visitor center, ranger station. Campsites 3/4 mile from Exit
Glacier. Food and lodging in Seward.

Free Print Material:
"Exit Glacier: A Window Into Time." 8-fold. Sketches, how
glaciers form, description of exit glacier, wildlife and wild
flowers, crevasses, interpretive programs, the retreat of Exit
Glacier.
"Kenai Fjords." 16-fold. Photos, maps, logistics, what to see
and do, weather, visitor safety, backcountry travel, description of the glacier-carved valleys filled with ocean waters.
"Kenai Fjords National Park Sightseeing Cruises from Seward,
Alaska." 8-fold. Photos, map, description of the sightseeing
cruise, special options.

Sales/Audiovisual List:
"Alaska Natural History Association Mail Order Catalog." 8 pages.
Publications and audiovisuals from various parks and other
sources in Alaska, sketches. Title, author, price annotation.
pages. Includes children's materials. Order blank, ordering
instructions.
"Alaska National Parklands: This Last Treasure." Brown, hard
$16.95, soft $5.95. 128 pages. Full-color publication describing the national significance of all national park service areas
in Alaska by means of a narrative by Brown and short writings
by individuals very familiar with the parks. 128 pages paperback and....

Suggested Curriculum Application:
ALASKA STATE AND LOCAL STUDIES
GEOGRAPHY

Suggested Sears Subject Heading:
ALASKA--DESCRIPTION AND TRAVEL--GUIDES
ALASKA--PUBLIC LANDS
GLACIERS
U.S.--DESCRIPTION AND TRAVEL--GUIDES
WILDERNESS AREAS

● MOUNT RAINIER
National Park. Tahoma Woods, Star Route, Ashford, WA 98304.
(206) 569-2211. 235,404 acres. 1899. Southwestern Washington,
95 miles southeast of Seattle, off of Route 706.

Largest single-peak glacial system in the United States, centering
from the dormant volcano's summit and slopes. The 14,410-foot
Mount Rainier has 35 square miles of ice in 25 named and about
50 unnamed glaciers and ice patches. Self-guiding nature trails,
bicycling, audiovisuals, horseback riding, ice cave formed by rivers
underneath a glacier, wildlife, climbing, sliding, snowshoeing, cross-
country skiing, exhibits. Interpretive programs such as flower
walks, map talks, alpine ecology hikes. Visitor centers, hiker information centers, supplies, picnicking, climbing guide service, campgrounds, food and lodging.

Free Print Material:
"Backcountry Trip Planner." 4 pages. A hikers' guide to the
wilderness of Mount Rainier National Park, map, photos.
"Birds of Mount Rainier National Park: A Checklist." 6-fold.
Grouped by such birds as waterfowl, swifts, warblers, and
many others. Seasonal checklist with symbols such as abundant, uncommon and others.
"Climbing Mount Rainier." 2 pages. Good climbing practices,
climbing regulations, recommended climbing equipment and
other tips.
"Common Mammals." 4 pages. Life zones, common mammals and
where to find them in the park. Includes common and scientific names, habits, where to see them.
"Flowers of the Sub-Alpine Meadows." 3 pages. Common name,
scientific name, family name. Sketches.
"Front Country Reservable Group Campside Information." 1 page.
Facilities at Ipsut Creek and Cougar Rock.
"Glaciers!" 1 page. Glacier advances and retreats, size, volume
on Mount Rainier.
"Indians in Mount Rainier National Park." 1 page. Indian
presence and activities. Bibliography.
"Kautz Creek Mudflow." 4 pages. Events preceding the 1947
flood, scope and character of the flood and other aspects.

"Mount Rainier." 24-fold. History, description. Visitor activities, map, photos.

"Mount Rainier National Park Fee Information." 1 page. Golden Eagle Passports, Golden Age Passports, Golden Access Passes, single entry fees.

"Mount Rainier News." 4 pages. Newspaper format. Guide to information, activities, programs.

"Self-Guiding Trails at Mount Rainier." 1 page. Name, location, length/time and description of various trails.

"Spotted Owl Study." 6 pages. Life cycle, sketch, habits of the spotted owl, research projects, donation form.

"Trees of Rainier." 1 page. Common, scientific name, family name.

"United States Peaks Over 14,000 Feet." 1 page. Names, heights, location of peaks in this country.

"What's In a Name?" 1 page. Map name, historic name and traditional name of Mount Rainier.

"Wildflowers of the Lower Forests." 1 page. Arranged by common name, scientific name, family name. Sketches.

Sales/Audiovisual List:

"Pacific Northwest National Parks and Forests Association Mail Order Price List." 8-fold. Grouped by: Mount Rainier guides and maps, backpacking, national parks--pictoral guides, history and exploration, geology, wildlife, plants, miscellaneous, 35mm color slides. Aims of the Pacific Northwest National Parks and Forests Association, order blank and order directions. Map, photo. Includes title, description, price.

"Exploring Mt. Rainier." 8-fold. Kirt, 1968, 112 pages. Concise guide with useful information for all visitors. $7.95.

Suggested Curriculum Application:
GEOGRAPHY
NATURAL HISTORY
RECREATION
SCIENCE
WASHINGTON STATE AND LOCAL STUDIES

Suggested Sears Subject Heading:
GLACIERS
MOUNT RAINIER NATIONAL PARK
NATIONAL PARKS AND RESERVES--U.S.
NATURAL HISTORY--WASHINGTON
OUTDOOR RECREATION
U.S.--DESCRIPTION AND TRAVEL--GUIDES
U.S.--GEOGRAPHY
WASHINGTON--DESCRIPTION AND TRAVEL--GUIDES
WASHINGTON--PUBLIC LANDS
WILDERNESS AREAS

- WRANGELL-ST. ELIAS

National Park/Preserve. P.O. Box 29, Glenn Allen, AK   99588.
(907) 822-5234. National Park, 8,945,000 acres; National Preserve,
4,255,000 acres; wilderness area, 8,700,000 acres. 1978. Southeastern Alaska, by highway, then 4-wheel-drive vehicle or
chartered aircraft.

The largest unit of the National Park System. Contains the continent's largest group of glaciers, peaks above 16,000 feet, including
the second highest peak in the United States. Backpacking; wildlife; scenic mountains, valleys, river basins; cross-country skiing
and other winter activity; historic mining sites. Lodges, cabins,
camps. Motels, restaurants in communities surrounding the park,
guide services.

Free Print Material:
   "Information--Copper River Basin." 2 pages. Roads, towns,
      services, emergency phone numbers of the river, the main
      artery draining the Wrangell Mountain region.
   "Wrangell-St. Elias." 2 pages. What to do and see, access,
      weather, services and other visitor information. Map, photo.

Bibliography:
   "Recommended Reading." 1 page. Materials grouped by:
      general, cultural, safety. Title, publisher, date; volume num-
      ber if magazine. Those available through the Alaska Natural
      History Association, Denali Branch, are indicated.

Suggested Curriculum Application:
   ALASKA STATE AND LOCAL STUDIES
   GEOGRAPHY
   RECREATION

Suggested Sears Subject Heading:
   ALASKA--DESCRIPTION AND TRAVEL--GUIDES
   ALASKA--PUBLIC LANDS
   NATIONAL PARKS AND RESERVES--U.S.
   OUTDOOR RECREATION
   U.S.--DESCRIPTION AND TRAVEL--GUIDES
   U.S.--GEOGRAPHY
   WILDERNESS AREAS
   WRANGELL-ST. ELIAS NATIONAL PARK AND PRESERVE

HAWAIIAN CULTURE

- PU'UHONUA O HONAUNAU

National Historical Park. P.O. Box 128, Honaunau, Kona, HI   96726.

(808) 328-2326. 181.80 acres. 1961. Western portion of the island of Hawaii, off of Highway 160.

Last remaining historical site of its type, aiming at restoration of 1700 appearance, a place set aside for vanished warriors, noncombatants, and breakers of the sacred rules of life where, after a purification ceremony, they could leave. Talks, cultural demonstrations. Self-guiding tours of palace grounds, house models, stone where you can play a game of old Hawaiian checkers, stone bowls, tree mold of a tree that fell in lava, royal canoe landing, royal fishpond, reconstructed temple, Keoua Stone, Ka'ahumanu Stone, Papamu, Old Temple, petroglyph, Halau. The Great Stone Wall is 1,000 feet long, 10 feet high, 17 feet wide and is built of stones formed from lava with no mortar used. Park amphitheatre, picnicking. Food and lodging 10 miles away.

Free Print Material:
"Pu'uhonua O Honaunau." 12-fold. Photos, map, features of the park, explanation of what the place of refuge was for Hawaiians.
"Pu'uhonua O Honaunau: Place of Refuge." 7 pages. Photos, map, background about the place of the sanctuary.
"Rules for Konane." 2 pages. How the game of konane, or Hawaiian checkers, is played: history and information about old Hawaiian culture, suggested reading.

Bibliography:
Suggested reading list included in "Rules for Konane" described above. Authors and titles about Hawaiian history and Hawaii, including books about the journals and life of Captain James Cook.

Audiovisual List:
Slide program on the park may be requested by a teacher on school stationery.

Sales/Audiovisual List:
"Pu'uhonua O Honaunau National Historical Park, Hawaii Natural History Association Sales." 1 page. Publications, slides, post cards, posters, map, lithographs, nose flute and other items. Title, price, ordering information.
"Atlas of Hawaii." $5.95.

Suggested Curriculum Application:
AMERICAN HISTORY
HAWAII STATE AND LOCAL STUDIES
SOCIAL STUDIES

Suggested Sears Subject Heading:
ARCHITECTURE--CONSERVATION AND RESTORATION
HAWAII--DESCRIPTION AND TRAVEL--GUIDES

HAWAII--HISTORY
HAWAII--PUBLIC LANDS
U.S.--DESCRIPTION AND TRAVEL--GUIDES

• PUUKOHOLA HEIAU
National Historic Site. P.O. Box 4963, Kawaihae, HI   96743.
(808) 882-7218. 77.71 acres. 1972. Northwestern part of the
island of Hawaii, near the village of Kawaihae.

Preserve the last major religious structure and other remains of the
ancient Hawaiian culture built in the islands by King Kamehameha
the Great and used from 1791 to 1819. Pu'ukohola Heiau ("heiau"
means temple), Mailekini Heiau, Hale-o-ka-puni Heiau, the Stone
Leaning Post, Pelekane, John Young's House site. Sites may be
viewed by foot or by taking the Spencer Beach Park Road. Visitor
center. Camping nearby. The Hawaii Visitors Bureau (a nonprofit
organization) with offices in Hawaii and an office in California will
supply information about trips: Hawaii Visitors Bureau, 209 Post St.,
San Francisco, CA   94108.

Free Print Material:
    "Puukohola Heiau." 16-fold. Kamehameha's struggle for power,
        island culture, description of sites to see, safety tips, trans-
        portation and services. Photo, sketches, map.
    "Watch Your Step." 8-fold. Sketches, visitor tips about smoking,
        trail use, wave action and winds, sharks.

Bibliography:
    "Reading List." 1 page. Title, author, publisher, place of
        publication, date. List is designed to develop or further
        interest in Hawaii history.

Sales/Audiovisual List:
    "Hawaii Natural History Association." 1 page. Name of item,
        tax, price. Books, arts and crafts, slides, map, post card,
        poster, and other items.
    "Atlas of Hawaii." .24 $5.95.

Suggested Curriculum Application:
    AMERICAN HISTORY
    HAWAII STATE AND LOCAL STUDIES

Suggested Sears Subject Heading:
    HAWAII--DESCRIPTION AND TRAVEL--GUIDES
    HAWAII--KINGS AND RULERS
    HAWAII--PUBLIC LANDS
    HAWAII--RELIGION
    U.S.--DESCRIPTION AND TRAVEL--GUIDES

INDUSTRIES

- HOPEWELL FURNACE

National Historic Site. R.D. #1, Box 345, Elverson, PA 19520.
(215) 582-8773. 848.06 acres. 1938. Eastern Pennsylvania, 5 miles
south of Birdsboro on PA Route 345, 45 miles northwest of Philadelphia.

Example of Early American ironmaking village built by Mark Bird, an
American patriot. Hopewell produced iron 1771-1883. Slide program,
exhibits, summer living history program. Walking tour includes:
village roads, cooling shed and charcoal house, anthracite furnace,
charcoal hearth, water wheel and blast machinery, connecting shed
and bridgehouse, the office store, cast house, tuyere arch, blacksmith shop, tenant houses, stone bridge, barn, spring house, bake-
ovens and kitchen, big house, east head race and garden. School
groups from grades 3-6 in groups of 15 or more may arrange for a
guided tour (not given during the summer) by writing or calling in
advance. Visitor center. Camping and recreational facilities nearby. Food and lodging in Reading, Pottstown, Morgantown.

Free Print Material:
    "Hopewell Village." 20-fold. Description, illustrations, biograph-
       ical sketch of Hopewell founder Mark Bird, iron-making pro-
       cess, description of village tour, visiting Hopewell Village.
    "National Park Service Travel Tips." 8-fold. Photos, what
       national parks have to offer the visitor, selecting parks to
       visit, making reservations and other visitor information.
    "Sand Cast Moulding at Hopewell Furnace." 8 pages. Photos,
       sketches. Description of the process of sand cast moulding
       that was used primarily between 1772 and 1844 at Hopewell.
       Brief history of ironmaking in America.

Suggested Curriculum Application:
    AMERICAN HISTORY
    INDUSTRIAL ARTS
    PENNSYLVANIA STATE AND LOCAL STUDIES

Suggested Sears Subject Heading:
    IRON INDUSTRY AND TRADE
    PENNSYLVANIA--DESCRIPTION AND TRAVEL--GUIDES
    PENNSYLVANIA--PUBLIC LANDS
    U.S.--DESCRIPTION AND TRAVEL--GUIDES

- LOWELL NATIONAL

Historical Park. 169 Merrimack St., Lowell, MA 01852.
(617) 459-1000. 137.08 acres. 1978. Northern Massachusetts, off
of I-495 or U.S. 3, visitor center is at 246 Market Street, Lowell.

Commemorate the country's first planned industrial community.
Multi-image slide show, tours, performances, displays. Visitor center. Food and lodging in Lowell.

Free Print Material:
"Directions to Lowell National Historical Park." 1 page. Maps of Massachusetts and Lowell. Narrative directions.
"Greater Lowell Massachusetts." 6-fold. History, photos, map of Lowell, background of Industrial Revolution.
"Lowell." 12-fold. Features, photos, history of Lowell, Massachusetts.
"Tour Schedule." 1 page. Description, schedule of tours.

Audiovisual List:
"Outreach Programs List." 2 pages. Grouped by slide shows, movies, filmstrips. Slides are available as live programs, while the movies and filmstrips are available on a mail-out basis. For more information call (617) 459-1000.
"Lowell History." A 45-minute introduction to America's first great industrial city. Themes such as technology, labor, and capital are revealed and discussed.

Suggested Curriculum Application:
AMERICAN HISTORY
MASSACHUSETTS STATE AND LOCAL STUDIES
SOCIAL STUDIES

Suggested Sears Subject Heading:
INDUSTRY--HISTORY
MASSACHUSETTS--DESCRIPTION AND TRAVEL--GUIDES
MASSACHUSETTS--HISTORY
MASSACHUSETTS--PUBLIC LANDS
U.S.--DESCRIPTION AND TRAVEL--GUIDES

• SALEM MARITIME
National Historic Site. 174 Derby St., Salem, MA 01970.
(617) 744-4323. 8.95 acres. 1938. Eastern Massachusetts, 20 miles northeast of Boston, off Route 1A.

Commemorate the shipping industry that prospered in Massachusetts Bay's oldest seaport. Salem was once the sixth largest city in the nation. Derby wharf, warehouses, the Custom House, the Scale House, West India Goods Store, Derby House, Hawkes House, Narbonne-Hale House, lighthouse. Guided tours of Derby House and some others. Groups may receive special service if advance arrangements are made at the site. Greater Boston's north shore area, Salem and others.

Free Print Material:
"Best of Salem." 8-fold. Maps (one includes the Heritage Trail,

a walking tour of some of Salem's historic sites), descriptions
of historic sites and attractions, sketch, business directory.
"The National Parks and the Bicentennial of the United States
Constitution." 12-fold. Photos, background history of the
making of the <u>Constitution</u>, parks connected with the framing
and early workings of the <u>Constitution</u>.
"Salem Maritime." 24-fold. Sketches, photos, history of the
seaport and the shipping industry. Illustration of a long boat
and stern boat with a cross section of contents amidst a wharf
scene. Items such as pepper, tallow, and sugar are marked.
Description and photos of cargo, map showing world trade
routes. Sketch with labeled descriptions of Salem Maritime
National Historic Site.

Suggested Curriculum Application:
AMERICAN HISTORY
MASSACHUSETTS STATE AND LOCAL STUDIES

Suggested Sears Subject Heading:
MASSACHUSETTS--DESCRIPTION AND TRAVEL--GUIDES
MASSACHUSETTS--PUBLIC LANDS
SHIPPING--U.S.
TRADE ROUTES
U.S.--DESCRIPTION AND TRAVEL--GUIDES

* SAUGUS IRON WORKS
National Historic Site. 244 Central Street, Saugus, MA 01906.
(617) 233-0050. 8.51 acres. 1968. Eastern Massachusetts, 10 miles
north of Boston, east of U.S. 1.

Commemorates America's first successful integrated ironworks. Reconstructed iron works of the 17th century shows water wheel, bel-
lows and other processes. Reconstructed furnace, forge, mill on
original foundations, furnished 17th-century house, museum, working
blacksmith, tours, demonstrations, film. Groups should call ahead.
Gift shop. Picnicking on the east bank of the river. Food and
lodging in greater Boston area.

Free Print Material:
"Adventures North of Boston." 44 pages. Accommodations listings,
attractions listed by towns, maps and adventure categories,
tourist council members, calendar of events, other Massachusetts
destinations. Sketches, photos, map.
"Information for Teachers." 4 pages. Audiovisuals, significance
of the Saugus iron works, activity sheet.
"Saugus Iron Works." 20-fold. Sketch, photos, life in the Puri-
tan colonies, ironworks on the Saugus, description of the iron-
making process.
"The Spirit of Massachusetts is the Spirit of America." 24 pages.
Photos, descriptions of historical places of importance, map,

mileage chart, name, address, telephone of regional tourist councils.

Audiovisual List:
 One page of movies, filmstrips available for free loan included in "Information for Teachers" described above.

Sales/Audiovisual List:
 "Sales List." 1 page. Coloring books, guide, books, post cards, notepaper, portfolio, slide strips, replicas, cookbook. Title, price. Ordering directions.

Suggested Curriculum Application:
 AMERICAN HISTORY
 INDUSTRIAL ARTS
 MASSACHUSETTS STATE AND LOCAL STUDIES

Suggested Sears Subject Heading:
 IRON INDUSTRY AND TRADE
 MASSACHUSETTS--DESCRIPTION AND TRAVEL--GUIDES
 MASSACHUSETTS--PUBLIC LANDS
 U.S.--DESCRIPTION AND TRAVEL--GUIDES

- SPRINGFIELD ARMORY
National Historic Site. One Armory Square, Springfield, MA   01105.
(413) 734-6477. 54.93 acres. 1974. Southwestern Massachusetts,
off Federal Street, within reach of several interstate highways.

Center for the manufacture, invention, and development of U.S. military small arms from 1794 to 1968. The weapons museum, begun about 1870, is regarded as one of the largest collections of small arms. Tours and self-guided tours. Historic buildings: commanding officer's quarter, master armorer's house, junior officer's quarters, west arsenal, east arsenal, administration, north and south shops, caserne. Accommodations in greater Springfield area.

Free Print Material:
 "Shay's Rebellion 1786-1787." 8-fold. Chronology and guide to sites in the Connecticut Valley. Map, places of related interest. Books for further reading, film, poster exhibit. Addresses and telephone numbers for obtaining the half-hour documentary and exhibit on Shay's Rebellion.
 "Springfield Armory." 16-fold. Photos, illustrations, maps. History of the manufacture of U.S. arms from President Washington's selection of the site as one of the two federal armories; development; quality control, assembly, operation of arms; closing in 1968. Visitor information.

Suggested Curriculum Application:
 AMERICAN HISTORY
 MASSACHUSETTS STATE AND LOCAL STUDIES

Suggested Sears Subject Heading:
    FIREARMS INDUSTRY AND TRADE
    MASSACHUSETTS--DESCRIPTION AND TRAVEL--GUIDES
    MASSACHUSETTS--PUBLIC LANDS
    U.S.--DESCRIPTION AND TRAVEL--GUIDES

INTERNATIONAL RELATIONS

- CHAMIZAL

National Memorial. 800 South San Marcial Street, El Paso, TX   79905.
(915) 541-7880. 54.90 acres. 1966. Western Texas, off I-10.

Memorializes signing of 1963 treaty settling a 99-year boundary
dispute between the United States and Mexico, presents international
boundary history, cultural heritages of both countries. Museum,
festivals, exhibits, film, graphic arts galleries, bicycling, theatrical
performances. Visitor center, picnicking. Food and lodging in El
Paso, TX and Juarez, Mexico.

Free Print Material:
    "Chamizal." (Also available in a Spanish version.) 14-fold.
    Maps, sketches, purpose of Chamizal National Memorial, es-
    tablishing an international boundary, the settlement problems
    of Chamizal, visitor information.

Suggested Curriculum Application:
    AMERICAN HISTORY
    GOVERNMENT
    SOCIAL STUDIES
    TEXAS STATE AND LOCAL STUDIES

Suggested Sears Subject Heading:
    INTERNATIONAL RELATIONS
    TEXAS--DESCRIPTION AND TRAVEL--GUIDES
    TEXAS--PUBLIC LANDS
    U.S.--BOUNDARIES
    U.S.--DESCRIPTION AND TRAVEL--GUIDES

- INTERNATIONAL PEACE GARDEN

P.O. Box 419, Dunseith, ND   58637. (701) 263-4390. 2,330.30
acres. 1931. Northern North Dakota, on the border of North
Dakota and Manitoba, 13 miles north of Dunseith on U.S. 281.

Commemorate peaceful relations between Canada and the United
States. Canadian natural drive tour, the United States Cultural

Drive tour, formal garden walking tour. Entrance gate, entrance area, hiking trail, arboretum, Ducks Unlimited Dam, Willis Pavilion, picnic areas, sunken garden, bell tower, peace tower, peace chapel, floral clock, greenhouse, music camp, sports camp, and other features. Visitor center, concessions, picnicking, souvenirs. International Peace Garden campground. Food and lodging in nearby Manitoba and North Dakota communities.

Free Print Material:
"A History of the International Peace Garden." 23 pages. Beginning and development. Description of various features such as the floral clock received by the peace garden in 1966 from the Bulova Watch Company. Photos.
"International Peace Garden." 12-fold. History and development, features of the garden, map, photos.

Audiovisual List:
A set of eighty slides with commentary is available for groups to view.

Suggested Curriculum Application:
NORTH DAKOTA STATE AND LOCAL STUDIES
SOCIAL STUDIES

Suggested Sears Subject Heading:
GARDENS
INTERNATIONAL RELATIONS
NORTH DAKOTA--DESCRIPTION AND TRAVEL--GUIDES
NORTH DAKOTA--PUBLIC LANDS
U.S.--BOUNDARIES
U.S.--DESCRIPTION AND TRAVEL--GUIDES

• SAN JUAN ISLAND
National Historical Park. P.O. Box 429, Friday Harbor, WA 98250. (206) 378-2240. 1,751.99 acres. 1966. Off northwestern Washington coast. Island is reached by ferries from Anacortes, WA, 83 miles north of Seattle; or from Sydney, British Columbia. Also accessible by private boats, or by commercial or private air flight.

Site of a military confrontation with Great Britain. San Juan Island was under British and American occupation for 12 years until the Treaty of Washington was signed. In 1872 the final boundary between Canada and the United States was set. Hiking trails, nature walk, south beach, wildlife. English camp in Garrison Bay has four historic buildings, restored garden, exhibit. The American camp on the southern tip of the island has two historic buildings, the remains of an earthwork gun implacement, with other building sites known, exhibit center. Picnic areas, information center in Friday Harbor. Campgrounds on the island. Friday Harbor and Roche Harbor have food and lodging.

Free Print Material:
  "Campgrounds and Accommodations." 2 pages. Name, description, location, facilities, telephone of various campgrounds, hotels, inns, lodges, resorts.
  "Maps of San Juan Island." 2 pages. Friday Harbor map and island map.
  "San Juan Island." 12-fold. Maps, photos, features and activities. Background of the boundary dispute. Includes photos of the English and American camps in the 1860's.

Suggested Curriculum Application:
  AMERICAN HISTORY
  SOCIAL STUDIES
  WASHINGTON STATE AND LOCAL STUDIES

Suggested Sears Subject Heading:
  INTERNATIONAL RELATIONS
  ISLANDS
  SAN JUAN ISLAND
  U.S.--DESCRIPTION AND TRAVEL--GUIDES
  U.S.--BOUNDARIES
  WASHINGTON--DESCRIPTION AND TRAVEL--GUIDES
  WASHINGTON--HISTORY
  WASHINGTON--PUBLIC LANDS

• SITKA
National Historical Park. P.O. Box 738, Sitka, AK 98836.
(907) 747-6281. 106.83 acres. 1910. West side of Baranof Island in southeast Alaska, 95 miles southwest from Juneau. Accessible only by air or boat.

Commemorate the battle for Sitka between Russian fur traders and Indians, interpret the story of the way of life of the Native American. Nine hiking trails, Tlingit Indian totem poles and crafts. The oldest intact piece of Russian-American architecture, the Russian bishop's house, built in 1842. Wildlife, Russian memorial, plaque. Visitor center, picnic tables. Campgrounds with picnic tables are located 7 miles north of town and six miles east of town. Lodging and food in Sitka.

Free Print Material:
  "Sitka Official Map and Guide." 16-fold. Illustrations, photos, map. Historical background about the Tlingit peoples and the coming of the Russians, development of the town of Sitka. Visitor information and park development.
  "Bird Checklist." 6-fold. Arranged by loons, grebes, cormorants, and many others. Includes seasonal symbols and relative abundance, nesting, species threatened or endangered in some part of its range in the United States, sketches.
  "Historic Sitka." 1 page. Map of the Russian-American capital.

"Is the Water Safe?" 8-fold. Precautions to take before drinking untreated water.

"Sitka National Historical Park Plant List." 8-fold, scientific and common name. Symbols used: introduced plant, in park herbarium, edible parts present, poisonous parts present.

"Sitka National Historical Park Trail Map." 1 page. Sketch, map, key.

"The Southeast Alaska Indian Cultural Center." 6-fold. Purpose and development of the cultural center housed in a wing of the Sitka visitor center at the edge of Sitka National Historical Park. Photos, hours.

Bibliography:
"Bibliography." 9 pages. Subjects of: history and culture of Tlingit Indians, Battle of Sitka, Russia-America, totem poles. Includes author, title, publisher, place of publication, date.

Audiovisual List:
"16mm Film List." 2 pages. Title, color, running length, annotation. Some include date.

"Age of Alaska." Color, 30 minutes, 1977. Explanation of the Alaska Native Claims Settlement Act as it pertains to federal land selection for national parks, refuges and forests in Alaska. Spectacular scenery.

Sales/Audiovisual List:
"Alaska Natural History Association Mail Order Catalog." 8 pages. Sketches, order form, ordering instructions. Items from Denali National Park and Preserve, Sitka National Historical Park and others. Grouped by: general-guide books; mountaineering, first aid; birds; mammals and much more. Sketches, order form and ordering information.

"Alaska National Parklands: This Last Treasure." Brown. Hardbound $16.95, soft $5.95. 128 pages. Full-color publication describing the national significance of all National Park Service areas in Alaska by means of a narrative by Brown and short writings by individuals....

Suggested Curriculum Application:
ALASKA STATE AND LOCAL STUDIES
NATIVE AMERICAN STUDIES
SOCIAL STUDIES

Suggested Sears Subject Heading:
ALASKA--DESCRIPTION AND TRAVEL--GUIDES
ALASKA--HISTORY
ALASKA--PUBLIC LANDS
INDIANS OF NORTH AMERICA--HISTORY
INTERNATIONAL RELATIONS
TLINGIT INDIANS
TOTEM AND TOTEMISM
U.S.--DESCRIPTION AND TRAVEL--GUIDES

INVENTORS

• EDISON

National Historic Site. Main Street and Lakeside Avenue, West Orange, NJ 07052. (201) 736-5050. 21.25 acres. 1955. Northeastern New Jersey.

Preserve the buildings, equipment, home, papers of Edison. Library, papers, models, home, laboratories, water tower, replica of the first motion picture studio, lab museum, guided tours, movies. At the time of compiling information, Glenmont, Edison's home was closed for renovations, so please inquire. Visitor center. Meals and lodging nearby.

Free Print Material:
"Edison." 12-fold. A guide to the site, maps, Edison's accomplishments, photos.
"National Park Sites: North Atlantic Region." 8-fold. History of national parks, sources of park information, regional sites, map, photos, chart.
"Welcome to Glenmont." 8 pages. Photos, description of Edison's 23-room home that he purchased in 1886 and in which he died.

Bibliography:
"Bibliography." 1 page. Books for adults arranged by author, title, publisher, date.

Sales List:
"Eastern National Park and Monument Association Order Blank." 4 pages. Grouped by: publications--adult, publications-- children, other sales items. Includes postcards, posters, stationery, reproduction cylinder boxes, buttons and other items. Ordering instructions, form.
"Edison: A Biography," Matthew Josephson, 511 pages, illustrated. $7.95.

Suggested Curriculum Application:
NEW JERSEY STATE AND LOCAL STUDIES
SCIENCE

Suggested Sears Subject Heading:
ARCHITECTURE--CONSERVATION AND RESTORATION
EDISON, THOMAS A., 1847-1931
INVENTORS
NEW JERSEY--DESCRIPTION AND TRAVEL--GUIDES
NEW JERSEY--PUBLIC LANDS
U.S.--DESCRIPTION AND TRAVEL--GUIDES

● WRIGHT BROTHERS
National Memorial. c/o Cape Hatteras National Seashore, Route 1,
Box 675, Manteo, NC 27954. (919) 441-7430. 431.40 acres.
National Memorial, 1927; transferred from War Department, 1933;
redesignated, 1953. Eastern North Carolina, on the outer banks of
North Carolina about midway between Kitty Hawk and Nags Head on
Byp. U.S. 158, about 10 miles from Cape Hatteras National Seashore.

Commemorate the first sustained flight in a heavier-than-air vehicle
in 1903 by Wilbur and Orville Wright. Exhibits, full-scale reproductions of 1902 glider and 1903 flying machine, 60-foot Wright Monument shaft standing on the site of many glider experiments, reconstruction of the Wrights' 1903 camp. Visitor center. Food and
lodging in Manteo.

Free Print Material:
    "Camping Information." 2 pages. Description of Cape Hatteras
        National Seashore, names of campgrounds, ranger-conducted
        activities, fees, reservations, and other user information.
    "In the Park." 12 pages. Newspaper format. Visitor informa-
        tion about Wright Brothers National Memorial, Fort Raleigh
        National Historic Site, Cape Hatteras National Seashore.
        Photos, schedules of activities, articles, maps, sales items.
    "Wright Brothers." 12-fold. Narrative chronology from Septem-
        ber 13, 1900 to the first flight December 17, 1903. Photos,
        maps, biographical information about the Wright brothers,
        what to see at the memorial.

Sales/Audiovisual List:
    Items from the Eastern National Park and Monument Association
        included in "In the Park" described above. Includes: books,
        miscellaneous, children's books, slides, puzzles, posters,
        note cards, model kits.

Suggested Curriculum Application:
    AMERICAN HISTORY
    NORTH CAROLINA STATE AND LOCAL STUDIES
    SOCIAL STUDIES

Suggested Sears Subject Heading:
    FLIGHT
    INVENTORS
    NORTH CAROLINA--DESCRIPTION AND TRAVEL--GUIDES
    NORTH CAROLINA--PUBLIC LANDS
    U.S.--DESCRIPTION AND TRAVEL--GUIDES
    WRIGHT, ORVILLE, 1871-1948
    WRIGHT, WILBUR, 1867-1912

ISLANDS

• APOSTLE ISLANDS
National Lakeshore. Route 1, Box 4, Bayfield, WI 54814.
(715) 779-3397. 67,884.84 acres. 1970. Northern tip of Wisconsin.
Islands and adjacent Bayfield Peninsula along the southern shore of
Lake Superior.

Islands, strip of shoreline, sandstone cliffs, sea caves, lighthouses,
sand beaches provide recreational area. Twenty islands, 12-mile
strip on Lake Superior's south shore, hiking trails, wildlife, sea
caves, lighthouse tours, cross-country skiing, Hokenson Brothers
Fishery Museum, beachcombing, abandoned brownstone quarries,
snowshoeing, winter camping, swimming, boating, exhibits, audiovisual programs, evening programs, nature walks, boat trips.
Visitor center, campsites, ranger stations. Food and lodging in
Bayfield, Washburn and others nearby.

Free Print Material:
    "Apostle Islands." 16-fold. Maps, boat trips, hiking, winter
        activities, wildlife, geology and history.
    "Apostle Islands Cruises." 6-fold. Maps, photos, information
        about various available cruises.
    "Around the Archipelago." 4 pages. Newspaper format.
        Articles, sketches, photos, maps, charts provide information
        on programs and activities at Apostle Islands National Lake-
        shore.
    "Boaters Guide." 2 pages. Map, name and description of public
        docks, boater information.
    "Camping in the Apostle Islands National Lakeshore." 4 pages.
        Getting to the islands, permits, groups, wildlife, fires and
        related information. Chart of various campgrounds with
        facilities.

Audiovisual List:
    "Film List." 1 page. Title of films.
    #0 "To Keep Our Liberty."

Sales/Audiovisual List:
    "Eastern National Park and Monument Association Mail Order Form
        for Apostle Islands National Lakeshore." 5 pages. Grouped
        by: Apostle Islands and the surrounding area, general inter-
        est, cultural history, recreation, children's books, natural
        history, field guides, maps, post cards, framing print, pass-
        port to your national parks, record albums, posters/prints,
        slides, miscellaneous. Title, author, description, date, type of
        cover (some), price. Order form, ordering instructions.
    "Sunrise on Morning Hill," Evadne Scott Beebe. Personal reflec-
        tions and memories about the area. 1980. $4.95.

Suggested Curriculum Application:
RECREATION
WISCONSIN STATE AND LOCAL STUDIES

Suggested Sears Subject Heading:
APOSTLE ISLANDS
ISLANDS
OUTDOOR RECREATION
U.S.--DESCRIPTION AND TRAVEL--GUIDES
WISCONSIN--DESCRIPTION AND TRAVEL--GUIDES
WISCONSIN--PUBLIC LANDS

• ASSATEAGUE ISLAND
National Seashore. Route 2, Box 294, Berlin, MD 21811.
(301) 641-2120. 39,630.93 acres. 1965. Off the coast of Maryland
and Virginia, about 150 miles from Baltimore or Washington.

Preserve the 37-mile barrier island, sandy beach, waterfowl and wild
ponies. Chincoteague National Wildlife Refuge guided programs, mi-
gratory birds, two herds of wild ponies, canoe-in campsites, shell
collecting, guided walks, talks, bicycle trails, hiking. Children's
programs and seashore recreation demonstrations daily in summer and
on weekends in fall and spring. Visitor centers, camping on the
island and nearby Chincoteague Island, oversand vehicle zones, picnic areas, boat launch.

Free Print Material:
"Assateague Island Backcountry Camping." 6 pages. Description
of sites and facilities offered, check-in time, regulations, map.
"Assateague Island Camping." 6 pages. What to expect, facilities, regulations, specialty camping, naturalist programs, off-
island campgrounds.
"Assateague Island Map and Guide." 16-fold. What the seashore,
wildlife refuge, lifeguarded beaches have to offer in activities.
Map, photos.
"Assateague Island the Wild Ponies." 6 pages. Questions and
answers about the descendants of domestic animals that re-
verted to a wild state. The two herds are separated and have
about 150 animals per herd.

Sales/Audiovisual List:
"Assateague Island National Seashore Sales Catalogue." 4 pages.
Publications grouped by: Assateague; plants, animals and
seashore, National Park Service, children's books. Ordering
information.
"Assateague," William H. Wroten, a human history of the island;
paperback, $2.95.

Suggested Curriculum Application:
ENVIRONMENTAL EDUCATION

GEOGRAPHY
VIRGINIA STATE AND LOCAL STUDIES

Suggested Sears Subject Heading:
ASSATEAGUE ISLAND
CHINCOTEAGUE NATIONAL WILDLIFE REFUGE
ISLANDS
MARYLAND--DESCRIPTION AND TRAVEL--GUIDES
MARYLAND--PUBLIC LANDS
PONIES
U.S.--DESCRIPTION AND TRAVEL--GUIDES
VIRGINIA--DESCRIPTION AND TRAVEL--GUIDES
VIRGINIA--PUBLIC LANDS
WILDLIFE--CONSERVATION

- CAPE HATTERAS

National Seashore. Route 1, Box 675, Manteo, NC 27954.
(919) 473-2111. 30,319.43 acres. 1937. Three islands in the
Atlantic off of eastern North Carolina. Motorists can reach the
park from the north by U.S. 17 and 158, or from the east by
U.S. 64 and 264. Ferries travel from the mainland.

Preserve beaches, wildlife, historic points of interest in this area
called the "Graveyard of the Atlantic." History and natural history
programs, observation platforms and walking trails in the Pea
Island National Wildlife Refuge, Ocracoke Island, Bodie Island,
Hatteras Island, lighthouses and life-saving reenactments, ranger-
conducted activities, water sports. Visitor centers, five campgrounds.

Free Print Material:
"Camping Information." 2 pages. Regulations, fees, campground
chart. Answers to frequently asked questions.
"Cape Hatteras." 12-fold. Map, photos, sketches, touring the
islands, history of the area, visitor tips.
"In the Park." 12 pages. Newspaper format covers what to see
and do in Wright Brothers National Memorial, Fort Raleigh
National Historic Site and Cape Hatteras National Seashore.
Photos, activity charts, schedules, program descriptions, maps,
articles, sales list.
"North Carolina Outer Banks Vacation Guide." 128 pages. Accommodations for beaches north of Oregon Inlet, Roanoke
Island, Hatteras Island, Ocracoke Island, places of worship,
emergency phone numbers, calendar, National Park Service
campgrounds, map, photos.

Sales List:
Order form and list of Eastern National Park and Monument Asso-
ciation composes one page of "In the Park" described above.
Includes books, children's books, miscellaneous such as

patches, puzzles, models, kits, maps.
"Cut and Assemble Paper Airplanes." $3.95.

Suggested Curriculum Application:
GEOGRAPHY
NORTH CAROLINA STATE AND LOCAL STUDIES

Suggested Sears Subject Heading:
HATTERAS ISLAND
ISLANDS
LIGHTHOUSES
NORTH CAROLINA--DESCRIPTION AND TRAVEL--GUIDES
NORTH CAROLINA--PUBLIC LANDS
PEA ISLAND NATIONAL WILDLIFE REFUGE
U.S.--DESCRIPTION AND TRAVEL--GUIDES
U.S.--GEOGRAPHY

• CHANNEL ISLANDS
National Park. 1901 Spinnaker Drive, Ventura, CA   93001.
(805) 644-8262. 249,353.77 acres. National Monument, 1938;
National Park, 1980. Five islands off the coast of Southern California, the closest island being 14 miles from Ventura, 11 miles
from Oxnard.

Preserve unique natural and cultural resources, conserving genetic
diversity and an environmental baseline for research and worldwide
monitoring. Film, boat tours, photo displays, exhibits, simulated
Caliche ghost forest, an indoor tidepool, native plant display,
self-guided nature trails, Frenchy's Cove, snorkeling, tidepools,
scuba and skin diving, ship wrecks, Cabrillo Monument, wildlife
and other features. An area extending six nautical miles around
each park island is designated the Channel Islands National Marine
Sanctuary, including the islands' submerged areas. Visitor centers,
ranger stations, campgrounds, picnicking. Food and lodging on the
mainland in Ventura, Oxnard.

Free Print Material:
"Channel Islands."   24-fold. Maps, photos, illustrations.
Visitor information, island life and ecology. Description,
features, map, photos of Anacapa Island, Santa Cruz Island,
Santa Rosa Island, San Miguel Island, Santa Barbara Island.
Labeled illustrations name and show giant squid, blue rock-
fish, soft coral, surf grass and many other ecological island
life features.
"Channel Islands Island Packers Inc., Ventura."   8-fold. Photos,
map, description, schedule, fares of various excursions, extended cruises.
"Channel Islands National Marine Sanctuary."   8-fold. Illustrations, map, description and purpose of the sanctuary.

Sales List:
   "Suggested Books on the Channel Islands National Park and Order
      Sheet." 2 pages. Title, price. One page order blank and
      ordering directions.
   "Channel Islands, the Story Behind the Scenery." $4.50.

Suggested Curriculum Application:
   CALIFORNIA STATE AND LOCAL STUDIES
   ENVIRONMENTAL EDUCATION
   GEOGRAPHY
   SCIENCE

Suggested Sears Subject Heading:
   CALIFORNIA--DESCRIPTION AND TRAVEL--GUIDES
   CALIFORNIA--PUBLIC LANDS
   CHANNEL ISLANDS NATIONAL PARK
   ECOLOGY
   ISLANDS
   MARINE RESOURCES
   NATIONAL PARKS AND RESERVES--U.S.
   NATURAL HISTORY--CALIFORNIA
   U.S.--DESCRIPTION AND TRAVEL--GUIDES
   WILDLIFE--CONSERVATION

● CUMBERLAND ISLAND
National Seashore. P.O. Box 806, St. Marys, GA 31558.
(912) 882-4335. 36,410.28 acres. 1972. Atlantic Ocean off the
southeastern Georgia coast.

Preserve unspoiled beaches, dunes, marshes, freshwater lakes.
Cumberland is 16 miles long by 3 miles at its widest point. Beach,
live-oak forest, backpacking, bird and wildlife, historical areas,
swimming. Ranger-conducted activities are available in peak season.
Accessible by tour boat only. An orientation talk before you board
the tour boat. Comfort stations and water are the only facilities
available on the island. Camping permitted in designated areas.
Motel accommodations, camping facilities and restaurants are available
on the mainland near St. Marys.

Free Print Material:
   "Cumberland Island." 12-fold. Sailing schedule, map, photos,
      visitor information.
   "Cumberland Island Information for Backpackers." 2 pages.
      Tips and regulations on camping, backpacking, information on
      campground.
   "Planning a Visit to Cumberland Island National Seashore." 2
      pages. Boat user fees, ticket purchase, reservations for
      ferry and campsites.

Suggested Curriculum Application:
GEORGIA STATE AND LOCAL STUDIES
RECREATION

Suggested Sears Subject Heading:
CUMBERLAND ISLAND
GEORGIA--DESCRIPTION AND TRAVEL--GUIDES
GEORGIA--PUBLIC LANDS
ISLANDS
NATURE CONSERVATION
OUTDOOR RECREATION
U.S.--DESCRIPTION AND TRAVEL--GUIDES

- FIRE ISLAND
National Seashore. 120 Laurel St., Patchogue, NY 11772.
(516) 289-4810. 19,578.55 acres. 1964. Off the southeastern
mainland of New York, access by car is limited to the eastern and
western ends of the seashore.

Island faces the Atlantic Ocean, protects Great South Bay and Long
Island, offers ecological observations and recreation. Lighthouse,
Watch Hill, William Floyd Estate, Sailors Haven Facility, Smith Point
West Facility. Nature trails, tours, interpretive activities, bird and
wildlife observation. Visitor centers, campground, marina, pic-
nicking, concessions, ferries. Food and lodging on the mainland.

Free Print Material:
"Fire Island." 12-fold. Description of the island and its wildlife,
features, access by car and ferries, map, photos.
"Fire Island Lighthouse--1858." 4 pages. History and future of
the lighthouse. Previous lighthouses, theories about how Fire
Island got its name.
"Fire Island National Seashore." 6-fold. Description of Fire
Island Lighthouse Facility, Watch Hill Facility, William Floyd
Estate, Sailors Haven Facility, Smith Point West Facility.
Sketch of the lighthouse, safety tips.
"An Introduction to the William Floyd Estate." 8-fold. Family
photos, background of the Floyd family. Sketches show growth
of the house from 1725 through eight generations.

Sales List:
"Interpretive Sales Publications." 1 page. List of items and
price. Includes postcards, buttons, books, stamps, calendar,
model kits, books, guides, emblems.
"Beachcraft Bonanza (Children's Activities). $8.95.

Suggested Curriculum Application:
ENVIRONMENTAL EDUCATION
GEOGRAPHY
NEW YORK STATE AND LOCAL STUDIES

Suggested Sears Subject Heading:
    ECOLOGY
    FIRE ISLAND
    ISLANDS
    LIGHTHOUSES
    NEW YORK--DESCRIPTION AND TRAVEL--GUIDES
    NEW YORK--PUBLIC LANDS
    U.S.--DESCRIPTION AND TRAVEL--GUIDES

- GULF ISLANDS
National Seashore. P.O. Box 100, Gulf Breeze, FL 32561.
(904) 932-5302. 65,816.64 acres. 1971. Southwestern Florida,
main entrance of the Pensacola Naval Air Station about one mile
south of Barrancas Avenue, FLA. 291.

Offshore islands and keys, white sand beaches, historic forts and
batteries, and mainland naval Live Oaks Reservation. Swimming,
various tours, programs, scuba diving, nature trails, beachcombing,
guided walks, interpretive programs, history and natural history
exhibits, boating, hiking. Visitor information station, ranger station, campgrounds, picnicking, concession store. Food and lodging
in Pensacola.

Free Print Material:
    "Advanced Redoubt." 8-fold. Construction from 1845-1859,
        location, facilities, function and use. Diagrams, maps.
    "Fort Barrancas and Water Battery." 6-fold. Chronology of the
        site from 1698, guide to the fort, water battery, Civil War
        action, seacoast defense, maps, photos.
    "Fort Massachusetts." 16-fold. Brief history of Ship Island,
        fort construction, fort tour, history of coastal fortifications,
        visitor information. Sketches, maps.
    "Fort Pickens." 8-fold. Photos, tour stops, maps, chronology
        of the site, Civil War action, the Apache Indians at Fort
        Pickens, modern coastal defenses.
    "Gulf Islands." 16-fold. Maps, photos. Description and illus-
        trations of life of the barrier island, visitor information, regu-
        lations and safety tips.
    "The Gulf Islands Barnacle." 4 pages. In newspaper format.
        Activities, maps, photos, visitor information.
    "Pensacola and Pensacola Beach." 8-fold. History, attractions,
        photos of the city of 5 flags.

Sales/Audiovisual List:
    "Eastern National Park and Monument Association Sales List."
        5 pages. Grouped by: general publications, historical publi-
        cations, children's publications, natural history books, golden
        guide publications, visual aids and general publications. In-
        cludes slide strips, posters, prints, photos, maps, post cards.
        Title, price.
    "Passport to Your National Parks." $2.95.

Suggested Curriculum Application:
AMERICAN HISTORY
FLORIDA STATE AND LOCAL STUDIES
GEOGRAPHY

Suggested Sears Subject Heading:
FLORIDA--DESCRIPTION AND TRAVEL--GUIDES
FLORIDA--PUBLIC LANDS
FORTIFICATION
GULF ISLANDS
ISLANDS
U.S.--DESCRIPTION AND TRAVEL--GUIDES

• GULF ISLANDS
National Seashore. 3500 Park Road, Ocean Springs, MS 39564.
(601) 875-9057. 73,958.82 acres. 1971. Northeastern Gulf of
Mexico from West Ship Island, Mississippi, 150 miles eastward to
Santa Rosa Island in Florida with mainland sections. Islands in the
Mississippi section are about 10 miles offshore.

Recreational beaches, wildlife sanctuary, historic remains. Audiovisual programs, hikes led by park rangers, exhibits, historic mainland Fort Massachusetts, variety of guided tours, sandbox-marine
museum, programs, illustrated talk, demonstrations, walks, self-
guiding trails, boating, swimming. Visitor center, picnicking,
snack bar, boat launch ramp, ranger stations, bathhouse, campgrounds.

Free Print Material:
"Activity Schedule." 1 page. Visitor hours, program descrip-
tions, maps.
"Fort Massachusetts." 16-fold. History of Ship Island, maps,
sketches, access, regulations, facilities, safety, fort construc-
tion, descriptive fort tour.
"Gulf Islands." 8-fold. Descriptions of the Mississippi and
Florida sections regarding facilities, recreation, visitor tips.
Map of each section.
"Gulf Islands." 16-fold. Photos, illustrations, maps, descrip-
tion and visitor information for visiting the Mississippi and
Florida sections. Ecology on the barrier island.
"The Gulf Islands Barnacles." 4 pages. In newspaper format
with photos, articles, activity schedule, facility listings,
camping and safety information.
"Wildlife Guide." 6-fold. Sketches with names of a variety of
birds, mammals, reptiles, amphibians, marine life.

Sales List:
"GUIS-MS District Eastern National Park and Monument Association
Items." 2 pages. Reproductions, handbooks, books, coloring
books, cookbook, guides, handbooks, kits, post cards, prints.

Title, price.
"Civil War Belt Plates" (2) U.S. and C.S. $4.00 each.

Audiovisual List:
"Film, Videotape List." 1 page. Title, indication if film or
videotape, number of copies, remarks/subject.
"Gulf Island." Old GUIS film tree film. 3 copies.

Suggested Curriculum Application:
AMERICAN HISTORY
FLORIDA STATE AND LOCAL STUDIES
GEOGRAPHY
MISSISSIPPI STATE AND LOCAL STUDIES

Suggested Sears Subject Heading:
FLORIDA--DESCRIPTION AND TRAVEL--GUIDES
FLORIDA--PUBLIC LANDS
GULF ISLANDS
ISLANDS
MISSISSIPPI--DESCRIPTION AND TRAVEL--GUIDES
MISSISSIPPI--PUBLIC LANDS
U.S.--DESCRIPTION AND TRAVEL--GUIDES
U.S.--HISTORY
WILDLIFE--CONSERVATION

KLONDIKE GOLD RUSH

• KLONDIKE GOLD RUSH
National Historical Park. P.O. Box 517, Skagway, AK 99840.
(907) 983-2921. 13,191.35 acres. 1976. Buildings in the Skagway
Historic District, Chilkoot and White Pass trails, visitor center is
at 2nd and Broadway. (Also in Seattle, Washington.)

Preserve historic buildings, parts of Chilkoot and White Pass trails
that were part of the 1898 Gold Rush. Thirty-three mile Chilkoot
Trail has historic ruins and artifacts and the White Pass Trail has
several turnouts and exhibits. Walking tours, interpretive pro-
grams, commercial tours, audiovisuals, Trail of '98 Museum, Gold
Rush cemetery. White Pass and Yukon Route Railroad depot and
general offices, Martin Itjen house, Arctic Brotherhood Hall,
Verbauwhede Confectionery, Boas tailoring shop, Pacific Clipper
Line Office, Mascot Saloon, Lynch and Kennedy dry goods store,
Pantheon Saloon, Ben Morre House, Captain Moore's cabin, Boss
bakery, Goldberg cigar store, Peniel mission, city hall and museum.
Campgrounds, food and lodging in Skagway.

Free Print Material:
  "Gold Rush Cemetery Guide." 8-fold. Names, dates of birth
    and death, biographical sketches of 12 persons. Sketch, map.
  "Klondike Gold Rush." 12-fold. Photos, maps, features, history,
    accommodations.
  "Skagway Alaska." 8-fold. Photos, map, history, features, lo-
    cation, visitor access, accommodations, climate of Skagway.
  "Walking Tour of the Historic District." 16 pages. Description,
    sketches of 16 sites reflecting the Gold Rush days. Map
    identifies sites, poem from "The Spell of the Yukon."

Bibliography:
  "A Bibliography of the Klondike Gold Rush." 2 pages. Grouped
    by: Gold Rush history, pictorials, human interest, suitable
    for young readers, suitable for junior high and high school.
    Includes author, title, publisher, date, number of pages.

Suggested Curriculum Application:
  AMERICAN HISTORY
  ALASKA STATE AND LOCAL STUDIES

Suggested Sears Subject Heading:
  ALASKA--DESCRIPTION AND TRAVEL--GUIDES
  ALASKA--PUBLIC LANDS
  ARCHITECTURE--CONSERVATION AND RESTORATION
  GOLD MINES AND MINING
  KLONDIKE GOLD FIELDS
  U.S.--DESCRIPTION AND TRAVEL--GUIDES

• KLONDIKE GOLD RUSH
National Historical Park. Seattle Unit, 117 South Main Street,
Seattle, WA 98104. (206) 442-7220. 13,191.35 acres. 1976.
Western Washington, in Seattle's historic Pioneer Square. There
is also an Alaskan unit in Skagway.

The Seattle unit recreates Seattle's role as a main supply center for
Alaska and Klondike gold miners in 1897-98 and the drama of the
Gold Rush. Mining exhibits, film and slide programs, artifacts,
photomurals. Visitor center. Food and lodging nearby.

Free Print Material:
  "Klondike Gold Rush." 12-fold. History, photos, maps. Illus-
    tration and list of a typical year's supplies of food, equipment,
    and clothing for a miner. Features of Pioneer Square,
    Seattle's historic legacy.
  "Klondike Gold Rush National Historical Park." 4 pages. What
    to see and do at the Seattle unit. Sketches, Gold Rush facts.

Sales/Audiovisual List:
  "Sales Items." 3 pages. Grouped by: Books, post cards. Maps

and guides, miscellaneous, theme-related, audiovisual (includes VHS). Books are described briefly. Some of these items under miscellaneous include brass "Gold" nuggets and a sourdough starter packet for making your own sourdough bread. "Alaska's Parklands: The Complete Guide." By Nancy Lange Simmerman; a comprehensive guide to the state and national parks in the last frontier. $13.95.

Suggested Curriculum Application:
  AMERICAN HISTORY
  WASHINGTON STATE AND LOCAL STUDIES

Suggested Sears Subject Heading:
  GOLD MINES AND MINING
  KLONDIKE GOLD FIELDS
  U.S.--DESCRIPTION AND TRAVEL--GUIDES
  WASHINGTON--DESCRIPTION AND TRAVEL--GUIDES
  WASHINGTON--HISTORY
  WASHINGTON--PUBLIC LANDS

MARINE RESOURCES

• BISCAYNE
National Park. P.O. Box 1369, Homestead, FL 33090. (305) 247-2044. 173,274.37 acres. 1968. Southern Florida, 21 miles east of Everglades National Park, 9 miles east of Homestead; park headquarters at Convoy Point, on S.W. 328.

Protect a rare combination of terrestrial and undersea life, preserve a scenic subtropical setting, provide a place for recreation. Swimming, snorkeling, nature hiking trails, Biscayne Bay, 45 keys (low islands), 20 miles of mainland mangrove shoreline, living coral reefs, interpretive activities on mainland, fish and birdlife, exhibits, glass-bottom boat tours, island boat excursions. For boat tour information/tour reservations inquire: Biscayne Aqua Center, Inc., P.O. Box 1270, Homestead, FL 33030, (305) 247-2400. Visitor center, information stations, picnicking, campground. Food and lodging in Homestead, Miami, Florida Keys.

Free Print Material:
  "Beneath Biscayne Waters." 8-fold. Sketches, map, safe water practices, descriptions of Biscayne Bay, mangrove tidal creeks, coral reefs and specific reefs.
  "Birds of Biscayne National Park." 6-fold. Bird checklist contains 179 species of birds observed within the park. Key

includes symbols for breeding status, seasons abundant and others. Common names of birds are given, sketches.

"Biscayne." 24-fold. Features of the mainland, bay, keys, reef, photos, maps, sketches, general information and regulations, nearby services and accommodations. Water safety tips, map key to navigational aids, boating markers and flags.

"Threatened and Endangered Species of South Florida's National Parks." 4-fold. Endangered Species Act of 1973, what "endangered" and "threatened" mean, list of endangered and threatened species, sketch. List includes scientific and common name, park location, status.

Sales/Audiovisual List:

"Everglades Natural History Association Sales Catalog." 8-fold. Grouped by: slides, embroidered patches, decals, post cards, wilderness waterway, everglades national park slide/cassette program, publications, children's books. Title, price, author/ publisher, description, number of papers, type of cover. Order form, ordering directions, purpose of the Everglades Natural History Association, sketch.

"The Alligator--Monarch of the Everglades." $3.95. By Connie M. Toops; publisher: Everglades Natural History Association, Inc. A book designed to erase some of the myths about alligators and emphasize their importance to the Everglades region. Illustrated in color, with maps and diagrams. 63 pages, paper.

Suggested Curriculum Application:
FLORIDA STATE AND LOCAL STUDIES
GEOGRAPHY
NATURAL HISTORY

Suggested Sears Subject Heading:
BISCAYNE NATIONAL PARK
CORAL REEFS AND ISLANDS
FLORIDA--DESCRIPTION AND TRAVEL--GUIDES
FLORIDA--PUBLIC LANDS
MARINE RESOURCES
NATIONAL PARKS AND RESERVES--U.S.
NATURAL HISTORY--FLORIDA
RARE ANIMALS
RARE BIRDS
UNDERWATER EXPLORATION
U.S.--DESCRIPTION AND TRAVEL--GUIDES
U.S.--GEOGRAPHY

• CANAVERAL
National Seashore. P.O. Box 6447, Titusville, FL   32782.
(305) 867-4675. 57,627.07 acres. 1975. Midway down Florida's east coast between Jacksonville and West Palm Beach, accessible by U.S. 1, I-95, I-4, I-75.

Preserve the natural beach, dune, lagoon and marsh of undeveloped barrier island for recreation and wildlife. Ranger-led programs on many seashore related topics, many species of birds and other wildlife, coastal hammocks, swimming, boating, surfing, seashells, coastal vegetation, interpretive and hiking trails, Indian shell middens, such as Turtle Mound, which is located 10 miles south of New Smyrna Beach on A1A. Playalinda Beach at the south and Apollo Beach on the north and the beach between them is accessible only by foot. Picnicking, Playalinda Beach ranger station, information station at Apollo Beach, boat rentals, boat launches. Campgrounds nearby. Food and lodging in Titusville, New Smyrna Beach.

Free Print Material:

"Canaveral National Seashore: Merritt Island National Wildlife Refuge." 12-fold. Photos, maps, visitor tips, facilities and area information.

"Canaveral National Seashore Guide to Seashells." 6-fold. Sketches and descriptions of various shells. Terminology of univalve and bivalve shells.

"Castle Windy Trail Guide." 6-fold. Tour features various plant life. The trail begins at the Castle Windy parking area and leads 1/2 mile to the shore of Mosquito Lagoon. Sketches.

"Common Birds of Canaveral National Seashore." 6-fold. Sketches and descriptions of wading birds, shore birds, soaring birds, duck-like birds.

"Guide to Coastal Vegetation in Canaveral National Seashore." 6-fold. Sketches, description of a sample of the over 700 species found at the Canaveral National Seashore.

"Hills of Sand: The First Defense." 6-fold. How various plants help the dunes. Sketches and description of various plants.

"Southeast National Parks and National Forests." 16-fold. Photos, map. Name, address, description, telephone number of national parks and national forests in: Alabama, Arkansas, Florida, Georgia, Kentucky, Louisiana, Mississippi, North Carolina, South Carolina, Tennessee.

"Turtle Mound." 12 pages. Map, sketches, list of plants, description of about a dozen plant species and animal inhabitants.

"Turtle Mound." 6-fold. Timucuan Indian life, coming of the Spanish. Historical drawings.

"Turtle Tracks and Facts." 8-fold. History, age, description and size, distribution and migration, nesting, sleep and breathing and other information.

"Visitor Information." 2 pages. Opening and closing times, rules and regulations, camping and motel accommodations, boating, hiking, naturalist programs and other information.

Sales List:

"Sales List." 1 page. Title, price of various items such as books, coloring books, cards, prints, poster, handbook, field guides.

"A Day at the Beach." $1.95.

Suggested Curriculum Application:
    FLORIDA STATE AND LOCAL STUDIES
    GEOGRAPHY
    NATURAL HISTORY
    SCIENCE

Suggested Sears Subject Heading:
    FLORIDA--DESCRIPTION AND TRAVEL--GUIDES
    FLORIDA--PUBLIC LANDS
    MARINE RESOURCES
    NATURE CONSERVATION
    NATURAL HISTORY--FLORIDA
    SEASHORE
    TIMUCUAN INDIANS
    U.S.--DESCRIPTION AND TRAVEL--GUIDES

• CAPE COD
National Seashore. South Wellfleet, MA   02663.   (617) 349-3785.
43,526.06 acres.   1961.   Eastern Massachusetts, Cape Cod Bay,
South Wellfleet, on U.S. 6.

Beaches, dunes, woodlands, ponds, marshes on outer Cape Cod
with examples of Cape Cod homes. Exhibits, audiovisuals, wayside
exhibits, onsite environmental living programs, swimming, horseback
riding trails, bicycling trails, guided walks, talks, evening programs.
Seven self-guiding nature trails provide a cross-section of forest,
upland, swamp environments. Check current activity schedule for
ranger-guided activities. Inquire about National Environmental Education Development program offered to 30 qualified school groups
annually: need coordinator, Cape Cod National Seashore, South
Wellfleet, MA   02663. Visitor centers, ranger station, park headquarters, picnicking. Campgrounds nearby. Youth hostels in
Hyannis, Eastham, Truro, Martha's Vineyard, Nantucket.

Free Print Material:
    "Camp, Tent Sites, Trailer Parks Directory." 4-fold. Name,
        address, number of sites, location, telephone.
    "Cape Cod." 12-fold. Sketch, maps, photos. Activities, visitor
        regulations, history.
    "Cape Cod." 8-fold. Activities, travel services, interpretive
        services, regulations, safety precautions, water and air
        temperatures.
    "Media Guide to Cape Cod National Seashore Interpretive Ser-
        vices." 2 pages. What the visitor centers offer, trails and
        exhibits, publications, talks and conducted walks, calendar
        of interpretive services.
    "Ranger-Guided Activities Calendar." 2 pages. Current des-
        cription of activities. Information and emergency telephone
        numbers.
    "What Can You Do at Cape Cod National Seashore?: Summary of

Services for Educational Groups." 1 page. What the National Environmental Education Development program offers, teacher's guides, Junior Ranger program, conducted programs.

Bibliography:
"Selected Bibliography." 9 pages. Grouped by: anthropology, archeology, history, regional guides; geology, oceanography; conservation, interpretation, park history, park management; natural history; selected bibliography addendum. Arranged alphabetically by author. Includes author, title, publisher, place of publication, date.

Sales List:
"Publications List." 8-fold. Grouped by: books for adults, books for children, new orientation packets, field guides, checklists, maps and charts, framing prints. Includes children's exploration kit, visit planner, teachers and leaders' orientation packet. Title, author, date, pages, price, some annotations. Ordering information, sketches, photos.
"The Archeology of Cape Cod National Seashore." McManamon and Borstel. 1982. 16 pages. $.80.

Suggested Curriculum Application:
ENVIRONMENTAL EDUCATION
GEOGRAPHY
MASSACHUSETTS STATE AND LOCAL STUDIES

Suggested Sears Subject Heading:
MARINE RESOURCES
MASSACHUSETTS--DESCRIPTION AND TRAVEL--GUIDES
MASSACHUSETTS--GEOGRAPHY
MASSACHUSETTS--PUBLIC LANDS
U.S.--DESCRIPTION AND TRAVEL--GUIDES

• CAPE LOOKOUT
National Seashore. P.O. Box 690, Beaufort, NC 28516. (919) 728-2121. 28,414.74 acres. 1966. Eastern North Carolina, off U.S. 70 with boats operating from Harkers Island, Davis, Atlantic, Ocracoke. Islands extend between Portsmouth Village and Cape Lookout.

Protects 55-mile stretch of natural barrier islands with extensive beaches, salt marshes, dunes, historic Portsmouth and lighthouse. Beachcombing, boating, history talks, swimming, naturalist-led walks, hiking. Visitor center, ranger stations, camping. Food and lodging in Beaufort, Morehead City, Atlantic Beach.

Free Print Material:
"Camping." 6-fold. Access, gear, sites, weather, swimming and other camper tips. Sketch.

"Cape Lookout." 12-fold. Maps, photos, description, importance, plants and animals, people on the barrier islands.

"Cape Lookout National Seashore." 1 page. Survey, visitor information, history, map.

"Carteret County." 12-fold. Photos, illustration map, visitor attractions, request form to check off for more information.

"Historic Importance of Cape Lookout Lighthouse." 3 pages. History and purpose of lighthouses constructed along the Atlantic with emphasis on the Cape Lookout lighthouse.

"N.C. State Ferries." 2 pages. Schedules, fares, maps.

"Portsmouth Village." 8-fold. History since 1753, attractions, maps, photos, sketch.

"Weather Summary for Cape Lookout National Seashore and Vicinity." 1 page. Temperature, beach weather, precipitation, winds, storms, forecast information.

Suggested Curriculum Application:
ENVIRONMENTAL EDUCATION
NORTH CAROLINA STATE AND LOCAL STUDIES

Suggested Sears Subject Heading:
ISLANDS
LIGHTHOUSES
MARINE RESOURCES
NATURAL HISTORY--NORTH CAROLINA
NORTH CAROLINA--DESCRIPTION AND TRAVEL--GUIDES
NORTH CAROLINA--PUBLIC LANDS
U.S.--DESCRIPTION AND TRAVEL--GUIDES

- PADRE ISLAND
National Seashore. 9405 South Padre Island Drive, Corpus Cristi, TX 78418. (512) 949-8068. 130,696.83 acres. 1962. Southeastern Texas, 113 miles along the Texas Gulf coast from Corpus Christi almost to Mexico.

North America's longest barrier island is known for its wide sand beaches, bird and marine life, recreational uses. The park boundaries include the undeveloped central part of the island. Swimming, bird watching, scuba diving, boating, beach walking and driving, wildlife, nature trail, underwater discovery walks, seining demonstrations, discovery walks, grasslands nature trail tours, programs. Audiovisuals loaned within Corpus Christi area. Educators wishing to arrange a program or wishing information are asked to call the chief naturalist at (512) 949-8173 Monday through Friday between 8 and 4, or the naturalist at (512) 949-8068 on weekends 9-4. Visitor center, ranger station. Gift shop, beach rental equipment, campground, picnicking, primitive camping, Malaquite Beach Pavilion. Food and lodging at both ends of the island and in Corpus Christi, Port Isabel.

Free Print Material:
   "Padre Island."   12-fold.   Description of the island, early
      visitors, map, what to do on the island, map, accommodations,
      regulations, safety advice.
   "Teachers and Group Leaders' Resources Available Through Padre
      Island National Seashore."   2 pages.   Description of such pro-
      grams as underwater discovery walks.
   "Things to See and Do."   4 pages.   Description of such activities
      as beachcombing, beach driving.   Accommodations, weather,
      park use guidelines.   Sketches.

Bibliography:
   "Bibliography of Basic Information."   2 pages.   Arranged by:
      surf and open gulf areas, interior grasslands and wildlife, mud
      flats, Laguna Madre and Spoil Banks, history, geology, ar-
      cheology and Indians.   Title, author, some annotations.

Sales List:
   "Southwest Parks and Monuments Association Sales List."   1 page.
      Title, price.   Includes coloring books and other children's
      publications, field guides.   Some publications include age
      levels.   Order form, ordering directions.
   "A Day at the Beach."   (Infant to age 7.) $1.95.

Suggested Curriculum Application:
   GEOGRAPHY
   NATURAL HISTORY
   SCIENCE
   TEXAS STATE AND LOCAL STUDIES

Suggested Sears Subject Heading:
   ISLANDS
   MARINE RESOURCES
   NATURAL HISTORY--TEXAS
   PADRE ISLAND
   TEXAS--DESCRIPTION AND TRAVEL--GUIDES
   TEXAS--PUBLIC LANDS
   UNDERWATER EXPLORATION
   U.S.--DESCRIPTION AND TRAVEL--GUIDES
   U.S.--GEOGRAPHY

• VIRGIN ISLANDS
National Park.   P.O. Box 7789, Charlotte Amalie, St. Thomas, VI
00801.   (809) 776-6201.   14,695.85 acres.   1956.   Most of St. John
Island, Hassel Island in St. Thomas Harbor, in the Caribbean Sea.
St. John is the smallest of the three major U.S. Virgin Islands.

Preserve the natural state of coves, coral reefs, beaches, hills,
tropical seas.   Remains of old sugar plantations.   Underwater nature
trail, historic bus tours, self-guiding nature trail, restored ruins of

Annaberg sugar mill factory complex, mangrove swamp, reef flat, snorkeling, swimming, boating, talks, exhibits, guided snorkel trips, hikes, and cultural demonstrations, evening programs, guided taxi tours, hiking trails, petroglyphs, ruins of Reef Bay estate house, steampowered sugar mill ruins. Visitor center, picnicking, camp store, tent sites, cottage units, campground, ranger station. Food at Cruz Bay, Trunk Bay, Cinnamon Bay. Church services at Caneel Bay Plantation and Cinnamon Bay campground.

Free Print Material:
"Animals." 2 pages. Domesticated mammals, reptiles, insects, birds. Description and names of various birds and animals.
"Geology." 2 pages. Record goes back some 100 million years.
"Here and Now in the Virgin Islands National Parks." 6 pages. Schedule of activities: historic programs, evening programs, exhibits, hikes and other activities. Sketches.
"Plants." 2 pages. Description of various plants found on the island of St. John.
"Safe Boating." 8-fold. Map, sketch, descriptions of north offshore areas and southside offshore areas. Regulations, charts and maps.
"St. John History." 2 pages. Indian culture, Danish influence, U.S. acquisition in 1917, administration.
"St. Thomas This Week." 74 pages. Weekly guide to island visitors including St. John. Maps, photos, background information on the Virgin Islands, island tours, U.S. customs, driving and others of interest.
"The Sea and the Shore." 2 pages. Description of coral reefs.
"Trail Guide for Safe Hiking." 4-fold. Map, tips on trail safety, hike planning and preparation, descriptions of north shore trails and south shore trails.
"Virgin Islands." 16-fold. Sketch, photos, maps, visitor information such as points of interest, safety tips, planning your visit, regulations and accommodations. History and uses of the Virgin Islands.
"Virgin Islands National Park." 2 pages. Legislation, development of the park, the only national park in the caribbean area.
"Where." 42 pages. Guide to shopping, events, dining and entertainment. Photos, maps.

Suggested Curriculum Application:
GEOGRAPHY
NATURAL HISTORY
VIRGIN ISLANDS LOCAL STUDIES

Suggested Sears Subject Heading:
CORAL REEFS AND ISLANDS
ISLANDS
HASSEL ISLAND
MARINE RESOURCES

NATIONAL PARKS AND RESERVES--U.S.
NATURAL HISTORY--VIRGIN ISLANDS
ST. JOHN ISLAND
UNDERWATER EXPLORATION
U.S.--DESCRIPTION AND TRAVEL--GUIDES
VIRGIN ISLANDS--DESCRIPTION AND TRAVEL--GUIDES
VIRGIN ISLANDS NATIONAL PARK
VIRGIN ISLANDS--PUBLIC LANDS

MISCELLANEOUS

- CAPE KRUSENSTERN
National Monument. P.O. Box 287, Kotzebue, AK 99752.
(907) 442-3890. 660,000 acres. 1980. Projecting into the Chukchi
Sea in northwest Alaska, about 450 miles west-northwest of Fairbanks.

Preserve 114 successive lateral beach ridge gravels containing artifacts from every known Eskimo occupation on the North American
continent dating from some 4,000 years ago. Geographical features,
wildlife and waterfowl. Backpacking and camping along the coast
and in the hills. Visitor center. Kotzebue has a hotel and stores.
Air taxi operators and boat owner services. Scheduled aircraft,
chartered aircraft, and boats provide access to the site. Camping
is permitted in most areas except in archeological zones and on
private land.

Free Print Material:
    "Cape Krusenstern." 2 pages. Description, location, what to
        see and do, access, weather and insects, clothing and pro-
        visions, precautions and courtesies. Map, photo.

Sales/Audiovisual List:
    "Alaska Natural History Association Mail Order Catalog." 8 pages.
        Newspaper format. Grouped by sources: Denali National Park
        and Preserve, Glacier Bay National Park and Preserve, Sitka
        National Historical Park, Katmai National Park/Preserve, park
        and forest information center, northwest national parks,
        Alaska Maritime National Wildlife, Chugach National Forest,
        Alaska Public Lands Information Center. Each is grouped
        under such headings as: general, plants--animals, maps--
        visual aids, habitat and vegetation, culture--history. For
        publications it includes: title, author, price, description,
        number of pages. Other materials are also annotated. State-
        ment of aims of the Alaska Natural History Association,
        sketches, order blank and ordering instructions.

"Alaska National Parklands: The Last Treasure." Brown.
Hard $16.95, Soft $5.95. 128 pages, full-color publication
describing the national significance of all National Park Service
areas in Alaska by means of a narrative by Brown and short
writings by individuals very familiar....

"Northwest Alaska Informational Resources." 2 pages. Grouped
by: books, children's books, slide set, poster, U.S. geological
survey maps. Information about the Alaska Natural History
Association, ordering directions. Includes title and price of
items.

"Alaska: A Pictorial Guide." $4.95.

Suggested Curriculum Application:
ALASKA STATE AND LOCAL STUDIES
ARCHEOLOGY
NATIVE AMERICAN STUDIES

Suggested Sears Subject Heading:
ALASKA--DESCRIPTION AND TRAVEL--GUIDES
ALASKA--HISTORY
ALASKA--PUBLIC LANDS
ARCHEOLOGY (EXCAVATIONS)
ESKIMO INDIANS
INDIANS OF NORTH AMERICA--HISTORY
U.S.--DESCRIPTION AND TRAVEL--GUIDES

• CASTLE CLINTON
National Monument. Manhattan Sites, National Park Service, 26 Wall
Street, New York, NY 10005. (212) 344-7220. 1 acre. 1946.
Eastern New York, Battery Park, at the tip of Manhattan Island in
New York City.

Built in 1808-11 for a New York Harbor defense; then served as a
promenade and entertainment center; an immigration depot from 1855
to 1890. Guided group tours by appointment. Gift shop, ferry
concessionaire runs every hour from nine till four. Food and
lodging in New York City.

Free Print Material:
"Castle Clinton." 12-fold. Photos, sketches, construction of the
fort, use and functions, development into a national park
facility.

Suggested Curriculum Application:
AMERICAN HISTORY
NEW YORK STATE AND LOCAL STUDIES

Suggested Sears Subject Heading:
FORTIFICATION
NEW YORK--DESCRIPTION AND TRAVEL--GUIDES

NEW YORK--HISTORY
NEW YORK--PUBLIC LANDS
U.S.--DESCRIPTION AND TRAVEL--GUIDES
U.S.--IMMIGRATION AND EMIGRATION

• DAVID BERGER
National Memorial. Jewish Community Center of Cleveland, 3505
Mayfield Road, Cleveland Heights, OH 44118. 0.5 acres. 1980.
Northeastern Ohio.

Honor the memory of eleven Israeli athletes killed at the 1972 Olympic
Games in Munich, Germany, one of whom, David Berger, was an
American citizen. Steel sculpture designed by David E. Davis. Food
and lodging nearby.

Free Print Material:
 "David Berger Memorial." 2 pages. Life and accomplishments of
   David Berger, description of the monument and what it repre-
   sents.

Suggested Curriculum Application:
 OHIO STATE AND LOCAL STUDIES
 SOCIAL STUDIES

Suggested Sears Subject Heading:
 JEWS--PERSECUTIONS
 OHIO--DESCRIPTION AND TRAVEL--GUIDES
 OHIO--PUBLIC LANDS
 OLYMPIC GAMES
 U.S.--DESCRIPTION AND TRAVEL--GUIDES

• EBEY'S LANDING
National Historical Reserve. Post Office Box 774, Coupeville, WA
98239. (206) 678-6084. 8,000 acres. 1978. Northwestern Washington, Whidbey Island in Puget Sound, reached by water or highway.

Preserve and protect a rural community which provides an unbroken
historic record from 19th-century exploration and settlement of
Puget Sound up to the present time. Exhibit, trails, walking tour
guides. Major historically significant vicinities within the reserve
are: Coupeville, Fort Casey State Park, Ebey's Landing, Grasser's
Hill and Lagoon, Fort Ebey State Park, Crockett Lake and Uplands,
Monroe's Landing, Smith Prairie. Information/orientation exhibit,
campgrounds, picnicking. Limited as the preservation management
project is just underway.

Free Print Material:
 "Comprehensive Plan for Ebey's Landing National Historical Reserve, Washington." 81 pages. Prepared to meet the require-

ments of the National Parks and Recreation Act of 1978
(P.L. 95-625). Photos, maps, aims, chart of preservation
priorities, preservation guidelines, land acquisition, natural
history, lists of birds, mammals, reptiles and amphibians,
history and various planning information. Appendix with
public law, ordinance, briefs, plan. Fold-out pages of blue-
print sketches.

"Design Considerations for Historic Properties." 20 pages. Aims
of the project, cultural landscape, standards, types of architectural designs, list of historic structures, financing,
sketches, preservation methods, project credits, bibliography.

"Ebey's Landing." 24-fold. Photos, history, maps, description
of the features of interest, administration.

"Introductory Sheet PNR-EBLA." 2 pages. Purpose and plans
of the National Historical Reserve Project.

"National Parks and National Forests in the Pacific Northwest."
24-fold. Chart of features and attractions, map, photos.
Information on the Forest Service, the National Park Service,
the Bureau of Land Management, tips for visitors.

Bibliography:
 Included in "Design Considerations for Historic Properties"
 described above.

Suggested Curriculum Application:
 AMERICAN HISTORY
 WASHINGTON STATE AND LOCAL STUDIES

Suggested Sears Subject Heading:
 ARCHITECTURE--CONSERVATION AND RESTORATION
 ISLANDS
 U.S.--DESCRIPTION AND TRAVEL--GUIDES
 WASHINGTON--HISTORY
 WASHINGTON--PUBLIC LANDS
 WIDBEY ISLAND

• GOLDEN GATE
National Recreation Area. Fort Mason, San Francisco, CA 94123.
(415) 556-0560. 45,618.03 acres. 1972. Western California, shoreline areas of San Francisco, Marin and San Mateo counties.

Preserve shoreline, ocean beaches, redwood forest, lagoons,
marshes, ships, historic military properties, cultural center, site
of Alcatraz. Alcatraz, National Maritime Museum, Aquatic Park, Fort
Mason, Marina Green, Crissy Field, Fort Point National Historic Site,
Cliff House area, Ocean Beach, Fort Funston, Muir Woods, Mt.
Tamalpais area, Angel Island, Olema Alley, Muir Beach, Stinson
Beach, Tennessee Valley. Hiking trails, wildlife, scenery, educa-
tional programs. At Fort Cronkhite are the California Marine Mammal
Center, the Golden Gate Energy Center and the Yosemite Institute--

Residential Environmental Center and Conference Facility. Near Battery Alexander is the YMCA Point Bonita Outdoor and Conference Center. Marin Headlands Visitor Center, Camping, Golden Gate hostel near Fort Barry.

Free Print Material:
"Golden Gate." 24-fold. Features, services, phone numbers, photos, maps, activities offered.

Suggested Curriculum Application:
AMERICAN HISTORY
CALIFORNIA STATE AND LOCAL STUDIES
ENVIRONMENTAL EDUCATION

Suggested Sears Subject Heading:
CALIFORNIA--DESCRIPTION AND TRAVEL--GUIDES
CALIFORNIA--PUBLIC LANDS
NATURAL HISTORY--CALIFORNIA
U.S.--DESCRIPTION AND TRAVEL--GUIDES

- JOHNSTOWN FLOOD
National Memorial. Box 247, Cresson, PA 16630. (814) 886-8176. 163.47 acres. 1964. Central Pennsylvania, northeast of Johnstown near St. Michael, PA, along U.S. 219 and Pa. 869.

Memorialize deaths of over 2,200 in Johnstown, Pennsylvania in 1889 flood, interpret the cause and effect. Interpretive talks, model of the dam and lake, remnants of the dam, self-guiding auto tour around the former lake bed to the north abutment, trails. Visitor center, picnicking. Food and lodging in Johnstown.

Free Print Material:
"Johnstown Flood." 16-fold. Narrative and personal account of the flood, photos, diagram, maps.
"Journey Around Lake Conemaugh." 12-fold. Sketches, map, photo, description of the three-mile drive to the north abutment of South Fork Dam, tracing almost the entire boundary of the lake as it existed in 1889.
"South Abutment Trail." 12 pages. Tour of the remains of South Fork Dam. Sketches, map, diagram.

Sales/Audiovisual List:
"Johnstown Flood National Memorial Sales List." 4 pages. Books, notecards, cachet envelopes, slides, post cards, coloring book, cookbook, leaflets. Title, author, date, price, some annotations. Ordering directions.
"The Old Portage Railroad 1834-1854." Floyd G. Hoestine and Mahlone J. Baumgardner, 1952. (Reprinted article, ceremonies, sketches and other documents.) $5.00.

Suggested Curriculum Application:
AMERICAN HISTORY
PENNSYLVANIA STATE AND LOCAL STUDIES

Suggested Sears Subject Heading:
FLOODS
JOHNSTOWN--FLOODS
NATURAL DISASTERS
PENNSYLVANIA--DESCRIPTION AND TRAVEL--GUIDES
PENNSYLVANIA--HISTORY
PENNSYLVANIA--PUBLIC LANDS
U.S.--DESCRIPTION AND TRAVEL--GUIDES

MISSION CHURCHES

- SALINAS

National Monument. P.O. Box 496, Mountainair, NM 87036.
(505) 847-2770. 1,076.94 acres. 1909. Central New Mexico,
75 miles southeast of Albuquerque, off U.S. 60 and NM 14.

Ruins of four 17th-century Franciscan churches, three large
Pueblo Indian (1100 A.D.-1670 A.D.) villages. (Salinas takes its
name from important salt lakes in the area.) Abo Ruins site
features church architecture and an unexcavated pueblo; quarai
ruins has the most complete Salinas church with artifacts on display;
Gran Quivira Ruins has two churches, excavated Indian structures,
exhibits, film. Visitor center, picnicking. Campgrounds in nearby
Manzano Mountains. Food and lodging at Mountainair.

Free Print Material:
"Camping Information." 1 page. Map, chart, address and phone
number of Manzano Mountain State Park and Cibola National
Forest. These six campgrounds are not within the boundaries
of Salinas National Monument.
"Salinas." 12-fold. Pueblos, history, coming of the Spaniards,
conflict of religions, Pueblo Indian culture, ruins, visitor information, photos, maps, illustrations.

Bibliography:
"Books Specifically Relating to Salinas." 1 page. States title
and price. Also includes three general books. Postage rates.

Suggested Curriculum Application:
AMERICAN HISTORY
ARCHEOLOGY
NATIVE AMERICAN STUDIES
NEW MEXICO STATE AND LOCAL STUDIES

Suggested Sears Subject Heading:
ARCHITECTURE--CONSERVATION AND RESTORATION
EXCAVATIONS (ARCHEOLOGY)
INDIANS OF NORTH AMERICA--HISTORY
INDIANS OF NORTH AMERICA--MISSIONS, CHRISTIAN
NEW MEXICO--DESCRIPTION AND TRAVEL
NEW MEXICO--PUBLIC LANDS
PUEBLO INDIANS
U.S.--DESCRIPTION AND TRAVEL--GUIDES

- SAN ANTONIO MISSIONS
National Historical Park. 2202 Roosevelt Avenue, San Antonio, TX
78210. (512) 229-5701. 477.43 acres. 1978. Central Texas, in
southern San Antonio. A signed driving trail that begins downtown
at Mission San Antonio Valero reaches all the park missions.

Four 18th-century Spanish missions, farms, irrigation systems.
Missions Concepcion, San Jose, San Juan, and Espada, the San Juan
and Espada Acequias, Espada Dam and Aqueduct. Tours by appointment, exhibits, museum, orientation talks, self-guided walks,
historical and nature trails. Teachers need to schedule their class
visits at least two weeks ahead and indicate if the class has limited
English-speaking or special education children. It is recommended
that one adult or teacher for every 10 students be used. The library at the park is open to the public during weekdays. Meals
and lodging in San Antonio. Parks nearby.

Free Print Material:
"General Information on the Missions." 1 page. Telephone numbers of the missions, hours.
"Mission Concepcion." 8-fold. Sketches, history, religious education, decline and reuse of the mission. The mission, built
on bedrock, was dedicated in 1755 and is used today as a
local church.
"Mission Espada." 8-fold. Purpose of the mission, building an
irrigation system that still works, sketches, decline in mission
activities, revival and current use, sketches.
"Mission San Jose." 8-fold. Strategic location of the mission
was used to help defend Spain's northern frontier and the
compound was a fortress. Indian life, importance of the mission, why the Spanish decided not to support it, sketches.
"Mission San Juan." 8-fold. Establishment, mission agricultural
efforts and economy. Impact on the Coahuiltecans Indian culture.
"Old Spanish Missions: Historical Research Library at Our Lady
of the Lake University of San Antonio." 6-fold. The beginning and goals of the library, collection and services. Materials are non-circulating but photocopies may be made from
microfilm. Inquiries about the collection may be directed to:
Maria Carolina Flores, C.D.P., Our Lady of the Lake University,

411 S.W. 24th Street, San Antonio, TX 78285, (512) 434-6711 ext. 325.

"Planning Your Visit." 2 pages. Teacher guide. Reservations, registration, refreshments, chaperones, hours, student "Do's and Don'ts" for class visits. A preview visit is recommended for teachers to help plan the trip and prepare students.

"Revolution and the Missions." 8-fold. The birth of the Republic of Texas, photos, the Battle at Concepcion, the missions under American rule.

"San Antonio Missions." 6-fold. Blending of Church and State in mission activities, sketches and description of the missions and aqueduct, function of the missions today.

Bibliography:
"Texas Bibliography." 20 pages. Extract from; "Texas Bibliography: A Manual on History Research Materials." In three sections that cover early explorations in Texas, mission period and Spanish colonization, Spanish decline and filibustering era. Arranged by date and includes author, title, place of publication, publisher, publication date.

1600 Alessio Robles, Vito. "Coahuila y Texas en la Epoca Colonial." 3 Vols. Mexico City: Editorial Cultural, 1938.

Suggested Curriculum Application:
AGRICULTURE
AMERICAN HISTORY
NATIVE AMERICAN STUDIES
TEXAS STATE AND LOCAL STUDIES

Suggested Sears Subject Heading:
ARCHITECTURE--CONSERVATION AND RESTORATION
CHURCHES--TEXAS
COAHUILTECANS INDIANS
INDIANS OF NORTH AMERICA--MISSIONS, CHRISTIAN
IRRIGATION--U.S.
MISSIONS, CHRISTIAN
TEXAS--DESCRIPTION AND TRAVEL--GUIDES
TEXAS--HISTORY
TEXAS--PUBLIC LANDS
U.S.--DESCRIPTION AND TRAVEL--GUIDES

- TUMACACORI
National Monument. P.O. Box 67, Tumacacori, AZ 85640. (602) 398-2341. 16.52 acres. 1908. Southern Arizona, 45 miles south of Tucson, off of Interstate 19.

Ruins of Spanish mission church. Self-guiding trails, ruins, museum, weekend craft demonstrations. Visitor center, picnicking. Campground 21 miles away. Food and lodging in Nogales, Rio Rico, Tucson.

Free Print Material:
  "Tumacacori National Monument." 12-fold. Photos, mission's
  purpose, history, visitor information. Sketches. Floorplan
  includes unexposed historic foundations, stabilized historic
  walls, stabilized historic structures.

Sales List:
  "Southwest Parks and Monuments Association Book List." 3
  pages. Grouped by: Native Americans; New Spain; plants
  and animals; local, regional, national, international. Title,
  author, date, pages, type of cover included on many. Note
  cards of Sonoran mission churches. Ordering instructions.
  "The Papago and Pima Indians of Arizona"; Underhill, 1941
  (1979), 60 pages, $2.00.

Suggested Curriculum Application:
  AMERICAN HISTORY
  ARIZONA STATE AND LOCAL STUDIES

Suggested Sears Subject Heading:
  ARCHITECTURE--CONSERVATION AND RESTORATION
  ARIZONA--DESCRIPTION AND TRAVEL--GUIDES
  ARIZONA--HISTORY
  ARIZONA--PUBLIC LANDS
  CHURCHES--ARIZONA
  INDIANS OF NORTH AMERICA--MISSIONS, CHRISTIAN
  MISSIONS, CHRISTIAN
  U.S.--DESCRIPTION AND TRAVEL--GUIDES

MOUNTAINS

• CATOCTIN
Mountain Park. 6602 Foxville Road, Thurmont, MD 21788.
(301) 663-9330. 5,770.22 acres. 1954. Northern Maryland, off
U.S. Route 15.

Streams, forests, and the ridge forming the eastern rampart of the
Appalachian Mountains offers panoramic views of the Monocacy
Valley. Cross-country ski seminars, winter carnival, charcoal
hikes, photo seminars, wildflower walks, campfire programs, natural
resource walks and seminars, orienteering, swimming, canoeing,
self-guiding auto tour with scenic overlook, trails for hiking, cross-
country skiing, snowshoeing, self-guiding nature trails, horse trail.
Arrangements for tours and ranger assistance for environmental
education for school groups should be made in advance. Visitor
center, campgrounds, picnicking, cabins, youth group tent camping,
group camping.

Free Print Material:
"Catoctin Mountains." 12-fold. Mountain heritage, things to
see and do, trail guide, map.
"Catoctin Mountain Park Calendar of Events." 4 pages. Seasonal
activities, camping and picnicking, cabins, tents.
"Family Cabins: Camp Misty Mount." 6-fold. General information, regulations and policies, applications and reservations,
camp etiquette.

Suggested Curriculum Application:
ENVIRONMENTAL EDUCATION
MARYLAND STATE AND LOCAL STUDIES
RECREATION

Suggested Sears Subject Heading:
CATOCTIN MOUNTAINS
MARYLAND--DESCRIPTION AND TRAVEL--GUIDES
MARYLAND--PUBLIC LANDS
OUTDOOR RECREATION
U.S.--DESCRIPTION AND TRAVEL--GUIDES

• DENALI
National Park and Preserve. P.O. Box 9, Denali National Park,
AK 99755. (907) 271-4243. 4,700,000 acres. 1917. Central
Alaska, 240 miles north of Anchorage and 129 miles south of Fair-
banks.

Contains North America's highest mountain, large glaciers, and a
wide variety of wildlife. Naturalist activities, air and bus tours,
backpacking, hiking, winter activities, mountaineering. Riley Creek
Information Center, campgrounds, hotel and auditorium, store,
showers, gas station, post office, youth hostel, trailer dump station.

Free Print Material:
"Denali." 24-fold. Features, history, wildlife of taiga and
tundra. Maps and photos.
"Denali Alpenglow." 8 pages. Current visitor information,
photos on services, accommodations, weather, hiking, campgrounds, wildlife.

Sales List:
For a free list of maps, books, and other publications, write:
Alaska Natural History Association, P.O. Box 9, McKinley
Park, AK 99755 or call (907) 683-2294.

Suggested Curriculum Application:
ALASKA STATE AND LOCAL STUDIES
GEOGRAPHY
RECREATION

Suggested Sears Subject Heading:
  ALASKA--DESCRIPTION AND TRAVEL--GUIDES
  ALASKA--PUBLIC LANDS
  DENALI NATIONAL PARK AND PRESERVE
  MOUNTAINS
  MOUNT MCKINLEY
  NATIONAL PARKS AND RESERVES--U.S.
  NATURAL HISTORY--ALASKA
  OUTDOOR LIFE
  U.S.--DESCRIPTION AND TRAVEL--GUIDES
  U.S.--GEOGRAPHY
  WILDERNESS AREAS

* GRAND TETON
National Park. P.O. Drawer 170, Moose, WY 83012.
(307) 733-2880. 310,520.94 acres. 1929. Western Wyoming,
visitor center is 13 miles north of Jackson on U.S. 26, 89, 191.

Site of a series of peaks over a mile above the sagebrush, once a
noted landmark. Includes part of Jackson Hole, winter feeding
ground of America's largest elk herd. Self-guided trails, float
trips, climbing, swimming, field seminars, special activities, programs,
hiking, boating, backpacking, guided walks and hikes. Visitor centers, campgrounds, cabins, restaurants, interdenominational Sunday
services, marina, kennels. Food and lodging in Jackson.

Free Print Material:
  "Teewinot." 8 pages. Issued three times a year by the Grand
Teton Natural History Association. Schedule of field seminars, services of worship, accommodations, camping, ranger-led activities,
safety and driving tips. Photos, map.

Sales/Audiovisual List:
  "Grand Teton Natural History Association Sales List." 8-fold.
    Material grouped by: guides and maps, wildlife, plants and
    wildflowers, history, mountaineering, geology, books for
    youth, guides, color slides, art, trip planner specials. Order
    form and mail order instructions.
  "Teton Trails" by Bryan Harry. Published by Grand Teton
    Natural History Association. A guide to hiking and horseback
    trails of Grand Teton. 56 pp., illus., maps show backcountry
    campsites. $1.50.

Suggested Curriculum Application:
  ENVIRONMENTAL EDUCATION
  GEOGRAPHY
  RECREATION
  WYOMING STATE AND LOCAL STUDIES

Suggested Sears Subject Heading:
  GRAND TETON NATIONAL PARK

MOUNTAINS
NATIONAL PARKS AND RESERVES--U.S.
OUTDOOR RECREATION
U.S.--DESCRIPTION AND TRAVEL--GUIDES
WYOMING--DESCRIPTION AND TRAVEL--GUIDES
WYOMING--PUBLIC LANDS

- GREAT SMOKY MOUNTAINS
National Park. Gatlinburg, TN 37738. (615) 436-5615. 520,269.44
acres. 1926. Eastern Tennessee, visitor center is 2 miles south of
Gatlinburg, U.S. 441.

Highest range east of the Black Hills, very old uplands have various plantlife, temperate deciduous forest. Restored log cabins and
barns, 1,500 kinds of flowering plants, smoke-like haze rolls over
the mountains, unspoiled forests, 900 miles of trails, naturalist activities, water-powered mill, exhibits, film, wildlife. Ten campgrounds, visitor centers. Most neighboring towns have supplies,
food, lodging. Campgrounds outside the park.

Free Print Material:
"General Form to Answer the Most Commonly Asked Questions."
2 pages. Accommodations, camping, weather, insects, wildflower blooming dates, public transportation and other visitor
information. Includes list of campgrounds, their elevations,
number of spaces, facilities, comments.
"Great Smoky Mountains." 8-fold. Features, activities, photos,
regulations, services, map.

Sales/Audiovisual List:
"Great Smoky Mountains Natural History Association, Inc. Publications List." 10-fold. Grouped by: general; natural
history; pictorial guides; nature study; hiking guides; backpacking; history; folk culture; southern Appalachian handicrafts; Cherokee Indians; for young people; audiovisual;
pamphlets; miscellaneous; maps; order form.
"Mountain Roads and Quiet Places." The park's official road
guide takes you step-by-step along the smokies' familiar
scenic highways and down the less-traveled backroads.
Beautifully illustrated with full-color photography, this comprehensive guidebook is keyed by colors and numbers to
roadside posts....

Suggested Curriculum Application:
GEOGRAPHY
NATURAL HISTORY
TENNESSEE STATE AND LOCAL STUDIES

Suggested Sears Subject Heading:
GREAT SMOKY MOUNTAINS NATIONAL PARK

MOUNTAINS
NATIONAL PARKS AND RESERVES--U.S.
NATURAL HISTORY--TENNESSEE
TENNESSEE--DESCRIPTION AND TRAVEL--GUIDES
TENNESSEE--PUBLIC LANDS
U.S.--DESCRIPTION AND TRAVEL--GUIDES

• ROCKY MOUNTAIN
National Park. Estes Park, CO 80517. (303) 586-2371 East Side,
near Estes Park, CO; (303) 627-3471 West Side, near Grand Lake,
CO. 265,192.86 acres. 1915. West central Colorado. U.S. 34
from Loveland, CO from the east; from the west by U.S. 34 from
Grand Lake.

Preserve and protect the Rocky Mountains with peaks over 14,000
feet. Scenic trail ridge road crosses the Continental divide. Walks,
campfire programs and other activities, hiking trails, wildlife,
horseback riding, weekend and weeklong seminars. For information
about seminars request "Seminar Brochure." Four visitor centers,
campgrounds, kennels. Food and lodging in Estes Park, Grand
Lake.

Free Print Material:
   "General Information." 2 pages. Facilities and services. Roads,
      locations of the various visitor centers, wildlife, and other
      visitor-interest information.
   "Lodging Guide." 40 pages. Photo and description, rates, tele-
      phone, location of various accommodations. Map, calendar of
      events, description and photos of various things and places to
      see and do.
   "Picture-Taking in Rocky Mountain National Park." 12-fold.
      Many photos showing park scenes, map, four tours with ap-
      proximate mileage between stops and picture taking, camera-
      handling hints.
   "Tundra World." 6-fold. Sketches, photos, map, character-
      istics of the tundra area, alpine climate, plants.

Sales/Audiovisual List:
   "Rocky Mountain Nature Association Publications List." 12 pages.
      Grouped by: Rocky Mountain National Park, national parks,
      ecology, flowers and trees, wildlife, geology, books for young
      people, backcountry guides, maps, road and nature trail
      guides, miscellaneous, post cards, slides, posters. Aims of
      the association, membership information, order form, description
      of free items. Title, description, pages, order number, price
      for publications. Miscellaneous items includes compasses, hand
      lens, mini-planisphere, wind meter, zip-o-gage.
   "Rocky Mountain National Park Panorama" by Ron Redfern and
      Dr. Richard Beidleman. A fresh concept in publications with a
      five-foot photographic panorama. Handsomely illustrated in full
      color. 8-1/2" by 12" opening to 59" by 12". 130-013. $2.95.

Suggested Curriculum Application:
COLORADO STATE AND LOCAL STUDIES
GEOGRAPHY

Suggested Sears Subject Heading:
COLORADO--DESCRIPTION AND TRAVEL--GUIDES
COLORADO--PUBLIC LANDS
MOUNTAINS
NATIONAL PARKS AND RESERVES--U.S.
ROCKY MOUNTAIN NATIONAL PARK
U.S.--DESCRIPTION AND TRAVEL--GUIDES
U.S.--GEOGRAPHY

NATIVE AMERICAN CULTURE

- ALIBATES FLINT QUARRIES

National Monument. Box 1438, Fritch, TX 79036. (806) 857-3151.
1,370.97 acres. 1965. Northern Texas (panhandle), near Lake
Meredith, 40 miles north of Amarillo, TX, off of Tex. 136.

Quarries used by Indians for thousands of years, in demand for
their high quality, rainbow-hued flint used for tools and weapons.
Guided tours leave from the Bates Canyon information station at
Lake Meredith during summer. Tours are by reservation at other
times by contacting: Lake Meredith National Recreation Area, P.O.
Box 1438, Fritch, TX 79036 or (806) 857-3151. The quarries now
consist of many small pits scattered along the edge of bluffs above
the Canadian River. Food and lodging in Fritch, Borger.

Free Print Material:
"Alibates Flint Quarries." 6-fold. Map, photos, type of weapons
and tools made by the Indians from the flint, history and use.
"Alibates National Monument--A History Sketch." 2 pages. Uses
of the flint by Indians in various time periods, map.
"Your Visit to the Alibates Flint Quarries." 2 pages. What the
quarries consist of, trail safety, tours, weather and other
visitor information.

Suggested Curriculum Application:
AMERICAN HISTORY
NATIVE AMERICAN STUDIES
TEXAS STATE AND LOCAL STUDIES

Suggested Sears Subject Heading:
INDIANS OF NORTH AMERICA--HISTORY
QUARRIES AND QUARRYING

STONE IMPLEMENTS
TEXAS--DESCRIPTION AND TRAVEL--GUIDES
TEXAS--PUBLIC LANDS
U.S.--DESCRIPTION AND TRAVEL--GUIDES

• AZTEC RUINS
National Monument. P.O. Box 640, Aztec, NM 87410.
(505) 334-6174. 27.14 acres. 1923. Northwestern New Mexico,
northwest of Aztec, near the junction of U.S. 550 and NM 44.

Preserve the 800-year-old Pueblo ruins built by Anasazi Indians.
When settlers began moving in they incorrectly thought that the
Aztecs of Mexico had built the ruins. Exhibits, self-guiding trail,
tours, talks, programs. Visitor center, picnicking. Camping nearby. Food and lodging available in nearby towns.

Free Print Material:
    "Aztec Ruins." 12-fold. Chronology of Indian settlement and
        culture, excavation of ruins. Sketches, maps.
    "Things to See and Do at Aztec Ruins." 1 page. Description,
        features, hours, map.

Sales/Audiovisual List:
    "Publication Sales List." 1 page. Titles, prices, authors of
        books, post cards, slides, coloring books, cookbooks, history
        books, crafts.
    $5.95 "Anasazi," Richard Ambler.

Audiovisual List:
    "National Park Videos." 4 pages. Grouped by: America's
        treasures; Alaska: the last frontier; man and nature: a
        delicate balance; along America's shores; Indian art and
        culture; westward expansion; Civil War; great Americans;
        national park handbooks; order form. All video are 1/2" VHS.
        For other sizes, call or write. No video rentals.
    "National Parks: Our Treasured Lands" narrated by Wally
        Schirra, this film explores the diverse nature of our national
        parks--small and large, historic and natural, backcountry and
        urban. An excellent introduction to America's treasures.
    (1983, 28 minutes). From Harpers Ferry Historical Association,
        Inc., Post Office Box 197, High Street, Harpers Ferry, WV
        25425. (304) 535-6881. The association is a non-profit co-
        operating association supporting the interpretive and preser-
        vation programs of Harpers Ferry National Historical Park and
        national park programs in general. The association operates a
        bookstore, publishes and distributes literature, films about
        national parks.

Suggested Curriculum Application:
    AMERICAN HISTORY

ARCHEOLOGY
NATIVE AMERICAN STUDIES
NEW MEXICO STATE AND LOCAL STUDIES

Suggested Sears Subject Heading:
ANASAZI INDIANS
EXCAVATIONS (ARCHEOLOGY)
INDIANS OF NORTH AMERICAN--HISTORY
NEW MEXICO--DESCRIPTION AND TRAVEL--GUIDES
NEW MEXICO--PUBLIC LANDS
U.S.--DESCRIPTION AND TRAVEL--GUIDES

- BANDELIER
National Monument. Los Alamos, NM 87544. (505) 672-3861.
36,916.89 acres. 1916. Central New Mexico, 46 miles west of Santa
Fe, reached from Santa Fe north on U.S. 285 to Pojoaque, then west
on NM 4.

Preserve ruins of cliff houses of Pueblo Indians, named in honor of
Swiss-American scholar who carried on extensive survey of prehistoric ruins in the region. Exhibits, self-guiding trails, slide programs, ranger-guided walks, unexcavated ruin, ruins in Frijoles
Canyon. Visitor center, campgrounds, curio store, snackbar. Food
and lodging nearby.

Free Print Material:
"Anasazi." 2 pages. Visitor tips for seeing archeological resources, weather, poisonous plants and animals.
"Bandelier." 10 pages. What to see and do, history of the
ruins, visitor tips. Photos, maps.
"Bandelier National Monument: Campground Information & Regulations." 2 pages. Camping guidelines, telephone numbers,
map.
"Selected Features of Los Alamos Climatology." 2 pages.
Temperatures by month showing average high, average low,
record high, record low, rain in inches, snow in inches,
and other climatic conditions.

Sales List:
"Backcountry Information." 2 pages. Hikers' aids for sale
include a book, water purification tablets, water bottles, maps.
Ordering by mail information.
"A Guide to Bandelier National Monument." (A paperbound hiking
guide book by Dorothy Hoard) $5.95.

Audiovisual List:
"Films and Other Materials Available for Free Loan from Bandelier
National Monument." 9 pages. Grouped by: environmental
films, films about national parks, bicentennial films, slide pro-
grams, filmstrips. User tips.
"Any Time, Any Place." 15 minutes. A film to be used with

teachers or students intending to begin working with environmental education. Beginning by looking at the world from outer space, the film points out how our modern lifestyle, as contrasted with more traditional ways of life, has artificially separated.

Suggested Curriculum Application:
AMERICAN HISTORY
ARCHEOLOGY
NATIVE AMERICAN STUDIES
NEW MEXICO STATE AND LOCAL STUDIES

Suggested Sears Subject Heading:
CLIFF DWELLERS AND CLIFF DWELLINGS
EXCAVATIONS (ARCHEOLOGY)
INDIANS OF NORTH AMERICA--HISTORY
NEW MEXICO--DESCRIPTION AND TRAVEL--GUIDES
NEW MEXICO--HISTORY
NEW MEXICO--PUBLIC LANDS
PUEBLO INDIANS
U.S.--DESCRIPTION AND TRAVEL--GUIDES

• CANYON DE CHELLY
National Monument. P.O. Box 588, Chinle, AZ 86503.
(602) 674-5436. 83,840 acres. 1931. Northeastern Arizona, from Gallup northwest on U.S. 666 to NM 264 to U.S. 191 to Chinle.

Maintain ruins of Indian villages built between 350-1300 A.D. at the base of sheer red cliffs and in canyon wall caves. South Rim Drive is a 36-mile round trip while North Rim Drive is a 32-mile round trip. The steep-walled canyons and many ruins of prehistoric Indian dwellings and present-day Navajo homes are scattered along the canyon floors. Pictographs, jeep tours, horseback riding, guide service, hikes, archeology walks, Junior Ranger programs, talks, programs. Meals and lodging, gift shop at Thunderbird Lodge, Chinle, AZ 86503. Cottonwood Campground is located 1/2 mile from the visitor center and is open year around. Talks and tours to school and community groups are available year around. To schedule a talk or tour call or write.

Free Print Material:
"Canyon De Chelly." 10-fold. Indian history, photos of baskets, ruins and attractions, travel tips, maps.
"Canyon Overlook." 4 pages. Visitor services and activities, map, photos. Includes lodging rates, tour rates and hours for various walks and programs, time of sunrise and sunset as well as other information for the visitor.

Suggested Curriculum Application:
AMERICAN HISTORY

ARCHEOLOGY
ARIZONA STATE AND LOCAL STUDIES
NATIVE AMERICAN STUDIES

Suggested Sears Subject Heading:
    ARIZONA--DESCRIPTION AND TRAVEL--GUIDES
    ARIZONA--PUBLIC LANDS
    CLIFF DWELLERS AND CLIFF DWELLINGS
    INDIANS OF NORTH AMERICA--HISTORY
    NAVAJO INDIANS
    U.S.--DESCRIPTION AND TRAVEL--GUIDES

• CASA GRANDE RUINS
National Monument. P.O. Box 518, Coolidge, AZ   85228.
(602) 723-7209.   472.50 acres.   1889.   Central Arizona, halfway
between Phoenix and Tucson, within Coolidge on highway 87.

Preserve the huge four-story building made of high-lime desert
soil by Indians who farmed 600 years ago in the Gila Valley.
Guided tours, museum, self-guiding trail, ranger talks.   Visitor
center, picnicking.   Private campground nearby.   Food and lodging
in Coolidge, Casa Grande.

Free Print Material:
    "Casa Grande Ruins."   2 pages.   History and culture of the
        Indians of the Gila Valley.   Theories about how the Casa
        Grande was used.   Maps and visitor information.

Bibliography:
    "Casa Grande Bibliography."   3 pages.   Author, date, title,
        publisher.   Materials include master's theses, journals,
        reports, manuscripts, books.

Sales/Audiovisual List:
    "Price List of Publications Sold as Casa Grande Ruins National
        Monument."   3 pages.   Title of item and price.   Ordering in-
        formation.
    "Ancient Ruins of the Southwest." $8.95.

Suggested Curriculum Application:
    AMERICAN HISTORY
    ARCHEOLOGY
    ARIZONA STATE AND LOCAL STUDIES
    NATIVE AMERICAN STUDIES

Suggested Sears Subject Heading:
    ARIZONA--DESCRIPTION AND TRAVEL--GUIDES
    ARIZONA--HISTORY
    ARIZONA--PUBLIC LANDS
    HOHOKAM INDIANS

INDIANS OF NORTH AMERICA--HISTORY
U.S.--DESCRIPTION AND TRAVEL--GUIDES

- CHACO CULTURE
National Historical Park. Star Route 4, Box 6500, Bloomfield, NM
87413. (505) 988-6716. 33,977.82 acres. 1907. Northwestern New
Mexico, 64 miles south of Aztec, on NM 57.

Preserve major ruins of Anasazi Indian pre-Columbian culture.
Self-guided trails go through major ruins on the canyon floor,
background trails go to further sites. Museum, programs. Visitor
center, campground. Food and lodging in Aztec.

Free Print Material:
   "Chaco." 16-fold. History, samples of masonry, photos of ruins,
      description and history of various ruins, ancient roads,
      visitor tips, maps, photos, painting.
   "Chaco Visitor Regulations." 2 pages. Visitor guidelines for
      roads, services, camping, weather, safety and other concerns.
      Map.

Sales/Audiovisual List:
   "Mail Order Sales Items." 2 pages. Items divided into: trail
      guides, post cards, books, miscellaneous, order form. Mis-
      cellaneous includes VHS videotape, map, cookbooks, calendar,
      game, stamps.
   "Pueblo Bonito, Chetro Ketl, Casa Rinconada, Pueblo Del Arroyo."
      Trail guides. 40 cents each.

Suggested Curriculum Application:
   AMERICAN HISTORY
   ARCHEOLOGY
   NATIVE AMERICAN STUDIES
   NEW MEXICO STATE AND LOCAL STUDIES

Suggested Sears Subject Heading:
   ANASAZI INDIANS
   INDIANS OF NORTH AMERICA--HISTORY
   NEW MEXICO--DESCRIPTION AND TRAVEL--GUIDES
   NEW MEXICO--HISTORY
   NEW MEXICO--PUBLIC LANDS
   U.S.--DESCRIPTION AND TRAVEL--GUIDES

- COLORADO
National Monument. Fruita, CO 81521. (303) 858-3617. 20,453.93
acres. 1911. West central Colorado, 4 miles west of Grand Junction
and about 3 miles south of Fruita on Colo. 340.

High monoliths, deep canyons, unique rocks, dinosaur fossils, remains of a prehistoric Indian culture. Hiking, climbing, scenic overlooks, interpretive and campfire programs, exhibits, slide program, trails, ancient Indian rock carvings and paintings. Visitor center. Campground and picnic area nearby. Private campgrounds, food and lodging in Grand Junction.

Free Print Material:
"Colorado National Monument." 12-fold. Wildlife, photos, features, activities, visitor facilities.
"Colorado National Monument Trails." 2 pages. Trail regulations, map, trail descriptions, safety tips.
"Colorado National Monument Visitor Planner." 2 pages. Features, safety suggestions, activities for the visitor, map.

Suggested Curriculum Application:
ARCHEOLOGY
ART
COLORADO STATE AND LOCAL STUDIES
NATIVE AMERICAN STUDIES

Suggested Sears Subject Heading:
COLORADO--DESCRIPTION AND TRAVEL--GUIDES
COLORADO--PUBLIC LANDS
FOSSILS
INDIANS OF NORTH AMERICA--HISTORY
MAN, PREHISTORIC
U.S.--DESCRIPTION AND TRAVEL--GUIDES

• EFFIGY MOUNDS
National Monument. McGregor, IA 52157. (319) 873-2356.
1,475.54 acres. 1949. Northeastern Iowa, 3 miles north of
Marquette on IA 76.

Preserve four kinds of prehistoric Indian burial mounds. Conical, linear, compound, and effigy mounds. Guided tours, self-guided trails, museum, film. Visitor center. Picnicking and camping at Pikes Peak State Park and Yellow River State Forest. Food and lodging in local communities.

Free Print Material:
"Effigy Mounds." 12-fold. Prehistory, history beginning with Joliet and Marquette, photos, map, description of mounds, visitor aids.
"Effigy Mounds National Monument." 3 pages. Description, location, hours, guided tours, services available, planning and safety tips.

Bibliography:
"Recommended Readings on Indian Mounds and Effigies." 2 pages. Author, title, publication, date. Magazine entries include volume, page numbers, month.

Audiovisual List:
  Inquire about 14-minute movie "Earthshapers."

Sales/Audiovisual List:
  "Sales Items." 2 pages. Books arranged by: prehistory,
      American Indians--general reading, plant life, animal life,
      geology, general reading (includes sticker book, coloring book,
      calendar), national park system travel guides, slides and post
      cards. Mail order information.
  "America's Ancient Treasures"; University of New Mexico Press.
      $17.50.

Suggested Curriculum Application:
  AMERICAN HISTORY
  ARCHEOLOGY
  IOWA STATE AND LOCAL STUDIES
  NATIVE AMERICAN STUDIES

Suggested Sears Subject Heading:
  INDIANS OF NORTH AMERICA--HISTORY
  IOWA--DESCRIPTION AND TRAVEL--GUIDES
  IOWA--PUBLIC LANDS
  MAN, PREHISTORIC
  MOUNDS AND MOUND BUILDERS
  U.S.--DESCRIPTION AND TRAVEL--GUIDES

• GILA CLIFF DWELLINGS
National Monument. Rt. 11, Box 100, Silver City, NM 88061.
(505) 536-9461. 533.13 acres. 1907. Western New Mexico, 44 miles
north of Silver City at the termination of State Highway 15.

Preserve cliff dwellings of Indians who lived there about 1300 A.D.
Natural and cultural history exhibits, audiovisual, interpretive talks,
self-guided loop trail, dwellings of Indians who built their homes in
natural caves and abandoned them by the early 1300's. Visitor
center, unlocked kennels. Campgrounds in the Gila River recreation
area and near the cliff dwellings. Food and lodging in Gila Hot
Springs, Silver City and others nearby.

Free Print Material:
  "Gila Cliff Dwellings." 8-fold. Maps, photos, history and des-
      cription, accommodations and services.
  "Information and Suggestions." 2 pages. Accommodations,
      features, location, map and other items of interest to the
      visitor.

Sales/Audiovisual List:
  "Sales List." 2 pages. Grouped by: publications, passport
      items, theme related, trail guides. Includes: color book,
      books, stamps, passport books, post cards, note cards, game,

maps, slide sets, posters, leaflets. Title, price, total price with tax, member price.
"American Food and Lore." $10.95 $11.48 $9.31.

Suggested Curriculum Application:
AMERICAN HISTORY
NATIVE AMERICAN STUDIES
NEW MEXICO STATE AND LOCAL STUDIES

Suggested Sears Subject Heading:
CLIFF DWELLERS AND CLIFF DWELLINGS
INDIANS OF NORTH AMERICA--HISTORY
NEW MEXICO--DESCRIPTION AND TRAVEL--GUIDES
NEW MEXICO--PUBLIC LANDS
U.S.--DESCRIPTION AND TRAVEL--GUIDES

- HOVENWEEP

National Monument. c/o Mesa Verde National Park, Mesa Verde National Park, CO 81330. 1923. (303) 529-4465. 784.93 acres. Southeastern Utah, southwestern Colorado, north of the San Juan River, 45 miles from Cortez, CO on Utah-Colorado border. Two groups are in Utah, four groups are in Colorado.

Six groups of towers, pueblos, cliff dwellings, built by pre-Columbian Pueblo Indians. Hovenweep is an Indian word meaning "Deserted Valley." Various ruins. Square Tower Ruin is the best preserved and a self-guiding trail leads through the ruin. Exhibits, short loop trails, wildlife, hiking trail. Inquire about campfire programs given by rangers. Campgrounds near the ranger station. Camping supplies are at Hatch Trading Post or Ismay Trading Post. Food and lodging at Blanding and Bluff in Utah and Cortez in Colorado.

Free Print Material:
"Exploring Hovenweep National Monument." 1 page. Trails, safety tips, provisions, accommodations, campground, ranger station, ruins.
"Hovenweep." 8-fold. Map, photos, description of the ruins, culture and history of the inhabitants of Hovenweep. Visitor information.

Sales List:
"Publications Sold by the Mesa Verde Museum Association, Inc." 6 pages. Grouped by: publications on Mesa Verde National Park, theme-related items on Mesa Verde National Park, archeology/Anasazi culture, ethnography (arts and crafts information), natural history, to provide interpretation and information on Mesa Verde National Park and other national park areas, children's books, miscellaneous items. Title, author, if paper or hardbound, annotation, price. Ordering instructions.

"Archaeological Techniques Used at Mesa Verde National Park,"
Wenger (paper), written for the layman and the average
visitor at Mesa Verde National Park. $3.95.

Suggested Curriculum Application:
AMERICAN HISTORY
ARCHEOLOGY
COLORADO STATE AND LOCAL STUDIES
NATIVE AMERICAN STUDIES
UTAH STATE AND LOCAL STUDIES

Suggested Sears Subject Heading:
ARCHITECTURE--CONSERVATION AND RESTORATION
CLIFF DWELLERS AND CLIFF DWELLINGS
COLORADO--DESCRIPTION AND TRAVEL--GUIDES
COLORADO--PUBLIC LANDS
INDIANS OF NORTH AMERICA--HISTORY
PUEBLO INDIANS
U.S.--DESCRIPTION AND TRAVEL--GUIDES
UTAH--DESCRIPTION AND TRAVEL--GUIDES
UTAH--PUBLIC LANDS

• KNIFE RIVER INDIAN VILLAGES
National Historic Site. R.R. I, Box 168, Stanton, ND 58571.
(701) 745-3309. 1,293.35 acres. 1974. Central North Dakota,
3 miles north of Stanton.

Preserve historic and archeological remnants of the culture and agricultural lifestyle of the Plains Indians. Interpretive tours, slide
program, exhibits, guided tours of the village areas available upon
request, self-guiding trails, reconstructed earthlodge, guided canoe
trips to archeological sites along the Knife River, wildlife, nature
trail, exhibits, fortification ditches, cache pits, cross-country ski
trails, cultural demonstrations, special programs, guided tour of the
Sakakawea Village site. Visitor center, picnicking. Camping nearby.
Food and lodging in Stanton, Beulah, Washburn.

Free Print Material:
"The Earthlodge." 8 pages. Hidatsa and Mandan Indian culture,
sketches, furnishings, construction of earthlodges, suggested
readings.
"Calendar of Activities." 1 page. Special programs, visitor
center hours, tours, trails.
"Frontier Fragments." 4 pages. Newspaper format information
about the national park areas in North Dakota. Photos, things
to see and do, articles, maps, sketches.
"Knife River Indian Villages National Historic Site." 6-fold. Culture, history of the Hidatsa Indians who lived along the Missouri River when explorers discovered them. Paintings by
George Catlin who visited the Indians, maps.

"Lewis and Clark Among the Earthlodge People." 6-fold.
Sketches, map, suggested readings, paintings, the role that
the villages played in the success of the Lewis and Clark
Expedition.

Bibliography:
Suggested readings included in "The Earthlodge" and "Lewis and
Clark Among the Earthlodge People" described above.

Suggested Curriculum Application:
AMERICAN HISTORY
ARCHEOLOGY
NATIVE AMERICAN STUDIES
NORTH DAKOTA STATE AND LOCAL STUDIES

Suggested Sears Subject Heading:
ARCHITECTURE--CONSERVATION AND RESTORATION
HIDATSA INDIANS
INDIANS OF NORTH AMERICA--HISTORY
MANDAN INDIANS
NORTH DAKOTA--DESCRIPTION AND TRAVEL--GUIDES
NORTH DAKOTA--HISTORY
NORTH DAKOTA--PUBLIC LANDS
PLAINS INDIANS
U.S.--DESCRIPTION AND TRAVEL--GUIDES

• MESA VERDE
National Park. Mesa Verde National Park, CO   81330.
(303) 529-4461. 52,085.14 acres. 1906. Southwestern Colorado,
the park entrance is between Cortez and Mancos, off U.S. 160.

Indian pre-Columbian cliff dwellings and other remains. Museum,
wayside exhibits, cross-country skiing, showshoeing, backpacking,
campfire program, hiking trails, general store, gift shop featuring
native american handicrafts, refreshment center, Indian craft demonstrations, multi-media show, hiking. Tours of Spruce Tree House,
Cliff Palace, Balcony House, Ruins Road, Far View Ruins and others.
For specific questions on tours, call the museum at (303) 529-4475.
Visitor center, campgrounds, bicycle rentals, seasonal food and
lodging, picnicking. Food and lodging in Durango, Cortez.

Free Print Material:
"Ara Mesa Verde Company Visitor Services and Information."
4-fold. Photos, map. Sketch. Description of Morefield Campground, Far View Terrace, Spruce Tree Terrace, Far View
Lodge.
"General Information for Visitors to Mesa Verde National Park."
2 pages. Lodging, camping, hiking, picnic facilities, tours,
weather. Name, address, telephone for information on surrounding area, nature and history association.

"Mesa Verde." 8-fold. Services available, visitor safety, description of features, regulations, maps.

"National Park Service Travel Tips." 8-fold. Types of National Park System attractions available to the visitor, photos, making reservations, selecting a park.

"Take Pride in America." 8-fold. Campaign to encourage everyone to take pride in the nation's natural and cultural resources. Photos.

Suggested Curriculum Application:
AMERICAN HISTORY
COLORADO STATE AND LOCAL STUDIES
NATIVE AMERICAN STUDIES

Suggested Sears Subject Heading:
ANASAZI INDIANS
CLIFF DWELLERS AND CLIFF DWELLINGS
COLORADO--DESCRIPTION AND TRAVEL--GUIDES
COLORADO--PUBLIC LANDS
INDIANS OF NORTH AMERICA--HISTORY
MESA VERDE NATIONAL PARK
NATIONAL PARKS AND RESERVES--U.S.
U.S.--DESCRIPTION AND TRAVEL--GUIDES

● MONTEZUMA CASTLE
National Monument. P.O. Box 219, Cape Verde, AZ 86322. (602) 567-3322. 857.69 acres. 1906. Central Arizona. Montezuma Castle is 2.5 miles off of I-17, about 50 miles south of Flagstaff and 90 miles north of Phoenix. Montezuma Well is 10 driving miles north of the castle on I-17 McGuireville exit.

Preserve Montezuma Castle and Montezuma Well. The five-story, 20-room castle (Sinagua Indian cliff dwelling) is 90 percent intact; the well is of archeological and geological importance. Castle that was begun early in the 12th century, and limestone sink well fed by springs have self-guided trails. Displays. Visitor center, picnic areas. Campgrounds nearby, food and lodging in Camp Verde, Cottonwood, Sedona.

Free Print Material:
"Come to Camp Verde." 6-fold. Photos, attractions. Description of Montezuma Castle and Montezuma Well.

"Verde Valley, Arizona." 8-fold. Description of Verde Valley, Cottonwood, Clarkdale, Jerome, Camp Verde, Lake Montezuma, Rimrock and other places. Map, photos.

"Montezuma Castle." 2 pages. Getting there, hours and fees, things to do, climate, accommodations. Maps includes points of interest.

"Montezuma Castle: Tuzigoot." 8-fold. Description of Montezuma Castle, Montezuma Well, Tuzigoot, daily life of the Sinagua Indians, history, photos.

Sales/Audiovisual List:
    "Southwestern Monuments Association Book List." 1 page. Books,
       post cards, slide sets, slide/cassette, coloring book, books,
       V.C.R., chart, guides, cookbook. Title, price.
    "Jerome." $.50

Suggested Curriculum Application:
    AMERICAN HISTORY
    ARCHEOLOGY
    ARIZONA STATE AND LOCAL STUDIES
    NATIVE AMERICAN STUDIES

Suggested Sears Subject Heading:
    ARIZONA--DESCRIPTION AND TRAVEL--GUIDES
    ARIZONA--PUBLIC LANDS
    CLIFF DWELLERS AND CLIFF DWELLINGS
    INDIANS OF NORTH AMERICA--HISTORY
    SINAGUA INDIANS
    U.S.--DESCRIPTION AND TRAVEL--GUIDES

● MOUND CITY GROUP
National Monument. 16062 State Route 104, Chillicothe, OH 45601.
(614) 774-1125. 217.50 acres. 1923. Southcentral Ohio, 3 miles
north of Chillicothe along the Scioto River on State Route 104, 45
miles south of Columbus on U.S. 23.

Twenty-three burial mounds of Hopewell Indians, 200 B.C. to 500
A.D., provides remains and information. Exhibits, self-guiding
tour, ranger-guided tours, videotape, Mica grave exhibit, charnel
house, Scioto River overlook, nature trail, interpretive talks, Mound
of the Pipes, Death Mask Mound, Elliptical Mound, special programs.
Rooftop observation provides a view of Mound City Necropolis with
tape-recorded interpretive message. Contact the monument in advance for ranger-led tours for educational groups. Visitor center,
picnicking. Campgrounds nearby. Food and lodging in Chillicothe.

Free Print Material:
    "Art and Burials in Ancient Ohio." 24 pages. Descriptive tour
       of the Mound City Necropolis with photos, maps, diagrams.
       Archeological findings, Hopewell culture.
    "Mound City Group." 8-fold. Location, facilities and services,
       maps, touring guide and other visitor aids.
    "Mound City Group." 12-fold. Hopewell Indian culture, maps,
       illustrations, visitor guide to Mound City.
    "Museum Exhibit Guide." 10 pages. Description of museum ex-
       hibits. Sketches, floor plan.
    "National Park Service Areas in Ohio." 6-fold. Descriptions,
       addresses, hours, telephones, photos.
    "Selected Campgrounds within a One-Hour Drive from Chillicothe."
       2 pages. Map, chart. Chart includes such information as

distance from Mound City, location, phone, daily rates, dates of operation, number of sites; laundry facilities, hot showers and many other facilities.

Audiovisual List:
"Educational Programs Available for Loan." 2 pages. Slide programs and 16mm films. Title, age level, length, description. Slide sets and films are mailed at no expense to the user.
"An Introduction to the Hopewell People" (all ages). A 15-minute program designed to introduce students to the Hopewell people and to the archeological story of Mound City. The program kit includes a written narrative, a cassette tape with recorded narrative and audible cues for slide changing, a replica of....

Sales/Audiovisual List:
"Eastern National Park and Monument Association Sales Items." 5 pages. Grouped by: publications, other items. Includes replicas, post cards, slide strips, stamps. Among the publications are included a coloring book, map, calendar, children's books. Purpose of the association, order blank, sketch.
"America's Ancient Treasures" by Franklin and Mary Folsom. 420 pages. A comprehensive travel guide to United States and Canadian archeological sites and museums of prehistoric Indian life. Paperback. $17.50.

Suggested Curriculum Application:
AMERICAN HISTORY
ARCHEOLOGY
NATIVE AMERICAN STUDIES
OHIO STATE AND LOCAL STUDIES

Suggested Sears Subject Heading:
FUNERAL RITES AND CEREMONIES
HOPEWELL INDIANS
INDIANS OF NORTH AMERICA--HISTORY
MOUNDS AND MOUND BUILDERS
OHIO--DESCRIPTION AND TRAVEL--GUIDES
OHIO--PUBLIC LANDS
U.S.--DESCRIPTION AND TRAVEL--GUIDES

• NAVAJO
National Monument. HC 63 Box 3, Tonalea, AZ 86044.
(602) 672-2366. 360 acres. 1909. Northeast Arizona, U.S. 160, 50 miles from Tuba City.

Preserve three of the largest and most elaborate cliff dwellings, abandoned about 1300 A.D. by Anasazi Indians but named for Navajos who discovered them afterwards. Audiovisuals, artifacts, self-guiding trail leading to Betatakin Ruin overlook, Keet Seel Ruin, Indian craftwork, campfire programs, Sandal Trail, horseback riding. Call or write for more information and reservations for your ruin entry permit. Visitor center, campground. Nearest food and fuel is at Black Mesa Trading Post at the junction of Ariz. 564 and U.S. 160. Food and lodging in Kayenta.

Free Print Material:
"Information for Hikers to Keet Seel." 2 pages. Reservations, time difference, groups, checklist for recommended supplies, safety precautions, sketches.
"Information for Horseback Riders to Keet Seel." 2 pages. Visitor information regarding reservations, organized groups, safety precautions, sketches.
"Information Letter." 1 page. Features, climate, tours, campground, visitor center hours.
"Navajo." 12-fold. Anazazi Indian culture, photos, diagrams, map, visiting the park, description of ruins, related sites.

Sales/Audiovisual List:
"Southwest Parks and Monuments Association Sales List." 2 pages. Publications, post cards, slide sets, films. Title, price.
"Flowers of the SW Deserts." $8.45.

Suggested Curriculum Application:
AMERICAN HISTORY
ARIZONA STATE AND LOCAL STUDIES
NATIVE AMERICAN STUDIES

Suggested Sears Subject Heading:
ANASAZI INDIANS
ARIZONA--DESCRIPTION AND TRAVEL--GUIDES
ARIZONA--PUBLIC LANDS
CLIFF DWELLERS AND CLIFF DWELLINGS
INDIANS OF NORTH AMERICA--HISTORY
U.S.--DESCRIPTION AND TRAVEL--GUIDES

• NEZ PERCE
National Historical Park. Box 93, Spalding, ID 83551. (208) 843-2261. 2,108.89 acres. 1965. Northcentral Idaho. Park headquarters at Spalding, 11 miles east of Lewiston, on U.S. 95.

Commemorate, preserve, interpret Nez Perce Indian history and culture through 24 individual sites scattered over a 12,000 square mile area. Scenic views, historic buildings, self-guided walk, film, natural formations, exhibits. Individual sites: Donald MacKenzie's Pacific Fur Company Trading Post, Coyote's Fishnet, Ant and Yellowjacket, Spalding, Spalding Home, Northern Idaho Indian Agency,

Fort Lapwai, Craig Donation Land Claim, St. Joseph's Mission, Cottonwood skirmishes, Weis Rockshelter, Camas Prairie, White Bird Battlefield, Clearwater Battlefield, East Kamiah, Asa Smith Mission, Lewis and Clark Long Camp, Canoe Camp, Lenore, Weippe Prairie, Pierce, Musselshell Meadow, Lolo Trail, Lolo Pass. Visitor center, picnicking. Campgrounds nearby. Food and lodging in Lewiston and others.

Free Print Material:

"The Appaloosa Horse." 1 page. Description, use, history of the Appaloosa horse.

"Bird List." 1 page. Common names of birds prepared for Nez Perce National Historical Park.

"A Brief History of the Tipi." 1 page. When the conical shelter was first mentioned by explorers, where it was used, use today.

"Buckskin." 1 page. Tanning process to make clothing.

"Camas." 1 page. Preparation of the bulbs for eating, preserving.

"Dances and Steps of the Nez Perce Indians." 1 page. Description of various dances most often done today.

"Dyes." 1 page. Color, native source, purpose. Table also for paints.

"Local Area Information Sheet." 1 page. Features, location, addresses and telephone numbers of national forests and national recreation area.

"Nez Perce." 24-fold. Map, description of the 24 individual sites, photos, visitor information, Nez Perce culture and the coming of white culture.

"The Nez Perce Tribe of Idaho." 1 page. History, culture, coming of the white man.

"Nez Perce Seasonal Calendar." 1 page. Monthly activities as determined by the season.

"Spalding Site." 1 page. Facilities of the headquarters of the Nez Perce National Historical Park, the work of Rev. Spalding among the Nez Perce.

"Present Day Costumes of the Nez Perce Indians." 1 page. Clothing for women and girls and for men and boys.

"Trees in Spalding Memorial Park." 1 page. List of common names of trees, some with comments.

Bibliography:

"Popular References on Nez Perce History and Culture." 1 page. Author, title, publisher, place of publication, date. Revised.

Sales List:

"Pacific Northwest National Parks and Forests Association Nez Perce Branch Price List." 2 pages. Grouped by: books and pamphlets, passport to your national parks, postcards and Nez Perce handicrafts. Most items include some description. Mail order directions.

"Chief Joseph's People and Their War," Josephy, Alvin M., Jr.,

Yellowstone Library and Museum Association, West Yellowstone, Montana, 1964. $.75.

Suggested Curriculum Application:
  AMERICAN HISTORY
  IDAHO STATE AND LOCAL STUDIES
  NATIVE AMERICAN STUDIES

Suggested Sears Subject Heading:
  IDAHO--DESCRIPTION AND TRAVEL--GUIDES
  IDAHO--HISTORY
  IDAHO--PUBLIC LANDS
  INDIANS OF NORTH AMERICA--HISTORY
  NEZ PERCE INDIANS
  U.S.--DESCRIPTION AND TRAVEL--GUIDES

• OCMULGEE
National Monument. 1207 Emery Highway, Macon, GA 31201.
(912) 742-0447. 683.48 acres. 1934. Central Georgia, east edge
of Macon on U.S. 80 East.

Preserve 10,000 years of American Indian heritage through platform mounds and ceremonial earthlodge, trenches. Archeological exhibits and film, guided tours, self-guiding trail, Indian handicraft demonstrations, mounds, trenches. Visitor center. Meals, lodging and campgrounds in Macon.

Free Print Material:
  "Calendar of Events." 1 page. List of recent events with date
    and hour.
  "Man on the Macon Plateau." 4 pages. Chronology beginning
    with 12,000 B.C. and ending with 1936.
  "Ocmulgee." 12-fold. Heritage and culture of the early Indians.
    Photos of artifacts and attractions, map, chart. Description
    of main features.

Sales/Audiovisual List:
  "Gift Shop Items." 1 page. Arranged by: post cards, maps,
    records, books. Name of item and price.
  "Funeral Mound Postcard." 25 cents.

Audiovisual List:
  "Film List." 4 pages. Description of films, length, color, level.
  "People of the Macon Plateau." People of the Macon Plateau de-
    picts the migration of Asiatic cultures across the North Ameri-
    can continent and the arrival of nomadic hunters into the south-
    east. Through time, southeastern Indian cultures advance and
    around A.D. 900 a mound-building culture....

Suggested Curriculum Application:
  AMERICAN HISTORY

ARCHEOLOGY
GEORGIA STATE AND LOCAL STUDIES
NATIVE AMERICAN STUDIES

Suggested Sears Subject Heading:
GEORGIA--DESCRIPTION AND TRAVEL--GUIDES
GEORGIA--PUBLIC LANDS
INDIANS OF NORTH AMERICA--HISTORY
MOUNDS AND MOUND BUILDERS
U.S.--DESCRIPTION AND TRAVEL--GUIDES

• PECOS
National Monument. P.O. Drawer 11, Pecos, NM 87552.
(505) 757-6414. 364.80 acres. 1965. Central Arizona, 25 miles
southeast of Santa Fe by Interstate 25.

Ruins of ancient pueblo of Pecos and remains of Spanish missions
built in the 17th and 18th centuries that became Santa Fe Trail
landmarks. Foundations, ruins of mission churches, remains of
pueblo, restored kivas, exhibits, mile and 1/4 self-guiding ruins
trail, film, cultural demonstrations. Guided tours are provided
when requested. Visitor center. Campgrounds from 5 to 21 miles
away. Food and lodging in Pecos, Santa Fe.

Free Print Material:
    "Birds of Pecos National Monument: The Habitat Approach to
        Birdwatching." 11 pages. Description of the monument's
        general environment as well as more specific habitat types;
        bird list includes species, probability of sighting season and
        other information. Birds are grouped such as: swallows;
        barn, cliff, violet-green, etc.
    "Happy 200th birthday to the Constitution of the United States."
        1 page. History of New Mexico and the Pecos National Monu-
        ment in relation to the Constitution.
    "Pecos." 16-fold. Pecos pueblo use and history, photos, Indian
        culture, Spanish exploration, excavations at North Pueblo,
        Pecos Ruins Trail, mission churches. Church and Convento
        ruins diagram, road map, tour map.
    "Plants of Pecos National Monument, New Mexico." 13 pages.
        Grouped by: trees, shrubs, herbs. Arranged by families.
        For example, under shrubs is first entered: Saxifrage family
        (Saxifragaceae) and then two are described with their common
        and scientific names included. List of suggested references.

Bibliography:
    "Pecos National Monument Bibliography." 21 pages. Grouped by:
        archeology and prehistory, ethnology, flora and fauna,
        geology, history: American, 1846-present, history: Civil War,
        history: Mexico Period, 1821-1846; history: Mexican War;
        history: Santa Fe Trail, 1821-1888; history: Spanish Period,
        1540-1821; management documents. Alphabetical arrangement

by author within each grouping. Includes author, title, publisher, place of publication and date. Many are reports,
papers, records, studies, notes, journal articles, bulletins,
master's theses, manuscripts, narratives, letters. Some include a brief annotation.

Sales/Audiovisual List:
"List of Publications Available from Pecos National Monument."
2 pages. Grouped by: Pecos National Monument, Southwestern
archeology, New Mexico--travel and history, Southwestern Indians, Hispanic culture, national parks, natural history,
children's books, maps and post cards. VHS videocassette in
English or Spanish. Ordering information. Title, author,
price.
"The Four Churches of Pecos." Alden C. Hayes. $2.50.

Suggested Curriculum Application:
AMERICAN HISTORY
ARCHEOLOGY
NATIVE AMERICAN STUDIES
NATURAL HISTORY
NEW MEXICO STATE AND LOCAL STUDIES

Suggested Sears Subject Heading:
EXCAVATIONS (ARCHEOLOGY)
INDIANS OF NORTH AMERICA--HISTORY
MISSIONS, CHRISTIAN
NATURAL HISTORY--NEW MEXICO
NEW MEXICO--DESCRIPTION AND TRAVEL--GUIDES
NEW MEXICO--PUBLIC LANDS
PECOS INDIANS
U.S.--DESCRIPTION AND TRAVEL--GUIDES

• PIPESTONE
National Monument. P.O. Box 727, Pipestone, MN   56164.
(507) 825-5463. 281.78 acres. 1937. Southwestern Minnesota,
north side of Pipestone, MN off of U.S. 75.

Well-known quarry for Indian ceremonial peace pipes. Indians often
traveled a thousand miles to obtain the sacred stone and the quarry
site was sacred ground. Upper Midwest Indian Cultural Center, exhibits, audiovisual program, interpretive programs, self-guiding
trail, demonstrations of Indian pipes being made from red pipestone,
wildlife, Nicollet Expedition marker. Visitor center. Food and
lodging in Pipestone and other nearby communities. Camping at
Split Rock Creek State Park and Blue Mounds State Park.

Free Print Material:
"Genuine Indian Made Handicrafts." 12-fold. History of the
quarries, photos and descriptions of various kinds of pipes,
photos of artifact reproductions and handicrafts, purpose of
the Pipestone Indian Shrine Association.

"Pipestone." 12-fold. Photos, maps, facilities, attractions, 1836 quotation of George Catlin, Indian culture, the Indian Cultural Center.

Sales List:
"Retail Price List." 6-fold. Grouped by: pipes, pipestone articles, books and miscellaneous. Name of item, example number, average length, price. Order blank, ordering instructions.
"Plains Pipe w/Feather." 1. 15". $27.00.

Suggested Curriculum Application:
AMERICAN HISTORY
ART
MINNESOTA STATE AND LOCAL STUDIES
NATIVE AMERICAN STUDIES

Suggested Sears Subject Heading:
INDIANS OF NORTH AMERICA--ART
MINNESOTA--DESCRIPTION AND TRAVEL--GUIDES
MINNESOTA--PUBLIC LANDS
QUARRIES AND QUARRYING
TOBACCO PIPES
U.S.--DESCRIPTION AND TRAVEL--GUIDES

• TONTO
National Monument. P.O. Box 707, Roosevelt, AZ 85545. (602) 467-2241. 1,120 acres. 1907. Central Arizona, the visitor center is two miles east of Roosevelt.

Preserve artifacts and major cliff dwellings of 13th-14th century Salado Indians. Displays, self-guiding trail with interpretive wayside markers, plants, ancient ruins, museum. Upper ruins guided tours require advance reservations. Visitor center, picnicking. Camping nearby. Food and lodging in Roosevelt, Roosevelt Lake Resort, and the Globe-Miami area.

Free Print Material:
"Checklist of Birds." 3 pages. Common, uncommon, occasional, endangered, permanent resident, summer, winter, migrant.
"Common Flowers of Tonto National Monument." 1 page. Arranged by color, common name, generic name, picture number.
"A Day in the Life of a Salado Family." 6 pages. Clothing, life expectancy, food, shelter and related information.
"Jojoba." 1 page. Description, use of evergreen shrub, sketch.
"Reptiles, Amphibians and Mammals of Tonto National Monument." 2 pages. Grouped by reptiles (snakes, lizards), amphibians (toads), mammals (bats, rabbits, rodents, carnivores, ungulates). Common, scientific name and if poisonous.
"Salado Craft Arts." 5 pages. Description of ceramics, textiles.

What the word "Tonto" means in Spanish.

"The Salado of the Tonto Basin." 6 pages. Development of Salado culture.

"Tonto National Monument." 16-fold. Salado Indian culture, visitor information, maps, photos.

"Questions about Natural History Subjects." 3 pages. Answers to such questions as "when do the cactus bloom?"

"Visiting the Monument." 9 pages. Location, hours, visitor center, walks, regulations, accommodations, safety and other visitor information. Questions and answers about the monument.

Bibliography:
"Master Bibliography." 13 pages. Salado archeology, natural history, cultural history. Arranged alphabetically by author. Author, date, annotation, place of publication, publisher.

Sales/Audiovisual List:
"Southwest Parks and Monuments Association Mail Order Sales List." 5 pages. Books arranged by: animals, archeology, children, desert, geology, history, Indians, national parks, plants, travel. Children's books include a workbook, coloring book, scratch-and-sniff book. Slides, post cards. Order form, ordering directions. Title, author/publisher.
"Birds of North America" (a golden guide) $7.95.

Suggested Curriculum Application:
AMERICAN HISTORY
ARIZONA STATE AND LOCAL STUDIES
NATIVE AMERICAN STUDIES
NATURAL HISTORY

Suggested Sears Subject Heading:
ARIZONA--DESCRIPTION AND TRAVEL--GUIDES
ARIZONA--PUBLIC LANDS
CLIFF DWELLERS AND CLIFF DWELLINGS
INDIANS OF NORTH AMERICAN--HISTORY
NATURAL HISTORY--ARIZONA
SALADO INDIANS
U.S.--DESCRIPTION AND TRAVEL--GUIDES

• TUZIGOOT
National Monument. P.O. Box 219, Camp Verde, AZ 86322. (602) 567-3322. 809.30 acres. 1939. Central Arizona, off of Alt. 89, near Clarkdale, AZ.

Preserve the remains of a Sinaguan Indian village built on the summit of a long ridge rising 120 feet above Verde Valley. The original pueblo was two stories high in places and had 77 ground-floor rooms; it was built between 1125 and 1400. Tuzigoot (Apache for "crooked water") ruins, exhibits. Visitor center. Campgrounds, food and lodging nearby.

Free Print Material:
"Montezuma Castle, Tuzigoot." 8-fold. Photos, map, descriptions of Montezuma Castle, Tuzigoot, Montezuma Well, ancient farmers of the Verde Valley, Tuzigoot pottery.

Suggested Curriculum Application:
AMERICAN HISTORY
ARIZONA STATE AND LOCAL STUDIES
NATIVE AMERICAN STUDIES

Suggested Sears Subject Heading:
ARIZONA--DESCRIPTION AND TRAVEL--GUIDES
ARIZONA--PUBLIC LANDS
CLIFF DWELLERS AND CLIFF DWELLINGS
INDIANS OF NORTH AMERICA--HISTORY
SINAGUA INDIANS
U.S.--DESCRIPTION AND TRAVEL--GUIDES

• WALNUT CANYON
National Monument. Walnut Canyon Road, Route 1, Box 25, Flagstaff, AZ 86001. (602) 526-3367. 2,249.46 acres. 1915. Central Arizona, 7 miles east of Flagstaff off I-40.

Cliff dwellings in caves under limestone ledges built by Sinagua Indians about 800 years ago. Canyon is named after the black walnut tree. Ruins trail is a self-guided trail to about 20 cliff dwellings. Rim trail is self-guided, along the canyon rim to scenic viewpoints and excavated/reconstructed surface dwellings. Exhibits. Visitor center, picnicking. Food and lodging in Flagstaff.

Free Print Material:
"Walnut Canyon National Monument." 16-fold. History, monument hours, Indian way of life, photos, map, administration.

Suggested Curriculum Application:
ARIZONA STATE AND LOCAL STUDIES
NATIVE AMERICAN STUDIES

Suggested Sears Subject Heading:
ARIZONA--DESCRIPTION AND TRAVEL--GUIDES
ARIZONA--PUBLIC LANDS
CLIFF DWELLERS AND CLIFF DWELLINGS
INDIANS OF NORTH AMERICA--HISTORY
SINAGUA INDIANS
U.S.--DESCRIPTION AND TRAVEL--GUIDES

● WUPATKI

National Monument. HC 33, Box 444A, Flagstaff, AZ 86001.
(602) 527-7040. 35,253.24 acres. 1924. Central Arizona, off U.S.
89, 30 miles north of Flagstaff.

Preserve the ruins of sandstone pueblos built by Indians between
100 A.D. and 1225 A.D. Over 2500 archeological sites are the remains of the Cohonina, Kayenta Anasazi, and the Sinagua Indian
groups. Self-guiding trails, field markers, pueblos, conducted
walks, demonstrations, activities, ranger-led hikes, displays.
Visitor center, picnic areas. Nearest campground is 20 miles. The
nearest food and lodging facilities are in Flagstaff and Gray Mountain.

Free Print Material:
    "Area Information Sheet." 2 pages. Features, activities.
        Description, services, weather, restrictions.
    "Ball Courts." 2 pages. Background, importance and type of
        games played, the excavated and reconstructed ball court in
        1965-66. Sketches of ball courts.
    "Birds of Wupatki National Monument." 2 pages. Commonly seen
        birds and their habits. Checklist of abundance and occur-
        rence.
    "Blowholes of the Wupatki Area." 1 page. Description of small
        openings in the rock layer which give out and take in air up
        to 35 miles per hour.
    "Help Save our Cultural Heritage!" 2 pages. Importance of
        helping to preserve prehistoric sites by leaving objects alone.
        Laws protecting materials, sketches.
    "The History of Excavation and Stabilization at Wupatki Ruin."
        1 page. Discovery, efforts at protection, importance of the
        ruin.
    "Mammals of Wupatki National Monument." 1 page. What the ani-
        mals are; the life cycles.
    "Perennial Plants of Wupatki National Monument." 1 page. Name,
        description, habitats of various plants.
    "Prehistoric Pottery Construction." 1 page. Description of pot-
        tery and how it was made by ancient Indians.
    "Reptiles of Wupatki National Monument." 1 page. Common
        names and scientific names of reptiles and their habits.
        Checklist of reptiles and amphibians.
    "Roadside Plants of Wupatki National Monument." 1 page. Des-
        criptions of various plants and their life cycles.
    "Wupati National Monument." 2 pages. Location, access, ar-
        cheological features, visitor/information center, weather,
        restrictions, services.
    "Wupatki-Sunset Crater." 2 pages. Description of Wupatki
        National Monument and Sunset Crater, map.

Sales List:
    "Publication List." 6-fold. Title, page and size, graphics, price,
        annotation. Ordering instructions and order form.

"Wupatki-Sunset Crater." (32 pages, 8-1/2 x 11" color and black and white photos, maps) $4.00. This book is actually an issue of Plateau magazine published by the Museum of Northern Arizona. There are three sections to the book: geology of Sunset Crater, archeology of Wupatki and biology of both areas.

Audiovisual List:
"Wupatki-Sunset Crater Slide Sets." 1 page. Number of set, title, price.
"Set #P548 "Sunset Crater in Winter," "Sunset Crater in Lava Flow," "Sunset Crater," "Sunset Crater from Air," "Sunset Crater from Lava Flow." $1.75.

Sales/Audiovisual List:
"Price List Wupatki." 2 pages. Title and price. Mostly publications but also video, slide cassettes.
"Pueblo Indian Cookbook." $5.95.

Suggested Curriculum Application:
AMERICAN HISTORY
ARCHEOLOGY
ARIZONA STATE AND LOCAL STUDIES
NATIVE AMERICAN STUDIES
NATURAL HISTORY

Suggested Sears Subject Heading:
ARIZONA--DESCRIPTION AND TRAVEL--GUIDES
ARIZONA--PUBLIC LANDS
COHONINA INDIANS
EXCAVATIONS (ARCHEOLOGY)
INDIANS OF NORTH AMERICA--HISTORY
KAYENTA ANASAZI INDIANS
NATURAL HISTORY--ARIZONA
SINAGUA INDIANS
U.S.--DESCRIPTION AND TRAVEL--GUIDES

NATURAL BRIDGES

• NATURAL BRIDGES
National Monument. Star Route, Blanding, UT 84511.
(801) 259-7164. 7,791 acres. 1908. Southeastern Utah, 40 miles west of Blanding, UT by Utah 95.

Three stream-eroded bridges from 180 to 268 feet in span, prehistoric pictographs. Exhibits, campfire programs, color slide

program, hiking, nature trails, scenic view, evidence of prehistoric
Indians, Sipapu Bridge, Owachomo Bridge, Kachina Bridge. Eight-
mile loop road from the visitor center links the trails to the three
bridges. Inquire about the huge photovoltaic power system dedicated at Natural Bridges in 1980 that converts sunlight directly into
electricity. Visitor center, campground, picnicking. Food and
lodging in Blanding, Mexican Hat.

Free Print Material:
　　"Grand Country Travel Council Information Request Postcard."
　　　　Postcard. Check-off items such as scenic flights, outdoor
　　　　education, retirement information, campgrounds or other
　　　　interests on which you would like to receive information.
　　"Natural Bridges." 8-fold. Photos, statistics, diagrams, map.
　　　　Visitor information for making the most of your stay, what to
　　　　see and do, geological background. Explains the difference
　　　　between natural bridges and arches, how they were formed.

Suggested Curriculum Application:
　　GEOGRAPHY
　　GEOLOGY
　　UTAH STATE AND LOCAL STUDIES

Suggested Sears Subject Heading:
　　GEOLOGY--U.S.
　　MAN, PREHISTORIC
　　NATURAL BRIDGES, UT
　　NATURAL MONUMENTS--U.S.
　　UTAH--DESCRIPTION AND TRAVEL--GUIDES
　　UTAH--PUBLIC LANDS
　　U.S.--DESCRIPTION AND TRAVEL--GUIDES
　　U.S.--GEOGRAPHY

• RAINBOW BRIDGE
National Monument. c/o Glen Canyon, National Recreation Area,
P.O. Box 1507, Page, AZ 86040. (602) 645-2471. 160 acres.
1910. Southern Utah, 24 miles from Navajo Mountain Trading Post
by foot or horse, but most people take the water route on Lake
Powell.

World's largest natural bridge, of salmon-pink sandstone, rising
290 feet above the floor of Bridge Canyon, called by the Navajos
"Rainbow of Stone." Trails begin on Navajo Reservation and permits are required and are not recommended for the beginning hiker.
Before beginning a trail trip be sure to ask a park ranger about
conditions. Boat tours on Lake Powell, boat rentals. Food and
lodging in Page, AZ.

Free Print Material:
　　"Anasazi." 2 pages. Antiquities Act of 1906 and Archeological

Resources Protection Act of 1979. Penalties for disregarding protection of archeological resources.

"Rainbow Bridge." 8-fold. How the bridge was formed, photos, illustrations, maps, how to reach the bridge by water, on foot, horseback. Information about the trailheads, trail ethics and regulations.

Suggested Curriculum Application:
GEOGRAPHY
GEOLOGY
UTAH STATE AND LOCAL STUDIES

Suggested Sears Subject Heading:
GEOLOGY--U.S.
NATURAL MONUMENTS--U.S.
RAINBOW BRIDGE, UT
U.S.--DESCRIPTION AND TRAVEL--GUIDES
U.S.--GEOGRAPHY
UTAH--DESCRIPTION AND TRAVEL--GUIDES
UTAH--PUBLIC LANDS

PARKWAYS

- BLUE RIDGE

Parkway. 700 Northwestern Bank Building, Asheville, NC 28801. (704) 259-0779. 82,117.37 acres. 1936. Southern Virginia and northern North Carolina, 469 miles long from Waynesboro, VA to Cherokee, NC.

Scenic parkway follows the crest of the Blue Ridge Mountains, preserving mountain folk culture and scenic areas. The first national parkway averages 3,000 feet above sea level. Wildflowers, hiking, forest-clad mountains, bicycling, wildlife, birdwatching, overlooks. Interpretive signs point out where there is a legend, old building, or place of scientific interest. Backpack camping, picnicking, campgrounds, ranger offices. Food and lodging on intersecting roads leaving the parkway.

Free Print Material:
"Bloom Calendar for the Parkway." 4 pages. Name of flower, months of peak bloom, location by milepost.
"Blue Ridge Parkway Campgrounds." 2 pages. General information, regulations, chart of campgrounds in Virginia and North Carolina.
"The Blue Ridge Parkway Directory." 36 pages. Parkway highlights, visitor tips, accommodations, attractions. Maps,

photos, sketches.

"The Blue Ridge Parkway Milepost." 20 pages. Parkway map and information, wildlife, vacation area guide, children's page, sketches, photos, articles.

"Parkway Tips." 1 page. Driving speed, reservations, visitor activities, weather, seasonal attractions.

"Take Pride in America." 8-fold. Public awareness campaign to encourage everyone to take pride in the nation's natural and cultural resources, photos.

Sales/Audiovisual List:

"Gift Catalog." 8 pages. Grouped by: of interest to the young, Blue Ridge Parkway and other parks, rockhounding for gems and minerals, American Indians, Appalachian folkways, natural history plants and flowers, hiking information and maps, music and bird songs, post cards, calendars, travel information. Includes coloring books, puzzles, records, cassette. Catalog number, title, price. Purpose of the Eastern National Park and Monument Association and how to join the association. Order blank. Sketches.

29568 "All About Trees" (Troll) $1.95.

Suggested Curriculum Application:

NORTH CAROLINA STATE AND LOCAL STUDIES
VIRGINIA STATE AND LOCAL STUDIES

Suggested Sears Subject Heading:

EXPRESS HIGHWAYS
NORTH CAROLINA--DESCRIPTION AND TRAVEL--GUIDES
NORTH CAROLINA--PUBLIC LANDS
U.S.--DESCRIPTION AND TRAVEL--GUIDES
VIRGINIA--DESCRIPTION AND TRAVEL--GUIDES
VIRGINIA--PUBLIC LANDS

- GEORGE WASHINGTON

Memorial Parkway. Turkey Run Park, McLean, VA 22101. (703) 285-2600. 7,141.63 acres. 1930. Along the Potomac River, through Virginia, Maryland, District of Columbia.

Preserves the natural scenery along the Potomac River, links various landmarks in the life of George Washington, includes natural, historical, and recreational areas from Mount Vernon to Great Falls. The first section was completed in 1932 to commemorate the bicentennial of George Washington's birth. Mount Vernon, Mount Vernon Trial, Great Falls Park, Patowmack Canal, Alexandria, Arlington House, Arlington National Cemetery, Memorial Bridge, The Netherlands Carillon, Theodore Roosevelt Island, Fort Marcy, Turkey Run Park, Glen Echo Park, Clara Barton National Historic Site, Mather Gorge, Belle Haven, Claude Moore Colonial Farm, Dyke Marsh, marinas, Fort Hunt, Fort Washington, Gravelly Point, Jones Point

Lighthouse, Lyndon Baines Johnson Grove, Navy and Marine
Memorial, Roaches Run Waterfowl Sanctuary, United States Marine
Corps War Memorial. Overlooks, hiking, water activities, boat
ramps. Visitor centers, picnicking, food and lodging.

Free Print Material:
"Arlington House." 8-fold. A Lee chronology, family history,
photos, hour tour map of the first and second floor, description of various tour rooms. The house overlooks the Potomac
River and Washington, DC and is memorial to Robert E. Lee.
"Clara Barton." 8-fold. Chronology, map, photos, personality
and accomplishments of Barton, Red Cross activities. The
house was built in 1891 of boards saved from Johnstown Flood
shelters and was first used for Red Cross purposes.
"George Washington Memorial Parkway." 12-fold. Map, photos,
features and description of parkway areas.
"Glen Echo Park." 8-fold. Sketch, map, photos, location, history, function. First a national Chautauqua assembly, then
an amusement park, now a park emphasizing arts and cultural
education.
"Great Falls Park." 8-fold. Photos, maps, description and
history of the park, what to see and do.
"Mount Vernon Trail." 8-fold. Photos, maps. Constructed in
1973, the trail in the Potomac River Valley parallels the
George Washington Memorial Parkway. Trail user ethics,
features to see, service accommodations along the way.
"Theodore Roosevelt Island." 10-fold. Map, photo, contribution
and life of Roosevelt, history of the island and the memorial.
Quotations by Roosevelt, visitor tips.
"The United States Marine Corps War Memorial: The Netherlands
Carillon." 10-fold. Description, history, statistics, location,
significance, administration. Both are located on the Virginia
shore of the Potomac River.

Suggested Curriculum Application:
AMERICAN HISTORY
DISTRICT OF COLUMBIA DISTRICT AND LOCAL STUDIES
MARYLAND STATE AND LOCAL STUDIES
VIRGINIA STATE AND LOCAL STUDIES

Suggested Sears Subject Heading:
DISTRICT OF COLUMBIA--DESCRIPTION AND TRAVEL--GUIDES
DISTRICT OF COLUMBIA--PUBLIC LANDS
EXPRESS HIGHWAYS
MARYLAND--DESCRIPTION AND TRAVEL--GUIDES
MARYLAND--PUBLIC LANDS
U.S.--DESCRIPTION AND TRAVEL--GUIDES
VIRGINIA--DESCRIPTION AND TRAVEL--GUIDES
VIRGINIA--PUBLIC LANDS
WASHINGTON, GEORGE, 1732-1799

● JOHN D. ROCKEFELLER, JR.
Memorial Parkway. c/o Grand Teton National Park, P.O. Drawer 170,
Moose, WY 83012. (307) 733-2880. 23,777.22 acres. 1972. Links
West Thumb in Yellowstone National Park with the south entrance of
Grand Teton National Park.

Scenic 82-mile corridor between Yellowstone and Grand Teton National
Parks commemorates Rockefeller's role in creating various parks, including Grand Teton. Continental Divide, Snake River, snowcoach
tours, wildlife, Mount Berry, Steamboat Mountain. Information services are located near the parkway. Campgrounds, trailer parks.
Flagg Ranch, Moran, WY.

Free Print Material:
    "Accommodations Information." 2 pages. Description, addresses
      of accommodations.
    "Animal Checklist." 4-fold. Sketches, checklist on mammals,
      reptiles and amphibians, visitor tips about animals found in
      the Teton Range and Valley of Jackson Hole.
    "Bear Us in Mind." 6-fold. Map, sketches, photos, tips on
      bears such as what to do if you encounter a bear.
    "Birds of Jackson Hole." 16 pages. Map, photo, checklist for
      birds. Checklist is grouped for such birds as loons, grebes,
      waterfowl, woodpeckers.
    "Historical Sketch of Jackson Hole." 2 pages. Archeological
      studies, fur trade, tourism, conservation movement. Sources.
    "John D. Rockefeller, Jr. Memorial Parkway." 8-fold. The de-
      velopment of the parkway, features to see, accommodations,
      map, photos, safety tips, contributions of John D. Rockefeller.
    "Natural Role of Fire." 6-fold. Advantages resulting to the eco-
      system from fire. Map, photos.
    "Pride of the Rockies: Bald Eagles of the Greater Yellowstone
      Ecosystem." 6-fold. Vital statistics, hunting and eating
      habits, mating and breeding, future of the bald eagle, what
      you can do to help. Maps, sketches.
    "Teewinot." 8 pages. Newspaper format. Photos, articles, ac-
      commodations, information about activities, schedule of field
      seminars, maps.

Sales/Audiovisual List:
    "Grand Teton Natural History Association." 8-fold. Grouped by:
      guides and maps, wildlife, plants and wildflowers, history,
      mountaineering, geology, books for youth, guides, color slides,
      art, trip planner specials. Title, author, publisher, annotation,
      number of pages, price. Aims of the Grand Teton Natural
      History Association, order blank, ordering instructions.
      Sketches.
    "Teton Trails." By Bryan Harry. Published by Grand Teton
      Natural History Association. A guide to hiking and horseback
      trails of Grand Teton. 56 pages, illustrated, maps show back-
      country campsites. $1.50.

Suggested Curriculum Application:
WYOMING STATE AND LOCAL STUDIES

Suggested Sears Subject Heading:
EXPRESS HIGHWAYS
ROCKEFELLER, JOHN D., JR., 1874-1960
U.S.--DESCRIPTION AND TRAVEL--GUIDES
WYOMING--DESCRIPTION AND TRAVEL--GUIDES
WYOMING--PUBLIC LANDS

• NATCHEZ TRACE NATIONAL PARKWAY
Rural Route 1, NT-143, Tupelo, MS 38801. (601) 842-1572.
50,189.33 acres. 1938. Alabama, Mississippi, Tennessee.

Preserve the estimated 449-mile historic Indian trail between Nashville,
TN and Natchez, MS, Chickasaw Village, Meriwether Lewis Park.
Old trace exhibits, annual anniversary celebration, nature trails,
natural features, historical features, water recreation, history exhibits. Mount Locust at milepost 15.5; Rocky Springs at milepost
54.8; Ridgeland Crafts Center at milepost 102.4; French Camp at
milepost 180.8; Colbert Ferry at milepost 327.3. Visitor center,
campgrounds, picnic areas. Food and lodging nearby.

Free Print Material:
"Chronology of the Natchez Trace." 5 pages. Events begin with
1541 with DeSoto spending part of the winter in Chickasaw villages and ends in 1961 with the Ackia Battleground National
Monument and Meriwether Lewis National Monument being included in the Natchez Trace Parkway.
"Natchez Trace Parkway." 24-fold. History and development of
the trace, milepost gazetteer, campgrounds, photos, facility
reference, map, photos.
"The Old Trail." 10 pages. History and development of the
trace, Mississippi Daughters of the American Revolution, road
development.
"Visitor Activity Planner." 8-fold. Safety tips, happenings and
highlights, points of interest by milepost location, map, photo,
sketch.

Sales/Audiovisual List:
A complete list of sales items may be obtained by writing:
Eastern National Park & Monument Association, Natchez Park-
way, Rural Route 1, NT-143, Tupelo, MS 38801.

Suggested Curriculum Application:
ALABAMA STATE AND LOCAL STUDIES
AMERICAN HISTORY
MISSISSIPPI STATE AND LOCAL STUDIES
TENNESSEE STATE AND LOCAL STUDIES

Suggested Sears Subject Heading:
ALABAMA--DESCRIPTION AND TRAVEL--GUIDES
ALABAMA--PUBLIC LANDS
EXPRESS HIGHWAYS
MISSISSIPPI--DESCRIPTION AND TRAVEL--GUIDES
MISSISSIPPI--PUBLIC LANDS
TENNESSEE--DESCRIPTION AND TRAVEL--GUIDES
TENNESSEE--PUBLIC LANDS
U.S.--DESCRIPTION AND TRAVEL--GUIDES

PERFORMING ARTS

• JOHN F. KENNEDY
Center for the Performing Arts. National Park Service, 2700 F
Street, NW, Washington, D.C. 20566. (202) 254-3760. 17.50 acres.
1958. District of Columbia, near the Potomac River, 2700 F Street,
NW, Washington, D.C.

National Cultural Center for the Performing Arts. Tours, roof terrace, exhibits, educational programs. The center's three theaters
are located on the main or plaza level: The Eisenhower Theater
seats 1,200; the Opera House seats 2,300; the Concert Hall seats
2,750. The Grand Foyer features a bronze bust of President
Kennedy. Three restaurants on the terrace. Parking three levels
below the auditoriums. Food and lodging nearby.

Free Print Material:
"The John F. Kennedy Center for the Performing Arts." 8-fold,
description of the purpose of the center, founding, its
theaters, restaurants, and other facilities. Tickets, administration.

Suggested Curriculum Application:
DISTRICT OF COLUMBIA STUDIES
PERFORMING ARTS

Suggested Sears Subject Heading:
CENTERS FOR THE PERFORMING ARTS
DISTRICT OF COLUMBIA--DESCRIPTION AND TRAVEL--GUIDES
DISTRICT OF COLUMBIA--PUBLIC LANDS
KENNEDY, JOHN F., 1917-1963
PRESIDENTS--U.S.
U.S.--DESCRIPTION AND TRAVEL--GUIDES

● WOLF TRAP FARM
Park for the Performing Arts. 1551 Trap Road, Vienna, VA 22180.
(703) 255-1827. 130.28 acres. 1966. Northern Virginia, west of
Washington, D.C. off I-495 (Capital Beltway).

Only national park for the performing arts in a setting of hills and
woods. Opera, ballet, jazz, pop, symphony orchestra, musical
theater, modern and folk dance performances. Filene Center ac-
commodates up to 7,000; two rustic, pre-revolutionary war barns
provide performances and other gatherings; children's theater-in-
the-woods provides an outdoor stage, 200-seat tented pavilion.
For information on workshops, master classes, and other programs
for students and adults call (703) 255-1939. Dining, shuttle bus.
Tickets for performances may be purchased by phone (703) 385-0044
or (800) 468-3540; in person at the Filene Center box office, or by
mail to 1624 Trap Road, adding $2.50 for handling and sending a
self-addressed, stamped, business-size envelope. Advance food
reservation at the pavilion at (703) 281-4256 or the American Cafe
at Wolf Trap at (202) 337-3604.

Free Print Material:
   "Interpretive Program." 6-fold. Current calendar of events.
   "Kodak and Wolf Trap Present." 12-fold. Tickets, map, sketches,
      guide to performances.
   "Welcome to Washington." 28-fold. Map, photos, downtown at-
      tractions and those within a day's reach. Includes name of at-
      traction, address, hours, tours, telephone.

Suggested Curriculum Application:
   PERFORMING ARTS
   VIRGINIA STATE AND LOCAL STUDIES

Suggested Sears Subject Heading:
   CENTER FOR THE PERFORMING ARTS
   PERFORMING ARTS
   U.S.--DESCRIPTION AND TRAVEL--GUIDES
   VIRGINIA--DESCRIPTION AND TRAVEL--GUIDES
   VIRGINIA--PUBLIC LANDS

PRESIDENTS

● ABRAHAM LINCOLN BIRTHPLACE
National Historic Site. R.F.D. 1, Hodgenville, KY 42748.
(502) 358-3874. 116.50 acres. 1916. Central Kentucky, 3 miles
south of Hodgenville on U.S. 31E and KY 61.

Cabin believed to be the one in which Lincoln was born in 1809. Groups may make advance arrangements for conducted tours. An environmental study area is for school use where trails of the birthplace farm are available and students can participate in special activities. Hiking trails, uniformed interpreters. Audiovisual program, exhibits, memorial building. Visitor center, picnicking. Camping nearby. Food and lodging in Hodgenville.

Free Print Material:
    "Lincoln Birthplace." 14-fold. Early family life of the Lincolns on a frontier farm. Sketches, maps, how the cabin was made into a site, visitor information.

Sales List:
    "Eastern National Park and Monument Association Sales List at the Abraham Lincoln Birthplace National Historic Site." 2 pages. Title, author, publisher, place of publication, date, price. Besides publications are items like photocard for framing, jigsaw puzzle, medals, stamp cachet, poster, print. Some books for children. Includes a fact book and teachers' guide on Lincoln. Ordering directions. Aims of the Eastern National Park and Monument Association.
    "Abraham Lincoln from his Own Words and Contemporary Accounts." Roy E. Appleman, Government Printing Office, Washington, D.C., reprint 1985. $1.75.

Audiovisual List:
    "Audiovisual List." 4 pages. Available for loan to schools and other organizations upon request on a first-come, first-served basis. Films are 16mm color except for one black-and-white film. Slide-tape sets are also available. Title, running time, description. A pre-site package of 40 slides is available for loan to school groups and clubs that provide a preview of the main features of the Abraham Lincoln birthplace.
    "Lincoln, the Kentucky Years"--18 minutes. This is the film shown at the Abraham Lincoln birthplace NHS Visitor Center. The film is an ecological approach to the influence of the Kentucky environment on the future president during the first seven years of his life. Some of the beautiful....

Suggested Curriculum Application:
    AMERICAN HISTORY
    GOVERNMENT
    KENTUCKY STATE AND LOCAL STUDIES

Suggested Sears Subject Heading:
    ARCHITECTURE--CONSERVATION AND RESTORATION
    KENTUCKY--DESCRIPTION AND TRAVEL--GUIDES
    KENTUCKY--PUBLIC LANDS
    LINCOLN, ABRAHAM--U.S.
    PRESIDENTS--U.S.
    U.S.--DESCRIPTION AND TRAVEL--GUIDES

- ADAMS

National Historic Site. 135 Adams Street, P.O. Box 531, Quincy,
MA 02269. (617) 773-1177. 9.82 acres. 1946. Eastern Massachusetts, about eight miles south of Boston.

Preserve the home of Presidents John Adams and John Quincy Adams
and other well-known members of the Adams family at 135 Adams
Street, the birthplaces of the two presidents on 133 Franklin Street
and 141 Franklin Street, and the United First Parish Church built
by the Adams family. Garden and grounds self-guiding walks,
house tours. Food and lodging in Quincy and greater Boston.

Free Print Material:
> "Adams National Historic Site, Massachusetts." 20-fold. Ac-
> complishments of four generations of the Adams family, photos,
> illustrations, map. The house was occupied by Adamses from
> 1788 to 1927.
> "John and John Quincy Adams Birthplaces." 4-fold. Portraits,
> history, touring schedule.
> "John Adams Birthplace." 2 pages. Sketches, early years of
> the second president of the United States.

Suggested Curriculum Application:
> AMERICAN HISTORY
> GOVERNMENT
> MASSACHUSETTS STATE AND LOCAL STUDIES

Suggested Sears Subject Heading:
> ADAMS, JOHN, 1735-1826
> ADAMS, JOHN QUINCY, 1767-1848
> ARCHITECTURE--CONSERVATION AND RESTORATION
> MASSACHUSETTS--DESCRIPTION AND TRAVEL--GUIDES
> MASSACHUSETTS--PUBLIC LANDS
> PRESIDENTS--U.S.
> U.S.--DESCRIPTION AND TRAVEL--GUIDES

- ANDREW JOHNSON

National Historic Site. College and Depot Streets, Greeneville, TN
37743. (615) 638-3551. 16.68 acres. 1935. Eastern Tennessee,
70 miles northeast of Knoxville, TN, off of U.S. I-81 in three
separate units.

Two homes, tailor shop of the 17th president as well as the Andrew
Johnson National Cemetery where the president, members of his
family and veterans of various wars are buried. Johnson's Tailor
Shop, his two Greeneville residences, cemetery in which he is
buried, museum. Several-weeks-in-advance reservations are required for class visits. Visitor center. Campgrounds nearby.
Food and lodging in Greeneville.

Free Print Material:
"Andrew Johnson." 16-fold. Career of Andrew Johnson from
tailor shop to White House, visitor information. Sketches, map,
photos.
"Andrew Johnson National Historic Site." 2 pages. Sketches,
map. What the site consists of, Johnson's accomplishments.
"Educational Group Visit Materials." 9 pages. Group visit suggestions and regulations, bibliography, post-visit activities
for older or advanced students, study and discussion questions and answers, identification of names and terms, word
search, scavenger hunt. Designed to be applicable to different grade levels.
"Litter-ally Speaking...." 2 pages. Litter pick-up and disposal
costs, how we can protect the land.

Bibliography:
Included in "Educational Group Visit Materials" described above.
Author, title, place of publication, publisher, date.

Sales/Audiovisual List:
"Eastern National Park and Monument Association Andrew Johnson
National Historic Site Sales List." 3 pages. Grouped by:
audio and visual aids, theme-related souvenirs, books. Title,
author, place of publication, date, price for books. Audio
and visual aids include post cards, slide sets. Ordering
directions.
"Portrait of Andrew Johnson." (c1860) color, 20 cents. Framing
print.

Suggested Curriculum Application:
AMERICAN HISTORY
GOVERNMENT
TENNESSEE STATE AND LOCAL STUDIES

Suggested Sears Subject Heading:
ANDREW JOHNSON NATIONAL CEMETERY
ARCHITECTURE--CONSERVATION AND RESTORATION
CEMETERIES
JOHNSON, ANDREW, 1808-1875
PRESIDENTS--U.S.
TENNESSEE--DESCRIPTION AND TRAVEL--GUIDES
TENNESSEE--PUBLIC LANDS
U.S.--DESCRIPTION AND TRAVEL--GUIDES

• EISENHOWER
National Historic Site. c/o Gettysburg National Military Park,
Gettysburg, PA 17325. (717) 334-1124. 690.46 acres. 1969.
Southern Pennsylvania, near Gettysburg National Military Park.
Tours begin at the lower end of the Gettysburg National Military
Park Information Center, located on PA 134 near its intersection
with U.S. 15.

Farmhouse and grounds purchased in 1951, the only home the
president and his wife owned. Orientation program, self-guided
walking tour of the grounds with points of interest being indicated
by red-and-white five-star symbols. All visits to the site are conducted through a reservation/shuttlebus system and begin at the
tour information center at the lower end of Gettysburg National
Military Park Visitor Center. A limited number of tours are available each day on a first-come, first-served basis. Organized groups
may make reservations at least 10 days in advance by calling the
telephone number given at extension 30. See the "Dear Tour Group
Leader Letter" described below for more information. Reception center. Food and lodging in Gettysburg.

Free Print Material:
   "Dear Tour Group Leader Letter." 1 page. Reservations, tours,
      fees, tickets and related visitor information.
   "Eisenhower." 8-fold. Photos and points of interest on the farm.
      Biographical survey with photos of President Eisenhower.
   "The Eisenhower Home: A Tour of the House." 2 pages. Nar-
      rative tour keyed to accompanying floor plans.
   "Gettysburg." 40 pages. Photos, maps, things to see and do,
      tours, accommodations, account of the Battle of Gettysburg.

Bibliography:
   "Selective Bibliography--Dwight Eisenhower." 1 page. Grouped
      by: books by Dwight Eisenhower, books about Dwight Eisen-
      hower, military, presidential, books for young readers.
      Author, title.

Suggested Curriculum Application:
   AMERICAN HISTORY
   GOVERNMENT
   PENNSYLVANIA STATE AND LOCAL STUDIES

Suggested Sears Subject Heading:
   ARCHITECTURE--CONSERVATION AND RESTORATION
   EISENHOWER, DWIGHT DAVID, 1890-1969
   PENNSYLVANIA--DESCRIPTION AND TRAVEL--GUIDES
   PENNSYLVANIA--PUBLIC LANDS
   PRESIDENTS--U.S.
   U.S.--DESCRIPTION AND TRAVEL--GUIDES

• FORD'S THEATRE
National Historic Site. 511 Tenth Street, N.W., Washington, D.C.
20004. (202) 426-6924. 0.29 acres. 1933. Washington, D.C.
between D and F streets, one block from the Metro Center Subway.

Theatre where Lincoln was shot April 14, 1865, and the house
across the street where he died the next day. Theatre, museum in
the theatre basement, first floor of the house where he died.

Programs, theatre performances are scheduled throughout the year.
Food and lodging in Washington, D.C.

Free Print Material:
"A Brief Chronological History of Abraham Lincoln's Life."
2 pages. Dates and events beginning with Lincoln's birth
on his father's farm February 12, 1809.
"Chronology of House Where Lincoln Died (Petersen House)."
2 pages. Dates and events connected with the Petersen
House beginning with February 5, 1849, until July 25, 1980,
when restoration work was completed.
"Ford's Theatre and the House Where Lincoln Died." 8-fold.
Photos, description of Lincoln's death, the restoration of the
theatre, what the museum offers, description of the house
where Lincoln died.
"Why Did Booth Kill Lincoln?" 4 pages. Biographical information
on John Wilkes Booth as to his motives.

Bibliography:
"Recommended Books on the Lincoln Assassination." 1 page.
Listed in order of priority. Title, author, place of publica-
tion, publisher, date, annotation. Most are included in the
Ford's Theatre library.
"Suggested Reading and Reference Works." 1 page. Title,
author.

Sales/Audiovisual List:
"Books and Other Publications Sold at Ford's Theatre." 2 pages.
Books, activity books, coloring books, guides, post cards,
slides, posters, brochures, songbook, cookbook and others.
Title, price.
"Lincoln Pilgrimage Trail Brochures." $.35.

Suggested Curriculum Application:
AMERICAN HISTORY
DISTRICT OF COLUMBIA STUDIES

Suggested Sears Subject Heading:
ARCHITECTURE--CONSERVATION AND RESTORATION
ASSASSINATION
BOOTH, JOHN WILKES, 1836-1865
DISTRICT OF COLUMBIA--DESCRIPTION AND TRAVEL--GUIDES
DISTRICT OF COLUMBIA--PUBLIC LANDS
LINCOLN, ABRAHAM, 1809-1865
PRESIDENTS--U.S.--ASSASSINATION
U.S.--DESCRIPTION AND TRAVEL--GUIDES

• GENERAL GRANT
National Memorial. c/o NPS Manhattan Sites, 26 Wall Street, New
York, NY 10005. (212) 666-1640. 0.76 acres. Dedicated 1897;

placed under National Park Service 1959. Eastern New York, New York City on a bluff overlooking the Hudson River, Riverside Drive near West 122nd Street and Henry Hudson Parkway.

Memorial to Ulysses S. Grant, Union commander and president. Popularly known as Grant's Tomb, it holds remains of Grant and his wife. It is the largest American Mausoleum. Large memorial building, rising 150 feet high composed of 8-1/2 tons of red granite. Telephone ahead to arrange for group visits. Food and lodging in New York City, upper Manhattan area.

Free Print Material:
"General Grant." 8-fold. Chronology of Grant the soldier/ citizen, the general, the statesman. Sketches, photos, description, and building of Grant's Memorial.
"Richard T. Greener." 6-fold. Life and accomplishments of prominant lawyer, educator, diplomat. Greener was the first black man to graduate form Harvard College and was promoter of Grant's Tomb. Photos.
"'Why Here?' The Entombment of Grant in New York." 2 pages. How Grant came to be buried in New York. Biographical sketch.

Sales/Audiovisual List:
"Sales List." 3 pages. Books, coloring books, calendar, post cards, slide sets, confederate currency sets, medal, map, and other items. Title, price.
"Concise History of the Civil War." $1.75 + .15 = $1.90.

Suggested Curriculum Application:
AMERICAN HISTORY
GOVERNMENT
NEW YORK STATE AND LOCAL STUDIES

Suggested Sears Subject Heading:
GRANT, ULYSSES, S., 1822-1885
NEW YORK--DESCRIPTION AND TRAVEL--GUIDES
NEW YORK--PUBLIC LANDS
PRESIDENTS--U.S.
TOMBS
U.S.--DESCRIPTION AND TRAVEL--GUIDES

• GEORGE WASHINGTON BIRTHPLACE
National Monument. Washington's Birthplace, VA 22575.
(804) 224-0196. 538.23 acres. 1930. Eastern Virginia, Potomac River, 38 miles east of Fredericksburg, VA, accessible over VA 3 and VA 204.

Birthplace of the first president includes memorial mansion and gardens and tombs of President Washington's father, grandfather, and great-grandfather. Restored and operating colonial farm, historic mansion area, colonial farm, burial grounds, hiking trails, gardens. Visitor center, picnicking. Food and lodging in Fredericksburg, Montross, Colonial Beach.

Free Print Material:
"George Washington Birthplace." 20-fold. Family tree, photos, map, family, plantation life, quotation of George Washington on farming, visitor features.

Suggested Curriculum Application:
AMERICAN HISTORY
GOVERNMENT
VIRGINIA STATE AND LOCAL STUDIES

Suggested Sears Subject Heading:
ARCHITECTURE--CONSERVATION AND RESTORATION
PRESIDENTS--U.S.
U.S.--DESCRIPTION AND TRAVEL--GUIDES
VIRGINIA--DESCRIPTION AND TRAVEL--GUIDES
VIRGINIA--HISTORY
VIRGINIA--PUBLIC LANDS
WASHINGTON, GEORGE, 1732-1799

• HARRY S TRUMAN
National Historic Site. 223 North Main St., Independence, MO 64050. (816) 254-7199. .78 acres. 1983. West central Missouri, 12 miles east of Kansas City, off I-70 or I-435.

Preserve and interpret the home of the 33rd president, known as the Summer White House from 1945-1953. Guided tours, slide program. Independence shuttle, food and lodging in Independence.

Free Print Material:
"Harry S Truman." 8-fold. Biographical sketch. Photos of various rooms of the president's house, map.
"Planning Your Visit." 1 page. Location, guided tours, photo, Truman related sites, house history, accommodations.

Bibliography:
Included in "Suggested Reading, Harry S Truman" described below.

Sales/Audiovisual List Annotation-First Entry:
"Suggested reading, Harry S Truman." 1 page. Grouped by: publications, post cards, slides. Title, author and if for sale price, type of book cover. Post cards include title and slides include number of slides in each set. Ordering instructions.
"The Autibiography of Harry S Truman." Robert H. Ferrell, editor.

Suggested Curriculum Application:
    AMERICAN HISTORY
    GOVERNMENT
    MISSOURI STATE AND LOCAL STUDIES

Suggested Sears Subject Heading:
    ARCHITECTURE--CONSERVATION AND RESTORATION
    MISSOURI--DESCRIPTION AND TRAVEL--GUIDES
    MISSOURI--PUBLIC LANDS
    PRESIDENTS--U.S.
    TRUMAN, HARRY S, 1884-1972
    U.S.--DESCRIPTION AND TRAVEL--GUIDES

• HERBERT HOOVER
National Historic Site. P.O. Box 607, West Branch, IA   52358.
(319) 643-2541. 186.80 acres. 1965. Central Iowa in West
Branch, the visitor center is on Parkside Drive and Main Street,
1/2 mile from exit 254 of Interstate 80.

Preserve the birthplace, home and boyhood neighborhood of President Hoover. Hoover Presidential Library and Museum, gravesite
of President and Mrs. Hoover, historic homes, prairie trail. Visitor
center. Food and lodging in West Branch.

Free Print Material:
    "Area Restaurants." 1 page. Name, address, phone number of
        restaurants and accommodations.
    "Herbert Hoover." 4 pages. What to see, background of the
        site, biographical facts of President Hoover and his parents.
    "Herbert Hoover Prairie Trail." 1 page. What to see on the
        1.3-mile trail. Map, visitor tips.
    "Historic Homes." 2 pages. Location, sketch and description of
        homes that are a part of the Herbert Hoover National Historic
        Site.
    "Iowa State Transportation Map." Folded map. Annual calendar
        of events, state parks, and recreation areas; other visitor
        information is included.

Bibliography:
    "Bibliography of Herbert Hoover." 1 page. Author, title, date
        of books. Includes juvenile books.

Suggested Curriculum Application:
    AMERICAN HISTORY
    GOVERNMENT
    IOWA STATE AND LOCAL STUDIES

Suggested Sears Subject Heading:
    ARCHITECTURE--CONSERVATION AND RESTORATION
    HOOVER, HERBERT, 1874-1964

IOWA--DESCRIPTION AND TRAVEL--GUIDES
IOWA--PUBLIC LANDS
PRESIDENTS--U.S.
U.S.--DESCRIPTION AND TRAVEL--GUIDES

• HOME OF FRANKLIN D. ROOSEVELT
National Historic Site. 249 Albany Post Road, Bellfield Headquarters,
Hyde Park, NY 12538. (914) 229-9115. 290.34 acres. 1944. East-
ern New York, Hyde Park, Hudson Valley, on Route 9.

Birthplace, lifetime residence, "Summer White House" of President
Franklin D. Roosevelt. Tour of house, grounds, exhibits, grave-
sites of President and Mrs. Roosevelt. Large groups are advised
to make advance reservations. Food and lodging nearby.

Free Print Material:
   "The Boy Franklin." 8-fold. Schooling, Roosevelt's love of the
      sea, Roosevelt as a conservationist and a father. Copy of
      Roosevelt's letter to his parents, drawing he made when he
      was 5 years old, photos, sketch, list of offices Roosevelt
      held with dates.
   "Home of Franklin D. Roosevelt." 16-fold. Photos, floor plans,
      life and accomplishments of Roosevelt, construction changes
      in the home.

Suggested Curriculum Application:
   AMERICAN HISTORY
   GOVERNMENT
   NEW YORK STATE AND LOCAL STUDIES

Suggested Sears Subject Heading:
   ARCHITECTURE--CONSERVATION AND RESTORATION
   NEW YORK--DESCRIPTION AND TRAVEL--GUIDES
   NEW YORK--PUBLIC LANDS
   PRESIDENTS--U.S.
   ROOSEVELT, FRANKLIN D., 1882-1945
   U.S.--DESCRIPTION AND TRAVEL--GUIDES

• JAMES A. GARFIELD
National Historic Site. Western Reserve Society, 8095 Mentor Avenue,
Mentor, OH 44060. (216) 255-8722. 7.82 acres. 1980. Northern
Ohio.

The home of James A. Garfield, the 20th president of the United
States, assassinated in 1881. The site is operated by the Western
Reserve Historical Society. Tours of Lawnfield, the three-story home
of President Garfield. Gift shop. Food and lodging nearby.

Free Print Material:
   "A Self Guided Tour of Lawnfield." 4 pages. Hours, admission

fees, biographical survey of Garfield, sketch, floor plans, descriptive tour of the house.

Suggested Curriculum Application:
    AMERICAN HISTORY
    GOVERNMENT
    OHIO STATE AND LOCAL STUDIES

Suggested Sears Subject Heading:
    ARCHITECTURE--CONSERVATION AND RESTORATION
    GARFIELD, JAMES A., 1831-1881
    OHIO--DESCRIPTION AND TRAVEL--GUIDES
    OHIO--PUBLIC LANDS
    PRESIDENTS--U.S.
    U.S.--DESCRIPTION AND TRAVEL--GUIDES

- JOHN F. KENNEDY

National Historic Site. 83 Beals Street, Brookline, MA 02146. (617) 566-7937. 0.09 acres. 1967. Eastern Massachusetts.

Preserve JFK's birthplace and early boyhood home. Audio and self-guiding home tours, walking tour of the neighborhood. Meals and lodging in greater Boston area.

Free Print Material:
    "John Fitzgerald Kennedy." 8-fold. Photo, map, floor plans, house tour, Kennedy family history.
    "The John F. Kennedy Library and Museum." 4-fold. What the museum contains, location, hours, photos.

Bibliography:
    "List of Books About John Fitzgerald Kennedy." 4 pages. Grouped by: books for children and young people; the Kennedy and Fitzgerald families; the Kennedy assassination; books written by J.F.K.; books written by members of J.F.K.'s staff; the Kennedy administration; the 1960 presidential election; photographic essays; other books of interest. Includes author, title, place of publication, publisher, year.
    Lee, Bruce, "J.F.K.: Boyhood to White House" (Greenwich, CT: Fawcett Publications, 1961)

Suggested Curriculum Application:
    AMERICAN HISTORY
    GOVERNMENT
    MASSACHUSETTS STATE AND LOCAL STUDIES

Suggested Sears Subject Heading:
    ARCHITECTURE--CONSERVATION AND RESTORATION
    KENNEDY, JOHN FITZGERALD, 1917-1963
    MASSACHUSETTS--DESCRIPTION AND TRAVEL--GUIDES

MASSACHUSETTS--PUBLIC LANDS
PRESIDENTS--U.S.
U.S.--DESCRIPTION AND TRAVEL--GUIDES

- LINCOLN BOYHOOD
National Memorial. Lincoln City, IN 47552. (812) 937-4757.
191.98 acres. 1962. Southern Indiana, 2 miles east of Gentryville,
on IN 162.

Commemorate President Abraham Lincoln's youthful life, 1816-1830,
with his pioneer family, his mother's grave. Wooded and landscaped
area, memorial visitor center, gravesite of Lincoln's mother, and the
Lincoln Living Historical Farm, Lincoln Boyhood Trail. Memorial
halls, exhibits, museum, film. Visitor center. Adjacent is Lincoln
State Park with facilities for camping, picnicking, hiking, swimming,
boating and fishing. Conducted tours for schools and other groups
can be arranged by advance reservations.

Free Print Material:
"Family Tree." 2 pages. Family tree of Abraham Lincoln traced.
"General Information." 1 page. Survey for the visitor of what
to do and see.
"Information for the Handicapped." 1 page. Accessibility of the
memorial.
"Lincoln Boyhood." 12-fold. Biographical information on Lincoln's
family and features of the memorial site. Map, illustrations.
"Lincoln Notebook" 21 topics, 1-2 pages. A wide variety of information on notebook-type pages such as an autobiographical
letter, Lincoln's sons, quizzes, chronological history, Lincoln's
beard, quotations.
"Lodging Campgrounds Restaurants." 2 pages. Name, phone,
facility information, price, miles, hours.
"Planning Package." 3 pages. Information designed for educators that includes tips for field trips, facilities, and programs
available.

Sales/Audiovisual List:
"Approved Sales List." 2 pages. Grouped by: audiovisuals,
publications. Name and price of such items as post cards,
slide strips, and books.
"Ford Theater" $3.25.

Audiovisual List:
"Film Library." 2 pages. Guidelines for film use and description.
"Here I Grew Up." In southern Indiana, one of the world's most
honored men grew to manhood. Here, too, is the grave of
his mother, Nancy Hanks Lincoln. In this area, young Abraham Lincoln learned his skilled axemanship and helped his
father, Thomas, farm. He lived here from 1816 to 1830,

fourteen formative years of education and experiences in the forest frontier. Narrated by the late senator Everett Dirksen. (27 minutes)

Suggested Curriculum Application:
AMERICAN HISTORY
INDIANA STATE AND LOCAL STUDIES

Suggested Sears Subject Heading:
INDIANA--DESCRIPTION AND TRAVEL--GUIDES
INDIANA--PUBLIC LANDS
LINCOLN, ABRAHAM, 1809-1865
PRESIDENTS--U.S.
U.S.--DESCRIPTION AND TRAVEL--GUIDES

• LINCOLN HOME
National Historic Site. 426 South 7th St., Springfield, IL 62703. (217) 789-2357. 12.24 acres. 1971. Central Illinois.

Home of Lincoln and his family for 17 years until he left to accept the presidency in 1861. Lincoln home, 12 homes of Lincoln's 1860 neighbors to maintain the atmosphere of Lincoln's neighborhood. Tours, program, bookshop, guides to provide information.

Free Print Material:
"Lincoln Home." 16-fold. Biographical sketch from birth to as-sassination, his home in Springfield, maps, photos, sketches.
"Mr. Lincoln's Hometown Visitors Guide." 8-fold. Visitor cen-ters; Lincoln attractions; other historic attractions, museums and sites; sightseeing; general information and other infor-mation.
"Mr. Lincoln's Springfield." 2 pages. History of the home, safety considerations, map, other Lincoln-related historic sites in the Springfield area.
"To Preserve the Past for the Future." 8-fold. Biographical Information of the Lincoln family, preservation efforts of the Lincoln home, sketches.

Suggested Curriculum Application:
AMERICAN HISTORY
GOVERNMENT
ILLINOIS STATE AND LOCAL STUDIES

Suggested Sears Subject Heading:
ARCHITECTURE--CONSERVATION AND RESTORATION
ILLINOIS--DESCRIPTION AND TRAVEL--GUIDES
ILLINOIS--PUBLIC LANDS
LINCOLN, ABRAHAM, 1809-1865
PRESIDENTS--U.S.
U.S.--DESCRIPTION AND TRAVEL--GUIDES

- **LINCOLN MEMORIAL**
c/o National Capital Region. National Park Service, 1100 Ohio
Drive, SW, Washington, D.C. 20242. (202) 426-6841. 163.63 acres.
1911. District of Columbia, West Potomac Park on the axis of the
Capitol and the Washington Monument, foot of 23rd Street, N.W.

Memorial to Abraham Lincoln, the 16th president of the United
States. White marble memorial building with doric outer columns.
Columns inside the great hall are 50-feet high. Nineteen-foot-high
statue of a seated Lincoln, two murals on the north and south walls
each 60-feet long and 12-feet high represent Lincoln's principles.
Names of states are cut into the frieze above the colonnade and attic
walls while the addition of Alaska and Hawaii is inscripted on the
terrace. Carved on marble walls are Lincoln's Gettysburg and
Second Inaugural addresses. Interpretive services. Guided tour-
mobiles--(202) 638-5371 for rates. A ranger is in attendance at the
memorial. Food and lodging in Washington, D.C.

Free Print Material:
    "The Lincoln Memorial." 8-fold. Biographical sketch of Lincoln,
       quotation from Lincoln's Gettysburg Address, construction of
       the memorial, architecture of the memorial, photos, description
       of the statue of Lincoln and the murals, memorial statistics,
       tourmobile service, administration.
    "Welcome to Washington." 28-fold. Description of attractions to
       see downtown and near Washington, D.C. such as the Kennedy
       Center, the Corcoran Gallery of Art, Clara Barton National
       Historic Site. Name of attractions, hours and other visitor in-
       formation, telephone. Maps, photos. General information sec-
       tion on camping, tourmobile sightseeing services, visitor infor-
       mation telephone numbers, picnic areas, recreation and sports,
       floral displays.

Suggested Curriculum Application:
    AMERICAN HISTORY
    DISTRICT OF COLUMBIA STATE AND LOCAL STUDIES
    GOVERNMENT

Suggested Sears Subject Heading:
    DISTRICT OF COLUMBIA--DESCRIPTION AND TRAVEL--GUIDES
    DISTRICT OF COLUMBIA--PUBLIC LANDS
    LINCOLN, ABRAHAM, 1809-1865
    PRESIDENTS--U.S.
    U.S.--DESCRIPTION AND TRAVEL--GUIDES

- **LYNDON B. JOHNSON**
National Historical Park. P.O. Box 329, Johnson City, TX   78636.
(512) 644-2252. 1,477.78 acres. 1969. Central Texas hill country
about 50 miles west of Austin. Two distinct areas compose the park
on U.S. 290: Johnson City and the LBJ Ranch.

Preserve the 36th president's birthplace, boyhood home, grand-
parents' ranch. Exhibits, programs. Living historical farm, outdoor
recreation, nature study, hiking trails, LBJ Ranch, boyhood home,
Johnson Settlement of restored historic structures, wildlife enclosures,
slide shows, self-guided walks, bus tours, guided tours. Visitor
center, picnic areas. Access to the LBJ Ranch is by tour bus only.

Free Print Material:
>"Johnson City." 6-fold. Map, photos, attractions, Johnson sites.
>"Lyndon B. Johnson." 16-fold. Johnson's family history, maps,
>photos, related sites, the hill country of Texas.
>"Lyndon B. Johnson State Historical Park." 6-fold. History,
>outstanding features, description and map. Nearby points of
>interest and recreational facilities.
>"Take Pride in America." 8-fold. Photos, national public aware-
>ness campaign to encourage everyone to take pride in the
>country's natural and cultural resources.
>"Visitor Hours." 1 page. Visitor information for Johnson City
>area, boyhood home, visitor center, Johnson Settlement, ranch
>bus tours, LBJ State Historical Park and LBJ Ranch area.
>Map, administration.

Suggested Curriculum Application:
>AMERICAN HISTORY
>GOVERNMENT
>TEXAS STATE AND LOCAL STUDIES

Suggested Sears Subject Heading:
>ARCHITECTURE--CONSERVATION AND RESTORATION
>JOHNSON, LYNDON B., 1908-1973
>PRESIDENTS--U.S.
>TEXAS--DESCRIPTION AND TRAVEL--GUIDES
>TEXAS--PUBLIC LANDS
>U.S.--DESCRIPTION AND TRAVEL--GUIDES

• MARTIN VAN BUREN
National Historic Site. P.O. Box 545, Kinderhook, NY 12106.
(518) 758-0689. 39.58 acres. 1974. Eastern New York, 25 miles
south of Albany off Rural Route 9H south of Kinderhook Village.

To commemorate the life and work of the eighth president of the
United States. Lindenwald, named after the linden trees on the
estate, was Van Buren's home from 1841 to 1862. Guided tours of
the home, self-guiding walks on the grounds. Advance group reservations are requested. Picnic tables located opposite the site.
Small towns nearby have food and lodging.

Free Print Material:
>"Martin Van Buren National Historic Site." 8-fold. Political and
>personal life of Van Buren, political chronology, photos, maps,
>development of Lindenwald, visitor information.

"Martin Van Buren Self-Guiding Tour." 8-fold. Guide is designed to introduce the visitor to various features of Van Buren's farmstead. Map and site descriptions help locate the features that have disappeared. Sketch of Van Buren.
"A Teacher's Guide to Martin Van Buren National Historic Site." 31 pages. Early life, political positions, contributions, activity suggestions, illustrations, puzzles, timetables, art work by 3rd and 4th graders.

Bibliography:
A one-page bibliography is included in "A Teacher's Guide to Martin Van Buren National Historic Site" described above.

Sales List:
"Order Form/Price List of Items Offered for Sale at Martin Van Buren National Historic Site." 1 page. Name of item and price, ordering information.
"The Complete Guide to America's National Parks." $7.95.

Suggested Curriculum Application:
AMERICAN HISTORY
GOVERNMENT
NEW YORK STATE AND LOCAL STUDIES

Suggested Sears Subject Heading:
ARCHITECTURE--CONSERVATION AND RESTORATION
NEW YORK--DESCRIPTION AND TRAVEL--GUIDES
NEW YORK--PUBLIC LANDS
PRESIDENTS--U.S.
U.S.--DESCRIPTION AND TRAVEL--GUIDES
VAN BUREN, MARTIN, 1782-1862

• PISCATAWAY PARK
National Capital Parks, East. 1900 Anacostia Drive, S.W., Washington, D.C. 20020. (301) 763-4600. 4,262.52 acres. 1961. Southern Maryland, about 10 miles south of Washington, D.C., accessible from the Capital Beltway exit 3-A.

Preserve the view of the Maryland shoreline as it would have been during the occupancy of Mount Vernon by George Washington. National Colonial Farm and Hard Bargain Farm tours, birdwatching. National Colonial Farm has a sales area in the gate house and Hard Bargain Farm has some publications for sale. Festivals, horseback riding. Picnicking, boat dock. Food and lodging in Oxon Hill, Washington, D.C.

Free Print Material:
"General Management Plan." 34 pages. Technical management document. Description of the park, park objectives and concerns, plan for land use and management, resources

management, visitor use and development, land protection, park operations, plan implementation. Appendix includes legislation. Folded maps. (When this plan was received it was indicated that the park had only a few remaining copies of the plan.)

Suggested Curriculum Application:
    AMERICAN GOVERNMENT
    MARYLAND STATE AND LOCAL STUDIES

Suggested Sears Subject Heading:
    LANDSCAPE PROTECTION
    MARYLAND--DESCRIPTION AND TRAVEL--GUIDES
    MARYLAND--PUBLIC LANDS
    U.S.--DESCRIPTION AND TRAVEL--GUIDES
    WASHINGTON, GEORGE, 1732-1799

• ROOSEVELT CAMPOBELLO
International Park. c/o Roosevelt Campobello, International Park Commission, P.O. Box 98, Lubec, ME 04652. (506) 752-2922. 2,721.50 acres. 1964. Island off eastern Maine, Canadian Island west of Nova Scotia. Main access is the Franklin D. Roosevelt Memorial Bridge at Lubec, ME. The Canadian address is: P.O. Box 9, Welshpool, New Brunswick E0G 3H0.

Cottage and the grounds where President Franklin D. Roosevelt spent summer vacations from 1883 to 1921 and where he was stricken with poliomyelitis when he was 39. The park is administered by a joint commission of three Canadian and three American members. Tour the Roosevelt cottage, Cranberry Point Drive, Eagle Hill Bog, Liberty Point Drive, Friar's Head, viewing areas, walking trails, beach. The park's reception center shows the films "Beloved Island" about the island and its impact on Roosevelt and "Campobello --the Outer Island" about the natural areas of the island and its shore. Picnicking. Camping nearby. Food and lodging on Campobello Island, Lubec area.

Free Print Material:
    "Roosevelt Campobello International Park." 6-fold. Photos, description of the park, map, visitor information.
    "Roosevelt Campobello International Park and Natural Area." 2 pages. Description, map of the natural area purchased by the park commission to protect the Roosevelt cottage and its surroundings.
    "Visitor Information." 1 page. Island visitor accommodations such as golf course, campgrounds, gift houses, theatre, guest houses and other information.

Suggested Curriculum Application:
    AMERICAN HISTORY
    GOVERNMENT

Suggested Sears Subject Heading:
CAMPOBELLO ISLAND
ISLANDS
ROOSEVELT, FRANKLIN D., 1882-1945
U.S.--DESCRIPTION AND TRAVEL--GUIDES

● SAGAMORE HILL
National Historic Site. Cove Neck Road, Box 304, Oyster Bay, NY
11771. (516) 922-4447. 78 acres. 1962. Southeastern New York,
on Cove Neck Road, 3 miles east of Oyster Bay.

Home of Theodore Roosevelt and used as the "Summer White House"
1901-08. Estate with original furnishings, Old Orchard Museum.
Meals and lodging on Long Island.

Free Print Material:
"Old Orchard Museum." 4-fold. When the museum was built, who
lived in it and when it was turned into a museum. Sketch.
"Sagamore Hill." 12-fold. Roosevelt family life, the home and its
furnishings, visitor tips, maps, photos.
"Sagamore Hill Welcomes You!" 4 pages. A room guide to the
home of Theodore Roosevelt covering the hall, library, drawing
room, dining room, the north room, piazza, and other floors.
"Theodore Roosevelt (1858-1919)." 1 page. Chronology of his
life and facts about his children and wives.

Suggested Curriculum Application:
AMERICAN HISTORY
GOVERNMENT
NEW YORK STATE AND LOCAL STUDIES

Suggested Sears Subject Heading:
ARCHITECTURE--CONSERVATION AND RESTORATION
NEW YORK--DESCRIPTION AND TRAVEL--GUIDES
NEW YORK--PUBLIC LANDS
PRESIDENTS--U.S.
ROOSEVELT, THEODORE, 1858-1919
U.S.--DESCRIPTION AND TRAVEL--GUIDES

● THEODORE ROOSEVELT
National Park. Medora, ND 58645. (701) 623-4466. 70,416.39
acres. 1947. Western North Dakota. The visitor center is about
7 miles east of Medora, off of I-94.

To remember Theodore Roosevelt's work as a conservationist. The
park includes part of his Elkhorn Ranch that he operated before be-
coming president, scenic badlands along the Little Missouri River.
Campfire programs, demonstrations, guided walks, trails for hiking
and horseback riding. Park consists of: North Unit, South Unit,

Elkhorn Ranch Site. Scenic drive from the entrance station to the Oxbow overlook with turnouts and interpretive signs at the North Unit, Squaw Creek Nature Trail, Achenbach Trail and other nature trails. The South Unit has a scenic loop road with interpretive signs; Scoria Point, Ridgeline Nature Trail, Peaceful Valley, Petrified Forest, trails, Wind Canyon Boicourt Overlook, Buck Hill and other attractions. Visitor centers, picnicking, campgrounds. Camping for organized groups is possible through a written reservation. Food and lodging nearby South and North units.

Free Print Material:
   "Buffalo." 2 pages. Name derivation, ancestors, habits, management today.
   "Checklist of Amphibians and Reptiles." 1 page. Common and scientific names of reptiles and amphibians.
   "Checklist of Flowering Plants." 2 pages. Family, common, scientific names. Sketch.
   "Checklist of Mammals." 2 pages. Family, common, scientific names of various mammals.
   "The Elkhorn Ranch Unit." 2 pages. Site that Roosevelt selected for his second ranch. Located 35 miles north of Medora, the ranch house was completed in 1885. Map, sketches.
   "Entrance and the User Fees." 1 page. Entrance fees and user fees, Golden Eagle Passport, Golden Age Passport, Golden Access Passport.
   "Frontier Fragments." 4 pages. Newspaper format. Articles, photos, sketches, maps about the national park areas in North Dakota.
   "Geology." 2 pages. Badlands past beginning during the Paleocene Epoch.
   "Little Missouri River Float Trips." 2 pages. Description and needs of float trips, visitor tips. Mileage chart, local guide services.
   "Prairie Dogs." 2 pages. Description, habits, prairie dog towns, diagram, photo.
   "Theodore Roosevelt National Park." 16-fold. What to see and do at the park, maps, photos, Roosevelt's activities as a cattle man in North Dakota.
   "Theodore Roosevelt Nature and History Association." Bookmark. Sketches. Memberships, purpose of the association, how you can help, address.

Sales List:
   "Maps Available." 1 page. Description of maps, scale, price, where to obtain.
   "Little Missouri National Grasslands." Displays federal, state, and private ownership; roads and trails; recreation sites and campgrounds; ranch locations. 1/2-1 mile. All federal lands open to public use. Cost $1.00. Available from: U.S. Forest Service, Route 3, Box 131-B, Dickinson, ND 58601.

Audiovisual List:

"Theodore Roosevelt National Park Film Library Guide." 20
pages. Films on: Roosevelt's life, conservation, wildlife,
other subjects. Also filmstrips, slides with cassette tape.
Also includes audiovisuals available from other sources.
Title, description, if black-and-white, running time for films.
Ordering directions. Sketches.

"Theodore Roosevelt." Shows vividly, with actual photographs
and movies, the life and times, successes and failures, of
Theodore Roosevelt, U.S. president and statesman. Narrated
by Mike Wallace. Black and white. 26 minutes.

Sales/Audiovisual List:

"Catalogue of Books and Other Interpretive Materials." 16 pages.
Sketches, map, order blank and ordering directions, aims of
the Theodore Roosevelt Nature and History Association and
benefits of membership. Arranged by: Theodore Roosevelt,
Western Americana, Fort Union, Natural History, Knife River,
children's corner, special interest books, art prints, Theodore
Roosevelt National Park, national parks, Upper Souris, animal
posters, scenic posters, post cards, antique documents,
topographic maps, maps, slide sets. Title, author, some include a descriptive phrase, price for publications.

"American Bears"--(hard cover). (Writings of Theodore Roosevelt.) $2.98.

Suggested Curriculum Application:

AMERICAN HISTORY
NATURAL HISTORY
NORTH DAKOTA STATE AND LOCAL STUDIES

Suggested Sears Subject Heading:

NATIONAL PARKS AND RESERVES--U.S.
NATURAL HISTORY--NORTH DAKOTA
NORTH DAKOTA--DESCRIPTION AND TRAVEL--GUIDES
NORTH DAKOTA--PUBLIC LANDS
PRESIDENTS--U.S.
RANCH LIFE
ROOSEVELT, THEODORE, 1858-1919
THEODORE ROOSEVELT NATIONAL PARK
U.S.--DESCRIPTION AND TRAVEL--GUIDES

• THEODORE ROOSEVELT BIRTHPLACE

National Historic Site. Manhattan Sites, 26 Wall St., New York,
NY 10005. (212) 260-1616. 0.11 acres. 1962. Eastern New York,
28 E. 20th Street, New York City.

Reconstructed house (includes museum and period rooms) where
Roosevelt was born in 1858. Guided tour of furnished home, museum,
movies, video tapes. Call to arrange for group visits. Meals and
lodging in New York City.

Free Print Material:
   "Following Teddy's Footsteps." 8-fold. A tour through Roose-
      velt's neighborhood when he was a boy. Sketches, map.
   "Sagamore Hill." 12-fold. Photos, maps, background regarding
      the house he built during 1884-1885.
   "Theodore Roosevelt Birthplace." 8-fold. Chronology of
      Roosevelt, family tree, Roosevelt's boyhood, what to see in
      the house, photos of inside and outside of the house.
   "Theodore Roosevelt Inaugural." 16-fold. Biographical back-
      ground on Roosevelt, photos, map.

Suggested Curriculum Application:
   AMERICAN HISTORY
   GOVERNMENT
   NEW YORK STATE AND LOCAL STUDIES

Suggested Sears Subject Heading:
   ARCHITECTURE--CONSERVATION AND RESTORATION
   NEW YORK--DESCRIPTION AND TRAVEL--GUIDES
   NEW YORK--PUBLIC LANDS
   PRESIDENTS--U.S.
   ROOSEVELT, THEODORE, 1858-1919
   U.S.--DESCRIPTION AND TRAVEL--GUIDES

● THEODORE ROOSEVELT INAUGURAL
National Historic Site. 641 Delaware Avenue, Buffalo, NY 14202.
(716) 884-0095. 1.03 acres. 1966. Western New York.

House where Theodore Roosevelt took the oath of office as president
in 1901 after President McKinley's assassination. The house is a
prime example of gothic revival architecture. Guided house tours.
Various educational tours aimed at grades 4-12 and adults are described in "Teachers' Guide" described below. Inquire about a cir-
culating book collection on Theodore Roosevelt and the presidency,
designed as a supplement to school and public library collections.
Inquire about 10,000-piece costume resource center in conjunction
with educational curriculum resources. Food and lodging in greater
Buffalo area.

Free Print Material:
   "Architectural Walking Tours." 1 page. Description of walking
      tours sponsored by the Theodore Roosevelt Inaugural National
      Historic Site. Fee and reservation information. Sketch.
   "Teachers' Guide." 14 pages. Educational programming, proper-
      ty history, events leading to the inauguration, description of
      the site, glossary, floor plan. Sketches.
   "Theodore Roosevelt Inaugural National Historic Site." 16-fold.
      Photos, map, the Ansley Wilcox House and its history, Roose-
      velt's inauguration in the house September 14, 1901.

"What Is the Rough Riders Association of the Theodore Roosevelt Inaugural Site Foundation?" Purpose of the association and what it does, advantages of membership. Sketches, membership application.

Audiovisual List:
  Description of audiovisuals included in "Teachers' Guide" described above.

Suggested Curriculum Application:
  AMERICAN HISTORY
  ART
  CLOTHING
  GOVERNMENT
  NEW YORK STATE AND LOCAL STUDIES

Suggested Sears Subject Heading:
  ARCHITECTURE--CONSERVATION AND RESTORATION
  NEW YORK--DESCRIPTION AND TRAVEL--GUIDES
  NEW YORK--PUBLIC LANDS
  PRESIDENTS--U.S.
  ROOSEVELT, THEODORE, 1858-1919
  U.S.--DESCRIPTION AND TRAVEL--GUIDES

• THEODORE ROOSEVELT ISLAND
c/o George Washington Memorial Parkway, Turkey Run Park, McLean, VA 22101. (202) 285-2601. 88.50 acres. 1932. In Potomac River in Washington, D.C., across from the Kennedy Center. Parking area may be reached from northbound lanes of George Washington Memorial Parkway on Potomac's Virginia side. Footbridge connects island to Virginia shore.

Eighty-eight acres of wilderness preserve memorializes President Theodore Roosevelt's contribution to conservation. Tours, interpretive programs, memorial with statue, self-guiding trails, wildlife. Food and lodging in Washington, D.C.

Free Print Material:
  "Theodore Roosevelt Island." 10-fold. History of the island; quotations on nature, manhood, youth, the state by Theodore Roosevelt; map; natural history of the island; visitor information.
  "Welcome to Washington." 28-fold. Maps, photos, description of attractions in the city and within a day's reach. Includes name of attraction, road directions, hours, telephone. Visitor information about camping, picnic areas, recreation and sports, floral displays, tourmobile sightseeing services, visitor information telephones.

Suggested Curriculum Application:
AMERICAN HISTORY
DISTRICT OF COLUMBIA STUDIES

Suggested Sears Subject Heading:
DISTRICT OF COLUMBIA--DESCRIPTION AND TRAVEL--GUIDES
DISTRICT OF COLUMBIA--PUBLIC LANDS
ISLANDS
NATURE CONSERVATION
PRESIDENTS--U.S.
ROOSEVELT, THEODORE, 1858-1919
THEODORE ROOSEVELT ISLAND
U.S.--DESCRIPTION AND TRAVEL--GUIDES

- THOMAS JEFFERSON MEMORIAL
c/o National Capital Region, 1100 Ohio Drive, SW, Washington,
D.C. 20242. (202) 426-6841. 18.36 acres. 1934. District of
Columbia, Washington, D.C., south bank of Tidal Basin on a line
with the south axis of the White House.

Memorial to Thomas Jefferson, chosen by his colleagues to draft
the Declaration of Independence and president of the United States
1801-1809. Circular colonnaded structure in the simple classic style
admired by Jefferson, 19-foot-high bronze statue, interior walls
have four carved excerpts from Jefferson's writings. Interpretive
services. Surrounding the memorial and the Tidal Basin are cherry
trees presented by the city of Tokyo in 1912. Ramp and interior
elevator are provided for the handicapped. Food and lodging in
Washington, D.C.

Free Print Material:
"Thomas Jefferson Memorial." 10-fold. Photos, quotations by
Jefferson, memorial site, description of the memorial building,
what writings are engraved on the four panels, accomplishments of Jefferson, Oriental flowering cherry trees, construction of the memorial, tourmobile service, administration.
"Welcome to Washington." 28-fold. What to see and do in downtown and in nearby Washington, D.C., such as the Library of
Congress, the Mall, Prince William Forest Park. Name of attraction, hours and other visitor information, telephone.
Maps, photos. General information section on floral displays,
recreation and sports, picnic areas, visitor information telephone numbers, tourmobile sightseeing services, camping.

Suggested Curriculum Application:
AMERICAN HISTORY
DISTRICT OF COLUMBIA STUDIES
GOVERNMENT

Suggested Sears Subject Heading:
DISTRICT OF COLUMBIA--DESCRIPTION AND TRAVEL--GUIDES

DISTRICT OF COLUMBIA--PUBLIC LANDS
JEFFERSON, THOMAS, 1743-1826
PRESIDENTS--U.S.
U.S.--DESCRIPTION AND TRAVEL--GUIDES

• WASHINGTON MONUMENT
c/o National Capital Region, National Park Service, 1100 Ohio Drive,
SW, Washington, D.C. 20242. (202) 426-6841. 106.01 acres.
1848. District of Columbia, Constitution Avenue at 15th Street, N.W.

Monument to honor George Washington, the first president. By
using the 898 steps visitors can see the 190 memorial stones donated
by local, state and foreign governments. The 555-foot, 5-1/8 inch
obelisk was opened to the public in 1888. The "ring" that is notice-
able on the shaft results from a different stratum of Maryland marble
used to complete the monument when work was resumed in 1880 after
ceasing in 1854. Inclined pathways from the parking lot and 15th
Street lead to the entrance and elevator. Food and lodging in
Washington, D.C.

Free Print Material:
"The Washington Monument." 8-fold. Monument construction in
intervals between 1848 and 1885, statistics, tourmobile service,
administration, biographical sketch of George Washington during the Revolutionary War and as president and retirement,
quotation of Washington, photo, type of marble used in the
monument.
"Welcome to Washington." 28-fold. Description of attractions to
see downtown and near Washington, D.C. such as Ford's
Theatre, the Corcoran Gallery of Art, Clara Barton National
Historic Site. Name of attraction, hours and other visitor information, telephone. Maps, photos. General information section on: camping, tourmobile sightseeing services, visitor
information telephone numbers, picnic areas, recreation and
sports, floral displays.

Suggested Curriculum Application:
AMERICAN HISTORY
DISTRICT OF COLUMBIA STUDIES
GOVERNMENT

Suggested Sears Subject Heading:
DISTRICT OF COLUMBIA--DESCRIPTION AND TRAVEL--GUIDES
DISTRICT OF COLUMBIA--PUBLIC LANDS
PRESIDENTS--U.S.
U.S.--DESCRIPTION AND TRAVEL--GUIDES
WASHINGTON, GEORGE, 1732-1799

• WHITE HOUSE
c/o National Capital Region, National Park Service, 1100 Ohio Drive,

SW, Washington, D.C.   20242.   (202) 456-7041.   18.07 acres.
Occupied since 1800; transferred to the National Park Service in
1933.   District of Columbia, 1600 Pennsylvania Avenue N.W.,
Washington, D.C.

Residence and office of the United States presidents, national museum.   The library, the vermeil room, the china room, the diplomatic
reception room, the state floor, the east room, the green room, the
blue room, the red room, the state dining room, lobby and cross
hall, gardens, grounds, commemorative plantings.   Tours from 10 a.m.
to 12 noon, Tuesday through Saturday.   Food and lodging in Washington, D.C.

Free Print Material:
  "The White House."   10-fold.   Sketches, photo, description of
    various rooms such as the red room, the library.   History,
    improvements, renovation, tour information.   Address to ob-
    tain more information: White House Historical Association,
    740 Jackson Place, NW, Washington, D.C.   20506.
  "The White House."   32 pages.   Photos, history, description of
    rooms, chronology of presidents, presidential activities.
  "The White House Gardens and Grounds."   22 pages.   Key plant-
    ings, garden ornaments, seasonal plantings, herbs and peren-
    nials in the east and west gardens in spring, summer, fall.
    Fold-out includes list and map of commemorative plantings since
    Thomas Jefferson.   Sketches.

Suggested Curriculum Application:
  AMERICAN HISTORY
  DISTRICT OF COLUMBIA LOCAL STUDIES
  GOVERNMENT

Suggested Sears Subject Heading:
  ARCHITECTURE--CONSERVATION AND RESTORATION
  DISTRICT OF COLUMBIA--DESCRIPTION AND TRAVEL--GUIDES
  DISTRICT OF COLUMBIA--PUBLIC LANDS
  PRESIDENTS--U.S.
  U.S.--DESCRIPTION AND TRAVEL--GUIDES
  WHITE HOUSE

• WILLIAM HOWARD TAFT
National Historic Site, 2038 Auburn Ave., Cincinnati, OH   45219.
(513) 684-3262.   3.07 acres.   1969.   Southwestern Ohio.

Preserve the birthplace and boyhood home of President Taft.
Historic home is being restored.   Food and lodging in Cincinnati.

Free Print Material:
  "Historic Auburn Avenue."   12-fold.   Photos, sketches, map,
    description of historic buildings on Auburn avenue.
  "William Howard Taft."   16-fold.   Biographical survey, photo, map.

Sales List:
"William Howard Taft National Historic Site-Publications and Related Products." 2 pages. Grouped by books, theme related
products, postcards.
"The Complete Guide to America's National Parks." $7.95. The
official visitor's guide to the National Park System includes
hours, services offered, addresses, and telephone numbers.
291 pages. Paperback.

Suggested Curriculum Application:
AMERICAN HISTORY
GOVERNMENT
OHIO STATE AND LOCAL STUDIES

Suggested Sears Subject Heading:
ARCHITECTURE--CONSERVATION AND RESTORATION
OHIO--DESCRIPTION AND TRAVEL--GUIDES
OHIO--PUBLIC LANDS
PRESIDENTS--U.S.
TAFT, WILLIAM HOWARD, 1857-1930
U.S.--DESCRIPTION AND TRAVEL--GUIDES

RAILROADS

- ALLEGHENY PORTAGE RAILROAD
National Historic Site. P.O. Box 247, Cresson, PA 16630.
(814) 886-8177. 1,134.91 acres. 1964. Central Pennsylvania, in
Blair and Cambria counties, U.S. 22, two miles east of Cresson.

Preserve and interpret the remains of the Allegheny Portage Railroad
built 1831-34 to carry passengers and cargoes of Pennsylvania Canal
boats over the Allegheny Mountains. The railroad was an inclined
plane railway system and allowed continuous transportation between
Philadelphia and Pittsburgh, serving in westward expansion.
Lemon House, rail planes, slide program, exhibits, ranger-conducted
interpretive programs, stone culverts, stone railroad ties, excavated
engine house foundations, Skew Arch bridge, Staple Bend Tunnel,
interpretive trails. Visitor center, picnicking. Food and lodging
in Cresson.

Free Print Material:
"The Allegheny Old Portage Railroad." 90 pages. A publication
commemorating a banquet and meeting at the Summit Mansion
House of the Sons of the American Revolution includes re-
prints, a reproduction of the Summit Mansion House register
for the month of June, 1852 that includes name of guest,

place of residence and destination. Charts, bibliography.

"Allegheny Portage Railroad." 24-fold. Photos, diagram, sketches, maps, history, description and construction of the portage railroad. Visitor information.

"The Lemon House." 4 pages. Biographical sketch of the Lemon family, why the house was constructed, its demise in the 1850's as a tavern and eatery. Sketch, map. It now serves as the visitor center.

"Profile of Old Allegheny Portage Railroad." 1 page. Charts, diagram, statistics.

"Sylvester Welch's Report on the Allegheny Portage Railroad." 22 pages. Report in 1833 to the superintendent of the western division of the Pennsylvania Canal and Allegheny Portage Railroad. Photos, sketches, bibliography, 6-fold pull-out pages include diagrams of the engine house, map.

"Trace Tracker ... for the Trails of Allegheny Portage Railroad National Historical Site." 32 pages. Numbered paragraphs correspond to the numbered posts on trails, sketches.

Bibliography:
Included in "The Allegheny Old Portage Railroad" and "Sylvester Welch's Report on the Allegheny Portage Railroad" described above. Both include: author, title, publisher, date, pages, annotation.

Audiovisual List:
Inquire about the 12-minute 16mm film on the Allegheny Portage Railroad and the Pennsylvania Mainline Canal which is loaned out for classroom use.

Sales/Audiovisual List:
"Allegheny Portage Railroad National Historic Site Sales List." 4 pages. Publications, notecards, cachet envelopes, slides, post cards, cookbook, coloring book. Title, author, date, price, some include annotations. Ordering directions.

"The Old Portage Railroad 1834-1854." Floyd G. Hoenstine and Mahlone J. Baumgardner, 1952. (Reprinted articles, ceremonies, sketches and other documents.) $5.00.

Suggested Curriculum Application:
AMERICAN HISTORY
PENNSYLVANIA STATE AND LOCAL STUDIES

Suggested Sears Subject Heading:
ALLEGHENY PORTAGE RAILROAD
PENNSYLVANIA--DESCRIPTION AND TRAVEL--GUIDES
PENNSYLVANIA--HISTORY
PENNSYLVANIA--PUBLIC LANDS
RAILROADS--PENNSYLVANIA
U.S.--DESCRIPTION AND TRAVEL--GUIDES

- GOLDEN SPIKE

National Historic Site, P.O. Box W, Brigham City, UT   84302.
(801) 471-2209.   2,735.28 acres.   National historic site nonfederal
ownership, 1957; National historic site for federal ownership, 1965.
Northcentral Utah, 32 miles west of Brigham City, UT, west on
Utah 83 and seven miles beyond Promontory Junction.

Site of the joining of the country's first transcontinental railroad.
In 1869 the Union Pacific and Central Pacific railroads met, joining
1,800 miles of railway from Sacramento to Omaha.   Interpretive
programs, slide presentation and movie, museum of railroad memorabilia, working replicas of the "Jupiter" and the "119" steam engines
are displayed May through September.   Visitor center, picnicking,
snack and beverage machines. Campgrounds nearby. Food and
lodging in Brigham City and Tremonton.

Free Print Material:
   "Golden Spike."   24-fold. Importance of rails coast to coast,
      origin of the Central Pacific, financing the railroad, construc-
      tion difficulties, the field organization, the great race to
      finish, the ceremony. Maps, illustrations, photos.
   "The Last Spikes." 2 pages. Description of the two gold, one
      silver, and one of gold and silver plated iron that were
      slipped into pre-drilled holes in a laurelwood crosstie and
      tapped with a silver-plated maul to signal the completion of
      the railroad. What happened to the spikes and tie after the
      ceremony. Sketches.
   "Utah National Parks and Monuments." 24-fold. Descriptions,
      photos of national monuments, national recreation areas,
      national historic site, national parks. Map, fees. Tempera-
      tures.

Audiovisual List:
   "Films Available on Free Loan--16mm." 1 page. Title, running
      length, color, description. Use of school stationery is re-
      quested.
   "The Golden Spike." 20 minutes. Color. Story of building of
      railroad.

Sales/Audiovisual List:
   "Golden Spike Sales List." 2 pages. Grouped by: railroad
      books, general history, geography, natural history, children's
      books, post cards, posters and prints, maps, rail memorabilia.
      Ordering information and aims of the Southwest Parks and
      Monuments Association. Books include title, author, date,
      pages, price, weight. Rail memorabilia includes steam sounds
      cassette, centennial gold medallion, Central Pacific baggage
      check reproduction, and various watchfobs.
   "American Locomotive Builders." White. 1982, 112 pages,
      $11.95, 9 ounces.

Suggested Curriculum Application:
    AMERICAN HISTORY
    SOCIAL STUDIES
    UTAH STATE AND LOCAL STUDIES

Suggested Sears Subject Heading:
    CENTRAL PACIFIC RAILROAD
    RAILROADS
    UNION PACIFIC RAILROAD
    U.S.--DESCRIPTION AND TRAVEL--GUIDES
    U.S.--HISTORY--1865-1898
    UTAH--DESCRIPTION AND TRAVEL--GUIDES
    UTAH--PUBLIC LANDS

RECREATION

- ALAGNAK

Wild River. c/o Katmai National Park and Preserve, P.O. Box 7,
King Salmon, AK 99613. (907) 246-3305. 24,038 acres. 1980.
Southern Alaska, scheduled airlines to King Salmon, charter flights
to the source of the Alagnak, Kukaklek Lake. Parts of the river
lie outside of Katmai National Park and Preserve.

Offers 69 miles of white-water floating, wildlife. Upper river is
rocky and moderately swift while lower down it slows for leisurely
floats through tundra. Accommodations at Brooks River Lodge and
Lake Grosvenor.

Free Print Material:
    "About Brown Bears...." 2 pages. Habits of bears, life cycle,
        safety tips.
    "Katmai." 24-fold. Photos, maps, weather, regulations and
        boating safety, wildlife, volcanics.

Sales/Audiovisual List:
    "Alaska Natural History Association Mail Order Catalog." 8 pages.
        Print and non-print sales items. Grouped by such sources as
        the Sitka National Historical Park, Denali National Park, and
        others. Sketches, aims of the Alaska Natural History Associa-
        tion, order blank, ordering instructions.
    "Alaska National Parklands: This Last Treasure." Brown. Hard
        $16.95. Soft $5.95. 128 pages, full-color publication describ-
        ing the national significance of all National Park Service areas
        in Alaska by means of a narrative by Brown and short writings
        by individuals....

Suggested Curriculum Application:
ALASKA STATE AND LOCAL STUDIES
RECREATION

Suggested Sears Subject Heading:
ALAGNAK WILD RIVER
ALASKA--DESCRIPTION AND TRAVEL--GUIDES
ALASKA--PUBLIC LANDS
CANOES AND CANOEING
OUTDOOR RECREATION
RIVERS
U.S.--DESCRIPTION AND TRAVEL--GUIDES
WILDERNESS AREAS

• AMISTAD
Recreation Area. U.S. Highway 90 West, Del Rio, TX 78840.
(512) 775-7491. 57,292.44 acres. 1965. Southern Texas, on the
United States-Mexican border, 12 miles from Del Rio, TX.

Cooperative recreation area with Mexico that provides general outdoor
enjoyment. Nature trail, amphitheater, lake with four main arms and
many coves, outdoor sports. Visitor center, campground, picnic
area. Food and lodging in Del Rio and along U.S. 90.

Free Print Material:
"Amistad." 20-fold. Photo, maps, what you can do at Amistad,
the Amistad Dam and Reservoir, safety tips.
"Delightful Del Rio, Amistad Lake, Ciudad Acuna." 24-fold.
Features, points of interest, photos, maps.
"For Your Information." 12-fold. History, population, border,
climate, Lake Amistad, tours and other information for the
visitor, climatological summary chart, Amistad Dam and Reservoir statistics.
"Take Pride in America." 8-fold. Campaign to encourage
everyone to take pride in the nation's natural and cultural
resources, photos.
"United States Department of the Interior, National Park Service,
Amistad Recreation Area." 2 pages. Regulations regarding
camping use, designated activity areas.
"Welcome to Amistad Lake." 2 pages. Boating, swimming, scuba
diving safety as well as tips about the cliffs area, abandoned
railroad, weather and alcohol use.

Suggested Curriculum Application:
RECREATION
TEXAS STATE AND LOCAL STUDIES

Suggested Sears Subject Heading:
AMISTAD LAKE
OUTDOOR RECREATION

TEXAS--DESCRIPTION AND TRAVEL--GUIDES
TEXAS--PUBLIC LANDS
U.S.--DESCRIPTION AND TRAVEL--GUIDES

● BIG SOUTH FORK
National River and Recreation Area. P.O. Drawer 630, Oneida, TN
37841. (615) 569-6389. 122,960 acres. 1974. Cumberland Plateau
bisected by Big South Fork of Cumberland River in south central
Kentucky, north central Tennessee. Between U.S. 27 and 127, 75
miles northwest of Knoxville, TN.

Recreational scenic route of calm and rough waters through gorges,
natural arches, waterfalls, diverse hardwood and coniferous forests,
valleys, variety of natural and historical features. Hiking, horseback riding, overlooks, canoeing, rafting, birdwatching. Visitor
center, ranger station, campground, picnicking. Food and lodging
in Oneida and Jamestown, TN, and Whitney City, KY.

Free Print Material:
"Big South Fork." 24-fold. Photos, map, description, develop-
ment. General travel tips, recreational activities.
"Big South Fork Streams and Trails." 8-fold. Photos, map.
Includes John Muir National Historic Trail, hiking trails,
horse trails, surface roads, gravel and unsurfaced roads.
"Brandy Creek." 2 pages. Camping information, regulations,
map.
"Horseback Riding." 1 page. Trails, camping, emergency information. Sketch.
"Litter-ally Speaking...." 2 pages. Cost of litter to the taxpayer, tips on preventing littering.
"Paddling the Gorge." 8-fold. Safety, hypothermia, paddlers'
schedule, whitewater rating definitions, map, trip registration form, photo.
"Take Pride in America." 8-fold. Campaign to encourage everyone to take pride in the nation's natural and cultural resources. Photos.

Suggested Curriculum Application:
KENTUCKY STATE AND LOCAL STUDIES
RECREATION
TENNESSEE STATE AND LOCAL STUDIES

Suggested Sears Subject Heading:
BIG SOUTH FORK RIVER
KENTUCKY--DESCRIPTION AND TRAVEL--GUIDES
KENTUCKY--PUBLIC LANDS
OUTDOOR RECREATION
RIVERS
TENNESSEE--DESCRIPTION AND TRAVEL--GUIDES
TENNESSEE--PUBLIC LANDS
U.S.--DESCRIPTION AND TRAVEL--GUIDES

- BUFFALO

National River. P.O. Box 1173, Harrison, AR 72601.
(501) 741-5443. 94,221.08 acres. 1972. Northcentral Arkansas,
17 miles south of Yellville, off AR 14.

Preserve one of the few remaining unpolluted rivers running through
bluffs, springs along its 132-mile wilderness course. Around 1,000
flowering plants, bluffs up to 500 feet, 200-foot waterfall, wilderness, guided hikes, canoe trips, demonstrations of Ozark crafts
and folk music, programs. Ranger stations, cabins, campgrounds,
restaurants. Food and lodging available in Harrison, Jasper and
other area communities.

Free Print Material:
"Backpacking and Wilderness Hiking at Buffalo River." 2 pages.
Wilderness area hiking, creek hiking, backpacking. Recommended techniques, safety and regulation tips.
"Buffalo River." 16-fold. Features, activities, photos, map,
visitor safety.
"Buffalo National River Currents." 16 pages. Articles for the
visitor, river mileages and levels, things to see, accommodations, trails, wildlife and other helps to enjoying the river.
"Dayhikes at Buffalo River." 8-fold. Name and description of
various trails, safety tips, regulations, where to obtain maps,
sketches.
"Survive the Buffalo River." 2 pages. Safety tips for swimming,
diving, canoeing, camping, cliffs and caves, thunderstorms and
other weather conditions.

Sales List:
"Buffalo National River Sales List." 1 page. Publications grouped
by: rivers, Ozarks, U.S. Geological Survey maps, hiking and
trail guides, field guides, national parks, flora and fauna, for
children, etc.
"Basic River Canoeing." $5.50.

Suggested Curriculum Application:
ARKANSAS STATE AND LOCAL STUDIES
GEOGRAPHY
RECREATION

Suggested Sears Subject Heading:
ARKANSAS--DESCRIPTION AND TRAVEL--GUIDES
ARKANSAS--PUBLIC LANDS
BUFFALO RIVER
OUTDOOR RECREATION
RIVERS
U.S.--DESCRIPTION AND TRAVEL--GUIDES
WILDERNESS AREAS

• CHATTAHOOCHEE RIVER
National Recreation Area. 1900 Northridge Road, Dunwoody, GA
30338. (404) 394-8325. 8,699.69 acres. 1978. Northcentral
Georgia off of Interstate 285 within the counties of Cobb, Fulton,
and Gwinnett.

Preserve and protect the national, scenic, recreation, historic, and
other values of a 48-mile segment of the Chattahoochee River and
certain adjoining lands from Buford Dam downstream to Peachtree
Creek. Boating, horseback riding, guided environmental walks,
trails, wildlife, historic structures and ruins, Palisades Unit,
Cochran Shoals Unit, Sope Creek Unit, Gold Branch Unit, Vickery
Creek Unit, Island Ford Unit. Ranger stations, picnicking. Food
and lodging in Atlanta.

Free Print Material:
  "The Chattahoochee Outdoor Center Information Sheet." 2 pages.
    Park concessionaire points of rental, take out points, safety
    tips, float times, operation hours, rental rates and other user
    information, map.
  "Chattahoochee River." 12-fold. Photos, maps, public access
    points chart, regulations, river safety tips. Description of
    such units as the Palisades Unit and others.
  "Chattahoochee River Guide: Buford Dam to Why. 20 Bridge."
    8-fold. River safety tips, telephone emergency numbers,
    facilities, map, sketch.
  "Golden Eagle, Golden Age, Golden Access Passports." 10-fold.
    Federal recreation fee program for persons under 62, 62 and
    older, for the blind and disabled person. Address of the
    National Park Service and other federal agencies.
  "Southeast National Parks and National Forests." 16-fold.
    Photos, map. Chart of national parks and national forests for
    Alabama, Arkansas, Florida, Georgia, Kentucky, Louisiana,
    Mississippi, North Carolina, South Carolina, Tennessee. Chart
    includes name, address, telephone and attractions.

Suggested Curriculum Application:
  GEORGIA STATE AND LOCAL STUDIES
  RECREATION

Suggested Sears Subject Heading:
  CHATTAHOOCHEE RIVER
  GEORGIA--DESCRIPTION AND TRAVEL--GUIDES
  GEORGIA--PUBLIC LANDS
  OUTDOOR RECREATION
  RIVERS
  U.S.--DESCRIPTION AND TRAVEL--GUIDES

• COULEE DAM
National Recreation Area. Box 37, Coulee Dam, WA   99116.

(509) 633-0881. 100,390.31 acres. 1946. Central Washington, headquarters on Columbia River, U.S. 2 to Wilbur, Wash. 174 to Coulee Dam.

Recreational lake area formed by Grand Coulee Dam. Special events, programs, activities, scenic roads, self-guiding trails around remaining buildings and foundations of Fort Spokane, scenic drives, water skiing, dam tours, boating, swimming. Visitor centers, campgrounds, boat dock and ramp, lifeguarded swim beach, picnic area, ferry service. Meals and lodging at Coulee Dam, Kettle Falls.

Free Print Material:
   "Boating on Lake Roosevelt." 1 page. Tips for boaters as to what to expect, description of charts and how to obtain them.
   "Camping in the Coulee Dam National Recreation Area." 2 pages. Coulee Dam district, Kettle Falls district, Fort Spokane district information, definition of campground types, chart of parks and campgrounds.
   "Coulee Dam." 24-fold. Land and water activities, a fishing primer, boating safety, chart of recreation area services, maps, photos.
   "Coulee Dam National Recreation Area Flora and Fauna." 1 page. Description of sagebrush, lichens, cheat grass and others.
   "Grand Coulee Dam Area Visitor Information and Area Map." 8-fold. Things to see and do, map, list of businesses.
   "Liquid Power." 2 pages. History, power of the Grand Coulee Dam. Spillway floodlighting program running during the summer, time schedule, color patterns.
   "Water in Action." 24 pages. Origin of Lake Roosevelt, how it serves the region. Map, chart, photos. Addresses and phone numbers to obtain more information from the U.S. Army Corps of Engineers, the U.S. Bureau of Reclamation and others.
   "Weeds of Eastern Washington." 1 page. Different families such as the pink family, the sunflower family, mustard family and others. Quick guide for identification. Suggests book and where it may be obtained.

Suggested Curriculum Application:
   GEOGRAPHY
   RECREATION
   SOCIAL STUDIES
   WASHINGTON STATE AND LOCAL STUDIES

Suggested Sears Subject Heading:
   COULEE DAM
   DAMS
   LAKE ROOSEVELT
   LAKES
   OUTDOOR RECREATION
   WASHINGTON--DESCRIPTION AND TRAVEL--GUIDES

WASHINGTON--PUBLIC LANDS
U.S.--DESCRIPTION AND TRAVEL--GUIDES

• CURECANTI
National Recreation Area. 102 Elk Creek, Gunnison, CO 81230.
(303) 641-2337. 42,114.47 acres. 1965. Central Colorado, Elk
Creek visitor center is 16 miles west of Gunnison on U.S. 50.

Blue Mesa Lake, Morrow Point Lake, Crystal Lake extends 40 miles
along the Gunnison River offering recreational opportunities. Boat
tours, scenic drives, birdwatching, cross-country skiing, snowmobiling, hiking, horseback riding, Morrow Point Dam Powerplant
tour, Pioneer Point, Cimarron Railroad exhibit, Gunnison Diversion
Tunnel, water, canyons, mesas, ranger-led walks and nature talks,
boating, windsurfing, exhibits, slide/tape program. Visitor center,
campgrounds, picnicking, marinas offer grocery store, boat rentals,
guide service, slips, showers. Restaurant at Elk Creek.

Free Print Material:
  "Boat-In Camping." 7 pages. Descriptions of facilities, regula-
    tions, visitor tips, maps.
  "Boating." 1 page. Safety checklist, emergency information,
    staying afloat on the lower lakes, enjoying Blue Mesa Lake.
  "Cimarron Canyon Exhibit." 4 pages. Terminology guide key
    sheet, sketches.
  "Camping." 1 page. Chart of major facilities, description of
    limited facilities.
  "Colorado Campground and Recreational Map and Facilities Chart."
    24-fold. Map, sketches, chart.
  "Cross Country Skiing." 1 page. Trails, safety, list of items
    for a survival pack.
  "Curecanti Official Map and Guide." 16-fold. Activities, pro-
    grams and services, boating and water safety, history, winter
    sports, photos, maps, illustrations.
  "The Gunnison Tunnel." 1 page. Exploration of the canyon and
    the beginning in 1904 of the construction of the Gunnison
    Diversion Tunnel.
  "Hiking." 1 page. Names, locations, descriptions of various
    hiking trails.
  "Information Sheet: Blue Mesa Dam and Powerplant, Blue Mesa
    Reservoir." 2 pages. Statistics such as dimensions, cost,
    first power generation, generating units.
  "Morrow Point Dam and Powerplant." 2 pages. Statistics to
    answer the most frequently asked questions. Map.
  "Narrow Gauge Railroad." 2 pages. Description of the railroad,
    history of the Cimarron area.
  "Scuba Diving." 2 pages. Regulations, depth charts, diving
    hazards, favorite diving areas.
  "Snowmobiling." 1 page. Safe loads on ice, regulations, hazards
    to watch out for.

Sales/Audiovisual List:
"Price List for Sales Items." 4 pages. Arranged by: Astronomy, birds, children's books, cookbooks, fishing, plants, geology, golden guides, history, maps, guides, post cards, posters, safety, miscellaneous items (slide set, calendar, note cards). Title, price. Purpose of the Southwest Parks and Monuments Association, mailing instructions.
"Field Guide to the Stars and Planets." $12.95.

Suggested Curriculum Application:
COLORADO STATE AND LOCAL STUDIES
GEOGRAPHY
RECREATION

Suggested Sears Subject Heading:
BLUE MESA LAKE
COLORADO--DESCRIPTION AND TRAVEL--GUIDES
COLORADO--PUBLIC LANDS
CRYSTAL LAKE
LAKES
MORROW POINT LAKE
OUTDOOR RECREATION
U.S.--DESCRIPTION AND TRAVEL--GUIDES
U.S.--GEOGRAPHY

• DELAWARE WATER GAP
National Recreation Area. Bushkill, PA 18324. (717) 588-6637. 66,696.97 acres. 1965. Eastern Pennsylvania and western New Jersey, visitor center is off U.S. 209, Int. 80 crosses the gap.

Preserve scenic Delaware River area on both the New Jersey and Pennsylvania sides in the famous gap in the Appalachian Mountains. Wildlife and bird watching, boating, scenic road trips, Peters Valley Craft Village, Millbrook Village, Pocono Environmental Education Center, hiking trails, ranger-conducted activities, Walpack Valley Environmental Education Center, guided canoe programs. Visitor centers, camping. Food and lodging in Bushkill.

Free Print Material:
"Canoeing and Boating on the Delaware River." 8-fold. River safety such as what to do if you capsize, types of life jackets.
"Delaware Water Gap." 12-fold. Features, things to do and see, map, photos.
"Hiking Trails." 8-fold. Description of 13 trails, camping for hikers, map, tips for hikers.
"Millbrook Village." 6-fold. What to see, map. A self-guiding tour of the century-old village.
"Spanning the Gap." 4 pages. Guide published for the Delaware Water Gap National Recreation Area, published three times a year. Schedule of activities, photos, maps, articles for visitors.

Suggested Curriculum Application:
ENVIRONMENTAL EDUCATION
GEOGRAPHY
PENNSYLVANIA STATE AND LOCAL STUDIES
RECREATION

Suggested Sears Subject Heading:
DELAWARE RIVER
NEW JERSEY--DESCRIPTION AND TRAVEL--GUIDES
NEW JERSEY--PUBLIC LANDS
OUTDOOR RECREATION
PENNSYLVANIA--DESCRIPTION AND TRAVEL--GUIDES
PENNSYLVANIA--PUBLIC LANDS
U.S.--DESCRIPTION AND TRAVEL--GUIDES

• GLEN CANYON
National Recreation Area. P.O. Box 1507, Page, AZ 86040.
(602) 745-2471. 1,236,880 acres. 1972. Northern Arizona, the
northern end of Glen Canyon can be seen from Utah 95.

Preserve recreational facilities and scenery of the Glen Canyon
area. Formed by the Colorado River, Lake Powell stretches for
186 miles behind one of the world's highest dams. Self-guiding
tours of Glen Canyon Dam, hiking, Lees Ferry, boat trips, water
sports. Visitor center, picnic tables, launching ramps, landing
strips, campgrounds. Food and lodging at developed areas on the
lake.

Free Print Material:
"Anasazi." 2 pages. Importance of protecting archeological re-
sources. What to do if you observe someone vandalizing or
removing antiquities, penalties, sketch.
"The Geology of Glen Canyon National Recreation Area." 3 pages.
Introduction, stratigraphy, development of today's scenery.
"Glen Canyon Dam and National Recreation Area." 24-fold.
Places to see, history, natural history, regulations and safety,
water sports and safety, facilities, map, photos.
"Glen Canyon Plant Life." 6 pages. Description of names of
plants of: streamside community, terrace community, hillside
community, hanging garden community, upper Sonora zone.
Suggested reading, typical transect of vegetation.
"History of Lee's Ferry." 4 pages. Corridor between Utah and
Arizona. Early explorers and efforts of Lee, one of Utah's
great pioneers. Suggested reading, map of historic sites of
Lee's Ferry.
"Lake Powell Weather and Lake Elevation." 1 page. 12-month
chart covering average and record: maximum temperature,
minimum temperature, precipitation, lake surface water temperature, wind. Also the surface elevation of lake beginning with
1963.

"1776 and Glen Canyon." 4 pages. Explorations of two Franciscan fathers and quotations of their exploration. Suggested reading, map of the Dominguez and Escalante 1776 Trail through Glen Canyon.

"Walking Softly in the Desert." 6-fold. A guide to low-impact camping, sketches.

Audiovisual List:

Inquire about "Adventure in Glen Canyon" about the dam and lake, and "Operation Glen Canyon" about the construction of the dam. These films are loaned out and requests/inquiries should be sent to: Film Management Center, Bureau of Reclamation, Building 67, Denver Federal Center, Denver, CO 80225.

Sales/Audiovisual List:

"The Glen Canyon Natural History Association Sales List." 2 pages. Grouped by: children, general information, history, national parks, Native American culture, natural history, video tapes, recreation. Ordering information.

"Animal Friends of the SW." $2.00.

Suggested Curriculum Application:

ARIZONA STATE AND LOCAL STUDIES
GEOGRAPHY
RECREATION

Suggested Sears Subject Heading:

ARIZONA--DESCRIPTION AND TRAVEL--GUIDES
ARIZONA--PUBLIC LANDS
DAMS
LAKE POWELL
OUTDOOR RECREATION
U.S.--DESCRIPTION AND TRAVEL--GUIDES

• GREENBELT PARK

6501 Greenbelt Road, Greenbelt, MD 20770. (301) 344-3948. 1,175.99 acres. 1950. Southern Maryland, 12 miles from Washington, D.C. off the Capital Beltway or the Baltimore-Washington Parkway.

Woodland park provides year-round outdoor recreation in a metropolitan area. Nature trails, bridle trail, guided walks, talks, programs, environmental study area, wildlife. Picnicking, campground. Food and lodging nearby.

Free Print Material:

"Greenbelt Park." 16-fold. Drawings, maps, description of trails, accommodations, and services, visitor tips.

"Welcome to Washington." 28 pages. Maps, photos, description

of places in and near Washington, D.C. Includes name of
attraction, location, what it offers, hours, telephone.

Suggested Curriculum Application:
ENVIRONMENTAL EDUCATION
MARYLAND STATE AND LOCAL STUDIES
RECREATION

Suggested Sears Subject Heading:
MARYLAND--DESCRIPTION AND TRAVEL--GUIDES
MARYLAND--PUBLIC LANDS
NATURE CONSERVATION
OUTDOOR RECREATION
U.S.--DESCRIPTION AND TRAVEL--GUIDES

• LAKE CHELAN
National Recreation Area. 800 State Street, Sedro Woolley, WA
98284. (509) 682-2549. 61,890.07 acres. 1968. Northcentral
Washington, 50 miles from Chelan by U.S. Highway 2 and 97 or 2
and State Highway 151.

Provide scenic recreational opportunities in Stehekin Valley and Lake
Chelan. Lake Chelan is one of the nation's deepest lakes. Boating,
hiking, interpretive programs, backpacking, nature walks and hikes,
Rainbow Falls, log school house, cross-country skiing, commercial
uplake boat trip, historic Buckner Homestead. Concession operations,
camping. Group campsites available but require reservations.
Seasonal shuttle bus. Charter floatplane service, ski tours, hiking-
pack trips. Food and lodging in Stehekin, Chelan.

Free Print Material:
  "Accommodations and Services." 2 pages. Overnight accommoda-
    tions, boating services, cabins for rent, ski tours, and other
    service addresses.
  "Backpacking from Stehekin." 8 pages. Descriptions of various
    trails; safety tips such as crossing streams, first aid kits,
    signaling devices.
  "Checklist of Trees in the North Cascades Complex." 2 pages.
    Common name, scientific name, forest type. Major forest types
    include: western hemlock, Pacific silver fir, subalpine-alpine
    zones, Engelmann spruce, grand fir--Douglas fir.
  "Cross Country Skiing in the Stehekin Valley." 4 pages.
    Guide to where to ski, skiing safety tips, map, description of
    trails, map.
  "Field's Point Landing." 1 page. Description of the landing
    designed to provide parking and orientation for travelers
    headed for the national forest and national park lands uplake.
  "Foods and Wilderness Survival." 6 pages. Edible plants, food
    testing, slugs, tea-making plants.
  "Four Lines of Defense Against Hypothermia." 6-fold. How to

guard against the rapid, progressive mental and physical collapse accompanying the chilling of the inner core of the human body, sketches.

"North Cascades National Park Complex." 24-fold. Photos, descriptions of North Cascades National Park, Ross Lake National Recreation Area, Lake Chelan National Recreation Area, maps, visitor information, driving in the park area, naturalist activities.

"Revegetation in North Cascades National Park." 6-fold. What revegetation is (restoring native plants to cover bare and overused campsites), examples of forest and subalpine revegetations. History of revegetation in the North Cascades, how you can help, sketches.

"Staying Warm." 2 pages. Tips for outdoor recreational visitors on guarding against cold.

"Stehekin Landing." 8-fold. Map, valley information, services, activities, access by ferry, charter air service, private boat, trail.

"Visitor Form Letter." 2 pages. Information to help answer visitor questions.

Sales/Audiovisual List:
"Pacific Northwest National Parks and Forests Association North Cascades Branch Order Form." 2 pages. Publications, maps, slide sets. Title, author, date, number of pages, price for books. Order form, ordering directions.

"Backpacking, one step at a time." Manning, 1980 revision, 414 pages, $6.95.

Suggested Curriculum Application:
NATURAL HISTORY
RECREATION
WASHINGTON STATE AND LOCAL STUDIES

Suggested Sears Subject Heading:
LAKE CHELAN
LAKES
NATURAL HISTORY--WASHINGTON
NATURE CONSERVATION
OUTDOOR RECREATION
U.S.--DESCRIPTION AND TRAVEL--GUIDES
WASHINGTON--DESCRIPTION AND TRAVEL--GUIDES
WASHINGTON--PUBLIC LANDS

● LAKE MEAD
National Recreation Area. 601 Nevada Highway, Boulder City, NV 89005. (702) 293-8932. 1,496,600.52 acres. 1964. Southern Nevada, visitor center is on U.S. Highway 93, 4 miles east of Boulder City.

Recreation area. Lake Mead, formed by Hoover Dam and Lake
Mohave by the Davis Dam, is the first national recreation area.
Hoover Dam Powerplant educational tour, Lake Mead and Lake
Mohave water sports, Davis Dam Powerplant educational tour, Hoover
Dam cruise, hiking. Special arrangements for guided group tours
may be made by writing to The Chief, Davis Dam Field Division,
Davis Dam, Bulhead City, Arizona 86430; and Chief, Parker Dam,
Field Division, P.O. Box 878, Parker Dam, CA 92267. Campgrounds,
food and lodging, docking facilities at Katherine's Landing, Cotton-
wood Cove.

Free Print Material:
  "Boating Regulations for Nevada-Arizona Interstate Waters."
    12 pages. Motorboat classification, definitions, personal flota-
    tion devices, numbering and registration, rules of the road
    and other boater information. Sketches, photos, Nevada water
    marker system.
  "Boulder City Has Your Place in the Sun." 12-fold. Photos and
    description of Hoover Dam, Lake Mead and other areas. Map,
    statistics, where to obtain more information.
  "Campground Regulations." 1 page. Fees, day-limits, areas,
    fires, quiet hours and other items.
  "Danger, Did You Know This Plant Can Kill?" 1 page. Descrip-
    tion and danger, precautions concerning the oleander bushes
    found in the area to people and pets. Emergency numbers,
    sketch.
  "Danger! Flash Flood: Checklist for Survival." Causes,
    seasons of flash floods, thunderstorm identification, safety
    tips, where to get information, photos.
  "Davis Dam and Powerplant." 8-fold. Photos, map, statistics,
    history of construction, transmission system, tours.
  "Flash Floods." 6-fold. Destruction of flash floods, what to do
    if a flash-flood watch is issued for your area, precautions to
    take when going into remote areas.
  "Golden Eagle, Golden Age, Golden Access Passports." 10-fold.
    What the passports do for persons under 62 and over 62, for
    those blind and disabled. How to get a passport, federal
    entrance fee areas, addresses, federal recreation fees.
  "Hiking and Temperatures (Lake Mead)." 1 page. Hiking tips,
    average temperature, average maximum temperature, average
    minimum temperature for each month.
  "Hoover Dam." 12-fold. History, engineering, physical data,
    maps, photos, multipurpose, tours. Includes information about
    a film and prints available on loan. Prints may be ordered
    from: U.S. Department of the Interior, Bureau of Reclamation,
    Code D-922, P.O. Box 25007, Denver, CO 80225. (No cost
    except return postage.)
  "National Park Service Safety Float." 1 sticker sheet. Sticker
    containing rules, storm warning flags, regulatory markers,
    channel buoy guide.
  "Nevada Map." 36-fold. Official highway map travel guide.

"Walk Softly, Walk Safely." 8 pages. Philosophy of backpacking that saves the wilderness for future users. Quotations, illustrations.

Audiovisual List:
See "Hoover Dam" Annotation above.

Sales/Audiovisual List:
"Publications List Southwest Parks and Monuments Association." 2 pages. Grouped by: Lake Mead and vicinity, boating and fishing, plants and animals, history and culture, geology, national parks, general, books for young people, maps and charts, post cards, slides, national parks calendar. Order form, ordering information.

"Auto Tour Guide to Lake Mead" by Evans--$.50. This booklet is a tour guide to the primary roads within the park that introduces the natural, historical, and recreational resources of this region. Black and white photos. 33 pages.

Suggested Curriculum Application:
GEOGRAPHY
NEVADA STATE AND LOCAL STUDIES
RECREATION

Suggested Sears Subject Heading:
DAMS
DAVIS DAM
HOOVER DAM
LAKE MEAD
LAKE MOHAVE
LAKES
NEVADA--DESCRIPTION AND TRAVEL--GUIDES
NEVADA--PUBLIC LANDS
OUTDOOR RECREATION
U.S.--DESCRIPTION AND TRAVEL--GUIDES

• LAKE MEREDITH
Recreation Area. P.O. Box 1438, Fritch, TX 79036. (806) 857-3151. 44,977.63 acres. 1965. Northern Texas (panhandle), near Alibates flint quarries, about 33 miles north of Amarillo, TX, off of State Route 136.

Manmade water-activity recreation area in the Southwest. Lake averages one-two miles wide and 14 miles long with a 100-mile shoreline. Public use is divided into eight areas: Sanford-Yake, Fritch Fortress, Alibates, McBride Canyon, Plum Creek, Blue West, Blue East, Bugbee. Swimming, off-road vehicles, boating, water skiing, wildlife. Picnicking, docks, launching ramps, campgrounds, marina with a store, snacks, and dry land boat storage and other facilities. Food and lodging in Fritch, Borger.

Free Print Material:

"Canadian River Project Texas." Description of the project that
linked eleven cities on the high plains of Texas, uses and
statistics of Sanford Dam and Lake Meredith.

"A Guide to a Safe Trip." 8-fold. Weather considerations, safe
boating and swimming, accident prevention, water skiing
safety. Sketches.

"Lake Meredith." 12-fold. Sketch, map, description of attractions, federal and state boating regulations, history and
wildlife of the area.

"Lake Meredith Recreation Area, Texas." 6-fold. What to see
and do, how to get there, some nearby attractions, overnight
accommodations, weather, safety.

"Off-Road Vehicle Use and Safety at Lake Meredith Recreation
Area." 8-fold. Safety tips, safety equipment, driving rules
to follow.

Sales List:

"List of Publications for Sale." 1 page. Includes publications,
post cards, posters, maps, guides. Title, author, price.

"American Indian Food and Lore" by Carolyn Niethammer.
$10.95.

Suggested Curriculum Application:
RECREATION
TEXAS STATE AND LOCAL STUDIES

Suggested Sears Subject Heading:
LAKE MEREDITH
LAKES
OUTDOOR RECREATION
TEXAS--DESCRIPTION AND TRAVEL--GUIDES
TEXAS--PUBLIC LANDS
U.S.--DESCRIPTION AND TRAVEL--GUIDES

• NEW RIVER GORGE
National River. P.O. Box 1189, Oak Hill, WV 25901.
(304) 465-0508. 62,024 acres. 1978. Southern West Virginia,
Appalachian Mountains through Summers, Raleigh and Fayette
counties. Visitor center 2 miles north of Fayetteville, on
east side of New River on U.S. 19.

Scenic, historic rugged river, flowing through deep canyons, among
the oldest rivers in North America. 50 miles of whitewater river,
historic railroading, coal mining, and lumbering. Exhibits, canoe
programs, interpretive programs, bus tours, slide program, kaymoor
overlook, bridge overlook, boardwalk overlook, educational programs.
Visitor centers, picnicking. Campgrounds nearby. Food and
lodging in nearby communities.

Free Print Material:
"Canyon Rim." 1 page. visitor center, Kaymoor Overlook,
bridge overlook, boardwalk overlooks, photo, map.
"Educational Programs at the New River Gorge National River
Canyon Rim Visitor Center." 6-fold. Program times, prerequisites and other information about educational programs
designed to involve your class in the cultural and natural
history of the New River.
"Educational Programs at New River Gorge National River Hinton
Visitor Center." 6-fold. Map, sketches. Program times,
prerequisites, reservations and other information about educational programs presented.
"Geologic Reflections." 8-fold. Geologic past, the making of a
gorge. Diagram, photos. Map of ancient river that was the
predecessor of New River.
"New River." 4 pages. Newspaper format publication by the
National Park Service for visitors. Photos, articles, map.
"New River Gorge." 8-fold. Diagram, bridge statistics, photos,
early transportation in the gorge.
"The New River Gorge Bridge." 1 page. Early history of the
gorge, bridge statistics. The bridge has the world's longest
steel arch span at 1,700 feet with a rise of 360 feet, and is
the second highest in the nation at 876 feet above the New
River. Sketch.
"New River Gorge National River Rafting and Canoeing Companies."
1 page. Name, address, telephone of companies offering
canoeing, camping for the general public, camping for guests.
"West Virginia State Parks and Forests." 51 pages. Descriptions
and photos of resort vacation parks, vacation parks, day
use/natural areas, historical parks, forests. Information
about camping, lodges and restaurants, skiing, special events,
statistics and other visitor aids.

Sales/Audiovisual List:
"Eastern National Park and Monument Association New River Gorge
National River Sales Items." 5 pages. Grouped by such headings as: Appalachia, New River, etc.--general; children's
publications; geology; early man; lumbering; industry, railroading; National Park Service, New River Gorge National River;
natural history; recreation; USGS topographical maps; West
Virginia--general; post cards; slide sleeves. Purpose of the
Eastern National Park and Monument Association. Title, author
included for some books. Order form, ordering information.
"Mountain Memories" (Deitz) $5.00.

Suggested Curriculum Application:
GEOGRAPHY
SOCIAL STUDIES
WEST VIRGINIA STATE AND LOCAL STUDIES

Suggested Sears Subject Heading:
BRIDGES

NEW RIVER
NEW RIVER GORGE BRIDGE
RIVERS
U.S.--DESCRIPTION AND TRAVEL--GUIDES
WEST VIRGINIA--DESCRIPTION AND TRAVEL--GUIDES
WEST VIRGINIA--PUBLIC LANDS

- OBED WILD AND SCENIC RIVER
P.O. Box 429, Wartburg, TN 37887. (404) 996-2520. 5,099.84
acres. 1976. Cumberland Plateau in central Tennessee. From
Nashville and west, take I-40 to U.S. 127 North.

Obed Wild and Scenic River has created a rugged landscape rarely
found east of the Mississippi River as it cuts deeply into the sandstone of the Cumberland Plateau with gorges as deep as 500 feet.
Forty-five miles of streams, wildlife, rugged scenery, Catoosa
Wildlife Management Area. Recreation such as canoeing and kayaking, swimming, camping, hiking. Cross-country buses and
scheduled airlines, rental cars in Knoxville and Nashville.

Free Print Material:
    "Parks for America." 16-fold. Sketches, photos, history and de-
        velopment of the national park service, variety and size of
        parks, recreational variety.
    "Obed." 16-fold. Map, photos, river chart, safety tips, things
        to do, river characteristics.
    "Southeast National Parks and National Forests." 16-fold. Des-
        cription and location of national parks and forests in: Alabama,
        Arkansas, Florida, Georgia, Kentucky, Louisiana, Mississippi,
        North Carolina, South Carolina, Tennessee. Map, photos,
        entrance and recreation use fees, passports and other charges.
    "Tennessee Rafting and Canoeing Guide." 18 pages. Tennessee's
        riverways whitewater and quietwater, heartland, plateaus and
        valleys, canoe clubs, guidebooks, principal floatable streams,
        whitewater ratings, maps, photos, first frontier, mountainous
        east.

Suggested Curriculum Application:
    GEOGRAPHY
    RECREATION
    TENNESSEE STATE AND LOCAL STUDIES

Suggested Sears Subject Heading:
    OBED WILD AND SCENIC RIVER
    OUTDOOR RECREATION
    RIVERS
    TENNESSEE--DESCRIPTION AND TRAVEL--GUIDES
    TENNESSEE--PUBLIC LANDS
    U.S.--DESCRIPTION AND TRAVEL--GUIDES
    WATER SPORTS

● RIO GRANDE

Wild and Scenic River. c/o Big Bend National Park, Big Bend
National Park, TX 79834. (915) 477-2251. Not established acreage.
1978. Southern Texas, beginning in Big Bend National Park and
downstream to the Terrell-Val Verde county line.

Preserve the river that borders the park for 118 miles where it
carves three major canyons. Scenic river trips by bringing your
own equipment, renting equipment, or hiring a guide service.
Campgrounds, lodge, concessions in Big Bend National Park.

Free Print Material:
    "General Information." 12-fold. Park services, average monthly
        river levels, types of river trips. Map, sketch, weather
        chart.

Sales List:
    "Big Bend Natural History Association Catalog of Sales Items."
        12-fold. Grouped by: guide books and maps, river guides,
        maps. Index to 7.5' minute maps, order form and instruc-
        tions, sketches.
    "Road Guide." $1.25. Describes points of interest visible from
        all paved and improved dirt roads in the park. 48 pages;
        black and white photographs.

Suggested Curriculum Application:
    RECREATION
    TEXAS STATE AND LOCAL STUDIES

Suggested Sears Subject Heading:
    OUTDOOR RECREATION
    RIO GRANDE RIVER
    RIVERS
    TEXAS--DESCRIPTION AND TRAVEL--GUIDES
    TEXAS--PUBLIC LANDS
    U.S.--DESCRIPTION AND TRAVEL--GUIDES

● ROCK CREEK PARK

5000 Glover Road, NW, Washington, D.C. 20015. (202) 426-6832.
1,754.37 acres. 1890. District of Columbia, Washington, D.C.,
south of East-West Highway, north of the White House.

Wooded preserve offers many natural, historical and recreational
facilities in the middle of the capital city. Various interpretive
activities--check "Rock Creek Park Interpretive Activities" described
below for current activities. Many hiking trails, playgrounds,
tennis courts, bicycle route. Fort Derussey, Rock Creek Nature
Center and Planetarium, Rock Creek Golf Course, Rock Creek Park
Horse Center, Fort Reno, Fort Bayard, Carter Barron Amphitheater,
Battery Kemble, flour mill, art barn, national zoological park,

Thompson's Boat House, Glover-Archbold Park, Montrose Park, Dumbarton Oaks Park, Old Stone House. School tours are available by reservation for the Old Stone House (believed to be the only surviving pre-Revolutionary building in D.C.) by calling (202) 426-6851. For talks, guided walks, planetarium shows, natural history slide shows, films and live animals demonstrations contact (202) 426-6829 or write Rock Creek Nature Center, 5200 Glover Road, N.W., Washington, D.C. 20015. Park headquarters and maintenance yard, park police substation and information center, picnic areas. Food and lodging in Washington, D.C.

Free Print Material:
   "Activity Guide for Organized Groups: Rock Creek Nature Center." 8 pages. Sketches, visiting hours, tours, how to
   schedule your group, natural science programs, planetarium
   programs.
   "The Old Stone House." 8-fold. History, furnishings, grounds
   of the house located at 3051 M St., N.W. in Georgetown.
   The house was begun apparently in 1764 and school tours may
   be arranged.
   "Pierce Mill." 12-fold. Flour milling beginning about 1820, development, milling process, map. Sketches, photos. The
   mill ceased operation in 1897.
   "Rock Creek Park." 12-fold. Features, photos, map, trail
   chart, regulations, telephone numbers.
   "Rock Creek Park Interpretive Activities." 2 pages. Monthly
   calendar of events. Name of event, description, date, hours,
   location, telephone.
   "Tales for Tots." 1 page. Selection of storytelling books with
   slide presentations for children ages four to six as an introduction to basic life science concepts. Title, description of
   presentations.

Suggested Curriculum Application:
   AMERICAN HISTORY
   DISTRICT OF COLUMBIA LOCAL STUDIES
   NATURAL HISTORY
   RECREATION
   SCIENCE

Suggested Sears Subject Heading:
   ARCHITECTURE--CONSERVATION AND RESTORATION
   DISTRICT OF COLUMBIA--DESCRIPTION AND TRAVEL--GUIDES
   DISTRICT OF COLUMBIA--PUBLIC LANDS
   NATURE STUDY--U.S.
   OUTDOOR RECREATION
   U.S.--DESCRIPTION AND TRAVEL--GUIDES

• ROSS LAKE
National Recreation Area. 800 State Street, Sedro Woolley, WA

98284. (206) 855-1331. 117,574.09 acres. 1968. Northern Washington, 61 miles from Sedro Woolley, access by WA 20.

Mountain-ringed reservoirs recreation area in Skagit River Canyon separating north and south units of North Cascades National Park. Boating, horse trails, boat tours, float trips, hiking, cross-country skiing. Meals and lodging, campgrounds. Food and lodging in Stehekin, Newhalem.

Free Print Material:
"Accommodations and Services." 2 pages. Name, address, phone number of overnight accommodations, boating services, ski tours, float trips, food service and groceries and others.
"Main Trails and Backcountry Camp Areas North Cascades Complex, Washington." 24-fold. Tips on hypothermia, wildlife, backcountry rules, revegetation, map, sketches.
"Vehicle Access Campgrounds." 2 pages. Descriptions of Newhalem Creek Campground, Goodell Creek Campground, Colonial Creek Campground.
"Visitor Letter." 3 pages. Description, activities on Lake Chelan and Ross Lake National Recreation Areas. Visitor information on camping, backcountry permits.

Suggested Curriculum Application:
RECREATION
WASHINGTON STATE AND LOCAL STUDIES

Suggested Sears Subject Heading:
LAKES
OUTDOOR RECREATION
ROSS LAKE
U.S.--DESCRIPTION AND TRAVEL--GUIDES
WASHINGTON--DESCRIPTION AND TRAVEL--GUIDES
WASHINGTON--PUBLIC LANDS

• SAINT CROIX
National Scenic Riverway. P.O. Box 708, St. Croix Falls, WI 54024. (715) 635-8346 from the headwaters of the Namekagon and St. Croix rivers to Riverside (WI Hwy. 35); (612) 629-2148 from Riverside (WI Hwy. 35) to St. Croix Falls; (715) 483-3284 from St. Croix Falls to Stillwater. 68,793.33 acres. 1968. St. Croix River and its Namekagon tributary flow 252 miles through westcentral Wisconsin and eastcentral Minnesota.

Recreational, scenic, free-flowing and unpolluted route through the upper Midwest. St. Croix means "sacred cross," deriving its name from a rock formation along the river. Canoeing, powerboating, water skiing, sailboating, tour boat rides, birdwatching, swimming. Inquire ahead of time about a short presentation and/or tour for students. Information centers, visitor center, canoe outfitters, picnicking, camping. Food and lodging along the riverway.

Free Print Material:
  "Cold Water Drowning." 14 pages. Sketches, information on how
    to help save a life in a drowning emergency.
  "The Dakota and Ojibway Indians of the St. Croix Valley Past."
    5 pages. Description and culture of Dakota and Ojibway
    Indians. Bibliography.
  "Geology of Interstate Park." 5 pages. The background of
    Interstate State Park formations going back a billion years.
  "The St. Croix: A Brief History." 7 pages. Topography,
    description of the river as it winds southward on its 174-mile
    journey from its source at Solon Springs, WI.
  "St. Croix Riverway." 24-fold. Description of upper St. Croix
    and Namekagon and lower St. Croix, map, photos, facilities,
    safety tips and regulations.
  "Take Pride in America." 8-fold. Campaign for public awareness
    to encourage pride in the nation's natural and cultural re-
    sources, photos.
  "Taylors Falls, MN, St. Croix Falls, WI, Dalles of the St. Croix
    and Gateway to the Wild River." 8-fold. Map, attractions,
    visitor accommodations.
  "Two Rivers Journal." 8 pages. Newspaper format. Photos,
    articles, telephone numbers, river trip checklist, outfitter
    listing, puzzles and games for children ("Kid's Corner").
  "Where Did the Energy Go??" 6-fold. Five ways to lose body
    heat, how outdoorsmen can cope with difficulties.
  "Wildlife on the St. Croix River." 3 pages. Variety of commonly
    seen wildlife in their habitats.

Sales/Audiovisual List:
  "Film List." 3 pages. Title, description, if color and sound,
    running length. Film request sheet.
  "Cold Can Kill": presents the dangers of overexposure (hypo-
    thermia) and demonstrates how to prepare for and avoid
    overexposures to the cold. A valuable safety film for sailors,
    mountain climbers, hikers, swimmers, skiers, and canoeists....

Suggested Curriculum Application:
  MINNESOTA STATE AND LOCAL STUDIES
  RECREATION
  WISCONSIN STATE AND LOCAL STUDIES

Suggested Sears Subject Heading:
  MINNESOTA--DESCRIPTION AND TRAVEL--GUIDES
  MINNESOTA--PUBLIC LANDS
  OUTDOOR RECREATION
  RIVERS
  ST. CROIX RIVER
  U.S.--DESCRIPTION AND TRAVEL--GUIDES
  WATER SPORTS
  WISCONSIN--DESCRIPTION AND TRAVEL--GUIDES
  WISCONSIN--PUBLIC LANDS

● SANTA MONICA MOUNTAINS
National Recreation Area. 22900 Ventura Boulevard, Suite 140,
Woodland Hills, CA 91364. (818) 888-3770. 150,000 acres. 1978.
Southwestern California, North of Los Angeles, from Griffith Park
to Point Mugu.

Preserve about 50 miles of mountains, chaparral and sage, woodlands,
grasslands, canyons, waterfalls, creeks, sandy beaches. Within the
national recreation area boundary are towns, developments, private
ranches and homes, private recreation areas and public parklands.
The National Park Service works with state, local agencies and private organizations. Paramount Ranch, site of western movie making,
is part of the Santa Monica Mountains National Recreation Area. It
is open for walking, horseback riding, evening programs, guided
tours, nature walks, folklife festival, organized activities.
Information center, picnicking. Food and lodging in nearby towns.

Free Print Material:
    "Give a Gift to the Mountains: Help Build Trails." 1 page.
        Work that the Sierra Club does, where to get information on
        membership and other information. Sketches.
    "Nursery Nature Walks." 1 page. Information about organized
        walks for infants and toddlers.
    "Paramount Ranch." 12-fold. Making of a movie ranch, uses
        today, maps, sketches, photos, visitor information.
    "Santa Monica Mountains." 24-fold. Maps, photos, description
        of the recreation area, visitor safety, features to explore.
    "Scheduled activities in the Santa Monica Mountains and Seashore."
        24 pages. Sketches, description of activities includes place
        event, hours, telephone and sponsoring agency or organiza-
        tion.
    "Take Pride in America." 8-fold. Campaign, photos to encourage
        everyone to take pride in the nation's natural and cultural
        resources.
    "Where You Can Hike and Ride in the Santa Monicas." 1 page.
        Description of various areas, future trails, map, where to call
        for the latest information.

Suggested Curriculum Application:
    CALIFORNIA STATE AND LOCAL STUDIES
    RECREATION

Suggested Sears Subject Heading:
    CALIFORNIA--DESCRIPTION AND TRAVEL--GUIDES
    CALIFORNIA--PUBLIC LANDS
    MOTION PICTURE INDUSTRY
    NATURE CONSERVATION
    OUTDOOR RECREATION
    SANTA MONICA MOUNTAINS
    U.S.--DESCRIPTION AND TRAVEL--GUIDES

- SHENANDOAH

National Park. Rt. 4, Box 292, Luray, VA 22835. (703) 999-2266.
195,072. 1926. Central Virginia, park headquarters is 4 miles west
of Thorton Gap and 4 miles east of Luray on U.S. 211.

Preserve many miles of scenic panoramas of the Piedmont and
Shenandoah Valley from the Blue Ridge Mountains. Naturalist programs, over 500 miles of hiking trails, 105-mile Skyline Drive with
interpretive signs at overlooks, waterfalls, self-guiding nature trails.
Visitor centers, picnic grounds, cabins, campgrounds, lodging and
food, supplies.

Free Print Material:
"Bear Friend or Foe?...." Safety considerations and visitor tips
regarding bears. Sketches.
"Exploring the Backcountry." 12-fold. Suggestions about how
to plan for a backcountry adventure, what to do when you
reach the park, trail aids, park rules. Sketches.
"Facilities and Services." 2 pages. Trails, backcountry camping,
campgrounds, backcountry cabins, lodges, park regulations,
guide books and maps, and others.
"Shenandoah." 24-fold. Features to enjoy, photos, safety tips,
chart of facilities and services, park history. Maps of Skyline
Drive that runs the full length of the park, along with descriptions of major points of interest.
"Shenandoah Overlook." 8 pages. Articles, maps, facilities and
services, ranger-conducted activities, games, visitor tips.
"Virginia Skyline Drive." 12-fold. Maps, photos, accommodations on Skyline Drive.

Sales/Audiovisual List:
"Shenandoah Natural History Association Price List and Order
Form." 2 pages. Items include: field guides; golden series;
finder series; golden guides; Shenandoah National Park; maps
and guides; general; video; children's selections; national
parks; audio-visuals; color prints and posters. Ordering information, order form.
"Natural History Field Guides--First Guide to Birds." $3.95.

Suggested Curriculum Application:
GEOGRAPHY
VIRGINIA STATE AND LOCAL STUDIES

Suggested Sears Subject Heading:
NATIONAL PARKS AND RESERVES--U.S.
SHENANDOAH NATIONAL PARK
U.S.--DESCRIPTION AND TRAVEL--GUIDES
VIRGINIA--DESCRIPTION AND TRAVEL--GUIDES
VIRGINIA--PUBLIC LANDS

- **UPPER DELAWARE**

Scenic and Recreational River. P.O. Box C, Narrowsburg, NY
12764. (914) 252-3947. 75,000 acres. 1978. Southern New York,
between Hancock and Sparrow Bath, NY along the Pennsylvania
border. Southern reaches accessible by N.Y. 17 and I-84; the
northern portion by N.Y. 17 and I-81.

Preserve 73 miles of varied landscape and free-flowing river.
Scale model of historic Roebling Delaware Aqueduct, basic canoe instruction at the Narrowsburg and Ten Mile River access areas, old
buildings, canal remains, oldest existing wire suspension bridge in
the country, wildlife, swimming, eel weirs, canoeing, rafting,
kayaking, inquire about off-site and special programs. Information
centers, ranger stations. Campgrounds, food and lodging, canoe
liveries, boat rentals, along the river. Recorded message about
river conditions: (914) 262-7100.

Free Print Material:

"The Battle of Minisink." 2 pages. The raid and the battle,
following events, sketches, map. Revolutionary War skirmish
of July 22, 1779, on the heights above Minisink Ford.

"Canoe Safety." 6-fold. Safety rules, courses available, sketches,
international scale of river difficulty.

"Hypothermia and Cold Water Survival." 6-fold. What hypothermia is and how it kills, what to do if an accident happens,
first aid for hypothermia victims, sketches.

"Minisink Battleground Park." 12-fold. Maps, sketches, administration, the Battle of Minisink, flora and fauna, use of
the park, visitor information.

"Personal Flotation Devices." 6-fold. Types, sketches of
personal floatation devices such as life preservers. Pennsylvania law requirements.

"Poison Plants." 2 pages. Description of poison ivy, poison
sumac, nettles, where they grow, symptoms, treatment.
Sketches.

"Roebling's Delaware Aqueduct." 6-fold. Building, purpose of
the bridge, now a historic feature.

"Snakes in Pennsylvania." 4 pages. Characteristics, reproduction and growth, food and feeding, snakebites and first aid,
sketches, maps, information on charts for sale on Pennsylvania
reptiles and amphibians.

"Upper Delaware." 12-fold. Photos, sketch, map, access,
facilities and accommodations, boating, wildlife, construction of
the Roebling Aqueduct.

"What Everyone Should Know About Boating Safety." 16 pages.
Narrative and sketches on swimming, safe boats, how to handle
a boat, how to prevent boat fires, traffic signs and other tips.

"Whitewater in an Open Canoe." 8-fold. International scale of
river difficulty, safety recommendation, tips, sketches, protec-
tive equipment.

Suggested Curriculum Application:
NEW YORK STATE AND LOCAL STUDIES
PENNSYLVANIA STATE AND LOCAL STUDIES
RECREATION

Suggested Sears Subject Heading:
NATURAL HISTORY--NEW YORK
NATURAL HISTORY--PENNSYLVANIA
NEW YORK--DESCRIPTION AND TRAVEL--GUIDES
NEW YORK--PUBLIC LANDS
PENNSYLVANIA--DESCRIPTION AND TRAVEL--GUIDES
PENNSYLVANIA--PUBLIC LANDS
OUTDOOR RECREATION
RIVERS
U.S.--DESCRIPTION AND TRAVEL--GUIDES
UPPER DELAWARE RIVER

* WHISKEYTOWN UNIT
National Recreation Area. P.O. Box 188, Whiskeytown, CA 96095.
(916) 241-6584. 42,500 acres. 1965. Northcentral California, on
California 299 off Interstate 5 near Redding, California.

Mountainous backcountry provides a variety of outdoor recreation
activities. Visitor center, exhibits, boating, water-skiing, scuba
diving, swimming, horseback riding, gold panning, National Environmental Education Development Camp, ranger-guided walks, wildlife,
demonstrations, programs. Nearby Trinity Unit and Shasta Lake
Unit are part of the national recreation area but are administered by
the U.S. Forest Service. Visitor center, amphitheater, campgrounds, picnicking. Food and lodging in Redding.

Free Print Material:
"Whiskeytown Unit." 16-fold. Photos, maps, access and services, description of the recreation area, activities and points
of interest.
"Whiskeytown Unit Area Information." 4 pages. Visitor survey
includes information in such areas as camping, interpretive
programs, hours, weather, wildlife.

Suggested Curriculum Application:
CALIFORNIA STATE AND LOCAL STUDIES
ENVIRONMENTAL EDUCATION
RECREATION

Suggested Sears Subject Heading:
CALIFORNIA--DESCRIPTION AND TRAVEL--GUIDES
CALIFORNIA--PUBLIC LANDS
OUTDOOR RECREATION
U.S.--DESCRIPTION AND TRAVEL--GUIDES

- YUKON-CHARLEY RIVERS

National Preserve. P.O. Box 64, Eagle, AK 99738. (907) 547-2233. 309,000 acres. National Monument, 1978; National Preserve, 1980. Central Alaska along the Canadian border, Taylor Highway to Eagle or Steese Highway from Fairbanks to Circle.

Protects 115 miles of the Yukon River and the 88-mile Charley River Basin, old cabins and relics of the 1898 Gold Rush, bird and wildlife. Historic remains, hiking, rafting, canoeing, powerboating, archeological and paleontological sites, wildlife, birdlife. The Yukon flows with glacial silt while the Charley flows clear and they merge between the early-day boom towns of Eagle and Circle. The two rivers provide nests for peregrine and gyrfalcons. Scheduled flights serve Eagle and Circle from Fairbanks. Food and lodging in Eagle and Circle in summer.

Free Print Material:
"National Parklands in Alaska." 24-fold. Maps, descriptions of various parklands, travel tips, parklands classifications, our lasting frontier, where to obtain more information, photos.
"Your Arctic Adventure." 10-fold. Campsites, trails, fires, sketches, wildlife, private property, litter, and other visitor tips.
"Yukon-Charley." 8-fold. Access, accommodations and services, weather, clothing, food, precautions and courtesies, map, photo, what to see and do.

Suggested Curriculum Application:
ALASKA STATE AND LOCAL STUDIES
RECREATION

Suggested Sears Subject Heading:
ALASKA--DESCRIPTION AND TRAVEL--GUIDES
ALASKA--PUBLIC LANDS
CHARLEY RIVER
OUTDOOR RECREATION
RIVERS
U.S.--DESCRIPTION AND TRAVEL--GUIDES
WILDERNESS AREAS
YUKON RIVER

REVOLUTIONARY PERIOD

- BOSTON

National Historical Park. Charlestown Navy Yard, Boston, MA 02129. (617) 242-5642. 41.03 acres. 1974. Eastern Massachusetts, downtown Boston and Charleston, mostly accessible by a 3-mile national recreation trail.

Sites at the center of the country's transformation from colony to independence, such as Faneuil Hall, Bunker Hill Monument, and Old North Church. State house and archives, Park Street Church, King's Chapel, Franklin Statue, Old Corner Bookstore, Old South Meeting House, Old State House, Quincy Market, Faneuil Hall, Paul Revere House, Pierce-Hichborn House, Old North Church, Copp's Hill Burying Ground, Charlestown Navy Yard, Bunker Hill Monument. The Freedom Trail begins at the Boston Common and ends at the Bunker Hill Monument in Charlestown; the marked trail takes about a day to tour the 16 sites along its route. The Black Heritage Trail is a walking tour exploring the history of Beacon Hill's 19th-century black community and begins at Shaw Memorial and is identified by signs along the route. Dorchester Heights in Thomas Park in South Boston is two miles from downtown Boston. Inquire about fieldtrips available for fourth grade Boston students if it applies to your grade level and you are in Boston. Visitor center, slide program, bus service between Boston and Charlestown. Food and lodging nearby.

Free Print Material:
"Boston." 16-fold. Photos and description of historic sites, history, illustration, map, traveling in historic Boston, touring trails, administration of the park complex.
"Massachusetts Calendar of Events." 24 pages. Map, sketches, things to do and see.
"Weekend Events and Package Guide." 44 pages. Weekend events and package guide. Getting to and around in Boston, museums and attractions, sightseeing tours and other visitor information.

Suggested Curriculum Application:
AMERICAN HISTORY
BLACK STUDIES
MASSACHUSETTS STATE AND LOCAL STUDIES

Suggested Sears Subject Heading:
MASSACHUSETTS--DESCRIPTION AND TRAVEL--GUIDES
MASSACHUSETTS--HISTORY
MASSACHUSETTS--PUBLIC LANDS
U.S.--DESCRIPTION AND TRAVEL--GUIDES
U.S.--HISTORY--REVOLUTION, 1775-1783

• COLONIAL
National Historical Park. P.O. Box 210, Yorktown, VA 23690. (804) 898-3400. 9,316.37 acres. 1930. Eastern Virginia. Jamestown and Yorktown are located on the Virginia Peninsula between the James and York rivers, off of Rte. 17 and I-64.

Preserve important American history sites. The 23-mile Colonial
Parkway connects Jamestown National Historic Site with Yorktown
Battlefield and along the way passes by restored Colonial Williams-
burg. Yorktown, the site of the culminating battle of the American
Revolution; Jamestown Island, the site of the first permanent
English settlement; parkway with turnouts and overlooks connects
with these and other colonial sites with Williamsburg; Cape Henry
Memorial marks the approximate site of the first landing of James-
town's colonists in 1607; Yorktown National Cemetery. Museum,
gift shop, theater, glasshouse, self-guiding auto tours, Moore
House, field displays, taped tour, reconstructed redoubts and bat-
teries, patriotic festivities, earthworks, Old Church Tower.
Visitor centers, gift shop. Campgrounds and picnicking nearby.
Food and lodging in Williamsburg, Yorktown.

Free Print Material:
   "Colonial National Historical Park." 16-fold. Maps, history of
      English colonization, photos, visitor information for exploring
      Jamestown National Historic Site and Yorktown Battlefield.
   "National Park Service Travel Tips." 8-fold. Variety of
      opportunities within the National Park System, selecting park
      areas to visit, making reservations, currency exchange for
      international visitors, photos, and other visitor information.

Sales/Audiovisual List:
   "Books and Gifts Sales List." 18 pages. Grouped by:
      Children's books, coloring books, adult books, cachets,
      cassettes and albums, maps, note paper, post cards, prints
      with mats, prints unmatted, soldier prints, slide strips,
      stamp sets, theme-related souvenir, needle kit, cross-stitch
      patterns, costumes of Williamsburg--patterns, pewter soldier--
      hand painted, pewter soldier--unpainted, cannons, documents
      and parchments, children's collectibles. Order form, sketches,
      purpose of the Eastern National Park and Monument Associa-
      tion. Paperback or hardback cover for books indicated.
      Stock number, title, author, description, price.
   "American Folk Toys." Dick Schnacke. Early American toys and
      how to make them. $7.95 pb.

Suggested Curriculum Application:
   AMERICAN HISTORY
   VIRGINIA STATE AND LOCAL STUDIES

Suggested Sears Subject Heading:
   U.S.--DESCRIPTION AND TRAVEL--GUIDES
   U.S.--HISTORY--COLONIAL PERIOD, 1600-1775
   U.S.--HISTORY--REVOLUTION, 1775-1783
   VIRGINIA--DESCRIPTION AND TRAVEL--GUIDES
   VIRGINIA--HISTORY
   VIRGINIA--PUBLIC LANDS

- COWPENS

National Battlefield. Post Office Box 308, Chesnee, SC 29323.
(803) 461-2828. 841.56 acres. 1929. Northern South Carolina,
11 miles west of Gaffney, SC, and 3 miles east of Chesnee, at the
intersection of highways 110 and 11.

Site of American Revolutionary War victory on January 17, 1781.
Cannons, weapons, paintings and exhibits, slide presentation,
fiber-optic map display. Battlefield Trail includes wayside exhibits,
1856 Washington Light Infantry Monument and Green River Road
which was the center line of the battle. Auto tour road travels
the perimeter of the battlefield and includes wayside exhibits and
overlooks with short trails. Visitor center, picnicking. Food and
lodging in Gaffney.

Free Print Material:
    "Available Resources and Facilities Information Sheet." 1 page.
        Description of what the visitor center offers, the battlefield
        trail, auto tour road, and picnic area.
    "Cowpens." 8-fold. Maps, photos. Account of the battle with
        diagrams of military tactics. Location, administration of the
        battlefield.

Sales/Audiovisual List:
    "Eastern National Park and Monument Association Sales List."
        6 pages. Alphabetically arranged by title or item. Includes
        books, prints, posters, medallions, calendar, post cards,
        maps, slides. Title or name of item, description, price.
        Order blank, ordering information.
    "The American Revolution," Bruce Bliven. A lively account of
        the buildup and major battles of the war (3.95).

Suggested Curriculum Application:
    AMERICAN HISTORY
    SOUTH CAROLINA STATE AND LOCAL STUDIES

Suggested Sears Subject Heading:
    COWPENS, BATTLE OF
    SOUTH CAROLINA--DESCRIPTION AND TRAVEL--GUIDES
    SOUTH CAROLINA--HISTORY
    SOUTH CAROLINA--PUBLIC LANDS
    U.S.--DESCRIPTION AND TRAVEL--GUIDES
    U.S.--HISTORY--REVOLUTION, 1775-1783

- FEDERAL HALL

National Memorial. Manhattan Sites. 26 Wall Street, New York, NY
10005. (212) 264-8711. 0.45 acres. National Historic Site, 1939;
National Memorial, 1955. Eastern New York, New York City, at the
corner of Wall and Nassau Streets, just off Broadway.

Site of the original federal hall where the Stamp Act Congress con-
vened and the Second Continental Congress met, where Washington
took the oath as the first president, where the Bill of Rights was
adopted, where John Peter Zenger's trial took place. Current building was completed in 1842 as a federal customs house. Museum,
historic building, film, displays and exhibits. Food and lodging in
New York City.

Free Print Material:
"Federal Hall." 16-fold. Historical events that have happened
on the site, sketches, how to reach the site, administration,
other areas in the national park system also in New York City.
"George Washington Stepped Here." 8-fold. A New York
Historical Society self-guided tour of George Washington's
New York. Maps, sketch.
"I Love New York City Visitors Guide and Map." 36-fold. Map
with guide grouped by: colleges and universities, museums
and galleries and other visitor items. Descriptions of attractions divided by areas such as: downtown Manhattan, Queens
and others. Photos.
"The National Parks and the Bicentennial of the United States
Constitution." 12-fold. Making of the Constitution, illustra-
tions, photos, national park facilities connected with the be-
ginnings of our federal system such as the Salem Maritime
National Historic Site and Montpelier, the home of James
Madison.

Audiovisual List:
"Films at Federal Hall." 5 pages. List of films to select to see
at Federal Hall or for schools and organizations to borrow
free of charge. Grouped by: American history, Independence
Day celebrations, national park sites, environmental topics.
American history category is grouped by two age levels. In-
cludes title, running time, description, sketches.
"George Washington Birthplace: A Childhood Place." 20:00.
Shows George Washington's birthplace in Virginia, and through
his words, describes his affection for it and for farm life.
Depicts some of the influences that may have shaped his
character.

Suggested Curriculum Application:
AMERICAN HISTORY
NEW YORK STATE AND LOCAL STUDIES

Suggested Sears Subject Heading:
ARCHITECTURE--CONSERVATION AND RESTORATION
FEDERAL HALL
NEW YORK--DESCRIPTION AND TRAVEL--GUIDES
NEW YORK--HISTORY
NEW YORK--PUBLIC LANDS
U.S.--DESCRIPTION AND TRAVEL--GUIDES
U.S.--HISTORY--COLONIAL PERIOD, 1600-1775

- FORT STANWIX

National Monument. 112 East Park St., Rome, NY 13440.
(315) 336-2090. 15.52 acres. 1935. Central New York, downtown
Rome, at intersection of State Routes 26, 46, 49, 69 and 365.

Reconstruction of a fort that was a major factor in resisting the
British invasion in 1777 from Canada, site of treaty of Fort Stanwix
and boundary line treaty. Living history program, exhibits,
guided fort tours. Group tours requested to make reservations.
Visitor center. Meals and lodging in Rome.

Free Print Material:
"Fort Stanwix." 16-fold. History of the site, photos, maps,
sketching, glossary of terms, visitor tips.

Audiovisual List:
"Film List." 4 pages. Arranged alphabetically by title.
Includes title, format, running time.
"Age of Alaska." The four systems of national forests, wildlife
refuges, parks and wild and scenic rivers which have been
recommended to Congress by the Secretary of the Interior
under terms of Alaska Native Claims Settlement Act. It depicts the beauty of Alaska, mining operations, fishing, logging
operations....

Suggested Curriculum Application:
AMERICAN HISTORY
NEW YORK STATE AND LOCAL STUDIES

Suggested Sears Subject Heading:
FORTIFICATION
NEW YORK--DESCRIPTION AND TRAVEL--GUIDES
NEW YORK--HISTORY
NEW YORK--PUBLIC LANDS
U.S.--DESCRIPTION AND TRAVEL--GUIDES
U.S.--HISTORY--REVOLUTION, 1775-1783

- GUILFORD COURTHOUSE

National Military Park. P.O. Box 9806. Greensboro, NC 27429.
(919) 288-1776. 220.25 acres. 1917. Northcentral North Carolina,
six miles north of downtown Greensboro, NC off of U.S. 220 on
New Garden Road.

Site of a 1781 battle that opened the campaign that led to Yorktown
and the ending of the Revolutionary War. Exhibits, film, 2-1/4 mile
automobile tour road with seven stops and displays, historic routes.
Greene Monument, American Third Line Monuments, Hooper-Pen
Monument, Cavalry Monument, Stuart Monument, Caldwell Monument,
and other monuments and graves. Special activities and seasonal
programs, self-guiding trails. Special services are available for

groups by arrangement by calling or writing. Visitor center. Food and lodging in Greensboro.

Free Print Material:
"Guilford Courthouse." 16-fold. Battle and personalities of the leaders, maps, photos, battlefield tour, illustrations.

"Take Pride in America." 8 pages. National public awareness campaign to encourage everyone to take pride in the country's natural and cultural resources, photos.

"Teacher Information Guide." 47 pages. Suggestions to use in planning a visit, description of the park's programs and services, suggested topics for study, park history, maps, many full-page sketches, chronology of events of the American Revolution, the battle action, Lord Charles Cornwallis, Thomas Carney, Peter Francisco, description of the continental soldier, Revolutionary War arms. Includes bibliography, film list, sales list.

Bibliography:
One page included in the "Teacher Information Guide" described above. Revolutionary reading is grouped by: biography, general history, primary sources. Includes author, title, city, date. Publisher and description are not included.

Audiovisual List:
2-page list included in the "Teacher Information Guide" described above. Includes film title, running length, description. Loan policy.

"George Washington's Birthplace" (20 minutes). An account of the early years of the future general and president, the many influences that shaped his character and the influences his family had in the Virginia Colony.

Sales/Audiovisual List:
Ten-page list included in the "Teacher Information Guide" described above. Grouped by: history books, history books for young historians, history related items, other sales items, national parks, national park passport program, the United States Constitution 1787-1987, ordering instructions, order form. History-related items and other sales items include slide sets, record, tape cassette, Colonial and Revolutionary currency, badges, buttons, and other items.

"The Monuments at Guilford Courthouse National Military Park" by Thomas E. Baker. 46 pages. $.95. An indispensable guide to the 28 monuments and graves located at Guilford Courthouse NMP. Each is covered by a brief history, the story of the person or event it commemorates....

Suggested Curriculum Application:
AMERICAN HISTORY
NORTH CAROLINA STATE AND LOCAL STUDIES

• HISTORIC CAMDEN

Camden District Heritage Foundation. Camden Historical Commission, Box 710, Camden, SC 29020. (803) 432-9841. 1982. Central South Carolina, in Camden, off of U.S. 1, I-20, 521 on Broad Street.

Preserve Camden history during the Revolutionary period of 1780-81. Cunningham House, Dogtrot, Craven House, Bradley House, Drakeford House, The Shed, archeological areas, nature trail, craft shop, slide presentation, exhibits, miniature dioramas. Picnic areas, visitor center. Food and lodging in Camden.

Free Print Material:
    "Historic Camden South Carolina." 6-fold. Photos, map, features
        to see, hours.
    "Historic Camden South Carolina." 12-fold. Sketches, map, tour
        features, restoration development. History of colonial and
        revolutionary Camden.

Suggested Curriculum Application:
    AMERICAN HISTORY
    ARCHEOLOGY
    SOUTH CAROLINA STATE AND LOCAL STUDIES

Suggested Sears Subject Heading:
    ARCHITECTURE--CONSERVATION AND RESTORATION
    EXCAVATIONS (ARCHEOLOGY)
    SOUTH CAROLINA--DESCRIPTION AND TRAVEL--GUIDES
    SOUTH CAROLINA--HISTORY
    SOUTH CAROLINA--PUBLIC LANDS
    U.S.--DESCRIPTION AND TRAVEL--GUIDES
    U.S.--HISTORY--REVOLUTION, 1775-1783

• INDEPENDENCE

National Historical Park. 313 Walnut Street, Philadelphia, PA 19106. (215) 597-8974. 44.85 acres. 1948. Eastern Pennsylvania, in central Philadelphia, the parking garage is on 2nd Street between Chestnut and Walnut streets.

Structures and sites associated with the American Revolution and the beginning of the country. Carpenters Hall, Independence Hall, Congress Hall, Old City Hall, Graff House, Liberty Bell Pavilion, Deshier-Morris House, Benjamin Franklin National Memorial, reconstructed city tavern, free Quaker Meeting House, Christ Church, Franklin Court, Second Bank of the United States, and others. Different audiovisuals at visitor center, Franklin Court, Second Bank; interactive computer programs; exhibits. Visitor center. Food and lodging in Philadelphia.

Free Print Material:
"Calendar of Events." 24 pages. What is currently going on in special events, historic sites, Fairmount Park, art museums/galleries, other museums and attractions, music and dance, sports, theater, tours. Includes the event, date, telephone number for admission information. Photos.
"Constitutional Exhibits." 2 pages. What is available at the visitor center, Second Bank, Old City Hall, Independence Hall in exhibits, dates, planning tips. List of names and addresses of bookstores and what is available with some items designed for classroom use and some free.
"Independence." 16-fold. Maps, touring information, history of Philadelphia including when it was the national capital.
"The National Parks and the Bicentennial of the United States Constitution." 12-fold. The making of the Constitution and the national park sites connected with it.
"Philadelphia Official Visitors Guide." 82 pages. Visitor facts and information, city and regional maps, photos, sightseeing, accommodations, historical information.

Sales List:
"Eastern National Park and Monument Association Sales List." 2 pages. Arranged by books, related materials. Title, price. Related materials include poster, medallions.
"Cobblestone: The History Magazine for Young People"; Vol. 3, No. 9; the Constitution of the United States. $3.50. Order form, order information, sketch, aims of the Eastern National Park and Monument Association.

Suggested Curriculum Application:
AMERICAN HISTORY
PENNSYLVANIA STATE AND LOCAL STUDIES

Suggested Sears Subject Heading:
ARCHITECTURE--CONSERVATION AND RESTORATION
PENNSYLVANIA--BUILDINGS
PENNSYLVANIA--DESCRIPTION AND TRAVEL--GUIDES
PENNSYLVANIA--HISTORY
PENNSYLVANIA--PUBLIC LANDS
U.S.--DESCRIPTION AND TRAVEL--GUIDES
U.S.--HISTORY--REVOLUTION, 1775-1783

• KINGS MOUNTAIN NATIONAL MILITARY PARK
P.O. Box 31, Kings Mountain, NC 28086. (803) 936-7921.
3,945.29 acres. 1931. Northern South Carolina, 35 miles northeast

of Spartanburg, SC on U.S. 29. Although the park is located in South Carolina, contact the North Carolina address above for information.

Site of important victory of over-mountain men against the British in the Revolutionary War. Museum, battlefield 1.5 mile self-guiding trail with exhibits, 1803 howser house, hiking and horse trails, programs, living history camp. Visitor center. Camping and picnicking in adjoining state park. Meals and lodging in Gaffney and Spartanburg.

Free Print Material:
    "Guide to Hiking and Horse Trails." 8-fold. Map, safety tips,
        park regulations.
    "King Mountain." 12-fold. Military campaign, maps, illustration.
    "Kings Mountain National Military Park." 6-fold. What to see
        and do, map, activities. Number to call about state park
        programs.

Sales/Audiovisual List:
    "Eastern National Park and Monument Association." 2 pages.
        Grouped by: publications, audio-visual aids, theme-related
        souvenirs. Ordering information.
    "American Revolution Bicentennial." $3.50.

Audiovisual List:
    "Films Available in Kings Mountain Visitor Center." 3 pages.
        Title, description, running time, type, date is usually in-
        cluded.
    "Age of Alaska." A pictorial explanation of the eleven proposed
        national parks and monuments in Alaska which would double
        the present size of the national park system, (5th grade and
        above), 21 minutes.

Suggested Curriculum Application:
    AMERICAN HISTORY
    SOUTH CAROLINA STATE AND LOCAL STUDIES

Suggested Sears Subject Heading:
    SOUTH CAROLINA--DESCRIPTION AND TRAVEL--GUIDES
    SOUTH CAROLINA--PUBLIC LANDS
    U.S.--DESCRIPTION AND TRAVEL--GUIDES
    U.S.--HISTORY--REVOLUTION, 1775-1783

• MINUTE MAN
National Historical Park. Post Office Box 160, Concord, MA 01742.
(617) 369-6993. 748.81 acres. 1959. Northeast Massachusetts,
visitor centers off Liberty Street in Concord and off Route 2A in
Lexington.

1775 site of fighting, the "Shot Heard Round the World," that was the beginning of the American Revolution. "Wayside," the house of the muster master for the Concord militia, later became the home of Louisa May Alcott, Nathaniel Hawthorne and others. Minute Man statue, Fiske House Site, the Bluff, Paul Revere Capture Site, Captain William Smith House, Hartwell Tavern, Bloodly Angles, Hardy's Hill, Meriam's Corner, Wayside, North Bridge, four miles of battle road between Lexington and Concord. Film, map program. Visitor centers. Food and lodging nearby.

Free Print Material:
"Concord Museum." 2 pages. Woodcut, map, description of the 15 period room museum, hours, visitor information.
"Great Meadows National Wildlife Refuge." 10-fold. History, areas, recreation, public use regulations, maps, photos. Information about the National Wildlife Refuge System and the U.S. Department of the Interior.
"Group Campsite Reservations." 2 pages. Making a reservation, charges, form, chart of national park campgrounds. Sketches, chart of camping equipment.
"In the Spirit of Walden." 14-fold. Sketches, photos, map. Quotations, life of Henry David Thoreau, origin of Walden Pond.
"Local Points of Interest." 2 pages. Place, telephone, address, location, features, and other visitor information. Grouped by various sites such as Minute Man National Historical Park, Lexington, MA.
"Lowell Massachusetts: History at Work." 12-fold. What to see at Lowell Heritage State Park and Lowell National Historical Park, photos, map, illustrations.
"Minute Man National Historical Park." 16-fold. Maps, photos, what to see, account of the beginning of the Revolution, historical drawings, military maps.
"National Park Sites: North Atlantic Region (New England, New York and New Jersey)." 12-fold. Map, photos, park description, phone and address. Grouped by state. Addresses for National Park Service, national forests, fish and wildlife.
"The Old Manse." 4-fold. Description of the Old Manse that was built in 1770 and purchased in 1939 by the trustees of reservations. Biographical information about Ralph Waldo Emerson.
"Orchard House." 6-fold. Photos, map, hours and description of the home of the Alcotts and setting for Little Women, biographical information of Louisa May Alcott's family.
"Scottish Rite Masonic Museum of Our National Heritage." 6-fold. Exhibitions, programs, library, photos, visitor information. Photos, map. The museum is located near Boston.

Bibliography:
"Basic Orientation Reading List-Minute Man National Historical Park." 7 pages. Designed to provide a guide in an initial reading program. Grouped by: issues and events preceding

the war, April 19, 1775, the war 1775-1783, weapons, the war at sea, loyalists, sociological and cultural, the Wayside, National Park Service, interpretation. Symbols denote the section of the park's collection, historian's office, where the publications can be found. Author, title, publisher, place of publication, date.

Sales List:
"Eastern National Park and Monument Association Book List: Minute Man National Historical Park." Grouped by: American Revolution, children's books, colonial living, Concord authors, Concord, travel and guide books, Peterson Field Guides, coloring books, posters, pewter statues, historic documents. Ordering information, order form, aims of the Eastern National Park and Monument Association. Title, author, pages, annotation, price.
"Battle Road Hour by Hour," Concord Chamber of Commerce, 39 pp. A detailed account of the events of April 19, 1775. $1.50.

Suggested Curriculum Application:
AMERICAN HISTORY
ENGLISH
MASSACHUSETTS STATE AND LOCAL STUDIES

Suggested Sears Subject Heading:
AMERICAN LITERATURE
CONCORD, BATTLE OF
LEXINGTON, BATTLE OF
MASSACHUSETTS--DESCRIPTION AND TRAVEL--GUIDES
MASSACHUSETTS--PUBLIC LANDS
U.S.--DESCRIPTION AND TRAVEL--GUIDES
U.S.--HISTORY--REVOLUTION, 1775-1783
WAYSIDE

• MOORES CREEK
National Battlefield. P.O. Box 69, Currie, NC 28435.
(919) 283-5591. 86.52 acres. 1926. Southern North Carolina, 20 miles northwest of Wilmington, NC, by U.S. 21 and N.C. 210.

Site of 1776 battle between North Carolina patriots and loyalists. The patriot victory aided the Revolutionary cause and North Carolina became the first colony to vote independence. Exhibits, diorama, history trail follows for a short distance the original alignment of the road used by both sides, the Patriot Monument, the Tarheel Trail has exhibits along the path, audiovisual program. Guide services are available for groups if advance arrangements are made. Visitor center, picnicking, meals and lodging in Wilmington.

Free Print Material:
"Litter-ally Speaking...." 2 pages. What littering costs the

taxpayer, importance of picking up, cleaning up.

"Moores Creek." 8-fold. Happenings at the February 27, 1776 battle, illustration, photos, maps, battlefield tour, visitor tips.

"National Park Service Travel Tips." 8-fold. Photos, making reservations, selecting park areas to visit, travel, accommodations, currency exchange for international visitors and other aids.

"Parks for America." 16-fold. Sketches, photos. History, development and uses of national parks.

"Trees Need Their Skin Too!" 6-fold. Appeal to campers to help protect trees when camping, illustrations, photos. Rules to follow to keep trees healthy.

"Wilmington, North Carolina Guide Map." 16-fold. Includes description of the battlefield, history and attractions of Cape Fear coast, maps, photos.

Bibliography:

"Source List." 1 page. Grouped by: author, title, publisher, city, date. Another list grouped by: author and title. Both are books for the general reader; the first had one magazine article and was alphabetically arranged by author.

Sales/Audiovisual List:

"Price List Eastern National Park and Monument Association." 2 pages. Grouped by: books, souvenirs. Souvenirs include reproductions such as musket balls and sets of colonial currency; post cards, parchments, slide and cassette of the American Revolution, stamps and other items. Ordering instructions.

Suggested Curriculum Application:

AMERICAN HISTORY

NORTH CAROLINA STATE AND LOCAL STUDIES

Suggested Sears Subject Heading:

MOORES CREEK BRIDGE, BATTLE OF

NORTH CAROLINA--DESCRIPTION AND TRAVEL--GUIDES

NORTH CAROLINA--PUBLIC LANDS

U.S.--DESCRIPTION AND TRAVEL--GUIDES

U.S.--HISTORY--REVOLUTION, 1775-1783

• MORRISTOWN

National Historical Park. P.O. Box 1136R, Washington Place, Morristown, NJ 07960. (201) 539-2085. 1,675.94 acres. 1933. Central New Jersey, off of I-287.

Continental Army quarters during the Revolutionary War, including Washington's winter headquarters, 1777 and 1779-80. Museum. Research library for scholars. Programs, talks, exhibits, audiovisual presentations, living history demonstrations, trail network. Visitor center. Food and lodging in Morristown.

Free Print Material:
> "Calendar of Events." 1 page. Dates, hours and description of events. Hours that the park buildings are open and other visitor information.
>
> "Morristown National Historical Park Library." 6-fold. Description and importance of: the Park Collection, the Lloyd W. Smith Collection, the Hessian Transcripts, the Ford Papers, the Diary of Sylvanus Seeley, additional collections. Sketches, photo, map, visitor hours.

Sales List:
> "Eastern National Park and Monument Association Order Blank and Publication Order Form." 2 pages. Grouped by: publications, coloring books, reproductions, artifacts, historical documents. Order blank and ordering information.
>
> "Adventures in Colonial America--The Village." $1.95.

Audiovisual List:
> "Film List." 2 pages. Describes films for loan to schools. Loan policy, ordering information, form.
>
> "Washington's Headquarters." This film depicts the life of Washington's officers while at the Ford Mansion in Morristown during the winter of 1779-1780. 20 minutes.

Suggested Curriculum Application:
> AMERICAN HISTORY
> NEW JERSEY STATE AND LOCAL STUDIES

Suggested Sears Subject Heading:
> NEW JERSEY--DESCRIPTION AND TRAVEL--GUIDES
> NEW JERSEY--PUBLIC LANDS
> U.S.--DESCRIPTION AND TRAVEL--GUIDES
> U.S.--HISTORY--REVOLUTION, 1775-1783

• NINETY SIX
National Historic Site. Post Office Box 496, Ninety Six, SC 29666. (803) 543-4068. 989.14 acres. 1976. West central South Carolina, 9 miles east of Greenwood and 2 miles south of Ninety Six on State Highway 248.

Crossroads hamlet in the 18th century, scene of Revolutionary War confrontations culminating in the longest siege of the war conducted by the Continental Army in 1781. Historic Island Ford Road, siege lines, the Star Fort, site of Ninety Six, jail site, stockage redoubt, site of Cambridge. Historical walking trail, Log House Trail, Wayside exhibits, library, guided tours, museum, special programs. Visitor center, picnicking. Campground 8 miles away. Meals and lodging in Greenwood.

Free Print Material:
"Interpretive Base Map." 1 page. Features, map legend, map.
"Ninety Six." 8-fold. Events of the 1781 siege, park features,
photos, map, history of Ninety Six as a frontier village.
"Ninety Six a Brief History." 11 pages. History and development of Ninety Six since 1540, sketches, 4 pages of historical
maps.

Audiovisual List:
"Films." 2 pages. List includes title, running length, annotation.
"The Americans 1776." 28 minutes. A film about the tough decision colonists had to make in 1776--whether to be patriots or
loyalists. A merchant who travels through the colonies takes
an in-depth look into the lives of several people as they
struggle with the decision.

Sales/Audiovisual List:
"Price List, Eastern National Parks and Monuments Association
Sales Outlet." 4 pages. Titles of books, post cards, slide
sets, posters, coin and currency set, and other items. Order
form and ordering information.
"Battleground of Freedom, South Carolina in the Revolution" by
Nat and Sam Hilborn, hardbound, 8-1/2 x 11, 239 pages. A
general history of the 137 Revolutionary War engagements
fought in South Carolina. $15.00.

Suggested Curriculum Application:
AMERICAN HISTORY
SOUTH CAROLINA STATE AND LOCAL STUDIES

Suggested Sears Subject Heading:
SOUTH CAROLINA--DESCRIPTION AND TRAVEL--GUIDES
SOUTH CAROLINA--HISTORY
SOUTH CAROLINA--PUBLIC LANDS
U.S.--DESCRIPTION AND TRAVEL
U.S.--HISTORY--REVOLUTION, 1775-1783

• ST. PAUL'S CHURCH
National Historic Site. 897 S. Columbus Ave., Mt. Vernon, NY
10550. (914) 667-4116. 6.09 acres. 1943. Southern New York,
897 S. Columbus Ave. in Mt. Vernon.

Church has architectural and historical importance associated with
the events leading to the John Peter Zenger trial involving freedom
of the press and also with the American Revolution. Guided tours
to colonial St. Paul's Church, Historic Churchyard Cemetery, Village
Green. Nearby Bill of Rights Museum is located in the former car-
riage shed/parish hall and contains a working replica of an 18th-
century printing press and dioramas about Zenger and his trial.
Guided student group tours for grades 4 up are available by

appointment. Food and lodging in New Rochelle, Yonkers, Larch-
mont, Mamaroneck.

Free Print Material:
"Bill of Rights Museum at Saint Paul's National Historic Site."
10 fold. Historical time line beginning with 1642, sketches,
administration, visitor information.

"Zenger's Journal." 6 pages. Official publication of the Society
of the National Shrine of the Bill of Rights at St. Paul's
Church. Newspaper format. Photos, articles.

Bibliography:
Suggested readings included in "St. Paul's Historic Site" described below. Includes author, title, place of publication,
publisher, date.

Sales List:
"St. Paul's Historic Site" (BCB). .50. 12-page children's
brochure that includes a puzzle, history, page of suggested
readings, sketches, vocabulary list.

Suggested Curriculum Application:
AMERICAN HISTORY
ENGLISH
GOVERNMENT
NEW YORK STATE AND LOCAL STUDIES

Suggested Sears Subject Heading:
CHURCHES--NEW YORK
FREEDOM OF THE PRESS
NEW YORK--DESCRIPTION AND TRAVEL--GUIDES
NEW YORK--PUBLIC LANDS
U.S.--DESCRIPTION AND TRAVEL--GUIDES
U.S.--HISTORY--REVOLUTION, 1775-1783
ZENGER, JOHN PETER, 1697-1746

• SARATOGA
National Historical Park. RD #2, Box 33, Stillwater, NY 12170.
(518) 664-9821. 3,415.08 acres. 1938. Eastern New York, 30 miles
north of Albany on U.S. 54 and N.Y. 32.

Site of turning point in the Revolutionary War in 1777. Schuyler
House, Saratoga Monument, 10-mile one-way tour road winds
through historic points of interest and has audio units, wayside
exhibits, walking trails, wildlife. Groups are requested to make
reservations. Visitor center has a museum and film, park rangers
and service facilities. Picnicking at designated areas. Food and
lodging in Schuylerville.

Free Print Material:
"The Philip Schuyler House." 4-fold. History, description of
the general's house, sketch, map.
"Saratoga." 16-fold. Military activity, maps, visitor information,
importance, features of the battlefield tour, sketches.
"The Saratoga Monument." 4-fold. Construction, significance
of the 155-foot memorial overlooking the Hudson Valley where
surrender of the Crown Forces took place, map, sketch.
"Round and About the Battlefield." 6-fold. Visitor information
about the visitor center, tour road, recreation, map, park
restrictions.

Bibliography:
"The Battles of Saratoga: A Bibliography and Suggested Reading
List." 3 pages. Author, title, place of publication, publisher,
date, description.

Sales/Audiovisual List:
"Eastern National Park and Monument Association Sales List."
3 pages. Items grouped by: books; visual aids, souvenirs.
Ordering information.
"The Battles of Saratoga" by John R. Cuneo. $4.95.

Suggested Curriculum Application:
AMERICAN HISTORY
NEW YORK STATE AND LOCAL STUDIES

Suggested Sears Subject Heading:
NEW YORK--DESCRIPTION AND TRAVEL--GUIDES
NEW YORK--PUBLIC LANDS
SARATOGA, BATTLE OF
U.S.--DESCRIPTION AND TRAVEL--GUIDES
U.S.--HISTORY--REVOLUTION, 1775-1783

• THADDEUS KOSCIUSZKO
National Memorial. c/o Independence National Historical Park, 313
Walnut Street, Philadelphia, PA 19106. (215) 597-8974. 0.02
acres. 1972. Eastern Pennsylvania, in Philadelphia, at 301 Pine
Street, at the corner of Third and Pine Streets.

The house is where Thaddeus Kosciuszko resided the winter of 1797-
1798, one of the first foreign volunteers to come to the aid of
the American Revolutionary Army. Restored outside of the house
and restored second floor bedroom to look much as it did when
Kosciuszko resided there. Food and lodging in Philadelphia.

Free Print Material:
"Thaddeus Kosciuszko." 8-fold. Biographical sketch of

Kosciuszko, painting, photos. One side of English and the other in Polish.

Audiovisual List:

"Film and Slide Kit Request." 1 page. Order form and ordering instructions to request "Independence" in film, VHS video-tape, closed-caption film, English slide program or Spanish slide program.

"Film Purchase." 1 page. Information about purchase of the 28-minute long film "Independence," also available in video-tape.

Sales List:

"Eastern National Park and Monument Association Sales List." 1 page. Arranged by books, related materials. Title, price. Related materials include poster, medallions.

"Cobblestone: The History Magazine for Young People"; vol. 3, no. 9; the Constitution of the United States. $3.50. Order-ing form and information. Sketch. Aims of the Eastern National Park and Monument Association.

Suggested Curriculum Application:

AMERICAN HISTORY
PENNSYLVANIA STATE AND LOCAL STUDIES

Suggested Sears Subject Heading:

ARCHITECTURE--CONSERVATION AND RESTORATION
KOSCIUSZKO, THADDEUS, 1746-1817
PENNSYLVANIA--DESCRIPTION AND TRAVEL--GUIDES
PENNSYLVANIA--PUBLIC LANDS
U.S.--DESCRIPTION AND TRAVEL--GUIDES
U.S.--HISTORY--REVOLUTION, 1775-1783

ROCK FORMATIONS

- ARCHES

National Park. 125 West Second, South, Moab, UT 84532. (801) 259-8161. 73,378.98 acres. National Monument, 1929; National Park, 1971. Southeastern Utah, north of Moab, off U.S. 163 and Utah 128. A bridge on U.S. Highway 191 connects the park with Moab.

Over 200 cataloged arches ranging from 3-foot openings to 105-foot openings up to 291 feet high, called the greatest density of arches in the world. It took about 100 million years of eroding sandstone to create the color changing arches, spires, pinnacles, balanced rocks. Park Avenue (resembles a city skyline) of balanced rocks, spires, eroded fins, courthouse towers, balanced rock, the windows section, Panorama Point, Wolfe Ranch, Delicate Arch, Salt Valley Overlook, Skyline Arch, Broken and Sand Dune arches, Klondike Bluffs, Herdina Park. Talks, self-guiding trails, hiking, rock climbing, backcountry trails, wildlife sanctuary, scenic turnouts, color slide program, geology museum, history exhibit, commercial tours, programs, numbered stops along the park road, naturalist-led fiery furnace walk. Visitor center, picnicking, campground. Food and lodging in Moab.

Free Print Material:

"Arches." 12-fold. Maps, photos, diagrams, sketch, safety tips. Points and features of interest, how the arches were formed and other geological information regarding the park, wildlife, flowers.

"Commercial Backcountry Tour Services." 6 pages. Name, address, telephone, type of service. Services include: white water river trip, calm water river trips and transportation service, hiking and backpacking trips, backcountry vehicle trip, horseback/pack stock trip, mountain bike tours, special emphasis workshop.

"Utah's Canyonlands Region." 24-fold. Where the region is, what they have to offer, photos, maps, accommodations. Addresses, and telephones of canyonlands visitor centers in Moab, Monticello, Thompson Information Center, Green River, and other visitor information.

Suggested Curriculum Application:
GEOGRAPHY
GEOLOGY
UTAH STATE AND LOCAL STUDIES

Suggested Sears Subject Heading:
ARCHES NATIONAL PARK
GEOLOGY--U.S.
NATIONAL PARKS AND RESERVES--U.S.
NATURAL MONUMENTS
ROCKS
SANDSTONE
U.S.--DESCRIPTION AND TRAVEL--GUIDES
U.S.--GEOGRAPHY
UTAH--DESCRIPTION AND TRAVEL--GUIDES
UTAH--PUBLIC LANDS

• CANYONLANDS
National Park. P.O. Box 40, 32 South 1st East, Monticello, UT 84532. (801) 259-7164. 337,570.43 acres. 1964. Central Utah, off Utah 191, north-southwest of Moab, confluence of Colorado and Green rivers.

Preserve wilderness of rock, Indian prehistoric rock art and ruins, at the heart of the Colorado Plateau. Wind and water have cut rock into hundreds of canyons, buttes, fins, arches, spires and 7,800-foot mesas. Guided tours, backcountry trails, prehistoric Indian rock art, chartered river rafting, 4-wheel drive tours, guided horseback tours, overlooks. Island in the Sky, the Maze, the Needles are regions of the park as divided up by the two great canyons carved by the Green and Colorado rivers. Picnicking, campgrounds. Ranger station and park headquarters in Moab, Monticello Information Center.

Free Print Material:
  "Commercial Backcountry Tour Services." 6 pages. Name, address, telephone, type of service. Services include: white water river trip, calm water river trips and transportation service, hiking and backpacking trips, backcountry vehicle trip, horseback/pack stock trip, mountain bike tours, special emphasis workshop.

Suggested Curriculum Application:
  ART
  GEOGRAPHY
  NATIVE AMERICAN STUDIES
  RECREATION
  UTAH STATE AND LOCAL STUDIES

Suggested Sears Subject Heading:
  ANASAZI INDIANS
  CANYONLANDS NATIONAL PARK
  INDIANS OF NORTH AMERICA--ART
  NATIONAL PARKS AND RESERVES--U.S.
  OUTDOOR RECREATION
  ROCKS
  U.S.--DESCRIPTION AND TRAVEL--GUIDES
  U.S.--GEOGRAPHY
  UTAH--DESCRIPTION AND TRAVEL--GUIDES
  UTAH--PUBLIC LANDS
  WILDERNESS AREAS

• CAPITOL REEF
National Park. Torrey, UT 84775. (801) 425-3871. 241,904.26 acres. 1971. Central Utah, visitor center is 11 miles east Torrey by Utah 24.

Preserve sandstone cliffs with colorful sedimentary formations cut through by gorges. The ridge of rock that forms a barrier is named for one of its high points that resembles the dome of the U.S. Capitol. Naturalist services such as walks and programs, scenic drives, exhibits, orientation program. Visitor center, campgrounds, backcountry camping. Meals and lodging in Torrey.

Free Print Material:

"Brief History Development and Administration of Capitol Reef National Park, Utah." 4 pages. Narrative traces such aspects as early history, the father of Capitol Reef National Monument, monument enlarged by presidents Eisenhower and Johnson, current administration.

"Capitol Reef." 20 pages. Geology, history. Visitor information about features to see, weather variations, park regulations, services. Map, charts.

"Capitol Reef Scene." 8 pages. Articles about getting the most of your visit, what to see and do, safety tips, history, general park information.

"Climate." 1 page. Month-by-month records for: average high, average low, recorded high, recorded low, rainfall average, rainfall range, snowfall range, snowfall chance, based on records.

"A Look at Capitol Reef for Students." 2 pages. Geological history, cultural history of the 378-square-mile Capitol Reef National Park.

"The One-Room Fruita Schoolhouse." 2 pages. History of the Mormon school gives evidence of the importance of education to Mormon settlers in the Fremont River Valley.

"Red Rock Eden: The Story of Fruita and the Orchards." 2 pages. Mormon settlement orchard efforts at the junction of the Fremont River and Sulphur Creek.

Sales/Audiovisual List:

"Capitol Reef Natural History Association Publication List." 5 pages. Grouped by: story behind the scenery series, field guides, golden guides, other publications, children's coloring books, miscellaneous items, posters, postcards, 35mm color slide strips, maps, miscellaneous. Mail order information and order form.

"Arches," Johnson. $4.50.

Suggested Curriculum Application:

GEOGRAPHY
GEOLOGY
UTAH STATE AND PUBLIC LANDS

Suggested Sears Subject Heading:

CAPITOL REEF NATIONAL PARK
NATIONAL PARKS AND RESERVES--U.S.
ROCKS
SANDSTONE
U.S.--DESCRIPTION AND TRAVEL--GUIDES
UTAH--DESCRIPTION AND TRAVEL--GUIDES
UTAH--PUBLIC LANDS

- CEDAR BREAKS
National Monument. P.O. Box 749, Cedar City, UT 84720.

(801) 586-9451. 6,154.60 acres. 1933. Southwestern Utah, 23
miles from Cedar City off Interstate 15.

Great natural rock amphitheater, shaped like a giant coliseum,
2,000 feet deep and 3 miles in diameter. Named "cedar" for the
cedar or juniper trees that grew nearby and for "breaks," which
was a word for badlands by Utah settlers. Exhibits, wildflowers,
drive and scenic overlooks, trails. Visitor center, campground,
picnicking. Cedar City, Brian Head has lodging and food.

Free Print Material:
  "Birds of Cedar Breaks National Monument and Vicinity." 2
    pages. 95 species of birds. Groups such as: hawks and
    eagles, gallinaceous birds, shorebirds and many others.
    Common names.
  "The Bristlecone Pine." 5 pages. Sketch, importance, location,
    age and how this is determined (some have been dated at over
    4,900 years in age), habitat, adaptations.
  "Cedar Breaks." 8-fold. Features and attractions, map, park
    guide, photos.
  "The Geologic History of Cedar Breaks." 6 pages. Cretaceous
    to the pliocene. Chart.
  "Mammals of Cedar Breaks National Monument." 1 page. Grouped
    by order. Includes common and scientific names.
  "Utah National Parks and Monuments." 24-fold. Description and
    photos, suggested itinerary, map, address and phone numbers.
  "The Vascular Plants of Cedar Breaks National Monument." 15
    pages. Comprehensive checklist. Scientific and common name,
    where they are found.

Sales/Audiovisual List:
  "Zion Natural History Association." 2 pages. Publications, color
    slides, bulletins, maps, slide program, posters, title, author,
    date, price, annotation. Mail order instructions.
  "Alpine Pond Trail Guide: Cedar Breaks National Monument" by
    Earle Curran and David Clark. Full color folder. 1978.
    $.25.

Suggested Curriculum Application:
  GEOGRAPHY
  GEOLOGY
  NATURAL HISTORY
  UTAH STATE AND LOCAL STUDIES

Suggested Sears Subject Heading:
  GEOLOGY--U.S.
  NATURAL HISTORY--UTAH
  ROCKS
  U.S.--DESCRIPTION AND TRAVEL--GUIDES
  UTAH--DESCRIPTION AND TRAVEL--GUIDES
  UTAH--PUBLIC LANDS

• CHIRICAHUA
National Monument. Don Cabezas Route, Box 6500, Willcox, AZ
85643. (602) 824-3560. 11,134.80 acres. 1924. Southeastern Arizona, 36 miles southeast of Willcox, off Rt. 186.

Preserve varied rock formations created by volcanic activity aided by erosion. Scenic drive with roadside pullouts and exhibits, many unusual rock formations, hiking, forests, displays, Faraway Ranch and Stafford Cabin, slide show, guided walks and talks, self-guiding trails, mountains. Trails provide views of all scenic features in the park. Visitor center, campgrounds, picnicking. Meals and lodging and commercial campground in Willcox.

Free Print Material:
"Chiricahua Official Map and Guide." 8-fold. History, attractions, regulations and visitor tips. Photos, maps.
"Hiking in Chiricahua National Monument." 2 pages. Descriptions of various trails. Trails are divided as to difficulty. Tips for hikers.
"Schedule of visitor activities for Chiricahua National Monument." 2 pages. What is available in the visitor center, camping, trails, hiking, ranger-conducted activities and other areas. safety tips.

Sales/Audiovisual List:
"Publications on the Chiricahua National Monument and Surrounding Areas." 5 pages. Materials are grouped into such divisions as plants, animals, geology, children's books, history, slide sets, posters, maps and others.
"The Chiricahua Mountains" by Weldon Heald. Heald's memories of living in the Chiricahua Mountains; Cave Creek area southeast of Chiricahua National Monument. $9.50.

Suggested Curriculum Application:
ARIZONA STATE AND LOCAL STUDIES
GEOGRAPHY

Suggested Sears Subject Heading:
ARIZONA--DESCRIPTION AND TRAVEL--GUIDES
ARIZONA--PUBLIC LANDS
ROCKS
U.S.--DESCRIPTION AND TRAVEL--GUIDES

• EL MORRO
National Monument. Ramah, NM 87321. (505) 783-5132. 1,278.72 acres. 1906. West central New Mexico, 58 miles southeast of Gallup by N. Mex. 32 and 53.

Preserve a 200-foot high soft sandstone monolith with historic inscriptions by Indians, Spanish, and Americans. "Morro" means bluff in

Spanish. Museum; inscription trail passes historic pool, Spanish and American inscriptions, Indian petroglyphs; Pueblo ruins and panoramic view on the Mesa Top Trail; campfire programs; wayside exhibits. Visitor center, campgrounds, picnicking. Food and lodging at Grants, Gallup.

Free Print Material:
"El Morro." 10-fold. Map, photos, visitor information, the seven cities of Cibola, the founding of New Mexico, coming of Americans.

"Teacher's Guide and Handbook." 8 pages. Guide to help the teacher when visiting with students. Sketches, concepts for students, ideas for classroom activities.

Sales/Audiovisual List:
"Southwest Parks and Monuments Association Sales List." 8 pages. Grouped by: children's books, flora and fauna, geology, history, Indians--cultural, national parks, travel and guide, miscellaneous, posters and maps, slides, post card strips. Price, title, date, author, publisher, place of publication.

$.50 "El Morro Trails" (trail guide). Southwest Parks and Monuments Association: Tucson, Arizona.

Suggested Curriculum Application:
AMERICAN HISTORY
NATIVE AMERICAN STUDIES
NEW MEXICO STATE AND LOCAL STUDIES

Suggested Sears Subject Heading:
AMERICA--EXPLORATION
EXPLORATIONS
INDIANS OF NORTH AMERICA--HISTORY
NEW MEXICO--DESCRIPTION AND TRAVEL--GUIDES
NEW MEXICO--HISTORY
NEW MEXICO--PUBLIC LANDS
ROCKS
SANDSTONE
U.S.--DESCRIPTION AND TRAVEL--GUIDES
ZUNI INDIANS

• PICTURED ROCKS
National Lakeshore. P.O. Box 40, Munising, MI 49862.
(906) 387-2607. 72,898.86 acres. 1966. Northern upper peninsula of Michigan, Lake Superior shoreline, southeast of Marquette, reached from Mich. 28 and Mich. 94 at Munising or Mich. 77 at Grand Marais.

Multicolored sandstone rocks rising directly from Lake Superior as high as 200 feet stretch 15 miles with caves, arches, varied formations. Sand dunes, waterfalls, Grand Sable Banks, inland lakes, ponds, marshes, forests, beach. Old logging roads, established trails, cross-country skiing, snowshoeing, motor boating, exhibits, birdwatching. Bridal Veil Falls, Twelvemile Beach, Sable Falls, Grand Sable Dunes. Log Slide, Beaver Basin, Chapel Basin, Miners Castle and Falls and Beach, Munising Falls, Ausable Light Station. Boat tours from June to mid-October. Visitor center, ranger stations, campgrounds, picnicking. Food and lodging in Munising, Grand Marais.

Free Print Material:
"Backcountry Camping and Hiking." 8-fold. Backcountry camping and permit system, regulations, sanitations, reservations, firewood, safety, map, North Country National Scenic Trail.
"Checklist of Birds." 7 pages. Bird groups such as loons, grebes, cormorants.
"Geology of Pictured Rocks National Lakeshore." 8-fold. Bedrock, glaciers, sketches, origin of Chapel Rock, evolution of Beaver Basin, origin of the Chapel/Mosquito Channels, waterfalls and other features.
"Michigan Amphibians." 1 page. Scientific and common names.
"Michigan Mammals." 2 pages. Scientific and common names.
"Michigan Reptiles." 1 page. Scientific and common names.
"Pictured Rocks." 12-fold. Photos, history and description, what the national lakeshore has to offer the visitor, map, points of interest.
"The Pictured Rocks National Lakeshore--An American First." 4 pages. Development and composition of America's first national lakeshore.
"Pictured Rocks National Lakeshore Vegetation." 2 pages. Upland soils, areas of outwash and well-drained sands, boggy areas and vegetation they support.
"Pictured Rocks National Lakeshore Wild Flowers." 6 pages. Common name, scientific name, places found, months they grow.
"Take Pride in America." 8-fold. Photos, public awareness campaign to encourage national pride in nation's natural and cultural resources.
"White Birch Trail." 12 pages. Narrative guide, sketches, map for the 1.6-mile-long White Birch Trail.
"White Pine Trail." 8-fold. Narrative guide to the 0.7-mile-long White Pine Trail, sketch, map.

Sales/Audiovisual List:
"Publications List." 1 page. Books, calendar, maps, guides, coloring books, prints, post cards, notecards, slide strips, star and planet locator, model of great lakes ship, buttons, patches, cross-stitch kit. Title, price. Ordering directions.
"Around the Shores of Lake Superior." $7.95.

Suggested Curriculum Application:
GEOGRAPHY

GEOLOGY
MICHIGAN STATE AND LOCAL STUDIES
NATURAL HISTORY

Suggested Sears Subject Heading:
GEOLOGY--U.S.
MICHIGAN--DESCRIPTION AND TRAVEL--GUIDES
MICHIGAN--PUBLIC LANDS
NATURAL HISTORY--MICHIGAN
ROCKS
SANDSTONE
U.S.--DESCRIPTION AND TRAVEL--GUIDES
U.S.--GEOGRAPHY

- PINNACLES

National Monument. Paicines, CA 95043. (408) 389-4578. 16,221.77
acres. 1908. West central California near the San Andreas Rift
Zone. East entrance 35 miles south of Hollister on Calif. Route 146.
West entrance 11 miles east of Soledad on Calif. Route 146.

Spires, caves, crags with rock remains up to 1,200 feet, the results
of an ancient volcano and movement along the San Andreas Rift Zone.
Coast range chaparral with distinctive plants and animals. Wildflowers in spring, interpretive talks, hiking and nature trails,
cave touring, spires and crags, climbing, exhibits, campfire programs, demonstrations. Inquire about special programs that may be
requested for educational groups. Visitor center, ranger station,
campground, picnicking. Camping nearby. Food and lodging in
Hollister, King City.

Free Print Material:
  "Hiking and Camping Information." 2 pages. Access, travel
    season, camping, backcountry use, safety, regulations and
    other user information.
  "Pinnacles." 12-fold. Photos, illustrations, map, description of
    hiking trails, safety tips, geological formation of the area,
    plant and animal communities.

Suggested Curriculum Application:
  CALIFORNIA STATE AND LOCAL STUDIES
  GEOGRAPHY
  GEOLOGY
  NATURAL HISTORY

Suggested Sears Subject Heading:
  CALIFORNIA--DESCRIPTION AND TRAVEL--GUIDES
  CALIFORNIA--PUBLIC LANDS
  GEOLOGY--U.S.
  NATURAL HISTORY--CALIFORNIA
  ROCKS
  U.S.--DESCRIPTION AND TRAVEL--GUIDES

U.S.--GEOGRAPHY

• ZION
National Park. Springdale, UT 84767. (801) 772-3256. 146,551.10
acres. 1919. Southwestern Utah, 60 miles from Cedar City, visitor
center at Kolob Canyons exit from I-15.

Spectacular cliffs, canyons, erosion and rock-fault patterns compose
unusual rock shapes. Tram tours, Checkerboard Mesa, naturalist-
guided walks, Kolob Terrace Road, bicycling, Virgin River, slide
program, wildlife, evening programs, talks, variety of trails, horseback riding, Zion Canyon Scenic Drive, Zion-Mt. Carmel Highway.
Visitor centers, ranger stations, campgrounds, picnicking, food and
lodging. Food and lodging in Springdale, Mt. Carmel, Hurricane.

Free Print Material:
  "Common Plant Checklist of Zion National Park." 2 pages.
    Name of plant and where it is found.
  "Footpaths in the Parks." 16 pages. Articles, photos, Junior
    Ranger program for children, aims of the Zion Natural History
    Association, selected publications.
  "The Geologic Story of the Zion National Park Area." 4 pages.
    Sedimentation, uplift and erosion.
  "Mammal Checklist of Zion National Park." 2 pages. Common
    name, scientific name, where mammal is found.
  "Recreation Fee Schedule." 2 pages. Entrance fees, camping
    fees, camping, miscellaneous.
  "Springdale." 4-fold. Sightseeing, facilities available in Spring-
    dale, UT located at the mouth of Zion National Park.
  "You Asked About the Geology." 2 pages. How the Zion Canyon
    was formed. Monthly chart of high temperatures, low tempera-
    tures, precipitation.
  "Zion." 24-fold. Maps, chart of trails, features to see, descrip-
    tion of Zion, general information and services, photos.

Sales/Audiovisual List:
  Two included in "Footpaths in the Parks" described above. Grouped
    by: guides to geology and trails, plants and animals, children's,
    historical, maps, posters, slides. Order form and order instruc-
    tions. Author, title, description, pages, date, price.
  "Alpine Pond Trail Guide: Cedar Breaks National Monument." By
    Earl Curran and David Clark. Full-color folder. 1978. .25.

Suggested Curriculum Application:
  GEOGRAPHY
  GEOLOGY
  NATURAL HISTORY
  UTAH STATE AND LOCAL STUDIES

Suggested Sears Subject Heading:
  GEOLOGY--U.S.

NATIONAL PARKS AND RESERVES-U.S.
NATURAL HISTORY--UTAH
ROCKS
U.S.--DESCRIPTION AND TRAVEL--GUIDES
U.S.--GEOGRAPHY
UTAH--DESCRIPTION AND TRAVEL--GUIDES
UTAH--PUBLIC LANDS
ZION NATIONAL PARK

SCULPTURE

• MOUNT RUSHMORE
National Memorial. P.O. Box 268, Keystone, SD 57761.
(605) 574-2523. 1,278.45 acres. 1925. Western South Dakota, 25
miles southwest of Rapid City and 3 miles from Keystone, SD.

Huge heads of Presidents George Washington, Thomas Jefferson,
Abraham Lincoln and Theodore Roosevelt sculpted on the face of
6,000-foot granite mountain. Ranger talks, programs, film, special
activities, trails, amphitheater summer evening sculpture lighting
program. Brochures are available in German, Spanish, Japanese,
French, Italian. Visitor center, gift shop, cafeteria, snack bar.
Picnicking, campgrounds, food and lodging in Keystone.

Free Print Material:
"Activities." 8-fold. Current visitor center hours, programs,
talks, special events, visitor services, map.
"Dimensions." 8-fold. Scale, length of nose and other dimensions, comparative size with Statue of Liberty, Washington
Monument.
"Mount Rushmore." 8-fold. How the monument was carved,
information about the sculptor, Gutzon Borglum. Photos,
map.
"Park Times." 12 pages. Newspaper format. Guide to South
Dakota's state parks and recreation areas. Includes a kids'
page of games.
"Rushmore: Monument to America." 8-fold. Significance of the
memorial and how it came to be carved, dimensions, quotations
of the four presidents represented and the sculptor of Mount
Rushmore.
"South Dakota Vacation Guide." 146 pages. Photos, maps,
articles, state symbols, museums, traveler's services directory,
travel planners, public campgrounds, state and natural parks
and other visitor aids.

Bibliography:
"Bibliography." 1 page. Arranged by: Mount Rushmore, Gutzon

Borglum, for young readers. Author, title, place of publication, publisher, date. Notation is made of those that are available at the Mount Rushmore Mountain Company Gift Shop.

Suggested Curriculum Application:
ART
GEOGRAPHY
SOUTH DAKOTA STATE AND LOCAL STUDIES

Suggested Sears Subject Heading:
PRESIDENTS--U.S.
SCULPTURE, AMERICAN
SOUTH DAKOTA--DESCRIPTION AND TRAVEL--GUIDES
SOUTH DAKOTA--PUBLIC LANDS
U.S.--DESCRIPTION AND TRAVEL--GUIDES

- SAINT-GAUDENS
National Historic Site. RR #2, Cornish, NH 03745. (603) 675-2175. 148.23 acres. 1964. Western New Hampshire, in Cornish, off N.H. 12A.

Home, studio, and gardens of sculptor, Augustus Saint-Gaudens. "Aspet," the sculptor's home, studios, gardens. Concerts, art exhibitions, sculptor-in-residence, nature trails. Food and lodging in surrounding areas.

Free Print Material:
"Ravine Trail." 12 pages. Natural features of a 1/4-mile walk, an old cart path often visited by the sculptor. Sketches of leaves, plants.
"Saint-Gaudens." 10-fold. The home, studios and gardens of the sculptor. Traces Saint-Gauden's life from his birth in Ireland to his death in 1907.
"The Saint-Gaudens National Historic Site." 6-fold. Features and tour, photos, maps.
"Woodlands and Wetlands." 18 pages. A guide to the Blow-Me-Down natural area. Walking through the ground forest, woodlands, wetlands and other areas. Photos, maps, list of birds, trees, ferns and fern allies.

Sales List:
"Order Form and Price List." 3 pages. Publications, postcards, coins, posters, calendar and other items. Order information.
"The Work of Augustus Saint-Gaudens," by John Dryfhout. The most complete compendium ever attempted on the life and works of Augustus Saint-Gaudens. 356 pages, over 500 illustrations. Hardcover $60.00: paperback $29.95.

Suggested Curriculum Application:
ART

NEW HAMPSHIRE STATE AND LOCAL STUDIES

Suggested Sears Subject Heading:
  NEW HAMPSHIRE--DESCRIPTION AND TRAVEL--GUIDES
  NEW HAMPSHIRE--PUBLIC LANDS
  SAINT-GAUDENS, AUGUSTUS, 1848-1907
  SCULPTORS, AMERICAN
  U.S.--DESCRIPTION AND TRAVEL--GUIDES

• STATUE OF LIBERTY
National Monument. Liberty Island, New York, NY   10004.
(212) 363-3200. 58.38 acres. 1924. Off eastern New York and
New Jersey coastline on Liberty Island.

Preserve the 152-foot copper Statue of Liberty given by France to
the United States in 1886. The monument includes the American
Museum of Immigration in the base of the statue and Ellis Island,
an immigration port from 1892 to 1954. Statue, museum, Ellis
Island. Ferry provides transportation to and from Liberty Island:
for rates and schedules contact (212) 265-5755.

Free Print Material:
  "Facts About the Statue of Liberty." 1 page. Statistics in
    standard and metric such as the length of the nose. Interest-
    ing facts such as how many windows are in the crown, what
    the roman numerals say.
  "The Statue of Liberty." 1 page. Construction, French and
    American financing, administrative changes, addition of Ellis
    Island in 1965.
  "Statue of Liberty Restoration." 1 page. Sketch with labeled
    portions indicating restoration process.

Suggested Curriculum Application:
  AMERICAN HISTORY
  ART
  GOVERNMENT
  NEW YORK STATE AND LOCAL STUDIES

Suggested Sears Subject Heading:
  AMERICAN MUSEUM OF IMMIGRATION
  ELLIS ISLAND
  IMMIGRATION AND EMIGRATION
  MONUMENTS
  NEW YORK--PUBLIC LANDS
  U.S.--DESCRIPTION AND TRAVEL--GUIDES

STATESMEN

- FRIENDSHIP HILL

National Historic Site, R.D. 2, Box 528, Farmington, PA   15437.
(412) 725-9190.   674.56 acres.   1978.   Southwestern Pennsylvania,
3 miles north of Point Marion, PA, along State Route 166.

Preserve the country estate of Albert Gallatin, a Swiss immigrant
who made vital contributions in finance, politics, diplomacy,
scholarship and served as treasury secretary under Presidents
Jefferson and Madison.   Guided tours of the house, exhibits, slide
program, gazebo, grave site, hiking trails, self-guiding tour of the
grounds.   Visitor center.   Food and lodging in Uniontown and
Morgantown.

Free Print Material:
  "Friendship Hill." 6-fold. Sketch, map, floorplan, contributions
      of Albert Gallatin, visitor information, construction history of
      the house.
  "Information Letter." 2 pages. Hours, description and purpose
      of Friendship Hill National Historic Site.

Sales/Audiovisual List:
  "Eastern National Parks and Monument Association Sales List."
      7 pages. Grouped by: publications, illustrative materials,
      slides, reproductions. Illustrative material includes post
      cards, maps, crewel kit, notecards. Reproductions include
      musket balls, dice, lead pencil, paper cartridge, wooden spin
      top. Trivia card game on national parks. Order sheet, or-
      dering directions. Publication annotations include title,
      author, annotation, publisher, date, pages, type of cover,
      price. Most other items are also annotated.
  "Advice to Officers." Sixth edition of a 1783 manual of humorous
      instructions. 134 pages, soft cover $2.50.

Suggested Curriculum Application:
  AMERICAN HISTORY
  PENNSYLVANIA STATE AND LOCAL STUDIES

Suggested Sears Subject Heading:
  GALLATIN, ALBERT, 1761-1849
  PENNSYLVANIA--DESCRIPTION AND TRAVEL--GUIDES
  PENNSYLVANIA--PUBLIC LANDS
  U.S.--DESCRIPTION AND TRAVEL--GUIDES
  U.S.--HISTORY--1783-1865

- HAMILTON GRANGE

National Memorial. c/o NPS Manhattan Sites, 26 Wall Street, New York, NY 10005. (212) 283-5154. 0.71 acres. 1962. Eastern New York, New York City, Convent Ave. and West 141st St.; can be reached by 85th Avenue IND Subway to West 145th Street.

Home of Alexander Hamilton, American statesman and first U.S. secretary of the treasury. The federal-style house, named in honor of the ancestral seat of the Hamilton family in Scotland, was completed in 1802 and had a view of Hudson and Harlem rivers. Interpretive programs, children's garden plots, guided house tour, exhibits. Food and lodging in New York City.

Free Print Material:
"Hamilton Grange." 12-fold. Boyhood, public and family life, patriot contributions of Alexander Hamilton, illustrations, the grange today.

Sales/Audiovisual List:
"Sales List." 2 pages. Title and price of maps, flags, currency, paper, biography, cookbook, quill pen, coloring book and other items.
"After the Revolution." $5.36.

Suggested Curriculum Application:
AMERICAN HISTORY
GOVERNMENT
NEW YORK STATE AND LOCAL STUDIES

Suggested Sears Subject Heading:
ARCHITECTURE--CONSERVATION AND RESTORATION
HAMILTON, ALEXANDER, 1755-1804
NEW YORK--DESCRIPTION AND TRAVEL--GUIDES
NEW YORK--PUBLIC LANDS
U.S.--DESCRIPTION AND TRAVEL--GUIDES
U.S.--HISTORY--REVOLUTION, 1775-1783

- ROGER WILLIAMS

National Memorial. P.O. Box 367, Annex Station, Providence, RI 02901. (401) 528-5385. 4.56 acres. 1965. Northeastern Rhode Island, 282 North Main Street in Providence.

Commemorates the life and work of Roger Williams, American statesman and 17th-century champion of religious freedom and democracy, founder of Rhode Island. Memorial is on the site of the original 1636 Providence settlement. (Providence means "gift of God" and the land was presented as a gift to Williams by two Narragansett chiefs). Exhibits, slide show, Roger Williams Spring Site, school and group tours, formal garden. Visitor center. Food and lodging in the greater Providence area.

Free Print Material:
 "A History of the Roger Williams National Memorial." 1 page.
  What the plot of land which is now the memorial was like in
  1636, changes in the land until it became a memorial.
 "A Map of the Providence Home Lots Showing Owners and Houses
  Erected 1636-1650." 1 page. Map taken from "The Civic and
  Architectural Development of Providence, 1636-1950" by John
  Hutchins Cady.
 "Providence the Walkable City Guide." 12-fold. Map, photos,
  descriptions of what to see, nearby attractions.
 "Roger Williams National Memorial." 12-fold. Life, accomplish-
  ments of Roger Williams. Maps, sketches. One map shows
  the dates and stages of Williams' travels.
 "Transcript of Audio-Visual Program at Roger Williams National
  Memorial." 2 pages. Accomplishments and career of Roger
  Williams.

Bibliography:
 "Works on Roger Williams." 2 pages. Arranged by: general,
  for young readers, pamphlet, writings of Roger Williams.
  Author, title, publisher, place of publication, date. Price
  and where to obtain some items. Books for young readers
  include grade level.

Sales List:
 "Roger Williams National Memorial Eastern National Agency Current Sales Items." 6 pages. Arranged by: Roger Williams,
  paperbacks on related history, Providence, Rhode Island,
  the nation, young visitors, National Park Service, post cards,
  scenic. Order number, title, author, price, description, publisher, date, number of pages.
 2-0921 "An Account of Roger Williams and the Narragansett
  Indians" by H. F. Davis $1.75. An 18-page pamphlet by a
  local historian. Pafnuty Press, 175 Freeman Parkway,
  Providence, RI 02906.

Suggested Curriculum Application:
 AMERICAN HISTORY
 RHODE ISLAND STATE AND LOCAL STUDIES

Suggested Sears Subject Heading:
 RELIGIOUS FREEDOM
 RHODE ISLAND--DESCRIPTION AND TRAVEL--GUIDES
 RHODE ISLAND--HISTORY
 RHODE ISLAND--PUBLIC LANDS
 U.S.--DESCRIPTION AND TRAVEL--GUIDES
 WILLIAMS, ROGER, 1603-1683

TRADING POSTS

- BENT'S OLD FORT
National Historic Site. 35110 Highway 194 East, La Junta, CO
81050. (303) 384-2596. 799.80 acres. 1960. Eastern Colorado,
68 miles east of Pueblo, 8 miles east of La Junta on Colo. 194.

Reconstructed fort and rooms of an important outpost that was a
trading center for Indians, a fur-trading post on the Santa Fe
Trail that was built in 1833-34. Self-guiding tour of the adobe fort
with rooms furnished in period style, archeological collection, living
history interpretation, annual rendezvous re-enactment. Picnicking.
Camping nearby. Food and lodging in La Junta and Los Animas.

Free Print Material:
    "Bent's Old Fort." 12-fold. Construction, purpose and function.
       Photos, map, floorplan. Biographical sketches of the leaders
       involved with the trading company.

Sales/Audiovisual List:
    "Commemorative Medal." 1 page. Description of a commemorative
       medal, the first of a continuing series to commemorate Bent's
       Old Fort. Sketch.
    "Commemorative Medal." $4.95 unnumbered. $8.95 numbered.
       Built in 1833-34 as the mountain-plains extension of St. Louis-
       based American commerce and fur trade into the Southwest,
       Bent's Old Fort was for 15 years the frontier hub from which
       American trade....
    "Publications List." 6 pages. $.30. Books arranged alphabetical-
       ly by title. Living history items arranged alphabetically by
       item. Living history items includes beads, blankets, bowls,
       bracelets, VHS video, post cards, posters, maps, cards and
       many other items.
    "American Fur Trade of the Far West" by Hiram Martin Critten-
       don. Introduction and notes by Stallo Vinton. Objective,
       detailed and comprehensive account of the fur trade of the
       trans-Mississippi West. Originally published in....
    "Teachers of Colorado History Sales List." 1 page. Description
       of "Bent's Old Fort Adventure Guide" that includes pictures
       and readings, puzzles; "VHS Castle on the Plains," a 31-minute
       video that also has a presentation on the great sand dunes.
       Order form and ordering information included.
    "Bent's Old Fort Adventure Guide." $2.00. Contains pictures
       and readings about: building of the fort, life of the fort,
       people at the fort, wildlife. Includes information on sign
       language, animal prints, recipes and map reading. Educational
       format includes crosswords, dot-to-dots, and creative pages.
       (29 pages)

Suggested Curriculum Application:
AMERICAN HISTORY
COLORADO STATE AND LOCAL STUDIES

Suggested Sears Subject Heading:
ARCHITECTURE--CONSERVATION AND RESTORATION
COLORADO--DESCRIPTION AND TRAVEL--GUIDES
COLORADO--HISTORY
COLORADO--PUBLIC LANDS
FORTIFICATION
FUR TRADE
SANTE FE TRAIL
U.S.--DESCRIPTION AND TRAVEL--GUIDES

- FORT LARAMIE
National Historic Site. Fort Laramie, WY 82212. (307) 837-2221.
832.45 acres. 1938. Southeastern Wyoming. 3.1 miles southwest
of the town of Fort Laramie, WY on U.S. 26.

Preserve the site of a fur-trade post, buildings of military post that
protected the trails to the west. Remains of 21 historic buildings,
restored buildings, visible founations, demonstrations, self-guiding
tours, portrayal of frontier fort life. Visitor center. Meals and
lodging in Fort Laramie.

Free Print Material:
"Discover the Wyoming State Museum and State Historic Sites."
8-fold. Description and photos of Wyoming's historic sites,
historical society, museum.
"Fort Laramie." 16-fold. History, features, visitor tips, photos,
map, description of historic buildings.
"Wyoming Travel Tips." 8-fold. Description of state symbols
such as the great seal, photos, state history, historic sites,
attractions, information centers.

Sales List:
"Fort Laramie Historical Association Mail Order Publications."
4-fold. Item no., title, postpaid price of publications.
"Fort Laramie and the Pageant of the West, 1834-1890" by Leroy
Hafen and Francis Marion Young. Covers entire scope of
fort's history. Newly reprinted. $10.00.

Sales/Audiovisual List:
Post cards, slides and theme-related items are available. Please
write for a complete listing.

Suggested Curriculum Application:
AMERICAN HISTORY
WYOMING STATE AND LOCAL STUDIES

Suggested Sears Subject Heading:
  ARCHITECTURE--CONSERVATION AND RESTORATION
  FORTIFICATION
  FRONTIER AND PIONEER LIFE
  FUR TRADE
  OVERLAND JOURNEYS TO THE PACIFIC (U.S.)
  U.S.--DESCRIPTION AND TRAVEL--GUIDES
  WYOMING--DESCRIPTION AND TRAVEL--GUIDES
  WYOMING--PUBLIC LANDS

• FORT UNION TRADING POST
National Historic Site. Buford Route, Williston, ND 58801.
(701) 572-9083. 434.04 acres. 1966. Eastern Montana, western
North Dakota, 25 miles southwest of Williston, on County Road
4 off of U.S. 2, 25.

Foundation ruins of the largest 19th-century trading post on the
Missouri River. The fort was established for the American Fur
Company. Exhibits, guided tours, slide shows, living history
programs. Long-term plans call for complete reconstruction of Fort
Union Trading Post but meanwhile the site provides an authentic
setting of mid-19th century river, plains, hills. Visitor center.
Camping nearby. Food and lodging in Williston.

Free Print Material:
  "Fort Union Trading Post." 16-fold. Sketches, maps. Descrip-
    tion of the fort, fort life, the Indians and the fur trade,
    the fort today.
  "Fort Union Trading Post National Historic Site: A Brief
    Historical and Developmental Summary." 24 pages. Maps,
    sketches, historical chronology from 1803, photos, annual
    visitation chart, events of the buckskinner rendezvous.
  "Friends of Fort Union Trading Post." 1 page. Purpose of the
    group, application and donation forms.
  "Interpretive Programming." 2 pages. Introductory letter to
    administrators and teachers. What is available off site and
    on site. Name of program, length, description. Reservations
    are requested, telephone.
  "Missouri-Yellowstone Confluence Area Dakota Territory 1873."
    1 page. Map, historical information.
  "Montana Highway Map." 24-fold. Mileage table, points of
    interest, maps, traffic regulations and safety rules, Montana
    attractions, photos, statistics.
  "The Mountain Man." 1 page. Description of what a mountain
    man was, sketch.
  "Psoralea Esculenta Pursh. Pomme Blanche, Tipsin." 1 page.
    Root of plant that was a vital part of the Plains Indian diet.
    Description of the plant.
  "Take Pride in America." 8-fold. National public awareness
    campaign, photos to encourage everyone to take pride in the

country's natural and cultural resources.
"Visitor Information." 3 pages. Visitor activities, history, weather, special events and other visitor information. Sketch of the site plan based on archeological excavations.

Bibliography:
"Fort Union Trading Post National Historic Site Bibliography." 4 pages. Arranged by: historical references, anthropological/ archeological references, natural science references, cultural resource management references. Author, title, place of publication, publisher, date.
"Selected Reading List on Fort Union." 5 pages. Arranged alphabetically by author. Includes author, date, title, place of publication, publisher, description.

Sales/Audiovisual List:
"Catalogue of Books and Other Interpretive Materials." 16 pages. Arranged by: Theodore Roosevelt, Western Americana, Fort Union, natural history, Knife River, children's corner (includes special interest books such as cookbooks, art prints), national parks, upper Souris, animal posters, scenic posters, post cards, antique document, topographic maps, maps, slide sets. Purpose of the Theodore Roosevelt Nature and History Association, order blank and ordering directions, map, sketches.
"American Bears." (hard cover). $2.98. Writings of Theodore Roosevelt.

Suggested Curriculum Application:
AMERICAN HISTORY
ARCHEOLOGY
MONTANA STATE AND LOCAL STUDIES
NORTH DAKOTA STATE AND LOCAL STUDIES

Suggested Sears Subject Heading:
EXCAVATIONS (ARCHEOLOGY)
FRONTIER AND PIONEER LIFE
FUR TRADE
MONTANA--DESCRIPTION AND TRAVEL--GUIDES
MONTANA--PUBLIC LANDS
NORTH DAKOTA--DESCRIPTION AND TRAVEL--GUIDES
NORTH DAKOTA--PUBLIC LANDS
U.S.--DESCRIPTION AND TRAVEL--GUIDES

• FORT VANCOUVER
National Historic Site. Vancouver, WA 98661. (206) 696-7655.
208.89 acres. National Monument, 1948; National Historic Site, 1961.
Southwestern Washington, in Vancouver off I-5.

Hudson Bay Company's fur trading western headquarters from 1825 to 1849, the center of Pacific Northwest activities. Beginning in 1948, archeologists excavated the site of the original fort, taking more than one million artifacts which were used for the basis of the current reconstructed fort. Museum exhibits, children's playground. Tours of: blacksmith's shop, bakery, Indian trade shop and dispensary, Wash House, Chief Factor's residence, kitchen, shipping needs, farming acreage, bastion, stockade. Visitor center. Picnicking and campground nearby. Food and lodging in greater Vancouver area.

Free Print Material:

"Campground Reservations." 10-fold. Description of various national park campgrounds, location, other information. Campsite reservation request form.

"Fort Vancouver." 12-fold. Reconstructed portions of the fort, activity in Fort Vancouver when it was in its power, painting, sketches, map. Portraits and activities of personalities important to the fort.

"National Parks and National Forests in the Pacific Northwest." 24-fold. Recreational opportunities, passports, photos, chart of features and attractions in Oregon, Idaho and Washington, map.

"National Park Service Travel Tips." 8-fold. Photos, selecting park areas to visit, making reservations, variety of traveler opportunities within the national park system.

"Vancouver and Clark County U.S.A. Recreational Review." 8-fold. Parks, campgrounds, swimming pools, theaters, special interests, historic attractions and other recreational information. Sketch.

Suggested Curriculum Application:
AMERICAN HISTORY
ARCHEOLOGY
WASHINGTON STATE AND LOCAL STUDIES

Suggested Sears Subject Heading:
ARCHITECTURE--CONSERVATION AND RESTORATION
EXCAVATIONS (ARCHEOLOGY)
FORTIFICATION
FUR TRADE
NORTHWEST, PACIFIC
U.S.--DESCRIPTION AND TRAVEL--GUIDES
U.S.--HISTORY--1815-1861
WASHINGTON--DESCRIPTION AND TRAVEL--GUIDES
WASHINGTON--HISTORY
WAHSINGTON--PUBLIC LANDS

• HUBBELL TRADING POST
National Historic Site. P.O. Box 150, Ganado, AZ 86505.
(602) 755-3475. 160.09 acres. 1965. Northeastern Arizona, 3 miles from Route 191 in Chinle.

Preserve the oldest continually active trading post, located on
Navajo Reservation. Self-guiding trail, interpretive programs,
weaving demonstrations, Indian crafts demonstrations, visitor's
loom, tours of the site, self-guided ground tour, the trading post
rooms. Inquire about additional tours and programs offered in the
summer. Special tours may be arranged for groups during the
months of October to May. Visitor center. Picnic tables are located near the visitor center. Food and lodging at Window Rock,
AZ.

Free Print Material:
> "Guide to Lodging & Camping." 2 pages. List of commercial
> lodging on and near the Navajo and Hopi resrevations ar-
> ranged by city. Includes name of lodging, how many units,
> address and telephone. Also covers campgrounds.
> "Hubbell Trading Post." 12-fold. Information about the trader
> John Lorenzo Hubbell, the importance of the trading post.
> Photos, map.
> "Traveling Among the Navajos." 2 pages. Background about
> the land, language, people, hogans. Travel tips when among
> the Navajos.
> "Visit Planner." 2 pages. What to see and do, hours of the
> Hubbell Trading Post, bus tours and groups, weather, im-
> paired visitor accessibility and other visitor tips.

Suggested Curriculum Application:
> AMERICAN HISTORY
> ARIZONA STATE AND LOCAL STUDIES
> NATIVE AMERICAN STUDIES

Suggested Sears Subject Heading:
> ARIZONA--DESCRIPTION AND TRAVEL--GUIDES
> ARIZONA--PUBLIC LANDS
> INDIANS OF NORTH AMERICA--ARIZONA
> NAVAJO INDIANS
> U.S.--DESCRIPTION AND TRAVEL--GUIDES

TRAILS

• APPALACHIAN
National Scenic Trail. P.O. Box 236, Harpers Ferry, WV   25425.
(304) 535-6331. 115,863.04 acres. 1968. From Mount Katahdin, ME
to Springer Mountain, GA.

America's first national scenic trail extends 2,100 miles through 14
states. It is primarily a backpacker's trail and follows mountain

ridgelines. Hiking, backpacking. The entire trail takes four to six months to complete. Campgrounds, food and lodging along the way.

Free Print Material:
 "The AMC Hut System: Hospitality in High Places." 12-fold. What Appalachian Mountain Club huts offer the hikers. Each summer thousands of people depend on these hostels as a basecamp. Descriptions of huts, map. Sketches, photos.
 "The Appalachian Trail: Maine to Georgia." 16-fold. What the Appalachian Trail Conference is and what it does, application form.
 "ATC Hiker Security Guidelines." 1 page. Ten guidelines for the hiker to follow.
 "Four Lines of Defense Against Hypothermia." 6-fold. Four ways of guarding against the cold, sketches.
 "Is the Water Safe?" 8-fold. Avoiding hazards encountered in drinking untreated water.

Sales List:
 "Sales List." 2 pages. Grouped by: Appalachian Trail guides, Appalachian Trail maps, T-shirts/patches/posters/miscellaneous products, maps and guides to other trails, books of general interest. Item number, name of item, price. Ordering directions, form.
 101 "Maine, '83." 10th ed., w/maps. $14.50 retail price; $12.35 member price.

Suggested Curriculum Application:
 CONNECTICUT STATE AND LOCAL STUDIES
 GEORGIA STATE AND LOCAL STUDIES
 MAINE STATE AND LOCAL STUDIES
 MARYLAND STATE AND LOCAL STUDIES
 MASSACHUSETTS STATE AND LOCAL STUDIES
 NEW HAMPSHIRE STATE AND LOCAL STUDIES
 NEW JERSEY STATE AND LOCAL STUDIES
 NEW YORK STATE AND LOCAL STUDIES
 NORTH CAROLINA STATE AND LOCAL STUDIES
 PENNSYLVANIA STATE AND LOCAL STUDIES
 RECREATION
 TENNESSEE STATE AND LOCAL STUDIES
 VERMONT STATE AND LOCAL STUDIES
 VIRGINIA STATE AND LOCAL STUDIES
 WEST VIRGINIA STATE AND LOCAL STUDIES

Suggested Sears Subject Heading:
 BACKPACKING
 CONNECTICUT--DESCRIPTION AND TRAVEL--GUIDES
 CONNECTICUT--PUBLIC LANDS
 GEORGIA--DESCRIPTION AND TRAVEL--GUIDES
 GEORGIA--PUBLIC LANDS

MAINE--DESCRIPTION AND TRAVEL--GUIDES
MAINE--PUBLIC LANDS
MARYLAND--DESCRIPTION AND TRAVEL--GUIDES
MARYLAND--PUBLIC LANDS
MASSACHUSETTS--DESCRIPTION AND TRAVEL--GUIDES
MASSACHUSETTS--PUBLIC LANDS
NEW HAMPSHIRE--DESCRIPTION AND TRAVEL--GUIDES
NEW HAMPSHIRE--PUBLIC LANDS
NEW JERSEY--DESCRIPTION AND TRAVEL--GUIDES
NER JERSEY--PUBLIC LANDS
NEW YORK--DESCRIPTION AND TRAVEL--GUIDES
NEW YORK--PUBLIC LANDS
NORTH CAROLINA--DESCRIPTION AND TRAVEL--GUIDES
NORTH CAROLINA--PUBLIC LANDS
OUTDOOR RECREATION
PENNSYLVANIA--DESCRIPTION AND TRAVEL--GUIDES
PENNSYLVANIA--PUBLIC LANDS
TENNESSEE--DESCRIPTION AND TRAVEL--GUIDES
TENNESSEE--PUBLIC LANDS
U.S.--DESCRIPTION AND TRAVEL--GUIDES
VERMONT--DESCRIPTION AND TRAVEL--GUIDES
VERMONT--PUBLIC LANDS
VIRGINIA--DESCRIPTION AND TRAVEL--GUIDES
VIRGINIA--PUBLIC LANDS
WEST VIRGINIA--DESCRIPTION AND TRAVEL--GUIDES
WEST VIRGINIA--PUBLIC LANDS

• GRAND PORTAGE
National Monument. Box 666, Grand Marais, MN 55604.
(218) 387-2788. 709.97 acres. National Historic Site, 1951;
National Monument, 1958. Northeast Minnesota, 146 miles northeast
of Duluth, 36 miles northeast of Grand Marais, off U.S. 61.

Preserve the historic Grand Portage Trail (the great carrying place)
and fur trade depot of the North West Company, providing interpretation of the fur trade era. The reconstructed fur trade post is
built upon the original site. Independent fur traders used the
Grand Portage as a depot from 1779-1802. Audiovisuals, exhibits,
Chippewa craft demonstrations and sales, ranger-conducted walks,
talks, activities, hiking trails, tours, Rendezvous Days events,
operating kitchen and pack warehouse, reconstructed fur trade
post. Campgrounds nearby. Food and lodging in Grand Portage,
Grand Marais.

Free Print Material:
"Grand Portage." 14-fold. Description of the fort, history and
development of the site, maps, sketches, the North West
Company, the fur trade, Grand Portage Trail, Mount Rose
Trail, the Dock.
"Grand Portage Chronology." 11 pages. Dates and events

beginning with: "2000 B.C.--Evidence of Use at the Mouth of the Pigeon River."

"National Park Service Travel Tips." 8-fold. What the park service offers the visitors, selecting park areas to visit, making reservations and other visitor tips.

"North West Company Courier." 4 pages. Newspaper format. Crossword puzzle, sketches, articles, photos, visitor activities.

Bibliography:

"Bibliography." 12 pages. Grouped by: books, collections, manuscripts and reports, periodicals, maps and atlas, lithographs. Alphabetical arrangement by author. Includes author, title, place of publication, publisher, date.

"Grand Portage National Monument Reading List." 1 page. Books grouped by: voyageurs and voyageur highway, the fur trade of North America, the North West Company, people of the North West Company, explorers of the North West Company, other companies at Grand Portage, western fur trade connections with Grand Portage. Author, title.

"References on Women." 1 page. books available through Grand Portage National Monument librarian services. Grouped by: those written by women, manuscripts by men with references to women on the frontier, records relating to women. Author, title, place of publication, publisher, date. Information about diaries and other documents related to the settlement of the area after 1850.

"Visit Planner." 6-fold. Visitor activities, safety, weather, camping, features of the monument. Map, sketch.

Audiovisual List:

"Film Program." 6-fold. Films available for free use by schools and other groups. Films cover such topics as: history of Grand Portage and the fur trade, lifestyle of the voyageurs, exploration, archeology, canoe-building. Viewing guides are enclosed with films. Film guidelines, sketch. Title of film description, running length.

"Northwest Passage--The Story of Grand Portage." Recreates the sights and sounds of life at the post, with narrative from early journals. Vivid photography and lively music make it an engaging film for all ages. (12 minutes)

Sales/Audiovisual List:

"Grand Portage National Monument Sales List." 2 pages. Grouped by: books, audio and visual aids, theme-related souvenirs, theme-related products, Jamestown glass. Audio and visual aids includes calendars, cassettes, prints, maps, notecards, playing cards, post cards, slide strips and other items. Title, price.

"101 Freshwater Fish Recipes." $4.95.

Suggested Curriculum Application:
  AMERICAN HISTORY
  MINNESOTA STATE AND LOCAL STUDIES

Suggested Sears Subject Heading:
  FRONTIER AND PIONEER LIFE
  FUR TRADE
  MINNESOTA--DESCRIPTION AND TRAVEL--GUIDES
  MINNESOTA--HISTORY
  MINNESOTA--PUBLIC LANDS
  U.S.--DESCRIPTION AND TRAVEL--GUIDES

- ICE AGE
National Scenic Trail. Midwest Region. National Park Service
1709 Jackson Street, Omaha, NE 68102. (402) 221-3471.
Under development. 1980. Southern, central, western Wisconsin.

Follow the path of Moraines marking the furthest advance of the last
glacier in Wisconsin, linking together the nine units of the Ice Age
National Scientific Reserve. Presently about 160 miles have been
certified as part of the Ice Age National Scenic Trail and 180 miles
of uncertified segments are open to public use. Interpretive centers
explaining the glacial history and geology of Wisconsin are located
along the trail in the northern unit of Kettle Moraine State Forest
and Interstate State Park. All segments are open to hiking and
backpacking. Inquire if bicycling, horseback riding, cross-country
skiing, snowshoeing, jogging, snowmobiling is allowed on the parti-
cular segment you may wish to use. Certified segments of the trail
are signed with markers and are supplemented by paint blazes and
routed wooden signs that give distance and directional information.
Other segments are marked similarly but lack the official Ice Age
National Scenic Trail symbol. The use of some segments and overnight facilities requires a fee payment and/or obtaining a permit.
Camping facilities vary greatly. For specific information on segments
on state lands inquire: Wisconsin Department of Natural Resources,
Box 7921, Madison, WI 53707. For information on trail segments on
county, municipal and private lands inquire: Ice Age Trail Council,
2302 Lakeland Avenue, Madison, WI 53704. Consult "Ice Age Trail"
described below for further sources.

Free Print Material:
  "Ice Age Trail." 24-fold. Photos, maps, description of the trail,
    glacial past in Wisconsin, development of the trail, information
    sources, user information.
  "Ice Age Trail Council Membership Application." 2 pages. Map
    shows names of established and proposed trails, membership
    application, description of the Ice Age Trail.

Suggested Curriculum Application:
  AMERICAN HISTORY

GEOGRAPHY
GEOLOGY
SCIENCE
WISCONSIN STATE AND LOCAL STUDIES

Suggested Sears Subject Heading:
GEOLOGY--U.S.
GLACIAL EPOCH
U.S.--DESCRIPTION AND TRAVEL--GUIDES
U.S.--GEOGRAPHY
WISCONSIN--DESCRIPTION AND TRAVEL--GUIDES
WISCONSIN--GEOGRAPHY
WISCONSIN--HISTORY
WISCONSIN--PUBLIC LANDS

- IDITAROD

National Historic Trail. Department of the Interior, Bureau of Land
Management, Box 13, 701 C St., Anchorage, AK   99513.
(907) 271-5076. 2,037-mile trail. 1978. Central Alaska, from
Seward to Nome.

Network of trails developed during the Gold Rush era connecting
Seward in southern Alaska with Nome in northwestern Alaska.
Iditarod Trail sled dog race, historic sites. Visitor accommodations
along the trail. Trail is not yet developed for public use.

Free Print Material:
"The Iditarod National Historic Trail Seward to Nome Route: A
Comprehensive Management Plan." 157 pages. Project background, historic overview, regional profile, significant sites
and segments, management opportunities. Appendices, maps,
tables, photos.
"The Iditarod National Historic Trail Seward to Nome Route:
Volume Two-Resource Inventories." 315 pages. Data-gathering
efforts of field crews working on the development of the proposed management plan. Historic/cultural resources, natural
resources, outdoor recreation resources. References, sources,
tables, maps, illustrations.

Suggested Curriculum Application:
ALASKA STATE AND LOCAL STUDIES
AMERICAN HISTORY

Suggested Sears Subject Heading:
ALASKA--DESCRIPTION AND TRAVEL--GUIDES
ALASKA--HISTORY
ALASKA--PUBLIC LANDS
GOLD MINES AND MINING
KLONDIKE GOLD FIELDS
U.S.--DESCRIPTION AND TRAVEL--GUIDES

● LEWIS AND CLARK
National Historic Trail. Midwest Region. National Park Service,
1709 Jackson Street, Omaha, NE 68102. (402) 221-3482. About
4,500 miles long. 1978. Water routes, planned trails, marked highways in: Illinois, Missouri, Kansas, Nebraska, Iowa, South Dakota,
North Dakota, Montana, Idaho, Washington, Oregon.

Commemorates the 1804-06 route of Meriwether Lewis and William
Clark from the Mississippi River to the Pacific Ocean. The over
8,000-mile expedition contributed new knowledge about the previously
unknown land. About 500 public and private recreation and historic
sites, eight National Park Service areas along the trail give the public use and interpretation of the expedition. Portions of the expedition can be traveled today by boat, car, or on foot. Three land
trail segments include the Roughrider Trail, the Lolo Trail, and the
Trail over Tillamook Head. Campgrounds, picnicking, food and
lodging along the route.

Free Print Material:
"Lewis and Clark Trail." 24-fold. Meriwether Lewis and William
Clark Expedition, biographical information, following the ex-
pedition footsteps today. Photos, map.

Suggested Curriculum Application:
AMERICAN HISTORY
IDAHO STATE AND LOCAL STUDIES
ILLINOIS STATE AND LOCAL STUDIES
IOWA STATE AND LOCAL STUDIES
KANSAS STATE AND LOCAL STUDIES
MISSOURI STATE AND LOCAL STUDIES
MONTANA STATE AND LOCAL STUDIES
NEBRASKA STATE AND LOCAL STUDIES
NORTH DAKOTA STATE AND LOCAL STUDIES
OREGON STATE AND LOCAL STUDIES
SOUTH DAKOTA STATE AND LOCAL STUDIES
WASHINGTON STATE AND LOCAL STUDIES

Suggested Sears Subject Heading:
CLARK, WILLIAM, 1770-1838
IDAHO--DESCRIPTION AND TRAVEL--GUIDES
IDAHO--PUBLIC LANDS
ILLINOIS--DESCRIPTION AND TRAVEL--GUIDES
ILLINOIS--PUBLIC LANDS
IOWA--DESCRIPTION AND TRAVEL--GUIDES
IOWA--PUBLIC LANDS
KANSAS--DESCRIPTION AND TRAVEL--GUIDES
KANSAS--PUBLIC LANDS
LEWIS, MERIWETHER, 1774-1809
MISSOURI--DESCRIPTION AND TRAVEL--GUIDES
MISSOURI--PUBLIC LANDS
MONTANA--DESCRIPTION AND TRAVEL--GUIDES

MONTANA--PUBLIC LANDS
NEBRASKA--DESCRIPTION AND TRAVEL--GUIDES
NEBRASKA--PUBLIC LANDS
NORTH DAKOTA--DESCRIPTION AND TRAVEL--GUIDES
NORTH DAKOTA--PUBLIC LANDS
OREGON--DESCRIPTION AND TRAVEL--GUIDES
OREGON--PUBLIC LANDS
OVERLAND JOURNEYS TO THE PACIFIC (U.S.)
SOUTH DAKOTA--DESCRIPTION AND TRAVEL--GUIDES
SOUTH DAKOTA--PUBLIC LANDS
U.S.--DESCRIPTION AND TRAVEL--GUIDES
WASHINGTON--DESCRIPTION AND TRAVEL--GUIDES
WASHINGTON--PUBLIC LANDS

● NORTH COUNTRY
National Scenic Trail. Midwest Region. National Park Service,
1709 Jackson Street, Omaha, NE 68102. (402) 221-3481.
Not completed. 1980. New York, Pennsylvania, Ohio, Michigan,
Wisconsin, Minnesota, North Dakota.

A footpath going through diverse landscapes of scenic, historic,
cultural and recreational features. When completed, the trail will
extend about 3,200 miles from Crown Point, New York to Lake
Sakakawea State Park in North Dakota. Presents a geographical
and cultural cross section of midwestern and northeastern America.
Accommodations along the trail.

Free Print Material:
    "The North Country National Scenic Trail Information for Users
        and Route Description." 30 pages. Overview of the trail,
        administration, trail marking, fees and permits, camping,
        route and segment descriptions, certified segments, chart.
    "Route and Key Map." 74 pages plus a 3-fold map. Topographic
        base maps show the route of the North Country National
        Scenic Trail.

Suggested Curriculum Application:
    GEOGRAPHY
    MICHIGAN STATE AND LOCAL STUDIES
    MINNESOTA STATE AND LOCAL STUDIES
    NEW YORK STATE AND LOCAL STUDIES
    NORTH DAKOTA STATE AND LOCAL STUDIES
    OHIO STATE AND LOCAL STUDIES
    PENNSYLVANIA STATE AND LOCAL STUDIES
    RECREATION
    WISCONSIN STATE AND LOCAL STUDIES

Suggested Sears Subject Heading:
    MICHIGAN--DESCRIPTION AND TRAVEL--GUIDES
    MINNESOTA--DESCRIPTION AND TRAVEL--GUIDES

- OREGON

National Historic Trail. Pacific Northwest Region. 83 South King
Street, Suite 212, Seattle, WA 98104. (206) 442-5565. Under de-
velopment. 1978. The trail begins in Missouri and extends through
Kansas, Nebraska, Wyoming, Idaho, Oregon. Cross-country seg-
ments include: South Pass segment in Lander, WY; Blue Mountain
Segment in Lagrande, OR; Boardman Segment in Seattle, WA; Barlow
Road Segment in Gresham, OR; Sinker Creek Segment in Boise, ID;
Bear River Divide Segment in Rock Springs, WY; North Trail Seg-
ment in Boise, ID. Numerous historic sites along the trail.

Commemorate and preserve 2,170-mile historic Oregon Trail from
western Missouri to Oregon and other locations in the Pacific Northwest. Most of the trail was yet to be marked. Long stretches of
the Oregon Trail has been lost to highways and other developments.
Those wishing to trace more extensive parts of the trail should plan
to travel by car between the historic sites and cross-country segments. Many of the historic sites and major portions of the cross-
country segments are for visitor use. The sites which are open to
the public can be reached by public roads or by footpaths from
nearby roads and the cross-country segments can be reached by
road at trailheads. Various state and federal agencies along the
trail offer maps and travel aids.

Free Print Material:
    "The Oregon Trail." 12-fold. Photos, map, description, ad-
        ministration, public use, selected bibliography.

Bibliography:
    Specific guides for the Oregon Trail and general histories of
        western expansion are included in "The Oregon Trail" des-
        cribed above. These references include author, title, place
        of publication, publisher, date, description.

Sales List:
    "A Catalog of High Adventure on the Oregon Trail." 5 pages.
        Books, map. Photos of covers, pages, ISBN number, type of
        cover, price, author, title, some reviews. Order blank and
        ordering instructions.
    "Historic Sites Along the Oregon Trail." Aubrey L. Haines.
        The second edition of this 453-page volume gives complete

information on virtually all sites of historic importance along the Oregon Trail, from Independence, Missouri, to Oregon City, Oregon. Each of the....

Suggested Curriculum Application:
AMERICAN HISTORY
IDAHO STATE AND LOCAL STUDIES
KANSAS STATE AND LOCAL STUDIES
MISSOURI STATE AND LOCAL STUDIES
NEBRASKA STATE AND LOCAL STUDIES
OREGON STATE AND LOCAL STUDIES
RECREATION
WYOMING STATE AND LOCAL STUDIES

Suggested Sears Subject Heading:
IDAHO--DESCRIPTION AND TRAVEL--GUIDES
IDAHO--PUBLIC LANDS
KANSAS--DESCRIPTION AND TRAVEL--GUIDES
KANSAS--PUBLIC LANDS
MISSOURI--DESCRIPTION AND TRAVEL--GUIDES
MISSOURI--PUBLIC LANDS
NEBRASKA--DESCRIPTION AND TRAVEL--GUIDES
NEBRASKA--PUBLIC LANDS
OREGON--DESCRIPTION AND TRAVEL--GUIDES
OREGON--PUBLIC LANDS
OUTDOOR RECREATION
OVERLAND JOURNEYS TO THE PACIFIC (U.S.)
U.S.--DESCRIPTION AND TRAVEL--GUIDES
WYOMING--DESCRIPTION AND TRAVEL--GUIDES
WYOMING--PUBLIC LANDS

• POTOMAC HERITAGE
National Scenic Trail. c/o C and O National Historical Park, P.O. Box 4, Sharpsburg, MD 21782. (301) 739-4200. In development. 1968. Georgetown, in the District of Columbia, to Cumberland, MD. This 184-mile-long trail is expected to be expanded.

Envisioned by Congress as "a corridor of approximately 704 miles following the route as generally depicted on a map identified as 'national trails system, proposed Potomac Heritage Trail' in The Potomac Trail, a report prepared by the Department of the Interior ...." Hiking, bicycling, horseback riding. Food and lodging in Sharpsburg.

Free Print Material:
"The Potomac Heritage Trail." 1 page. Establishment of the trail, development, where to obtain written guides.
"Towpath Update." 1 page. Location of the towpath along the C&O Canal National Historical Park, facilities.

Sales List:
    "Publications." 1 page. Grouped by: trail guides, canal read-
        ing. Author, title, date, cost, some annotations.
    "Boy Scouts of America." 184 miles of adventure, hiker's guide
        to the C&O Canal, 1977. Cost: $1.75. (Contains brief
        historical highlights of the entire canal.)

Suggested Curriculum Application:
    DISTRICT OF COLUMBIA LOCAL STUDIES
    MARYLAND STATE AND LOCAL STUDIES
    RECREATION

Suggested Sears Subject Heading:
    DISTRICT OF COLUMBIA--DESCRIPTION AND TRAVEL--GUIDES
    DISTRICT OF COLUMBIA--PUBLIC LANDS
    MARYLAND--DESCRIPTION AND TRAVEL--GUIDES
    MARYLAND--PUBLIC LANDS
    OUTDOOR RECREATION
    U.S.--DESCRIPTION AND TRAVEL--GUIDES

TREES

• BIG CYPRESS NATIONAL PRESERVE
S.R. Box 110, Ochopee, FL 33943. (813) 695-2000. 570,000 acres.
1974. Southern Florida, Oasis Ranger Station is located on U.S.
Highway 41, 55 miles east of Naples, FL and 50 miles west of Miami.
The preserve adjoins the northwest portion of Everglades National
Park.

Preserve subtropical plant and animal life with about one-third of
the area covered with cypress trees, including some of today's few
remaining great bald-cypresses, some 600-700 years old. Wildlife,
hiking, canoeing. Off-road vehicles licensed by the National Park
Service are allowed. Visitor centers, a privately owned campground,
backcountry camping. Road frontage campgrounds. Food and
lodging in Naples, Everglades, Ochopee.

Free Print Material:
    "Big Cypress." 16-fold. Map, diagram, photos, uses of cypress.
    "Florida Trail." 1 page. Map of Big Cypress Florida Trail.
    "Trail Data--Big Cypress Section." 1 page. Progress from north
        terminus to southern terminus, 29.7 miles. Hiking tips and
        where to get answers to your questions.

Suggested Curriculum Application:
    FLORIDA STATE AND LOCAL STUDIES

GEOGRAPHY
NATURAL HISTORY
RECREATION

Suggested Sears Subject Heading:
CYPRESS
FLORIDA--DESCRIPTION AND TRAVEL--GUIDES
FLORIDA--PUBLIC LANDS
NATURE CONSERVATION
OUTDOOR RECREATION
TREES--U.S.
U.S.--DESCRIPTION AND TRAVEL--GUIDES
WILDERNESS AREAS

• CONGAREE
National Monument. P.O. Box 11938, Columbia, SC   29211.
(803) 765-5571. 15,138.25 acres. 1976. Central South Carolina,
20 miles southeast of Columbia off S.C. 48.

Last important tract of virgin southern bottomland hardwoods in
Southeast United States. Hiking trails, canoeing, guided walking
tours, guided canoe tours. Boardwalk under construction. For
special group tours, group camping, call to make arrangements.
Visitor contact and first-aid station, primitive camping by permit.

Free Print Material:
    "Authorized Boundary." 2 pages. Map, visitor information.
    "Trail Map." 2 pages. Map, names and distances and marker
        color of trails, visitor activities.

Suggested Curriculum Application:
GEOGRAPHY
SOUTH CAROLINA STATE AND LOCAL STUDIES

Suggested Sears Subject Heading:
FORESTS AND FORESTRY
SOUTH CAROLINA--DESCRIPTION AND TRAVEL--GUIDES
SOUTH CAROLINA--PUBLIC LANDS
TREES--U.S.
U.S.--DESCRIPTION AND TRAVEL--GUIDES
U.S.--GEOGRAPHY

• MUIR WOODS
National Monument. Mill Valley, CA   94941. (415) 388-2595.
553.55 acres. 1908. Western California, 17 miles north of San
Francisco in a box canyon, off California Route 1.

Virgin stand of coastal redwoods named in honor of John Muir,
writer and conservationist. Redwoods first appeared when

dinosaurs walked the earth and were widespread but the only remaining redwoods are located in a narrow band along California's coast. Trails, wildlife. The largest trees are in Bohemian Grove--the tallest is 250 feet while the widest is 13-1/2 feet. Visitor center. Snacks and souvenirs near the visitor center. Picnicking in nearby park areas. Food and lodging nearby.

Free Print Material:
    "Muir Woods." 12-fold. Location, visitor information, maps, photos, history of redwood trees, development of Muir Woods National Monument.

Suggested Curriculum Application:
    CALIFORNIA STATE AND LOCAL STUDIES
    ENVIRONMENTAL EDUCATION
    GEOGRAPHY

Suggested Sears Subject Heading:
    CALIFORNIA--DESCRIPTION AND TRAVEL--GUIDES
    CALIFORNIA--PUBLIC LANDS
    FORESTS AND FORESTRY
    MUIR, JOHN, 1838-1914
    NATURE CONSERVATION
    REDWOOD
    TREES--U.S.
    U.S.--DESCRIPTION AND TRAVEL--GUIDES

● PETRIFIED FOREST
National Park. Petrified Forest National Park, AZ 86028. (602) 524-6228. 93,492.57 acres. National Monument 1906; National Park 1962. East-central Arizona, painted desert. Take U.S. 180 from Holbrook or I-40.

Preserve tree remains changed to stone about 200 million years ago. Indian ruins and petroglyphs, part of the Painted Desert are also part of the park as well as 50,000 acres of wilderness. Film, rainbow forest museum, 27-mile scenic drive with many pullouts, two wilderness areas offer cross-country hiking and backpack camping with permits, eight overlooks, Chinde Point, Puerco Indian ruins, newspaper rock, tepees, blue mesa, Jasper Forest Overlook, Crystal Forest, the flattops, long logs, Agate House. Mountain trails, cross-country hiking, conducted activities, special events. Picnic area, restaurant and soda fountain, visitor center, wilderness backpack camping. Restaurant, fountain, gift store. Food and lodging in nearby communities.

Free Print Material:
    "Area Campgrounds." 2 pages. Name, services, address, telephone of area campgrounds. Addresses for petrified wood sales. Name, address, telephone of accommodations.

"Hours and Information." 2 pages. Activities, hours of the
   park, Painted Desert Visitor Center, Rainbow Forest Museum,
   access, services, weather chart, visitor regulations.
"Petrified Forest." 12-fold. Discovery in 1985 of the world's
   oldest dinosaur skeleton, geology of the petrified trees, commercial sources of petrified wood, features of the park.
   Photos, map, illustrations, health and safety regulations.

Sales/Audiovisual List:
   "Publications of the Petrified Forest Museum Association." 6-fold.
   Grouped by: publications, slides, flowers, maps. Order
   blank and ordering instructions. Title, description, price.
   Slides cover park features. Publications include the "story
   behind the scenery" series and the Parkway series.
   "Bryce Canyon." John Bezy: 48 pages. $3.75.

Suggested Curriculum Application:
   ARIZONA STATE AND LOCAL STUDIES
   GEOGRAPHY
   GEOLOGY
   NATIVE AMERICAN STUDIES
   SCIENCE

Suggested Sears Subject Heading:
   ARIZONA--DESCRIPTION AND TRAVEL--GUIDES
   ARIZONA--PUBLIC LANDS
   DESERTS
   GEOLOGY--U.S.
   INDIANS OF NORTH AMERICA--HISTORY
   NATIONAL PARKS AND RESERVES--U.S.
   PETRIFIED FOREST NATIONAL PARK
   TREES--U.S.
   U.S.--DESCRIPTION AND TRAVEL--GUIDES

● REDWOOD
National Park. 1111 Second St., Crescent City, CA 95531.
(707) 464-6101. 34,853.07 acres. 1968. Northwest California.
Stretches along California's north coast from north of Eureka to
just south of the Oregon border. U.S. 101 runs north and south
through the park.

Preserve coast redwoods that grow only along the Pacific Coast,
including the world's tallest known tree at 367.8 feet as well as the
second, third, and sixth tallest. Interpretive walks and talks,
water activities, virgin redwood groves and those including the
world's tallest tree, hiking trails, scenic drives, conducted tidepool
and seashore walks, exhibits, scenic viewpoints, whale-watching,
beachcombing activities, nature trails. Information center, ranger
station, picnicking, campgrounds, shuttle bus. Food and lodging
in Smith River, Crescent City, Klamath and others.

Free Print Material:
  "Amphibians and Reptiles and Mammals of Redwood National Park."
    8 pages. Common and scientific names of snakes, lizards,
    turtles, frogs and toads, salamanders, mammals, sketches.
  "Burls." 1 page. Description, illustration.
  "Geology of the Redwood Parks." 5 pages. Sketches, map,
    geological survey.
  "Redwood." 8-fold. History of the move to make Redwood Nation-
    al Park, visitor tips, illustrations and life cycle of the red-
    wood, photos, the role of fog, map.
  "Redwood Map and Guide." 12-fold. Map, description of the park
    divided into Hiouchi area, Crescent City area, Klamath area,
    Prairie Creek area, Orick area. Visitor information including
    camping facilities and safety tips.
  "Redwood Renaissance." 8-fold. Photos, description of the
    stabilizing and reforesting of logged-over lands in the Redwood
    National Park.
  "Seasons of Visitation at Redwood National Park." 2 pages.
    Temperature, wind, storms, wildflowers, poison oak, roads.
  "Tall Trees Grove." 2 pages. The discovery of the grove along
    Redwood Creek, the efforts of expanding the park despite
    logging efforts. Shuttle bus information, camping and camp-
    ground information.

Sales/Audiovisual List:
  "Redwood Natural History Association Publications List." 2 pages.
    Grouped by: trees, other plants, mammals and reptiles, birds,
    fish, insects, nature studies, oceans, geology, recreation,
    travel, national parks, Indians, environmental literature, his-
    tory, sky, maps, calendars, post cards, slides, special items,
    posters, video. Includes order form, shipping label, shipping
    instructions. Aims of the Redwood Natural History Association.
    Within each category, book titles are listed from the general to
    the specific and hardbacks are noted. Sketches. Title,
    author, price.
  "Trees." Usborne first nature series. $2.95.

Suggested Curriculum Application:
  CALIFORNIA STATE AND LOCAL STUDIES
  ENVIRONMENTAL EDUCATION
  GEOGRAPHY
  NATURAL HISTORY
  SCIENCE

Suggested Sears Subject Heading:
  CALIFORNIA--DESCRIPTION AND TRAVEL--GUIDES
  CALIFORNIA--PUBLIC LANDS
  FORESTS AND FORESTRY
  NATIONAL PARKS AND RESERVES--U.S.
  NATURAL HISTORY--CALIFORNIA
  NATURE CONSERVATION

REDWOOD
REDWOOD NATIONAL PARK
TREES--U.S.
U.S.--DESCRIPTION AND TRAVEL--GUIDES
U.S.--GEOGRAPHY

VOLCANOES

• ANIAKCHAK
National Monument and Preserve. P.O. Box 7, King Salmon, AK
99613. (907) 246-3305. National Monument, 139,500 acres; National
Preserve, 475,500 acres. National Monument, 1978; National Monu-
ment and Preserve, 1980. Southern Alaska, 400 miles southwest of
Anchorage.

Crater includes lava flows, cinder cones, explosion pits. Surprise
Lake has a 6-mile average diameter, one of the largest dry calderas
in the world. Located in the volcanically active Aleutian Mountains,
Aniakchak last erupted in 1931. Surprise Lake's waters cascade
through the crater wall to form Aniakchak Wild River, wildlife,
geology and plant succession, inside of the caldera. Access is
scheduled, then chartered airplane or floatplane. Food and lodging
in King Salmon.

Free Print Material:
"Aniakchak." 2 pages. Photos, map, access, features, weather.
"Transportation." 1 page. Information about air flights and
other visitor information.

Suggested Curriculum Application:
ALASKA STATE AND LOCAL STUDIES
GEOGRAPHY
GEOLOGY

Suggested Sears Subject Heading:
ALASKA--DESCRIPTION AND TRAVEL--GUIDES
ALASKA--PUBLIC LANDS
GEOLOGY--U.S.
U.S.--DESCRIPTION AND TRAVEL--GUIDES
VOLCANOES

• CAPULIN MOUNTAIN
National Monument. Capulin, NM 88414. (505) 278-2201. 775.38 acres.
1916. Northeast New Mexico, 3 miles north of Capulin, off of 325.

10,000-year-old volcano, a recent symmetrical cone rising 1,000 feet
above its 8,182-foot base. Capulin is taken from the Spanish word
for chokecherry, a shrub found on the mountain. Audiovisual,
200-foot trail with plaques describing plants and volcanic happenings,
volcanic cone, plant and animal life. A 2-mile road spirals to the
summit where one trail goes down to the bottom of the crater to the
vent and the other follows the rim all the way around providing
scenic viewing. Visitor center, picnicking. Campgrounds nearby.
Food and lodging in Capulin.

Free Print Material:
 "Bird Checklist." 2 pages. Names of birds with two notations,
  1) showing if they are summer, winter, resident, transient;
  2) if common, abundant, rare, unknown.
 "Birth of a Volcano." 1 page. Activity above the surface and
  below the surface. How a cinder cone is formed. Diagram.
 "Capulin Mountain." 8-fold. Photos, maps, description of the
  volcano today, general park information with safety tips, wildlife.
 "Folsom Man." 1 page. Evidence of prehistoric man found in
  Folsom, New Mexico, drawings, discovery of a spear-point
  made by man.
 "Visitor Information." 10 pages. Building the road, rim shelter
  and other developments, statistics, area information about accommodations, area history and facts, volcanic rock, types of
  volcanoes. Diagrams of shield, strato and cinder cone volcanoes, photos.

Audiovisual List:
 "Movies and Slide Programs Available for Loan at Capulin Mountain National Monument." 2 pages. One page for slides, one
  page for movies. Title, number of minutes, description,
  amount of money to insure.
 "Mount St. Helens." 20 minutes. A slide program telling the
  story of the eruption of Mt. St. Helens. It contains 40 slides
  of the eruption, cassette tape with slide-advance sounds. Also
  available in reel-to-reel tape. Please insure for $100.00.

Sales/Audiovisual List:
 "Southwest Parks and Monuments Association Sales List." 1 page.
  Grouped by: natural history; archeology, people, and
  history; post cards; slides; film; volcanoes and geology;
  general; wildlife prints; maps. Ordering information. Title,
  price.
 "Birds of North America." $7.95.

Suggested Curriculum Application:
 GEOGRAPHY
 GEOLOGY
 NEW MEXICO STATE AND LOCAL STUDIES
 SCIENCE

Suggested Sears Subject Heading:
CAPULIN MOUNTAIN, NM
GEOLOGY--U.S.
MOUNTAINS
NEW MEXICO--DESCRIPTION AND TRAVEL--GUIDES
NEW MEXICO--PUBLIC LANDS
U.S.--DESCRIPTION AND TRAVEL--GUIDES
U.S.--GEOGRAPHY
VOLCANOES

● CRATER LAKE
National Park. P.O. Box 7, Crater Lake, OR 97604.
(503) 594-2211. 183,227.05 acres. 1902. Southwestern Oregon,
southeast of Eugene, north of Klamath Falls, off of Oregon Highway
Route 62.

Scenic blue lake, the nation's deepest (1,996 feet deepest point)
surrounded by rolling mountains, volcanic peaks, and evergreen
forests. Lake was formed by springs, snow and rain after volcanic
eruption about 6,800 years ago created a huge bowl. Displays, activities, overlooks, van tours, trails, ranger talks, campfire programs, ranger-led hikes, rim drive (33 miles) circles the Caldera
Rim, special activities for children, snowshoe hikes and other winter
activities, Sinnot Memorial, boat tours, Wizard Island. Visitor
center, campgrounds, coffee/gift shop, camper store, food and
lodging. Limousines between the park and Klamath Falls.

Free Print Material:
"Crater Lake." 24-fold. What to do and see, geology of the
lake, maps, accommodations, photos, sketches, block diagrams,
discovery and development.

Sales List:
"Crater Lake Natural History Association Sales List." 2 pages.
Map, guides, poster. Mail order form and instructions, mem-
bership information, goals of the association, application form.
"USGS Topographic Map of Crater Lake National Park." $4.00.
Scale 1:62,500. Available folded.

Suggested Curriculum Application:
GEOGRAPHY
GEOLOGY
OREGON STATE AND LOCAL STUDIES
SCIENCE

Suggested Sears Subject Heading:
CRATER LAKE NATIONAL PARK
LAKES
NATIONAL PARKS AND RESERVES--U.S.
OREGON--DESCRIPTION AND TRAVEL--GUIDES

OREGON--PUBLIC LANDS
U.S.--DESCRIPTION AND TRAVEL--GUIDES

• CRATERS OF THE MOON
National Monument. P.O. Box 20, Arco, ID 83213. (208) 527-3257.
53,120 acres. 1924. Central Idaho, 18 miles southwest of Arco,
Idaho on Highway 26.

Preserve the fissure vents, volcanic cones, and lava flows that began 15,000 years ago. Seven-mile loop road of moon-like landscape,
conducted walks and talks, film, displays. Visitor center. Campground near monument headquarters. Campgrounds are available
in Arco and other nearby communities. Food and lodging in Arco.

Free Print Material:
    "Craters of the Moon." 8-fold. Photos, points of interest along
        the loop road, maps, visitor services, geological information,
        safety and management regulations.
    "Visitor Information Sheet." 2 pages. Camping information,
        safety and visitor tips, services, park hours, weather.

Sales/Audiovisual List:
    Request from: Craters of the Moon Natural History Association,
        P.O. Box 29, Arco, ID 83213.

Suggested Curriculum Application:
    GEOGRAPHY
    GEOLOGY
    IDAHO STATE AND LOCAL STUDIES
    SCIENCE

Suggested Sears Subject Heading:
    GEOLOGY--U.S.
    IDAHO--DESCRIPTION AND TRAVEL--GUIDES
    IDAHO--PUBLIC LANDS
    U.S.--DESCRIPTION AND TRAVEL--GUIDES
    U.S.--GEOGRAPHY
    VOLCANOES

• DEVILS TOWER
National Monument. Devils Tower, WY 82714. (307) 467-5370.
1,346.91 acres. 1906. Northeast Wyoming, Gillette is 65 miles from
the monument, Sundance is 27 miles. Park entrance is from
Wyoming 24, 7 miles north of U.S. 14.

Preserve the 865-foot tower of columnar rock, the remains of a volcanic intrusion. Exhibits, programs, year around recreational activities, wildlife, self-guiding nature trail. More than 1,000 people
climb the tower annually. Visitor center, campground. Food and
lodging in Sundance and Hulett.

Free Print Material:
 "Devils Tower." 8-fold. Geological story of the tower, cultural
  history, visitor and safety tips, map, photos, illustration.
 "Facilities." 2 pages. Map, sketch, visitor facilities and accommodations.

Sales/Audiovisual List:
 "Price List Devils Tower Natural History Association." 1 page.
  Books, and theme-related items. Includes games, slides, post
  cards, posters, photos, maps, medallion, and other items.
  Gives title and price, mail order information and form.
 "Story of the Prairie Dog." $.05.

Suggested Curriculum Application:
 GEOGRAPHY
 GEOLOGY
 SCIENCE
 WYOMING STATE AND LOCAL STUDIES

Suggested Sears Subject Heading:
 DEVILS TOWER, WY
 NATURAL MONUMENTS--U.S.
 U.S.--DESCRIPTION AND TRAVEL--GUIDES
 VOLCANOES
 WYOMING--DESCRIPTION AND TRAVEL--GUIDES
 WYOMING--PUBLIC LANDS

• HAWAII VOLCANOES
National Park. Hawaii National Park, HI 96718. (808) 967-7311.
11,878.98 acres. 1916. On the eastern-central portion of the island
of Hawaii from Mauna Loa to the seacoast near Kalapana.

Preserve the natural setting of Mauna Loa and Kilauea, refuge for
native plants and animals, physical remains of old Hawaiian temple.
Crater rim drive, film, temple of the Red Mouth, overlooks, trails,
volcano art center, Hulina Pali, displays, bird park, chain of craters
road, coastal section, talks, nature walks, activities. Up-to-date
information about on-going eruptions or potential activity:
(808) 967-7977. Visitor center, campgrounds, cabins, hotel, hikers
shelters: reservations are advised for accommodations. Food and
lodging nearby.

Free Print Material:
 "Backcountry Travel." 12-fold. Tips for visitors such as a
  chart showing boiling point of water for different sea levels,
  wind chill chart, trail markers, sketches, wilderness ethic,
  regulations and others.
 "Hawaii Volcanoes." 12-fold. Hiking Mauna Loa's summit trails,
  volcanic action, hiking tips. Map, photos, sketch.
 "Hawaii Volcanoes National Park." 20-fold. Volcanic history,

Hawaian history, visitor features, maps, photos.
"Hawaii Volcanoes National Park." 2 pages. Suggestions on
what to do if you have: limited time, moderate time, half-
day, full day. Maps, safety tips.
"Trail Map-Coastal District." 2 pages. Hiker's checklist includes
such information as facilities, weather hazards. Map includes
type of roads, location of fresh water supply, shelter.
"Waha'ula Heiau." 16-fold. Waha'ula (Temple of the Red Mouth)
Visitor Center, Hawaian history. Maps, glossary of Hawaiian
words used in text, trail information, sketches.

Bibliography:
A "for more reading" section is included in "Waha'ula Heiau"
described above.

Sales/Audiovisual List:
"Sales List." 3 pages. Items grouped by: art prints, Hawaii
Natural History Association publications, posters, other publi-
cations, 8mm movie films, slide sets, video tapes. Title, price,
4th class book rate.
"Madame Pele" by Hitchcock.

Suggested Curriculum Application:
AMERICAN HISTORY
GEOGRAPHY
GEOLOGY
HAWAII STATE AND LOCAL STUDIES
NATURAL HISTORY

Suggested Sears Subject Heading:
HAWAII--DESCRIPTION AND TRAVEL--GUIDES
HAWAII--HISTORY
HAWAII--PUBLIC LANDS
HAWAII VOLCANOES NATIONAL PARK
NATIONAL PARK AND RESERVES--U.S.
NATURAL HISTORY--HAWAII
U.S.--DESCRIPTION AND TRAVEL--GUIDES
VOLCANOES

• LASSEN VOLCANIC
National Park. P.O. Box 100, Mineral, CA 96063. (916) 595-4444.
106,372.36 acres. 1916. Northcentral California, accessible by
Calif. 89 or Calif. 36 and 44.

Volcanoes, active hot springs, steaming fumaroles, sulfurous vents,
coniferous forest, wilderness lakes and mountain area. Lassen
Peak erupted intermittently 1914-1921. Plug-dome Lassen Peak
volcano, Cinder Cone volcano, interpretive programs such as nature
walks and hikes, talks, evening programs, self-guiding trails, exhibits, skiing, overlook, wildlife, foot trails, Lassen Park Road.

Visitor centers, guest ranch, fast food service, supplies, campgrounds, picnicking, rental ski equipment. Food and lodging in
Mineral, Old Station, Mill Creek and others.

Free Print Material:
  "Lassen Park Guide." 8 pages. Newspaper format. Articles,
    visitor information, photos, sketches, maps.
  "Lassen Volcanic National Park." 20-fold. Description, ad-
    ministration, map, what to do, regulations, accommodations
    and services, how to reach the park.
  "Picture Taking in Northern California." 28-fold. Description,
    photos of 83 sites. Map, photo taking tips.

Sales List:
  "List of Publications for Sale by Loomis Museum Association."
    6-fold. Grouped by: guide books to Lassen Volcanic National
    Park, history. Natural history, rocks and minerals, Indians,
    hiking, books for young people, national parks, maps, post
    cards. Title, author, price description. Order blank, order-
    ing instructions, aims of the Loomis Museum Association.
  "Road Guide to Lassen Volcanic National Park." Schulz. $1.65.
    Illustrated guide to the park's major natural features as seen
    from the park road.

Audiovisual List:
  "Filmstrip Announcement." 2 pages. Description of filmstrip and
    accompanying script available for free loan to schools. Recom-
    mended grade levels, number of frames. Covers grades 1-12.
  "Life of a Tree." Grades 1-4. Describes in simple language the
    life of a tree from the seed through death and beyond. In-
    cludes various parts of a tree and the functions they perform;
    how a tree grows; how seeds are....

Suggested Curriculum Application:
  CALIFORNIA STATE AND LOCAL STUDIES
  GEOGRAPHY
  GEOLOGY
  SCIENCE

Suggested Sears Subject Heading:
  CALIFORNIA--DESCRIPTION AND TRAVEL--GUIDES
  CALIFORNIA--PUBLIC LANDS
  GEOLOGY--U.S.
  LESSEN VOLCANIC NATIONAL PARK
  NATIONAL PARKS AND RESERVES--U.S.
  NATURAL MONUMENTS
  U.S.--DESCRIPTION AND TRAVEL--GUIDES
  VOLCANOES

• LAVA BEDS
National Monument. Box 867, Tulelake, CA 96134. (916) 667-2282.

46,559.87 acres. 1925. Northern California, 30 miles south of Tulelake and 60 miles south of Klamath Falls, or, off California Route 139.

Rugged landscape resulting from volcanic activity, site of Modoc Indian War of 1872-73. Hiking, Hidden Valley, exhibits, Canby's Cross, audiovisuals, Captain Jack's Stronghold, Hospital Rock, wildlife overlooks, pictographs, museum, nature trails, Cinder Cone, summer interpretive programs, petroglyphs, Thomas-Wright Battlefield, Mammoth Crater, Fleener Chimneys, Black Crater, Devil's Homestead, Gillem's Camp, Mushpot Cave. Visitor center, picnicking, campgrounds. Food and lodging in Tulelake.

Free Print Material:
"Addresses for Campgrounds and General Information." 2 pages. Addresses and telephone numbers for National Park Service facilities, U.S. Forest Service, Fish and Wildlife Service, chambers of commerce, private campgrounds, boarding kennels and others.

"A Brief History of the Modoc War." 3 pages. Account of the war that ended June 1, 1873, the only major Indian war fought in California.

"The Geology of Lava Beds National Monument." 4 pages. Describes the rocks formed by lava found in the monument.

"Lava Beds." 12-fold. Formation of the lava tube caves, photos, maps, visitor information, wildlife. Account of the Modoc Indian War where warriors held off the U.S. Army in the safety of the lava beds.

"Ranger-Guided Tours and Activities." 4 pages. Description of programs offered from Memorial Day weekend through Labor Day. Safety and visitor tips.

"The Rock Art of Lava Beds National Monument." 3 pages. Description of the pictographs and petroglyphs found in Lava Beds National Monument.

"Things to See and Do at Lava Beds National Monument." 2 pages. Descriptions of attractions such as Fleener Chimneys, Hidden Valley and many others. Other visitor information about what to see north of the monument as well as other government lands.

Audiovisual List:
"Lava Beds National Monument Film List." 1 page. Title description, running time. Films on forests, wildlife, Alaska and other topics.

"The Age of Alaska." Alaska: old vs. new, and preservation of its heritage. 35 minutes.

Sales/Audiovisual List:
"Sales List." 1 page. Books, maps, post cards, slide sets, and other items. Title, price.

"Ancient Modocs of California and Oregon." $9.95.

Suggested Curriculum Application:
AMERICAN HISTORY
CALIFORNIA STATE AND LOCAL STUDIES
GEOGRAPHY
GEOLOGY
NATIVE AMERICAN STUDIES
SCIENCE

Suggested Sears Subject Heading:
CALIFORNIA--DESCRIPTION AND TRAVEL--GUIDES
CALIFORNIA--PUBLIC LANDS
GEOLOGY--U.S.
INDIANS OF NORTH AMERICA--HISTORY
MODOC INDIAN WAR, 1872-73
U.S.--DESCRIPTION AND TRAVEL--GUIDES
VOLCANOES

• SUNSET CRATER
National Monument. Rt. 3, Box 149, Flagstaff, AZ 86001.
(602) 527-7042. 3,040 acres. 1930. Central Arizona, 13 miles north
of Flagstaff, on U.S. 89.

Preserve 1,000-foot volcanic cinder cone formed 1064-65 A.D. The
cinders give an illusion of a sunset. It is the newest volcano in
Arizona and is over a mile wide at the base. Conducted walks,
programs, activities, self-guiding nature trail, volcanic crater, bus
or aerial tours. Visitor center, picnic areas. Camping across the
road from the visitor center. Meals and lodging in Flagstaff.

Free Print Material:
"Arizona Road Map." 32-fold. Points of interest, state symbols,
    photos, map with index, mile chart, list of campgrounds.
"Dating Sunset Crater." 2 pages. Dating methods used to date
    Sunset Crater's eruption.
"Geology of Sunset Crater." 2 pages. Eruption process, lava
    flows, future eruptions.
"Museum Notes: Hopi legends of the sunset crater region."
    4 pages. Various legends associated with the Sunset Crater
    region such as "Yaponcha, the Wind God."
"Nature Notes: Sunset Crater Biology." 1 page. Volcanic lava
    breakdown into a life supporting soil, adaptation of life.
"Sunset Crater National Monument." 2 pages. Location, access,
    natural features, visitor center, interpretive programs,
    weather, restrictions, and other services.
"Sunset Crater Weather." 1 page. Seasonal look, weather chart
    by month showing temperature and precipitation.
"Wupatki-Sunset Crater." 2 pages. Description of both national
    monuments, map, visitor centers, trails.
"Wupatki, Sunset Crater Official Map and Guide." 16-fold. Map,
    diagrams, photos, description and features. Includes a forma-
    tion of a cinder cone.

Sales List:
"Publication List." 6-fold. Title, number of pages, size,
graphics, price, annotation.
"Wupatki-Sunset Crater." (32 pages, 8-1/2" x 11", color and
black-and-white photos, maps) $4.00. This book is actually
an issue of Plateau magazine published by the Museum of
Northern Arizona. There are three sections to the book:
geology of Sunset Crater, archeology of Wupatki, and biology
of both areas.

Audiovisual List:
"Wupatki-Sunset Crater Slide Sets." 1 page. Number of set,
titles, price.
"Set #P548." Sunset Crater in winter, Sunset Crater and lava
flow, Sunset Crater, Sunset Crater from air. $1.75.

Suggested Curriculum Application:
ARIZONA STATE AND LOCAL STUDIES
GEOGRAPHY
GEOLOGY
SCIENCE

Suggested Sears Subject Heading:
ARIZONA--DESCRIPTION AND TRAVEL--GUIDES
ARIZONA--PUBLIC LANDS
GEOLOGY--U.S.
NATURAL MONUMENTS
U.S.--DESCRIPTION AND TRAVEL--GUIDES
U.S.--GEOGRAPHY
VOLCANOES

WAR OF 1812

• FORT McHENRY
National Monument and Historic Shrine. Baltimore, MD 21230.
(301) 962-4290. 43.26 acres. 1925. Central Maryland, three miles
from the center of Baltimore, reached on East Fort Avenue.

Defense of this fort during the War of 1812 inspired Francis Scott
Key to compose "The Star Spangled Banner." Ranger-guided activities, military demonstrations, narrated cruises, film, guided tours,
programs, exhibits, fort and grounds, statue. Visitor center, gift
shop. Food and lodging in Baltimore.

Free Print Material:
"Fort McHenry." 12-fold. The War of 1812 and what happened

at the Battle of Baltimore. Layout, map of Fort McHenry.
"Teacher's Guide, Pre-Visit Package." 17 pages. Outlines the
recommended grade levels, lengths of programs, numbers of
participants; states behavioral objectives; describes programs
and recommends pre-visit activities. Includes bibliography,
scheduling procedures for group reservations.

Bibliography:
"Bibliography" included in "Teacher's Guide, Pre-Visit Package"
described above. Grouped by: the flag, the War of 1812,
artillery, uniforms, the Civil War. Author, title, publisher,
date, pages, annotation.

Sales/Audiovisual List:
"Film and Video Sales List." 1 page. Where "Defense of Fort
McHenry" in video cassette or film is available for rent or
purchase.
Harpers Ferry Historical Association, P.O. Box 147, Harpers
Ferry, WV 25425, Attention: Film Librarian. Phone number:
(304) 535-6881. 16mm film "Defense of Fort McHenry." Rent:
$18 + $2 shipping for a 3-day period. Purchase: $142.
Video cassette "Defense of Fort McHenry" 1/2" VHS (special
orders are taken for video cassettes in other formats).
Purchase....

Suggested Curriculum Application:
AMERICAN HISTORY
MARYLAND STATE AND LOCAL STUDIES

Suggested Sears Subject Heading:
MARYLAND--DESCRIPTION AND TRAVEL--GUIDES
MARYLAND--PUBLIC LANDS
NATIONAL SONGS
U.S.--DESCRIPTION AND TRAVEL--GUIDES
U.S.--HISTORY--WAR OF 1812

• JEAN LAFITTE
National Historical Park. 423 Canal St., Room 210, New Orleans,
LA 70130. (504) 689-2002. 20,000 acres. 1978. Southeastern
Louisiana, three different units located in separate parts of the
greater New Orleans area.

Preserve the natural, cultural, historical resources of the Mississippi
Delta region. Jean Lafitte, from his headquarters on Barataria Bay
led his followers in privateering and smuggling and helped the
American forces over the British in 1815. The Chalmette Unit marks
the Battle of New Orleans and contains the Chalmette National
Cemetery. The French Quarter Unit provides an introduction to the
culture of the delta. The Barataria Unit preserves bayous, freshwater swamps and marshes. Variety of programs and presentations,

museum, audiovisuals, walking tours, holiday events, exhibits,
battlefield road tour, Chalmette National Cemetery, demonstrations,
folklife center, hiking and canoe trails, birdlife. Visitor centers,
picnicking. Campground 10 miles from Chalmette. Food and
lodging in New Orleans.

Free Print Material:
    "About the Park." 2 pages. Information about Jean Lafitte
        National Historical Park and how to get to the various units
        and what each offers.
    "Barataria Unit." 1 page. What the unit consists of, information
        about trails, tours. map.
    "Chalmette." 8-fold. Background about Andrew Jackson's vic-
        tory over the British in 1815. Photos of Chalmette Monument,
        Beauregard House, Chalmette National Cemetery, maps.
    "Folklife Center." 8-fold. What the center has to offer, photos,
        sampling of activities, performances, demonstrations.
    "French Quarter Unit Walking Tours." 1 page. Information about
        regularly scheduled, free walking tours offered by rangers
        such as the City of the Dead, Faubourg Promenade, History
        of New Orleans and Tour de Jour. Tours require reservations,
        for more information call (504) 589-2636.

Suggested Curriculum Application:
    AMERICAN HISTORY
    LOUISIANA STATE AND LOCAL STUDIES

Suggested Sears Subject Heading:
    CEMETERIES
    CHALMETTE NATIONAL CEMETERY
    LAFITTE, JEAN, 1780-1826
    LOUISIANA--HISTORY
    LOUISIANA--DESCRIPTION AND TRAVEL--GUIDES
    LOUISIANA--PUBLIC LANDS
    NEW ORLEANS, BATTLE OF
    U.S.--DESCRIPTION AND TRAVEL--GUIDES
    U.S.--HISTORY--WAR OF 1812

• PERRY'S
Victory and International Peace Memorial. P.O. Box 549, Put-in-Bay,
OH 43456. (419) 285-2184. 25.38 acres. 1936. Northern Ohio,
39 miles from Toledo, on South Bass Island in Lake Erie about 3
miles from the mainland.

Commemorate Commodore Oliver Hazard Perry's War of 1812 naval
battle against the British and memorialize the principle of maintain-
ing peace among nations through arbitration and disarmament.
Perry's victory resulted in Americans taking control of Lake Erie
and most of the old northwest. 352-foot-high doric column made
from pink granite and topped by an 11-ton bronze urn. Elevator

ride for a small fee to the observation platform from late April to mid-October, audiovisual presentation, exhibits, ranger activities in July and August such as demonstrations, evening programs, talks. Perry's battle site is 10 miles northwest and can be seen on a clear day from the observation platform. Visitor center. Campgrounds, picnicking nearby. Autoferry and air service. Food and lodging on South Bass Island and on mainland.

Free Print Material:
  "Perry's Victory." 12-fold. War in the northwest, battle action, significance of the victory. Description of the memorial and visitor information. Photos, maps, illustrations.
  "Your Island Guide: Put-In-Bay." 52 pages. Sketches, map, photos, articles, calendar of events, tips for travelers. Information about Bass Island and Perry's victory and International Peace Memorial.

Suggested Curriculum Application:
  AMERICAN HISTORY
  OHIO STATE AND LOCAL STUDIES

Suggested Sears Subject Heading:
  INTERNATIONAL RELATIONS
  NORTHWEST, OLD
  OHIO--DESCRIPTION AND TRAVEL--GUIDES
  OHIO--HISTORY
  OHIO--PUBLIC LANDS
  PERRY, OLIVER HAZARD, 1785-1819
  SOUTH BASS ISLAND
  U.S.--DESCRIPTION AND TRAVEL--GUIDES
  U.S.--HISTORY--WAR OF 1812

WESTERN EXPANSION

• BIG HOLE
National Battlefield. Box 237, Wisdom, MT 59761. (406) 689-3155. 655.61 acres. 1910. Western Montana, 12 miles west of Wisdom on Mont. 43.

Site of Nez Perce Indians and U.S. Army troops battle. Battlefield tour, hiking, museum exhibits, audiovisual program. Visitor center, picnicking. Camping nearby. Lodging and food, supplies at Wisdom, Butte, Hamilton, Mt.

Free Print Material:
  "Big Hole National Battlefield." 20-fold. The first treaty, the

second treaty and then the conflict between the Nez Perce
and westward expansion. Events of the Battle of the Big
Hole. What to do and see. Maps, photos.

Sales List:
   "Big Hole National Battlefield Items for Sale." 1 page. Grouped
      by post cards, pamphlets, books. You are requested to write
      first to inquire about postage due for mailing.
   "3-1/2 x 5-1/2 inch Post Card in Color Depicting Battle Mountain
      from a Distance." 10 cents each.

Suggested Curriculum Application:
   AMERICAN HISTORY
   MONTANA STATE AND LOCAL STUDIES
   NATIVE AMERICAN STUDIES

Suggested Sears Subject Heading:
   BIG HOLE, BATTLE OF
   INDIANS OF NORTH AMERICA--HISTORY
   MONTANA--DESCRIPTION AND TRAVEL--GUIDES
   MONTANA--PUBLIC LANDS
   NEZ PERCE INDIAN WAR, 1877
   NEZ PERCE INDIANS
   U.S.--DESCRIPTION AND TRAVEL--GUIDES

• CHIMNEY ROCK
National Historic Site. c/o Scotts Bluff National Monument, P.O.
Box 427, Gering, NE 69341. (402) 471-4755. 83.86 acres. 1956.
Western Nebraska, 3-1/2 miles southwest of Bayard, off Nebr. 92.

Famous landmark on the Oregon Trail. 500-foot spire of rock above
the Platte River, exhibits on Nebr. 92 from Memorial Day through
Labor Day by the Nebraska State Historical Society. Exhibits about
Chimney Rock at Scotts Bluff National Monument, 23 miles west.
Boots and hiking clothes are essential in reaching the half-mile walk
from Nebr. 92. Food and lodging in Gering and Scottsbluff.

Free Print Material:
   "Chimney Rock National Historic Site, Nebraska." 6-fold. Map,
      illustration, photo, visitor and administration information.
      Historical significance.

Suggested Curriculum Application:
   AMERICAN HISTORY
   NEBRASKA STATE AND LOCAL STUDIES

Suggested Sears Subject Heading:
   FRONTIER AND PIONEER LIFE
   NEBRASKA--DESCRIPTION AND TRAVEL--GUIDES
   NEBRASKA--PUBLIC LANDS

OVERLAND JOURNEYS TO THE PACIFIC (U.S.)
U.S.--DESCRIPTION AND TRAVEL--GUIDES

- **CUMBERLAND GAP**
National Historical Park. P.O. Box 1848, Middlesboro, KY 40965.
(606) 248-2817. 20,274.42 acres. 1940. Southeastern Kentucky,
60 mile south of Louisville, 3 miles south of Hodgenville on U.S.
31E and KY 61.

Historic site, on wilderness road explored by Daniel Boone, used to
cross the Appalachians by settlers heading west; important in
military strategy in the Revolutionary and Civil wars. Museum,
scenic overlooks, wilderness road, self-guiding trails, hiking trails,
restored settlement. Visitor center, campgrounds, picnicking. Food
and lodging in Middlesboro, KY and Cumberland Gap, TN.

Free Print Material:
"Camping and Lodging Facilities in the Cumberland Gap." 1 page.
Name, address, telephone.
"Cumberland Gap." 16-fold. Maps, photos, history, visitor in-
formation.
"Hensley Settlement." 6-fold. History and significance of the
small settlement of people, map of the settlement today, photo.
"The Iron Industry at Cumberland Gap." 6-fold. How iron is
produced, history of production in Cumberland Gap.
"The Pinnacle." 6-fold. Historic importance of this location,
the legend of Long Tom and Civil War times, sketches, map.
"Wilderness Road Campground Season." 6-fold. Fees, facilities,
safety tips, regulations, map.

Audiovisual List:
"Catalog of Audio-Visual Materials." 9 pages. No charge to
schools, clubs, civic groups. Sound/slide programs, films.
Films grouped by: history, nature, general.
"Orientation to Cumberland Gap." (sound/slide). This program
explains the history of the Cumberland Gap area, illustrated
with historic drawings, photographs, and modern scenes.
Although it is used primarily to orient park visitors to the
history and points of interest available....

Sales/Audiovisual List:
"Eastern National Park & Monument Association Mail Order Listing." 3 pages. Children's books, cassettes, records, slide
sets and other items. Schools and libraries are entitled to a
20 percent discount on items used for an educational purpose.
Postage and packing information.
"A Brittle Sword (Kentucky Militia)." $6.95.

Suggested Curriculum Application:
AMERICAN HISTORY

GEOGRAPHY
KENTUCKY STATE AND LOCAL STUDIES

Suggested Sears Subject Heading:
KENTUCKY--DESCRIPTION AND TRAVEL--GUIDES
KENTUCKY--HISTORY
KENTUCKY--PUBLIC LANDS
OVERLAND JOURNEYS TO THE PACIFIC (U.S.)
U.S.--DESCRIPTION AND TRAVEL--GUIDES
U.S.--GEOGRAPHY

- CUSTER BATTLEFIELD
National Monument. Post Office Box 39, Crow Agency, MT 59022.
(406) 638-2622. 765.34 acres. 1879 as a national cemetery; 1946 as
a national monument. Southeastern Montana, 17 miles from Hardin,
MT by Interstate 90.

Preserve the site of the Battle of the Little Big Horn between the
U.S. Cavalry and Sioux and Cheyenne Indians; Custer Battlefield
National Cemetery. Battlefield tour with interpretive markers of
Reno-Benteen Battlefield, Weir Point, Calhoun Ridge, National
Cemetery, Custer Hill. Exhibits, programs, audiovisual programs,
guided bus and van tours of the battlefield, Native American
presentations, cemetery walks, special events, trails. Visitor cen-
ters. Meals and lodging in Hardin. Camping in Crow Agency and
Hardin.

Free Print Material:
"Current Programs." 2 pages. What is offered, hours, descrip-
tion. Map, daily program schedule.
"Custer Battlefield." 16-fold. Background and action of the
battle, description and photos of battlefield tour, maps.
"Montana Highway Map." 24-fold. Points of interest described
and numbered on map, mileage table, Montana attractions
by area, photos, map, state information.
"The National Parks and the Bicentennial of the United States
Constitution." 12-fold. Constitutional history, photos of
national landmarks.
"Old West Trail Country." 32-fold. Map of Montana, Nebraska,
North Dakota, South Dakota, Wyoming. Areas and attractions,
photos, maps, phone numbers and addresses, state information.
"Take Pride in America." 8-fold. National public awareness campaign to encourage taking pride in our nation's natural and
cultural resources, photos.

Bibliography:
"Little Bighorn Battle Bibliography." 1 page. Grouped by:
general comprehensive, Indian, children. By author, title,
place of publication, publisher, date.

Audiovisual List:
  Inquire about a VCR tape of a 28-minute documentary movie
    about the Battle of the Little Big Horn. The tape is loaned
    free to schools.

Sales/Audiovisual List:
  "Council on America's Military Past." 10-fold. Information about
    the purposes of the organization includes materials for sale.
  "Back Issues." Issues of all publications are available, although
    some are in facsimile versions. They are $3 a copy for the
    "periodical," $1.50 for "Heliogram" (50 percent discount for
    members). Specify issue numbers. (Some facsimiles cost
    more). Double for facsimile.
  "Custer Battlefield Land Drive in High Gear." 4 pages. Custer
    battlefield preservation committee efforts to raise funds, items
    for sale. Includes sculptor, video tapes, pictures.
  "Contrasts." The weapons, dress and equipment of the 1876
    U.S. cavalryman and the Plains Indian warrior. Filmed on site
    at the Reno Crossing. 48 minutes. $43.00.
  "Merchandise Catalog." $1.50. From: Custer Battlefield
    Historical and Museum Association, P.O. Box 39, Crow Agency,
    MT 59022.

Suggested Curriculum Application:
  AMERICAN HISTORY
  MONTANA STATE AND LOCAL STUDIES
  NATIVE AMERICAN STUDIES

Suggested Sears Subject Heading:
  CEMETERIES
  CHEYENNE INDIANS
  CUSTER BATTLEFIELD NATIONAL CEMETERY
  CUSTER, GEORGE, 1839-1876
  INDIANS OF NORTH AMERICA--WARS
  LITTLE BIG HORN, BATTLE OF
  MONTANA--DESCRIPTION AND TRAVEL--GUIDES
  MONTANA--PUBLIC LANDS
  SIOUX INDIANS
  U.S.--DESCRIPTION AND TRAVEL--GUIDES

• FORT BOWIE
National Historic Site. P.O. Box 158, Bowie, AZ 85605.
(602) 847-2500. 1,000 acres. 1972. Southeastern Arizona, from
Willcox on Interstate 10.

Preserve the ruins of the fort that was the center of military operations against Geronimo, the Butterfield Overland Mail Route, the
Apache Pass Stage Station and Apache Spring. Museum, hiking,
Butterfield Overland Mail Route, Apache Pass Stage Station, ruins
of Fort Bowie. Picnicking. Food and lodging, stores, trailer parks
and campgrounds can be found in nearby towns of Willcox and Bowie.

Free Print Material:
"Fort Bowie." 16-fold. History of the site, photos, map, tips
for visitors.
"Your Visit to Fort Bowie National Historic Site." 1 page. What
to expect as to weather, services, the ranger station and
museum. A few history books, slides, trail guide and post
cards are for sale.

Suggested Curriculum Application:
AMERICAN HISTORY
ARIZONA STATE AND LOCAL STUDIES

Suggested Sears Subject Heading:
ARIZONA--DESCRIPTION AND TRAVEL--GUIDES
ARIZONA--HISTORY
ARIZONA--PUBLIC LANDS
FORTIFICATION
U.S.--DESCRIPTION AND TRAVEL--GUIDES

- FORT DAVIS
National Historic Site. P.O. Box 1456, Fort Davis, TX 79734.
(915) 426-3224. 460 acres. 1961. Western Texas, northern edge
of Fort Davis, by Interstate 10 by Tex. 17 and 118 or from U.S.
90 by 505 and 166 or 17.

Key post in guarding San Antonio-El Paso Road, 1854-1891. Half
of the 50 original structures, museum, audiovisual programs, self-
guiding tours of the grounds and buildings, nature trail system,
demonstrations and programs. Visitor center, picnicking. Food
and lodging in Fort Davis. Campgrounds nearby.

Free Print Material:
"Fort Davis." 10-fold. Sketches, map, founding and history
including the black soldiers that served in the Indian wars.
"Sights and Places of Interest in Fort Davis." 1 page. Descrip-
tion of Fort Davis National Historic Site, Davis Mountains
State Park, the Old Overland Trail Museum, the University of
Texas McDonald Observatory, the Scenic Drive. Name and
telephone of lodging, names of restaurants.

Bibliography:
"Fort Davis, Texas Bibliography." 3 pages. Grouped by:
secondary source books, articles. Author, title, place of
publication, publisher, date for books; author, title, periodical, volume number, date, pages for articles.

Sales/Audiovisual List:
"Fort Davis National Historic Site: Southwest Parks and Monu-
ments Association List of Books and Items for Sale." 4 pages.
Books, coloring books, guides, notecards, maps, prints,

slides, reproductions of post canteen tokens and other items.
Title, author, pages, price. Ordering instructions.
"An Army of Marksmen." Douglas C. McChristian, 94 pages
$4.95.

Suggested Curriculum Application:
AMERICAN HISTORY
BLACK STUDIES
TEXAS STATE AND LOCAL STUDIES

Suggested Sears Subject Heading:
ARCHITECTURE--CONSERVATION AND RESTORATION
FORTIFICATION
TEXAS--DESCRIPTION AND TRAVEL--GUIDES
TEXAS--HISTORY
TEXAS--PUBLIC LANDS
U.S.--DESCRIPTION AND TRAVEL--GUIDES

- FORT LARNED

National Historic Site. Route 3, Larned, KS 67550. (316) 285-3571.
718.39 acres. 1964. Central Kansas, 7 miles west of Larned, on
U.S. 156.

Protected Santa Fe Trail traffic from 1859-1878, key military base in
the 1868-69 Indian War and also functioned as an Indian agency.
Various historic military buildings, exhibits and furnished rooms,
self-guiding tour, guided tour, special events, walking trail.
Visitor center with audiovisual program, museum and other services,
picnic area. Meals, lodging and campgrounds in Larned and Great
Bend.

Free Print Material:
"Fort Larned." 12-fold. History of the fort and the Santa Fe
Trail, Indian Bureau Agency. Description of fort buildings,
maps, photos.
"Fort Larned History Trail." 4 pages. Map, sketches, list of
wildlife prairie inhabitants, description of points of interest
on the Fort Larned History Trail.

Suggested Curriculum Application:
AMERICAN HISTORY
KANSAS STATE AND LOCAL STUDIES
NATIVE AMERICAN STUDIES

Suggested Sears Subject Heading:
ARCHITECTURE--CONSERVATION AND RESTORATION
FORTIFICATION
INDIANS OF NORTH AMERICA--HISTORY
KANSAS--HISTORY
KANSAS--DESCRIPTION AND TRAVEL--GUIDES

KANSAS--PUBLIC LANDS
OVERLAND JOURNEYS TO THE PACIFIC (U.S.)
U.S.--DESCRIPTION AND TRAVEL--GUIDES

- FORT UNION
National Monument. Watrous, NM 87753. (506) 425-8025. 720.60
acres. 1954.

Site of three U.S. Army forts on a vital Santa Fe Trail location.
Ruins of the last fort, the largest military post in the Southwest.
Self-guiding trails, 100 acres of ruins, trail ruts of the Santa Fe
Trail still visible on the prairie, museum. Visitor center, picnic
area. Meals and lodging in Las Vegas.

Free Print Material:
"Fort Union." 16-fold. Descriptions of first Fort Union, the
Star Fort and third Fort Union that stood 1851-1893. Touring
guide to the remains of forts, visitor tips, photos, maps.

Sales/Audiovisual List:
"SPMA Mail Order List." 3 pages. Alphabetically arranged by
title and grouped under: books, maps, post cards, souvenirs.
Order form and shipping information.
"An Army of Marksmen." $4.95.

Suggested Curriculum Application:
AMERICAN HISTORY
NEW MEXICO STATE AND LOCAL STUDIES

Suggested Sears Subject Heading:
FORTIFICATION
NEW MEXICO--DESCRIPTION AND TRAVEL--GUIDES
NEW MEXICO--PUBLIC LANDS
OVERLAND JOURNEYS TO THE PACIFIC (U.S.)
U.S.--DESCRIPTION AND TRAVEL--GUIDES

- GEORGE ROGERS CLARK
National Historical Park. 401 South Second Street, Vincennes, IN
47591. (812) 882-1776. 24.30 acres. 1966. Southwestern Indiana,
at junction of U.S. Highways 50 and 41.

Commemorates the role George Rogers Clark and his frontiersmen
played in the American Revolution and also the development of the
region north of the Ohio River during the territorial period from
1787 to 1815. The rotunda is located on the site of Fort Sackville,
which Rogers captured from the British in 1779. Marble rotunda
contains seven large murals, landscaped grounds, Wabash River
view, audio tape, Lincoln Memorial Bridge, Francis Vigo statue,
Father Pierre Gibault statue, war memorials. Film about the George

Rogers Clark Campaign is preceded by an introductory talk. Visitor center. Campgrounds and picnicking nearby. Food and lodging in Vincennes.

Free Print Material:
  "Teacher Information Guide." 16 pages. Maps, sketches. Park use information, park facilities, interpretive programs, extended tour ideas, general suggestions for your visit, films, suggested reading, book and other sales items.
  "Wander Vincennes." 14 pages. Map, photos, sketches. Attractions such as the Indiana Territorial State Memorial, Sonotabac Prehistoric Indian Mound. Accommodations, tours, brief history of Vincennes from 1732 to 1838.

Bibliography:
  Appears in "Teacher Information Guide" described above. Two pages of suggested reading grouped by: Indians, French, British, Americans. Sketches. Author, title.

Audiovisual List:
  Appears in "Teacher Information Guide" described above. Two pages of films offered for loan to schools at no cost on a first-request basis. Request them by calling in advance. Title, running length, description, age level.
  "French Exploration in the New World." (11 minutes). Describes the earliest settlement of French trading centers in the new land. (Jr. High)

Sales/Audiovisual List:
  Appears in "Teacher Information Guide" described above. Two pages plus order blank page with ordering directions. Title, author, price. Arranged by: books, posters, post cards. Also lists: slide strip, button, Revolutionary War battlefield map.
  "Alice of Old Vincennes." (Thompson) $3.50.

Suggested Curriculum Application:
  AMERICAN HISTORY
  INDIANA STATE AND LOCAL STUDIES

Suggested Sears Subject Heading:
  CLARK, GEORGE ROGERS, 1752-1818
  INDIANA--DESCRIPTION AND TRAVEL--GUIDES
  INDIANA--HISTORY
  INDIANA--PUBLIC LANDS
  NORTHWEST, OLD
  U.S.--DESCRIPTION AND TRAVEL--GUIDES

• GRANT-KOHRS RANCH
National Historic Site. P.O. Box 790, Deer Lodge, MT 59722.

(406) 846-2070. 1,498.65 acres. 1972. Western Montana, at the north edge of Deer Lodge, on Interstate 90.

One of the largest and best known cattle ranch headquarters operated in the West between 1850 and 1910. Exhibits, guided tours, demonstrations. Ranch house, bunkhouse row, ice house, garage-blacksmith shop, thoroughbred barn, Leeds Lion barn, feed lot and sheds, chicken coop, buggy shed, granary, draft horse barn, oxen barn, dairy, Bielenberg barn. Visitor contact station. Food and lodging in Deer Lodge.

Free Print Material:
"Grant-Kohrs Ranch." 12-fold. Sketch, photos, map. Frontier cattle industry, ranch life. Description and illustration of ranch buildings.
"Montana Accommodations Guide." 36 pages. Motels, hotels, ranches and resorts, hostels, hot springs, private campgrounds. Maps, sketches, photos, charts. Description, order form about guides, books on Montana.

Bibliography:
"Bibliography." 1 page. Title, author, publisher, place of publication. Also comments on other books.

Sales List:
"Sales Items Available from Grant-Kohrs Ranch NHS." 1 page. Grouped by: books, cards, miscellaneous. Title, price. Ordering information. Books are mostly paperback with some hardcover.
"Birds of North America." $7.95.

Suggested Curriculum Application:
AMERICAN HISTORY
MONTANA STATE AND LOCAL STUDIES

Suggested Sears Subject Heading:
MONTANA--DESCRIPTION AND TRAVEL--GUIDES
MONTANA--PUBLIC LANDS
RANCH LIFE
U.S.--DESCRIPTION AND TRAVEL--GUIDES

● HOMESTEAD
National Monument. Route 3, Box 47, Beatrice, NE 68310.
(402) 223-3414. 194.57 acres. 1936. Southern Nebraska, 50 miles south of Lincoln and about 5 miles northwest of Beatrice, off Nebr. 4.

Where one of the first claims filed under the Homestead Act took place. The act, signed in 1862, made it possible for settlers to claim farms of 160 acres by paying a minor filing fee. Exhibits,

restored cabin and schoolhouses, self-guiding trail, guided tours
arranged for groups, demonstrations of pioneer arts and crafts,
gardens, programs, prairie remnants, woods, Cub Creek, home-style
grist mill for visitors to use. School groups should phone or write
ahead to make arrangements. Visitor center. Campgrounds nearby.
Food and lodging in Beatrice.

Free Print Material:
  "Homestead." 8-fold. Photos of prairie life, education on the
    frontier, the Homestead Act of 1862. Visitor information, map.
  "Prairie Whisper." 8 pages. Visitor activities, sketches, how
    you can help the monument. Monthly local weather chart.

Sales/Audiovisual List:
  "Books Available at Homestead National Monument." 2 pages.
    Grouped by: historical, natural history, travel. Historical
    sections includes Plains Indians coloring book, pioneer cook-
    book. Title, price.
  "Boy Life on the Prairie." $9.95.

Suggested Curriculum Application:
  AMERICAN HISTORY
  NEBRASKA STATE AND LOCAL STUDIES

Suggested Sears Subject Heading:
  FRONTIER AND PIONEER LIFE
  LAND SETTLEMENT--U.S.
  NEBRASKA--DESCRIPTION AND TRAVEL--GUIDES
  NEBRASKA--HISTORY
  NEBRASKA--PUBLIC LANDS
  U.S.--DESCRIPTION AND TRAVEL--GUIDES

• JEFFERSON NATIONAL EXPANSION MEMORIAL
National Historic Site. 11 North 4th St., St. Louis, MO 63102.
(314) 425-4465. 90.96 acres. 1954. Eastern Missouri, near
downtown St. Louis.

Memorialize Thomas Jefferson and others leading western expansion.
630-foot-high arch (tram rides available), court house where Dred
Scott sought his freedom, football field size exhibit area, films,
tours. For teachers: traveling exhibits, slide packets and films,
ranger/docent-conducted tours on a variety of topics, specifically
geared for each age level, special programs. For more information
call (314) 425-6010. Visitor center. Food and lodging in St. Louis.

Free Print Material:
  "Gateway Today." 16 pages. Lists some of the publications
    available from the museum shop under the Gateway Arch, pro-
    vides visitor tips, schedules, articles. Photos, maps,
    sketches.

"JNEM." 24-fold. History of westward expansion, western
settlement. Steps of construction illustration, photos of the
Gateway Arch.

"Missouri Facts and Figures." 28 pages. Climate, forest resources, names and dates and many other areas of interest
are covered. Photos and background about state flower,
state song and other state symbols. Telephone numbers and
addresses to obtain more information.

"Missouri Lodging Directory and Travel Map." 36-fold. Map,
photos, travel directory.

"St. Louis Metropolitan Area Illustrated Pocket Map." 24-fold.
Points of interest such as historical, retail shopping centers,
recreation and sports, are grouped together in the map index.

Sales List:
Sales items and form included in "Gateway Today" described
above. Grouped by: western exploration and expansion,
the western tradition, personalities of the West, Indians,
cookbooks, St. Louis and Missouri: history and character,
children's West. Title, author, type of cover, order number,
price.
"The Military in Dakota" 13180. $9.95.

Suggested Curriculum Application:
AMERICAN HISTORY
MISSOURI STATE AND LOCAL STUDIES

Suggested Sears Subject Heading:
JEFFERSON, THOMAS, 1743-1826
MISSOURI--DESCRIPTION AND TRAVEL--GUIDES
MISSOURI--PUBLIC LANDS
OVERLAND JOURNEYS TO THE PACIFIC (U.S.)
U.S.--DESCRIPTION AND TRAVEL--GUIDES

• McLOUGHLIN HOUSE
National Historic Site. 713 Center Street, Oregon City, OR 97045.
(503) 656-5146. 0.63 acres. 1941. Northwestern Oregon, 13 miles
from Portland, off U.S. 99, between 7th and 8th Streets in Oregon
City.

Home of Dr. John McLoughlin, often called the "Father of Oregon."
McLoughlin was superintendent of Fort Vancouver, prominent in the
development of the Pacific Northwest. The house was built by
McLoughlin, who lived in it 1846-1857. House tour featuring
McLoughlin's personal belongings and other period pieces. The
house is owned and administered by the McLoughlin Memorial Association. Lodging in Oregon City, others 6-10 miles.

Bibliography:
"Reading List." 1 page. Title, author. Adult and children.

Sales List:
    "Sales List." 1 page. Grouped by: books, beaver coin,
       jewelry, kits, litho, maps, post cards, other.
    "1846-Texas, Oregon, California." $4.00.

Suggested Curriculum Application:
    AMERICAN HISTORY
    OREGON STATE AND LOCAL STUDIES

Suggested Sears Subject Heading:
    McLOUGHLIN, JOHN, 1784-1857
    NORTHWEST, PACIFIC
    OREGON--DESCRIPTION AND TRAVEL--GUIDES
    OREGON--HISTORY
    OREGON--PUBLIC LANDS
    U.S.--DESCRIPTION AND TRAVEL--GUIDES

• THE MORMON PIONEER TRAIL
National Historic Trail. Rocky Mountain Region. National Park
Service, P.O. Box 25287, Denver, CO 80225. (303) 236-8720.
In miles: 1,300-mile trail. 1978. Begins in Illinois in Nauvoo and
ends in Salt Lake City, Utah.

Retrace the historical route that thousands of Mormons took to Utah
between 1847 and 1869. The Mormon Pioneer National Historic Trail
begins with Nauvoo National Historic District, the trail has 73
historic sites, six cross-country trails for recreational use, ends
with Pioneer Trail State Park in Salt Lake City, Utah. Although
nearly two-thirds of the trail is privately owned, many of the
places and events connected with the trail can be seen or visited.
Food and lodging, campgrounds along the trail.

Free Print Material:
    "The Mormon Pioneer Trail." 12-fold. Photos, map, history,
      description and features of the trail. Addresses of nine state
      and federal agencies to inquire about access and travel.

Bibliography:
    "Bibliography." 3 pages. Arranged by author, name of book or
      article, date of periodical, pages of periodical, date and city
      of book publication. Some describe contents. Includes
      diaries, journals, Mormon guide, letters along with books and
      periodicals.

Suggested Curriculum Application:
    AMERICAN HISTORY
    ILLINOIS STATE AND LOCAL STUDIES
    IOWA STATE AND LOCAL STUDIES
    NEBRASKA STATE AND LOCAL STUDIES
    UTAH STATE AND LOCAL STUDIES
    WYOMING STATE AND LOCAL STUDIES

Suggested Sears Subject Heading:
<u>ILLINOIS--DESCRIPTION AND TRAVEL--GUIDES</u>
ILLINOIS--PUBLIC LANDS
IOWA--DESCRIPTION AND TRAVEL--GUIDES
IOWA--PUBLIC LANDS
MORMONS AND MORMONISM
NEBRASKA--DESCRIPTION AND TRAVEL--GUIDES
NEBRASKA--PUBLIC LANDS
OVERLAND JOURNEYS TO THE PACIFIC (U.S.)
U.S.--DESCRIPTION AND TRAVEL--GUIDES
UTAH--DESCRIPTION AND TRAVEL--GUIDES
UTAH--PUBLIC LANDS
WYOMING--DESCRIPTION AND TRAVEL--GUIDES
WYOMING--PUBLIC LANDS

- PIPE SPRING

National Monument. Moccasin, AZ 86022. (602) 643-7105. 40 acres.
1923. Northern Arizona, 15 miles south of Fredonia, from U.S. 89
by Ariz. 398.

Nineteenth-century fort and other buildings built by Mormon pioneers. Tours, living history demonstrations, special events.
Campground nearby. Food and lodging in Fredonia, Hurricane.

Free Print Material:
"Pipe Spring." 12-fold. Description of cowboy life with sketches
and photos. Touring information with sketches and photos.
History and construction.

Audiovisual List:
Inquire about movie on Arizona Strip and movie on Death Valley
Days: series and taped interviews of old pioneers of the area.

Sales/Audiovisual List:
"Zion Natural History Association Sales List." 4 pages. Books
alphabetically arranged by author, color slides by set number,
posters by title, post cards are listed by title. Books and
items include a brief description. Aims of the Zion Natural
History Association and mail order instruction included.
"Bright Edge, The" by Stephen Trimble. The Museum of Northern
Arizona Press. 1979. An overall look at the red rock country.
$5.95.

Suggested Curriculum Application:
AMERICAN HISTORY
ARIZONA STATE AND LOCAL STUDIES

Suggested Sears Subject Heading:
ARIZONA--DESCRIPTION AND TRAVEL--GUIDES
ARIZONA--PUBLIC LANDS

FRONTIER AND PIONEER LIFE
MORMONS AND MORMONISM
U.S.--DESCRIPTION AND TRAVEL--GUIDES

● SCOTTS BLUFF
National Monument. P.O. Box 427, Gering, NE 69341.
(308) 436-4340. 2,997.08 acres. 1919. Western Nebraska, three
miles west of Gering, on Nebr. 92.

Sandstone and clay rock promontory landmark associated with overland migration on the Oregon Trail. 800-foot rock formation, exhibits, museum, Oregon Trail ruts, covered wagons, living history
demonstrations, interpretive programs, self-guiding trail, bicycle
trail. Visitor center. Camping and picnicking nearby. Food and
lodging in Gering and Scottsbluff.

Free Print Material:
    "Scotts Bluff Official Map and Guide." 8-fold. Illustrations,
        photos, map, diagram. Visitor information, geological and
        historical features of Scotts Bluff.

Suggested Curriculum Application:
    AMERICAN HISTORY
    NEBRASKA STATE AND LOCAL STUDIES

Suggested Sears Subject Heading:
    FRONTIER AND PIONEER LIFE
    NEBRASKA--DESCRIPTION AND TRAVEL--GUIDES
    NEBRASKA--PUBLIC LANDS
    OVERLAND JOURNEYS TO THE PACIFIC (U.S.)
    U.S.--DESCRIPTION AND TRAVEL--GUIDES

● VOYAGEURS
National Park. P.O. Box 50, International Falls, MN 56649.
(218) 283-9821. 217,892.01 acres. 1971. Northern Minnesota,
from Duluth follow Route 53 north to the park.

Preserve the scenery, geological conditions and waterway system
of the voyageurs who contributed to the opening of the northwestern
part of the country. Interconnected lakes (over 30) surrounded by
forests. Swimming, waterskiing, bird watching, boating, naturalist-
guided boat tours, cross-country ski trips and evening programs,
winter activities, wildlife, exhibits, trail system. Boat-in campsites
and interior campsites, public launching ramps. Boat and canoe
camping outfitters. Inquire about Kettle Falls Hotel, on the National
Register of Historic Places, and operated as a park concession.
Campgrounds nearby. Food and lodging in International Falls.

Free Print Material:
    "Caution: Bears." 4-fold. Tips on treating bears, life cycle.

"Cruiser Lake Hiking Trail." 6-fold. Map, sketches. Hiking and backpacking in Voyageurs National Park. The longest hiking trail is Cruiser Lake Trail.

"Naturalist-Guided Activities." 8-fold. Description and schedule of current activities such as island campfire program, north canoe voyage, kids explore Voyageurs.

"A Peek at the Park...." 13 pages. Sketches, human history, Voyageurs ecosystem, park ecology, 101 things to do in Voyageurs National Park, the act to authorize the creation of the park.

"Rendezvous." 8 pages. Newspaper format. Information on activities, accommodations, services in the park. Photos, maps, sketches. Articles and schedules for visitors.

"Voyageurs." 16-fold. Photos, maps, chart of resort services, activities, safety tips, description of the park, fur trade and life of the Voyageur.

"Voyageurs National Park Area Climate." 1 page. Description, monthly chart of average temperatures and precipitation.

Audiovisual List:

"Video Program." 1 page. Description, running time, and other information. The free 1/2"-tape, 16-minute program is on enjoying Voyageurs National Park the year around and includes a brief history. You are asked to call or write for more details.

Sales/Audiovisual List:

"Lake States Interpretive Association Catalog." 8-fold. Grouped by: history, general reading, general science, animals and plants, children's books, Peterson Field Guides, Golden Guides, records and cassettes, prints, Voyageurs National Park map list, Voyageurs National Park, Superior National Forest, Ottawa National Forest. Order blank and ordering directions. Sketches. Title, author, description, price.

"A Toast to the Fur Trade." Wheeler. A picture essay with illustrations by David Christopherson.

Suggested Curriculum Application:

AMERICAN HISTORY
MINNESOTA STATE AND LOCAL STUDIES
NATURAL HISTORY
RECREATION

Suggested Sears Subject Heading:

FUR TRADE
LAKES
MINNESOTA--DESCRIPTION AND TRAVEL--GUIDES
MINNESOTA--PUBLIC LANDS
NATIONAL PARKS AND RESERVES--U.S.
NATURAL HISTORY--MINNESOTA
NATURAL CONSERVATION

OUTDOOR RECREATION
U.S.--DESCRIPTION AND TRAVEL--GUIDES
VOYAGEURS NATIONAL PARK
WATERWAYS

- WHITMAN MISSION
National Historic Site. Route 2, Box 247, Walla Walla, WA 99362.
(509) 522-6360. 98.15 acres. 1936. Southern Washington, 7 miles
west of Walla Walla off U.S. 12.

Commemorates Marcus and Narcissa Whitman's 11 years among
Indians when settlers began coming down the Oregon Trail. The
Protestant missionary and his wife and others were killed in 1847
by a band of Cayuse. Exhibits, museum, self-guiding trails, common
grave for massacre victims, mission site, pioneer and Indian cultural
demonstrations, memorial monument built in 1897, audiovisuals.
Visitor center, picnicking. Food and lodging in Walla Walla.

Free Print Material:
  "A Guide to Food, Fun and Lodging in Walla Walla, Washington."
    8-fold. Things to see and do includes historic sites of inter-
    est, art galleries, mileage chart, map, sketch.
  "Teacher's Guide." 32 pages. Designed to help teachers who
    are going to visit the Whitman Mission as a field trip. Spelling
    words, sample questions, Indian children, traditional games,
    trail map, trail guide, Cayuse Indians, suggested activities
    and others.
  "Waiilatpu Press." 4 pages. Sketches, photos, maps, schedules
    of events, articles, visitor information, Waiilatpu, meaning
    "Place of the People of the Rye Grass" is the site of Whitman's
    Mission founded in 1836.
  "Walla Walla." 12-fold. Map, photos of the city as a place of
    history, recreation, accommodations and to live and do business.
    Calendar of annual events, telephones and addresses of where
    to obtain more information.
  "Whitman Mission." 8-fold. Founding in 1836 among the Cayuse
    Indians by Marcus and Narcissa Whitman, importance to the
    Oregon Trail, western advances. Maps. photos.

Bibliography:
  "Suggested Reading List." 1 page. Thirty-three general reading
    adult level books. Includes author, title. Alphabetically ar-
    ranged by author.

Audiovisual List:
  One page in "Teacher's Guide" described above.
  "The Whitmans and Waiilatpus." 14 minutes. The story of
    Whitman Mission and the Waiilatpu Indians as seen through
    the eyes of children. Although designed for children, the
    film has been well received by adult audiences. It deals with
    the major significance of ....

Sales/Audiovisual List:
  Last 6 pages of "Teacher's Guide" described above. Grouped by:
    books, pamphlets, maps, slides, post cards, notecards, patches,
    reading kits, wool kits.
  "Allen, Opal Sweazea, "Narcissa Whitman." $8.95. Copyright
    1959; hardbound; 6" x 9"; 325 pages. A historical biography
    of Narcissa Whitman.

Suggested Curriculum Application:
  AMERICAN HISTORY
  NATIVE AMERICAN STUDIES
  WASHINGTON STATE AND LOCAL STUDIES

Suggested Sears Subject Heading:
  CAYUSE INDIANS
  INDIANS OF NORTH AMERICA--MISSIONS, CHRISTIAN
  MISSIONS, CHRISTIAN
  U.S.--DESCRIPTION AND TRAVEL--GUIDES
  WASHINGTON--DESCRIPTION AND TRAVEL--GUIDES
  WASHINGTON--HISTORY
  WASHINGTON--PUBLIC LANDS
  WHITMAN, MARCUS, 1802-1847

WILDERNESS

- EVERGLADES
National Park. P.O. Box 279, Homestead, FL   33030.
(305) 247-6211. 1,398,939.19 acres. 1934. Southern tip of Florida,
with the main park entrance about 10 miles southwest of Homestead
on Route 9336.

Protect the unique features and wildlife of the largest remaining
subtropical wilderness in the coterminous United States. Wildlife,
film, displays, dwarf cypress forests, ponds, walking trails, board-
walks, exhibits, Shark Valley, Florida Bay, Lone Pine Key, Pa-hay-
okee Overlook Trail, boat tours, tram tours, sightseeing cruises,
birdwatching, ranger-guided activities such as talks, demonstrations,
canoe trips, and campfire programs, hiking, boating. Visitor centers, ranger station, campgrounds, picnicking, food and lodging,
equipment rental, church services in amphitheaters, gift shops.
Food and lodging in surrounding communities.

Free Print Material:
  "Endangered and Threatened Species in South Florida National
    Parks." 1 page. Common and scientific name, status in the
    Everglades National Park, Biscayne National Park, Fort
    Jefferson National Monument, Big Cypress National Preserve.

"Everglades." 24-fold. Ecology, wildlife, things to see and do, facilities and services, photos, sketches, chart, map, points of interest, road distance chart, walking trails. Photos and map indications of the areas of: marine and estuarine, mangrove, cypress, coastal prairie, fresh water slough, pinelands, freshwater marl prairie, hardwood hammocks.

"Everglades National Park Visitor Information Letter." 2 pages. Seasonal temperatures, visitor facilities, accommodations and services.

"Fire in Shark Valley." 2 pages. History of fire and its effects.

"Flamingo Lodge Marina and Outpost Resort in Everglades National Park." 16-fold. Illustration, photos, map, features and services.

"Pa-hay-okee." 8-pages. Newspaper format visitor guide to south Florida's national park areas. Articles, schedules, photos, services.

"Purpose of the Park." 2 pages. History of the formation of the park, importance of the park.

"Research in the National Parks." 2 pages. Purpose and type of research underway at the Everglades in hydrology, wildlife ecology, marine ecology, plant ecology and fire ecology.

Sales/Audiovisual List:

"Florida National Parks and Monuments Association, Inc." 8-fold. Grouped by: publications, children's books, post cards, wilderness waterway, slides. Title, price, author, publisher, descriptive annotation includes page number and if hardback or paper. Order form, mail order instructions.

"The Alligator--Monarch of the Everglades." $3.95 by Connie M. Toops. Publisher: Everglades Natural History Association, Inc. A book designed to erase some of the myths about alligators and emphasize their importance to the everglades....

Suggested Curriculum Application:
FLORIDA STATE AND LOCAL STUDIES
GEOGRAPHY
SCIENCE

Suggested Sears Subject Heading:
EVERGLADES NATIONAL PARK
FLORIDA--DESCRIPTION AND TRAVEL--GUIDES
FLORIDA--PUBLIC LANDS
NATIONAL PARKS AND RESERVES--U.S.
NATURAL HISTORY--FLORIDA
NATURE CONSERVATION
U.S.--DESCRIPTION AND TRAVEL--GUIDES
WILDERNESS AREAS
WILDLIFE--CONSERVATION

• GATES OF THE ARCTIC
National Park and Preserve. Box 74680, Fairbanks, AK 99707.

(907) 456-0281. National Park, 7,500,000; national preserve, 940,000; wilderness area, 7,052,000. Proclaimed a national monument 1978; established a national park and preserve 1980. North-central Alaska, 200 miles northwest of Fairbanks, reached by scheduled flights from Fairbanks to Bettles or Anaktuvuk Pass and then chartered small aircraft to the park and preserve.

Preserve 8.5 million acres (second largest unit of the national park system), one of the finest remaining wilderness areas, located in the Central Brooks Range above the Arctic Circle, it includes jagged peaks, arctic valleys, wild rivers, many lakes, forested slopes. Foothills, ragged peaks, glacially-carved valleys, clearwater rivers and alpine lakes, wildlife, backpacking, floating the rivers, rock and mountain climbing. The Central Brooks Range is the northernmost part of the Rocky Mountains. No established facilities. Food and lodging in Fairbanks.

Free Print Material:
"Gates of the Arctic." 2 pages. Accommodations and services, weather, trip planning, subsistence, safety, description and park resources, access, sketches.

Suggested Curriculum Application:
ALASKA STATE AND LOCAL STUDIES
RECREATION

Suggested Sears Subject Heading:
ALASKA--DESCRIPTION AND TRAVEL--GUIDES
ALASKA--PUBLIC LANDS
GATES OF THE ARCTIC NATIONAL PARK AND PRESERVE
NATIONAL PARKS AND RESERVES--U.S.
OUTDOOR RECREATION
U.S.--DESCRIPTION AND TRAVEL--GUIDES
WILDERNESS AREAS

• ISLE ROYALE
National Park. 87 North Ripley St., Houghton, MI 49931. (906) 482-0984. 571,790.11 acres. 1931. Lake Superior off the northern coast of Michigan's upper peninsula. The main island is 45 miles long and 9 miles wide. Island is 73 miles north of Houghton, MI and 15 miles from Canada.

Preserve the wilderness of this 210-square-mile, French-named island with its timber wolves, moose, and copper mines used by Indians at least 3500 years ago. Wildlife, self-guiding trails, exhibits, field seminars, boating, copper mines, swimming, guided walks, interpretive programs. Programs that include touring a passenger vessel and seeing a film are offered January through March in Houghton, MI, and teachers should write ahead or call the park historian. Campgrounds, food, lodging, supplies, marina. Transportation by float-plane or boat.

Free Print Material:
  "Camping Hiking Boating." 8-fold. Where to camp, regulations,
    facilities chart of campgrounds, group camping, hiking, back-
    packing and boating.
  "Disabled Visitors Special Notice." 4-fold. Accessibility tips,
    guide dog certification, tips for planning your trip.
  "Drinking Water Special Notice." 4-fold. How to avoid hydadid
    tapeworm, giardia, intestinal bacteria. Information on filters
    and a list that meets the 25-micron requirement.
  "Field Seminars." 6-fold. Seminars offered by professional in-
    structors with academic credit available. Describes seminars,
    gives session schedule, fee, registration form.
  "Getting There." 6-fold. Transportation to Isle Royale. Rates
    and schedules from various points of departure.
  "Isle Royale." 16-fold. Access and accommodations, activities,
    map, sketches, photos, the island's wilderness world.
  "Isle Royale Birds." 2 pages. Common names of numerous birds.
    Where to obtain more information. Sketches.
  "Isle Royale Facts." 2 pages. Includes such facts as how many
    kinds of birds have been seen on the island, when the Indians
    sold the island, how many species of orchids the island has.
  "Isle Royale Mammals." 1 page. Scientific and common name,
    habitat, occurrence.
  "Isle Royale National Park: An International Biosphere Reserve."
    2 pages. Questions and answers about a biosphere, such as
    what it is, why Isle Royale is a biosphere reserve.
  "Isle Royale Orchids by Genus." 1 page. Scientific name, com-
    mon name, bloom period. Reading list.
  "Isle Royale Trees List." 2 pages. Scientific and common name,
    habitat, occurrence.
  "Outline of the Geological History of Isle Royale." 2 pages.
    Begins with the rifting that began 1.1 billion years ago through
    the retreat of the last ice age. Includes selected advanced
    references on Isle Royale geology.
  "Rock Harbor Lodge." 10-fold. Facilities offered by Rock Harbor
    Lodge, activities on the island, photos, map. Rate schedule
    and reservation form.

Bibliography:
  "Recent Periodicals on Isle Royale National Park." 1 page. Lists
    name and date of magazine articles about the island.

Audiovisual List:
  "Film Loans." 1 page. Movies and slide programs available
    between November and May. Loaned without charge except
    user must pay return postage and insurance. Grouped by
    35mm slide/cassette tape sets and 16mm movies. Includes
    title, running length, annotation, sketch.
  "Acid Rain, the Choice is Ours." 19 minutes. Story of acid
    rain in the midwest and particularly the northern Minnesota
    lakes region.

Sales/Audiovisual List:
  "Publications." 8-fold. Includes: Games, poster, animal prints, publications, maps and charts, color transparencies. Order form and mailing information. Publications include annotation. Information and membership form for the Isle Royale Natural History Association.
  "Isle Royale Adventure Game." $14.95. Informative, educational, and fun for the whole family.

Suggested Curriculum Application:
  ENVIRONMENTAL EDUCATION
  GEOGRAPHY
  MICHIGAN STATE AND LOCAL STUDIES
  NATURAL HISTORY
  RECREATION

Suggested Sears Subject Heading:
  ISLANDS
  ISLE ROYALE NATIONAL PARK
  MICHIGAN--DESCRIPTION AND TRAVEL--GUIDES
  MICHIGAN--PUBLIC LANDS
  NATIONAL PARKS AND RESERVES--U.S.
  NATURAL HISTORY--MICHIGAN
  OUTDOOR RECREATION
  U.S.--DESCRIPTION AND TRAVEL--GUIDES
  WILDERNESS AREAS

- KOBUK VALLEY
National Park. P.O. Box 287, Kotzebue, AK 99752. (907) 442-3890. 1,750,000 acres. National Monument, 1978; National Park, 1980. Northwestern Alaska, 25 miles north of the Arctic Circle, 350 miles west-northwest of Fairbanks, 75 miles east of Kotzebue. Broad valley along the central Kobuk River.

Wilderness area north of the Arctic Circle, rich in wildlife, includes the northernmost extent of the boreal forest, the Great Kobuk and Little Kobuk sand dunes, central valley of the Kobuk River. This area reveals sites showing over 10,000 years of human life with current inland Eskimos living here. Twenty-five square miles of sand dunes reaching 100 feet high, hiking, boating on the Kobuk and Salmon rivers, wildlife, backpacking in the Baird and Waring mountains and along their foothills and valleys. Visitor center. Camping is permitted except in sensitive archeological areas or on private land along the Kobuk River. Hotel in Kotzebue and stores. Lodging in Kiana, Ambler. Air taxi operators and boat owners offer some services as well as limited guiding and outfitting. Access to the park is by air.

Free Print Material:
  "Kobuk Valley." 2 pages. Description, photos, map, what to

see and do, access, accommodations and services, weather and insects, clothing and provisions, visitor tips.

Sales/Audiovisual List:
"Alaska Natural History Association Mail Order Catalog." 8 pages. Newspaper format. Grouped by sources: Denali National Park and Preserve, Glacier Bay National Park and Preserve, Sitka National Historical Park, Katmai National Park/Reserve, Park and Forest Information Center, Northwest National Parks, Alaska Maritime National Wildlife, Chagach National Forest, Alaska Public Lands Information Center. Each is grouped under such headings as: general, plants--animals, maps--visual aids, habitat and vegetation culture--history. Title, author, price, description, number of pages for publications. Other materials are also annotated. Statement of aims of the Alaska Natural History Association, sketches, order blank and ordering instructions.
"Alaska National Parklands: The Last Treasure." Brown. Hard $16.95, soft $5.95. 128 pages, full-color publication describing the national significance of all National Park Service areas in Alaska by means of a narrative by Brown and short writings by individuals very familiar....

Suggested Curriculum Application:
ALASKA STATE AND LOCAL STUDIES
GEOGRAPHY
RECREATION

Suggested Sears Subject Heading:
ALASKA--DESCRIPTION AND TRAVEL--GUIDES
ALASKA--PUBLIC LANDS
KOBUK VALLEY NATIONAL PARK
NATIONAL PARKS AND RESERVES--U.S.
OUTDOOR RECREATION
SAND DUNES
U.S.--DESCRIPTION AND TRAVEL--GUIDES
WILDERNESS AREAS

• NOATAK
National Preserve. Box 287, Kotzebue, AK 99752.
(907) 442-3890. 6,560,000 acres. National Monument, 1978;
National Preserve, 1980. Northwestern Alaska, 350 miles northwest of Fairbanks. Access by air.

Preserve one of the world's finest remaining vast wilderness areas. The 425-mile-long Noatak River has the largest undisturbed mountain-ringed watershed on this continent. Backpacking the mountain foot-hills, canoeing and kayaking the Noatak, wildlife. The Noatak River flows within a broad sloping valley where boreal forest merges into treeless tundra. Visitor center. Two summer ranger stations.

Kotzebue has a hotel and stores. Camping is permitted except on private inholdings along the lower Noatak River. A few guides and outfitters available. Food and lodging in Fairbanks and Anchorage.

Free Print Material:

"Alaska National Parklands 3 Steps to Bear Safety." 8-fold. Planning ahead, preventing close encounters, what to do if you see a grizzly or brown bear. Sketches.

"Noatak." 2 pages. Access, description, map, what to do and see, photo, accommodations and services, weather and insects, clothing and provisions, visitor tips.

"The Noatak National Preserve." 4 pages. Maps, sketches, description of the preserve, when to visit, planning your trip, flight cost estimates and other visitor information.

"Take Pride in America." 8-fold. Campaign, photos with the message to encourage everyone to take pride in the nation's natural and cultural resources.

"Your Arctic Adventure." 10-fold. Trails, campsites, wildlife, water, private property and other topics for wilderness visitors to ensure your visit has minimum impact on the environment. Sketches.

Sales/Audiovisual List:

"Alaska Natural History Association Mail Order Catalog." 8 pages. Newspaper format. Grouped by sources: Denali National Park and Preserve, Glacier Bay National Park and Preserve, Sitka National Historical Park, Katmai National Park/Reserve, Park and Forest Information Center, Northwest National Parks, Alaska Maritime National Wildlife, Chagach National Forest, Alaska Public Lands Information Center. Each source is grouped under such headings as: general, plants--animals, maps--visual aids, habitat and vegetation, culture--history. Title, author, price, description, number of pages for publications. Other materials are also annotated. Statement of aims of the Alaska Natural History Association, sketches, order blank and ordering instructions.

"Alaska National Parklands: The Last Treasure." Brown. Hard $16.95, soft $5.95. 128 pages, full-color publication describing the national significance of all National Park Service areas in Alaska by means of a narrative by Brown and short writings by individuals very familiar....

Suggested Curriculum Application:

ALASKA STATE AND LOCAL STUDIES
RECREATION

Suggested Sears Subject Heading:

ALASKA--DESCRIPTION AND TRAVEL--GUIDES
ALASKA--PUBLIC LANDS
NOATAK RIVER
OUTDOOR RECREATION

U.S.--DESCRIPTION AND TRAVEL--GUIDES
WILDERNESS AREAS

WOMEN

- CLARA BARTON

National Historic Site. 5801 Oxford Road, Glen Echo, MD 20812.
(301) 492-6245. 8.59 acres. 1974. Eight miles from downtown
Washington, D.C.

Home of American Red Cross founder, organization headquarters.
Guided tour of restored home and furnishings. If planning to visit
the area contact: Montgomery County Travel Council, Red Brick
Courthouse, 27 Courthouse Square, Rockville, MD 20850 for more
information. Food and lodging in greater Washington, D.C. area.

Free Print Material:
> "Clara Barton." 8-fold. Chronology of Clara Barton's life, map,
> photos, development of the Red Cross, Barton's personality
> and work.

Bibliography:
> "Bibliography of Basic Information." 2 pages. Grouped by:
> primary interpretive themes, secondary interpretive themes,
> tertiary interpretive themes. Divisions of primary interpretive
> themes: early history of the American Red Cross, life and
> times of Clara Barton (adult books), life and times of Clara
> Barton (juvenile books). Secondary interpretive themes divi-
> sions: emergency services in the 19th-century, women's
> history in the 19th century, minorities and ethnic/cultural
> groups. Tertiary interpretive themes are grouped by: pres-
> ervation of historic structures, NPS sites associated with
> Clara Barton, Victorian lifestyle. Author, title, publisher,
> date.

Sales List:
> Inquire about handbook on Clara Barton (stock number 024-005-
> 00806-3). On sale from: The Superintendent of Documents,
> U.S. Government Printing Office, Washington, D.C. 20402.

Suggested Curriculum Application:
> AMERICAN HISTORY
> MARYLAND STATE AND LOCAL STUDIES
> SOCIAL STUDIES
> WOMEN'S STUDIES

Suggested Sears Subject Heading:
    BARTON, CLARA, 1821-1912
    MARYLAND--DESCRIPTION AND TRAVEL--GUIDES
    MARYLAND--PUBLIC LANDS
    RED CROSS
    U.S.--DESCRIPTION AND TRAVEL--GUIDES
    WOMEN--U.S.

• ELEANOR ROOSEVELT
National Historic Site. 249 Albany Post Road, Bellfield
Headquarters, Hyde Park, NY 12538. (914) 229-9115.
180.50 acres. 1977. Eastern New York, Hyde Park,
about 3 miles from the Franklin Roosevelt home, off
Route 9G.

Val-Kill (named after nearby stream), country retreat home of
Eleanor Roosevelt. Film, tour of Val-Kill cottage, tour of stone
cottage, Depression factory, outbuildings, flower gardens, swimming
pool, Val-Kill Pond, trails. The site is closed from Thanksgiving
Day through the last day of February. From April through October
transportation to the site is by shuttle bus only and departs from
the home of Franklin Roosevelt National Historic Site. Food and
lodging nearby.

Free Print Material:
    "Eleanor Roosevelt." 8-fold. Photos, map, life and accomplish-
        ments, visitor information, development of craftsmen's work-
        shop, country retreat.

Suggested Curriculum Application:
    AMERICAN HISTORY
    NEW YORK STATE AND LOCAL STUDIES
    WOMEN'S STUDIES

Suggested Sears Subject Heading:
    NEW YORK--DESCRIPTION AND TRAVEL--GUIDES
    NEW YORK--PUBLIC LANDS
    ROOSEVELT, ELEANOR, 1884-1962
    U.S.--DESCRIPTION AND TRAVEL--GUIDES
    WOMEN--U.S.

• MAGGIE L. WALKER
National Historic Site. c/o Richmond National Battlefield Park,
3215 East Broad Street, Richmond, VA 23223.
(804) 226-1981. 1.29 acres. 1978. Eastern Virginia, in downtown Richmond at 110-1/2 East Leigh Street, in Jackson Ward
National Historic Landmark District, accessible from Interstate 95
north and south.

Restored home of black leader, the first woman president of a U.S. financial institution. Guided tours of the 22-room, two-story home arranged, please call before visit. Advance notice for groups of five or more are required. Public transportation to the house. Food and lodging in Richmond.

Free Print Material:
"Maggie L. Walker." 4 pages. Biographical sketch and accomplishments of Maggie L. Walker, map, photos of various rooms in her house.
"Maggie L. Walker National Historic Site." 8-fold. Life and career, photos of her house, sketch.
"An Orientation." 30 pages. Business and public service career, family life, early construction of the house, various additions, renovations, paint colors, floors, light fixtures, bibliography. Floor plans.
"Reservations." 2 pages. Reservation requirements, student visitor behavior, reservation request form.
"Summary of Environmental Assessment." 28 pages. Six alternative uses, public response sheet.

Bibliography:
Included in "An Orientation" described above. A four-page bibliography includes books, oral interviews, newspapers, reports and others.

Suggested Curriculum Application:
BLACK STUDIES
VIRGINIA STATE AND LOCAL STUDIES
WOMEN'S STUDIES

Suggested Sears Subject Heading:
ARCHITECTURE--CONSERVATION AND RESTORATION
BLACK BUSINESS PEOPLE
U.S.--DESCRIPTION AND TRAVEL--GUIDES
VIRGINIA--DESCRIPTION AND TRAVEL--GUIDES
VIRGINIA--PUBLIC LANDS
WALKER, MAGGIE LENA, 1867-1934
WOMEN--U.S.

• MARY McLEOD BETHUNE COUNCIL HOUSE
National Historic Site. 1318 Vermont Avenue, NW, Washington, D.C. 20005. (202) 332-1233. 1982. 1318 Vermont Avenue N.W., Washington, D.C.

Largest manuscript collection of materials pertaining to the organizational and individual contributions of black women in America, named for the founder and first president of the National Council of Negro Women. Bethune was a pioneer black political and civil rights leader and noted educator. Guided tours of the museum may be arranged

for groups. Inquire about special children's programs, traveling
exhibits, lectures, special educational programs, use of meeting
rooms, audiovisual facilities and other special services. Museum
shop offers books, cards, photographs, color slides, posters.
Food and lodging in Washington, D.C.

Free Print Material:
"Bethune Museum and Archives for Black Women's History."
8-fold. Description of the beginning, purpose, location,
exhibits, tours, archives, programs, hours, public service,
museum shop. Photos, membership application.

Audiovisual List:
"Black Women Organized for Social Change: 1800-1920--Special
Educational Video Cassette (V.H.S.)." 1 page. Description,
sales order form. Sketch.
"Black Women: Organizing for Social Change." This unusual
educational video tape, written and produced by the Bethune
Museum-Archives, examines the role of black women in the
development of extensive social service programs and as power-
ful advocates for....

Sales/Audiovisual List:
"Black Women in Print." 5 pages. Grouped by: books, kits,
posters, films, exhibits. Also includes buttons, bibliographies,
teaching units. Application to join the Bethune Museum-
Archives, order form, ordering information. Title, author,
annotation, price.
"A Black Woman Speaks" by Beah Richards. This book of stun-
ning prose poems exploring the experience of the black woman
was written by Academy Award-Nominee, actress Beah
Richards. $6.00.

Suggested Curriculum Application:
BLACK STUDIES
DISTRICT OF COLUMBIA LOCAL STUDIES
WOMEN'S STUDIES

Suggested Sears Subject Heading:
BETHUNE, MARY McLEOD, 1875-1955
BLACK STUDIES
DISTRICT OF COLUMBIA--DESCRIPTION AND TRAVEL--GUIDES
DISTRICT OF COLUMBIA--PUBLIC LANDS
U.S.--DESCRIPTION AND TRAVEL--GUIDES
WOMEN--U.S.

• WOMEN'S RIGHTS
National Historical Park. P.O. Box 70, Seneca Falls, NY 13148.
(315) 568-2991. 4.99 acres. 1980. Central New York, near junction
of Rts. 414 and 20; New York State Thruway Exit 41 is about 15
miles from the park.

Commemorate the Women's Rights Movement and its founders. Site of 1848 convention, the first women's rights convention. Stanton House tours, exhibits, audiovisual programs, walking tours of Seneca Falls. Wesleyan Chapel was just purchased by the National Park Service in 1985. In Waterloo the Hunt House and McClintock House are not open to the public. The Mumford House is also closed to the public. (The park is in the early stages of development in Seneca Falls and Waterloo.) Visitor center. Towns in the Finger Lakes section.

Free Print Material:

"Answers to Frequently Asked Questions About the Park." 2 pages. Answers to such questions as: What is the Women's Rights National Historical Park? Who organized the convention, and where?

"The 'Bloomer Costume' and Dress Reform." 6-fold. How baggy pantaloons caused great controversy, illustrations, bibliography.

"Central New York Traveling Trivia and Other Information About Waterloo, Seneca Falls, Auburn." 10-fold. Description and photos of historical features of importance and interest. Maps, questions and answers.

"Frederick Douglass and the Women's Rights Movement." 6-fold. Photo, bibliography, Douglass's contributions to the Women's Movement, his friendship with Elizabeth Cady Stanton.

"I Love New York Seneca County Travel Guide Finger Lakes Region." 16 pages. Map, photos, Seneca County attractions, accommodations.

"Invitation to the Park." 1 page. What to do and see, map.

"Lucretia Mott." 8-fold. Mott's reform work, religious issues, early life, abolitionist and women's rights advocacy efforts. Illustration, bibliography.

"The Park and Its Purpose." 1 page. What the park contains, sketches of the four separate sites.

"Women's Rights National Historical Park." 6-fold. History of the convention, map, sketches, park features.

Bibliography:

"Grade Level Suggested Reading List." 3 pages. Grouped by: grades 2 and 3; grades 4 and 5; grade 6; grades 7 and 8; grades 9-12. Title, author, publisher, date.

"A Recommended Reading List on the 19th Century Women's Rights Movement." 2 pages. Arranged alphabetically by author. Includes title, place of publication, publisher, date, annotation.

Sales List:

"Publications Order Form." 1 page. Form and ordering information, including discounts for schools and libraries.

"Women's Rights National Historical Park." 4 pages. Grouped by: 2 government publications; 33 other publications.

Indication is made if publication is designed for or related to
children. Includes title and price, some are annotated.
"Camping in the National Park System" (pamphlet describing
specific resources) $.60.

Audiovisual List:
  "Suggested Film List." 1 page. Grouped by elementary, middle
  school and high school. Includes title, running length, color,
  price, ordering information. Elementary: The Women's
  Rights National Historical Park offers slide programs of various lengths and levels of complexity. Please phone
  (315) 568-2991 for information.
Middle school (grades 5-9): "You Are There: Harriet Tubman
  and the Underground Railroad." 22 minutes, color. $14.50.
  To order call University of Illinois Film Center at
  1-800-367-3456. Please specify film #53766.

Suggested Curriculum Application:
  AMERICAN HISTORY
  NEW YORK STATE AND LOCAL STUDIES
  WOMEN'S STUDIES

Suggested Sears Subject Heading:
  MOTT, LUCRETIA, 1793-1880
  NEW YORK--DESCRIPTION AND TRAVEL--GUIDES
  NEW YORK--PUBLIC LANDS
  STANTON, ELIZABETH CADY, 1815-1902
  U.S.--DESCRIPTION AND TRAVEL--GUIDES
  WOMEN--CIVIL RIGHTS
  WOMEN--U.S.

WORLD WAR II AND VIETNAMESE CONFLICT

• USS ARIZONA
Memorial. c/o Pacific Area Office, National Park Service, Box 50165,
Honolulu, HI 96850. (808) 422-2771. 1980. Southern part of the
island of Oahu, suburbs of Honolulu. The visitor center is directly
off State Highway 99, the memorial spans the sunken battleship
U.S.S. Arizona and is within the boundaries of the Pearl Harbor
Naval Base.

Floating memorial over the U.S.S. Arizona where it was sunk in
Pearl Harbor, December 7, 1941, by a Japanese attack. The visitor
center is on nearby shoreline. The 184-foot long Arizona Memorial
includes a shrine chamber with the names of 1,177 killed. Tours,
museum, interpretive program, shuttle boat trip, museum shop.

Landscaped area provides view of the focal point of the 1941 attack. Visitor center. Food and lodging in Honolulu.

Free Print Material:
  "U.S.S. Arizona." 10-fold. Maps, photos, table of American and Japanese losses, the attack, visitor services, transportation and features.

Sales/Audiovisual List:
  Grouped by: publications, cassette tapes/audiovisual, miscellaneous, flags. Items annotated. Cassette tapes/audiovisual includes cassette tape, slides with cassette tape, video tapes VHS or Beta. Miscellaneous includes a calendar and newspaper. Includes member blank and aims of the Arizona Memorial Museum Association. Sales order blank and ordering information. Publications include order number, title, author, annotation, pages, price, postage and handling charges first class and fourth class.
  "Pearl Harbor and the U.S.S. Arizona Memorial," by Richard A. Wisniewski. A 64-page pictorial history of Pearl Harbor and the U.S.S. Arizona Memorial before it became a harbor, taking you into, through and out of the war, and the actual conception and building.... List price: $4.50 + postage and handling--$1.90 1st class, $1.20 4th class.

Suggested Curriculum Application:
  AMERICAN HISTORY
  HAWAII STATE AND LOCAL STUDIES

Suggested Sears Subject Heading:
  HAWAII--DESCRIPTION AND TRAVEL--GUIDES
  HAWAII--HISTORY
  PEARL HARBOR, ATTACK ON
  HAWAII--PUBLIC LANDS
  U.S.--DESCRIPTION AND TRAVEL--GUIDES
  WORLD WAR, 1939-1945--U.S.

• VIETNAM VETERANS MEMORIAL
c/o National Capital Parks--Central, National Park Service, 900 Ohio Drive, S.W., Washington, D.C. 20242. (202) 426-6841. 2 acres. 1980. District of Columbia, near Lincoln Memorial at the west end of Constitution Gardens on the National Mall.

Memorial to those who lost their lives or remain missing as a result of the Vietnamese conflict. Polished black granite wall inscribed with names of 58,007 persons. Each of the walls is 246.75 feet long and each at its vertex is 10.1 feet high. Flagstaff and bronze statue. The flag flies from a 60-foot staff and its base contains emblems of the five services. Food and lodging in Washington D.C. area.

Free Print Material:
   "Vietnam Veterans Memorial." 8-fold. How the memorial came
      about, arrangement of names and how to locate a name, photos,
      memorial design and statistics, the Vietnam conflict.

Sales List:
   "List of Suppliers for Commemorative Items of the Vietnam Veterans
      Memorial." 3 pages. Memorial statue, Vietnam service ban-
      nerette, tee-shirts, buttons, bumper stickers, posters and other
      items. Item, price, description, address of supplier.
   "Memorial Statue." (A) Exact replica 7" high in bonded bronze.
      $122.50.
   "Parks and History Association Publications Sales List." 1 page.
      Booklets, books, post card, first-day cover for postal stamp
      issued November 10, 1984. Inquire about others not included
      in the list.
   "Let us Remember," a 32-page booklet about the memorial, pub-
      lished by the association, tells the story of the building of the
      memorial in text and pictures for only $3.50. There is a 20
      percent discount on lots of 100 or more to a single address.

Suggested Curriculum Application:
   AMERICAN HISTORY
   DISTRICT OF COLUMBIA LOCAL STUDIES
   GOVERNMENT

Suggested Sears Subject Heading:
   DISTRICT OF COLUMBIA--DESCRIPTION AND TRAVEL--GUIDES
   DISTRICT OF COLUMBIA--PUBLIC LANDS
   U.S.--DESCRIPTION AND TRAVEL--GUIDES
   VIETNAMESE CONFLICT, 1961-1975

• WAR IN THE PACIFIC
National Historical Park. P.O. Box FA, Agana, GU 96910.
(671) 477-8528. 1,957.89 acres. 1978. In Guam Agana Harbor area
in seven separate units, near the villages of Asan, Piti and Agat, on
the west side of the island.

Interprets events in the Pacific area during World War II. Museum,
major invasion beaches. Each of the separate units provides a different insight into the Pacific war: Asan Beach Unit, Asan Island
Unit, Piti Unit, Mt. Tenjo/Mt. Chachao Unit, Agat Unit, Mount
Alifan Unit, Fonte Plateau Unit. Visitor center. Food and lodging
nearby.

Free Print Material:
   "Guam." 16-fold. Maps, war activity in Guam, summary of
      events for 1941-1945. Visitor information.
   "Guam, USA: Gateway to Micronesia." 12-fold. Photos, map,

places to see, things to know before visiting Guam, list of hotels and number of rooms, statistics and attractions.

Suggested Curriculum Application:
AMERICAN HISTORY
GUAM LOCAL STUDIES

Suggested Sears Subject Heading:
GUAM--DESCRIPTION AND TRAVEL--GUIDES
GUAM--PUBLIC LANDS
U.S.--DESCRIPTION AND TRAVEL--GUIDES
WORLD WAR, 1939-1945--CAMPAIGNS AND BATTLES--GUAM

NATIONAL PARK SERVICE REGIONAL OFFICES

Region	State(s)	Address and Telephone Number
Alaska	Alaska	2525 Gambell Street, Anchorage, AK 99503. (907) 271-4196
Pacific Northwest	Washington Oregon Idaho	83 South King Street, Suite 212, Seattle, WA 98104. (206) 442-0170
Western	California Nevada Arizona Guam Hawaii	450 Golden Gate Avenue, San Francisco, CA 94102. (415) 556-4122
Rocky Mountain	Montana Wyoming Utah Colorado North Dakota South Dakota	P.O. Box 25287, 655 Parfet Street, Denver, CO 80225. (303) 234-3095
Southwest	New Mexico Texas Oklahoma Arkansas Louisiana	P.O. Box 728, Santa Fe, NM 87501. (505) 988-6375
Midwest	Nebraska Kansas Minnesota Iowa Missouri Wisconsin Illinois Michigan Indiana Ohio	1709 Jackson Street, Omaha, NE 68102. (402) 221-3471

Region	State(s)	Address and Telephone Number
Southeast	Mississippi Alabama Tennessee Kentucky Georgia South Carolina North Carolina Florida Puerto Rico Virgin Islands	75 Spring Street, S.W., Atlanta, GA 30303. (404) 221-5187
National Capital	Washington, D.C.	1100 Ohio Drive, S.W., Washington, D.C. 20242. (202) 426-6700
Mid-Atlantic	West Virginia Virginia Delaware Pennsylvania	143 South Third Street, Philadelphia, PA 19106. (215) 597-7018.
North Atlantic	New York Vermont New Hampshire Maine Massachusetts Connecticut Rhode Island New Jersey	15 State Street, Boston, MA 02109. (617) 223-0058

SAMPLING OF REGIONAL OFFICE MATERIALS

ALASKA

Free Print Material:

"Alaska Lands." 16-fold. Names of state parks, state historical parks, state recreation areas, state trails, state recreation sites, state game refuges, state critical habitat areas, state game sanctuaries. Addresses to obtain information. Alaska lands use key. Photos, map.

"Aniakchak." 8-fold. Photos, weather, map, clothing, food and gear, precautions, location, access, accommodations, inside the caldera, discovery of the 6-mile average diameter caldera.

"Bering Land Bridge." 8-fold. Photo, map, what to wear, food and supplies, weather and insects, safety, user courtesies, historical significance of Bering Land Bridge, access, accommodations and services.

"Cape Krusenstern." 8-fold. Weather and insects, map, what to wear, food and gear, safety tips, what to see and do, access, accommodations and services, location, wildlife, historic use.

"Denali Alpenglow." 8 pages. Newspaper format. Naturalist activities, photos, schedules, programs, campgrounds, wildlife, articles of visitor interest about Denali National Park and Preserve.

"Denali National Park and Preserve." 24-fold. Photos, wildlife of taiga and tundra, geographical features, how to get to Denali, what to do in the park and preserve, regulations, chart of campgrounds, maps.

"The Fairweather." 4 pages. Newspaper format. Articles, photos, sketches, map, wildlife, information about Glacier Bay National Park and Preserve.

"Four Lines of Defense Against Hypothermia." 6-fold. How to protect yourself against the rapid, progressive, mental and physical collapse accompanying the chilling of the inner core of your body.

"Gates of the Arctic." 8-fold. Park resources, sketches, access, location, wildlife, taiga forests, accommodations and services, weather, trip planning, subsistence, precautions, map and other visitor information.

"Glacier Bay." 24-fold. Maps, photos, access and services information, backcountry travel, boating, hazards, weather, regulations, tidewater glaciers, illustrations and descriptions of types of whales, plant and animal life.

"Iditarod--An Historic Trial." 19 pages. Historical significance of the Iditarod Trail located from Seward to Nome. Trail use today, maps, photos, administration.

"Is the Water Safe?" 8-fold. Dangers of drinking untreated water. Symptoms and treatment of Giardia lamblia.

"Katmai." 24-fold. Volcanoes, wildlife, 1912 eruption of Novarupta volcano, diagram, photos, access and information, maps, accommodations and services, backcountry travel, regulations and safety.

"Kenai Fjords." 16-fold. Logistics, information sources, what to see and do, weather and clothing, backcountry travel, boating safety, park land features, maps, plant and wildlife, birds.

"Klondike Gold Rush." 12-fold. Historical background of the gold rush, photos, maps, what to see and do, Chilkoot and White Pass Trails, regulations, how to reach the park, Skagway and Dyea.

"Kobuk Valley." 8-fold. Location, what to see and do, access, accommodations and services, weather and insects, clothing, food and gear, map, precautions and courtesies, photos.

"Lake Clark." 16-fold. Logistics, what to see and do, weather, safety, guides and outfitting, park's scenic diversity, photos, maps, recreational opportunities.

"Minimum Impact Camping." 8-fold. Techniques for wilderness ethics, sketches. How to travel lightly and leave the wilderness in its natural state when you leave.

"National Parklands in Alaska." 24-fold. Maps, travel tips, Alaskan landscape, description of various parklands, parkland classifications, where to obtain more information, national rivers.

"Noatak." 8-fold. Map, what to do and see, photo, access, accommodations and services, description of geographical features, weather, safety, clothing, food and gear, user consideration.

"Sitka." 12-fold. The coming of the Russians, totem pole use and meaning, description of Crane people totem pole, map, photos, Tlingit Indian culture--beliefs and identification with nature.

"Three Steps to Bear Safety." 8-fold. Visitor tips about safety with grizzly and brown bears, sketches.

"Wrangell-St. Elias." 8-fold. Accommodations and services, map, safety, weather, photo, clothing, supplies, what to do and see, access, locations, geographical features and mountain peaks.

"Your Arctic Adventure." 10-fold. Trails, groups, campsites, fires, arctic ecosystem, wildlife, sketches, water, respecting private property and other visitor tips.

"Yukon-Charley." 8-fold. Geographical features, photo, what to see and do, map, access, accommodations and services, weather, clothing, supplies, safety, user courtesies, where to obtain further information.

Audiovisual List:

"Public Film List." 7 pages. Videotapes, films. Use policies. Title, running time, age level, description. Includes an oral history narrated by pioneer Alaskan women.

Sales/Audiovisual List:

"Alaska Natural History Association Mail Order Catalog." 8 pages. What is available from: Denali National Park and Preserve, Glacier Bay National Park and Preserve, Sitka National Historical Park and others. Title, author, type of book cover, price, pages, description of books. Includes videos, posters, coloring books, T-shirts, cassettes, maps, photos, slide sets. Purpose of the Alaska Natural History Association, order blank, ordering directions, map, sketches.

"Alaska National Parklands: This Last Treasure." Brown. Hard, $16.95; soft, $5.95. 128 pages. Full-color publication describing the national significance of all National Park Service areas in Alaska by means of a narrative by Brown and short writings by individuals very familiar with the parks. 128 pages paper....

MIDWEST

Free Print Material:

"Campground Reservations." 10-fold. Reservation procedures by mail, in person. List of various national park campgrounds with facilities and location/special information. Campside reservation request. Camping trips, sketches.

"Golden Eagle, Golden Age, Golden Access Passports, Federal Recreation Fee Program." 10-fold. What they are and how to get: Golden Eagle Passports for persons under 62; Golden Age Passport for persons 62 and older; Golden Access Passport for blind and disabled persons. Federal recreation fees, information services, addresses of other federal agencies.

"Guide and Map: National Parks of the United States." 30-fold. Maps, photos, charts. Alphabetically arranged by state. Charts for each facility to show if accommodations are provided for visitors such as: swimming, exhibits, guides for hire, boat rentals, guided tours, restrooms, campgrounds and many others.

"Ice Age Trail." 24-fold. Photos, Wisconsin's glacial past and landscape, illustration, development of the trail, trail facilities, maps, description of the trail route.

"Index of the National Park System and Related Areas." 97 pages. Background and nomenclature of the park system, designation of wilderness areas, statistics, descriptive listing of national park system areas by state, affiliated areas, wild and scenic rivers system, national trail system. Alphabetical list/index, photos, maps.

"Lewis and Clark Trail." 24-fold. Description of water-land-motor route segments, features along the trail, illustration, photos, account of Meriwether Lewis and William Clark's expedition.

"National Park Service Areas in the Midwest Region." 20-fold. Armchair sampling of national parks, lakeshore, scenic riverways, recreation areas and historic sites in a 10-state area extending from Nebraska to Ohio and from Missouri to the Great Lakes. Photos, map.

"National Park System." 30-fold. Maps, photos. Guide to national parks arranged alphabetically by state. Charts such visitor interest accommodations as: swimming, exhibits, entrance fees, campgrounds and many others.

"The National Parks: Camping Guide." 115 pages. Safety and regulations, planning tips. A by-state description, charts of sites. Alphabetical list/index, photos, maps.

"The National Parks: Lesser-Known Areas." 50 pages. Preparing for a park visit, maps. Areas that are less familiar to the average traveler are described by state. Alphabetical index, photos.

"Volunteers in Parks." 10-fold. Addresses and states covered for national park regional offices, how to apply, living in the parks, types of jobs volunteers do. Prospective volunteer application. Maps.

SOUTHEAST

Free Print Material:

"Golden Eagle, Golden Age, Golden Access Passports, Federal Recreation Fee Program." 10-fold. What they are and how to get: Golden Eagle Passports for persons under 62; Golden Age Passport for persons 62 and older; Golden Access Passport for blind and disabled persons. Federal recreation fees, information services, addresses of other federal agencies.

"Guide and Map: National Parks of the United States." 30-fold. Alphabetically arranged by state. Maps, photos, charts. Charts for each facility shows what accommodations are provided for visitors such as: swimming, exhibits, guides for hire, boat rentals, guided tours, restrooms, campgrounds, and many others.

"Index of the National Park System and Related Areas." 98 pages. Background and nomenclature of the park system, designation of wilderness areas, statistics, descriptive listing of national park system areas by: state, affiliated areas, wild and scenic rivers system, national trail system. Alphabetical list/index, photos, maps.

"The National Parks: Camping Guide." 115 pages. Safety and regulations, planning tips. A by-state description, charts of sites. Alphabetical list/index, photos, maps.

"The National Parks: Lesser-Known Areas." 50 pages. Preparing for a park visit, maps. Areas that are less familiar to the average traveler are described by state. Alphabetical index, photos.

"National Parks Visitor Facilities and Services." 98 pages. Overnight lodging and other facilities and services that concessioners provide for travelers in the national park system. Arranged alphabetically by the name of the facility. Index by state, photos. History of concessions in U.S. national parks, provisions of the 1916 National Park Service Act (30 Sta. 535) and other public laws that followed.

"Southeast National Parks and National Forests." 16-fold. Photos, map. Facilities for: Alabama, Arkansas, Florida, Georgia, Kentucky, Mississippi, North Carolina, South Carolina, Tennessee. Name of national park or national forest, address, telephone number, description. Description of the kinds of entrance fees.

Audiovisual List:

"General Films." 6 pages. Title of films arranged alphabetically. Wide variety of films such as "Smokey Bear," "Lincoln: The Kentucky Years," "Gulf Islands," "Why Man Creates," "Age of Alaska."

MATERIALS AVAILABLE IN BULK

"National Park Service Handbooks." 9 pages. Free. Most of the publications are available in bulk. Includes title, number of pages, stock number, price per 100, retail and wholesale price per copy. Order form, ordering directions. Available from: National Park Service, P.O. Box 37127, Washington, D.C. 20013.

First entry: "Abraham Lincoln in His Own Words" (64 pages). $88 per 100--stock number 024-005-00954-0. $2.25 per copy, retail-stock number 024-005-00156-5. $1.69 per copy, wholesale.

"Subject Bibliography SB-170." 1 page. Free. National Park Service folders available from the United States Government Printing Office. Includes title, description, price, format, stock number. Includes order form, ordering information. Some items sold in packets of 100 only. Request from: United States Government Printing Office, Superintendent of Documents, Washington, D.C. 20402.

First entry: "Ironmaking." Illustrates the history of iron-making technology. 1980: Folder: Ill. Sold in packages of 100 only. 1 29.2:1R 6 S/N 024-005-00787-3 $35.00.

NATIONAL PARK SERVICE POSTERS

[Available from: Superintendent of Documents, Government Printing Office, Washington, D.C. 20402-9325. (202) 783-3238.]

All posters are in full color and prices include regular domestic postage and handling. Include S/N number listed, quantity, price, title when ordering. Prices may change so please verify by calling or writing. Payment method may be: Check payable to the Superintendent of Documents; GPO Deposit Account; Visa, Choice, Mastercard credit card. To see reproductions, request "Posters Order Form" from address above.

"Glacier Bay National Monument, Alaska." 29" x 39". S/N 024-005-00667-2. $4.50.

"The Coral Reef: Virgin Islands National Park, Biscayne, Fort Jefferson, and Buck Island Reef National Monuments." 29" x 39". S/N 024-005-00751-2. $4.50.

"Atlantic Barrier Islands." 30" x 37". S/N 024-005-00965-5. $3.75.

"The Rocky Mountains." 30" x 37". S/N 024-005-00967-1. $3.75.

"Hawaii (Volcanoes)." 30" x 37". S/N 024-005-00966-3. $3.75.

ALABAMA

Horseshoe Bend
National Military Park
Route 1, Box 103
Daviston, AL   36256

Russell Cave
National Monument
Route 1, Box 175
Bridgeport, AL   35740

Tuskegee Institute
National Historic Site
P.O. Drawer 10
Tuskegee Institute, AL   36088

ALASKA

Alagnak Wild River
c/o Katmai National Park and
   Preserve
P.O. Box 7
King Salmon, AK   99613

Aniakchak
National Monument and Preserve
P.O. Box 7
King Salmon, AK   99613

Bering Land Bridge
National Preserve
P.O. Box 220
Nome, AK   99762

Cape Krusenstern
National Monument
P.O. Box 287
Kotzebue, AK   99752

Denali
National Park and Preserve
P.O. Box 9
McKinley Park, AK   99755

Gates of the Arctic
National Park and Preserve
P.O. Box 74680
Fairbanks, AK   99707

Glacier Bay
National Park and Preserve
Juneau, AK   99802
   or--in summer
Bartlett Cove
Gustavus, AK   99826

Iditarod
National Historic Trail
Alaska Region
National Park Service
2525 Gambell Street
Anchorage, AK   99503

Katmai
National Park and Preserve
P.O. Box 7
King Salmon, AK   99613

Kenai Fjords National Park
P.O. Box 1727
Seward, AK   99664

Klondike Gold Rush
National Historical Park
P.O. Box 517
Skagway, AK   99840

Kobuk Valley National Park
P.O. Box 287
Kotzebue, AK   99752

Lake Clark
National Park and Preserve
701 C St., Box 61
Anchorage, AK   99513

Noatak National Preserve
P.O. Box 287
Kotzebue, AK   99752

Sitka
National Historical Park
P.O. Box 738
Sitka, AK 99835

Wrangell-St. Elias
National Park and Preserve
P.O. Box 29
Glenn Allen, AK 99588

Yukon-Charley Rivers
National Preserve
P.O. Box 64
Eagle, AK 99738

ARIZONA

Canyon de Chelly
National Monument
P.O. Box 588
Chinle, AZ 86503

Casa Grande
National Monument
P.O. Box 518
Coolidge, AZ 85228

Chiricahua
National Monument
Dos Cabezas Star Route
Box 6500
Willcox, AZ 85643

Coronado
National Memorial
Route 1, Box 126
Hereford, AZ 85615

Fort Bowie
National Historic Site
P.O. Box 158
Bowie, AZ 85605

Glen Canyon
National Recreation Area
P.O. Box 1507
Page, AZ 86040

Grand Canyon
National Park
P.O. Box 129
Grand Canyon, AZ 86023

Hohokam Pima
National Monument
c/o Casa Grande National Monument

P.O. Box 518
Coolidge, AZ 85228

Hubbell Trading Post
National Historic Site
P.O. Box 150
Ganado, AZ 86505

Montezuma Castle
National Monument
P.O. Box 219
Camp Verde, AZ 86322

Rainbow Bridge National Monument
c/o Glen Canyon
P.O. Box 1507
Page, AZ 86040

Navajo
National Monument
HC63, Box 3
Tonalea, AZ 86044

Organ Pipe Cactus
National Monument
Route 1, Box 100
Ajo, AZ 85321

Petrified Forest
National Park
Petrified National Forest
Park, AZ 86028

Pipe Spring
National Monument
Moccasin, AZ 86022

Saguaro National Monument
Old Spanish Trail
Route 8, Box 695
Tucson, AZ 85730

Sunset Crater
National Monument
Route 3, Box 149
Flagstaff, AZ 86001

Tonto National Monument
P.O. Box 707
Roosevelt, AZ 85545

Tumacacori National Monument
P.O. Box 67
Tumacacori, AZ 85640

Tuzigoot
National Monument

P.O. Box 68
Clarkdale, AZ 86324

Walnut Canyon
National Monument
Walnut Canyon Rd.
Flagstaff, AZ 86001

Wupatki National Monument
HC 33, Box 444A
Flagstaff, AZ 86001

ARKANSAS

Arkansas Post National Memorial
Route 1, Box 16
Gillett, AR 72055

Buffalo National River
P.O. Box 1173
Harrison, AR 72601

Fort Smith
National Historic Site
P.O. Box 1406
Fort Smith, AR 72902

Hot Springs National Park
P.O. Box 1860
Hot Springs National Park, AR
  71901

Pea Ridge
National Military Park
Pea Ridge, AR 72751

CALIFORNIA

Cabrillo National Monument
P.O. Box 6670
San Diego, CA 92106

Channel Islands
National Park
1699 Anchors Way Drive
Ventura, CA 93003

Death Valley
National Monument
Death Valley, CA 92328

Devils Postpile
National Monument
c/o Sequoia and Kings
Canyon National Parks
Three Rivers, CA 93271

Eugene O'Neill
National Historic Site
c/o John Muir NHS
4202 Alhambra Ave.
Martinez, CA 94553

Fort Point
National Historic Site
P.O. Box 29333
Presidio of San Francisco, CA 94129

Golden Gate
National Recreation Area
Fort Mason
San Francisco, CA 94123

John Muir
National Historic Site
4202 Alhambra Ave.
Martinez, CA 94553

Joshua Tree National Monument
74485 National Monument Dr.
Twentynine Palms, CA 92277

Kings Canyon National Park
Three Rivers, CA 93271

Lassen Volcanic
National Park
Mineral, CA 96063

Lava Beds
National Monument
P.O. Box 867
Tulelake, CA 96134

Muir Woods
National Monument
Mill Valley, CA 94941

Pinnacles National Monument
Paicines, CA 95043

Point Reyes
National Seashore
Point Reyes, CA 94956

Redwood National Park
1111 Second St.
Crescent City, CA 95531

Santa Monica Mountains
National Recreation Area
22900 Ventura Blvd.
Suite 140
Woodland Hills, CA 91364

Sequoia National Park
Three Rivers, CA   93271

Whiskeytown-Shasta-Trinity
National Recreation Area
P.O. Box 188
Whiskeytown, CA   96095

Yosemite National Park
P.O. Box 577
Yosemite National Park, CA   95389

COLORADO

Bent's Old Fort National Historic
   Site
35110 Highway 194 East
La Junta, CO   81050

Black Canyon of the Gunnison
National Monument
P.O. Box 1648
Montrose, CO   81402

Colorado National Monument
Fruita, CO   81521

Curecanti National Recreation Area
P.O. Box 1040
Gunnison, CO   81230

Dinosaur National Monument
P.O. Box 210
Dinosaur, CO   81610

Florissant Fossil Beds
National Monument
P.O. Box 185
Florissant, CO   80816

Great Sand Dunes
National Monument
Mosca, CO   81146

Hovenweep National Monument
c/o Mesa Verda National Park
Mesa Verde National Park, CO
   81330

Mormon Pioneer
National Historic Trail
Rocky Mountain Region
National Park Service
P.O. Box 25287
Denver, CO   80225

Mesa Verde National Park

Mesa Verde National Park, CO   81330

Rocky Mountain National Park
Estes Park, CO   80517

Yucca House National Monument
c/o Mesa Verde National Park
Mesa Verde National Park, CO   81330

DISTRICT OF COLUMBIA

Constitution Gardens
c/o National Capital Region
National Park Service
1100 Ohio Drive, S.W.
Washington, D.C.   20242

Ford's Theatre
National Historic Site
511 Tenth St., N.W.
Washington, D.C.   20004

Fort Washington Park
National Capital Parks, East
1900 Anacostia Drive, S.E.
Washington, D.C.   20019

Frederick Douglass Home
1411 W St. S.E.
Washington, D.C.   20020

John F. Kennedy Center
   for the Performing Arts
National Park Service
2700 F St., N.W.
Washington, D.C.   20566

Lincoln Memorial
c/o National Capital Region
National Park Service
1100 Ohio Drive, S.W.
Washington, D.C.   20242

Lyndon Baines Johnson Memorial
Grove on the Potomac
c/o George Washington Memorial
   Parkway
Turkey Run Park
McLean, VA   22101

Mary McLeod Bethune Council House
National Historic Site
1318 Vermont Avenue, N.W.
Washington, D.C.   20005

National Capital Parks
1100 Ohio Drive, S.W.

Washington, D.C. 20242

National Mall
c/o National Capital Region
National Park Service
1100 Ohio Drive, S.W.
Washington, D.C. 20242

Old Post Office Tower
c/o National Capital Region
National Park Service
1100 Ohio Drive, S.W.
Washington, D.C. 20242

Pennsylvania Avenue National
    Historic Site
c/o Penn. Ave. Dev. Corp.
Suite 1148, 425 13th St., N.W.
Washington, D.C. 20004

Piscataway Park
National Capital Parks, East
1900 Anacostia Drive, S.E.
Washington, D.C. 20019

Potomac Heritage
National Scenic Trail
c/o National Capital Region
National Park Service
1100 Ohio Drive, S.W.
Washington, D.C. 20242

Rock Creek Park
5000 Glover Rd., N.W.
Washington, D.C. 20015

Sewall-Belmont House
National Historic Site
144 Constitution Ave. N.E.
Washington, D.C. 20002

Thomas Jefferson Memorial
c/o National Capital Region
National Park Service
1100 Ohio Drive, S.W.
Washington, D.C. 20242

Vietnam Veterans Memorial
c/o National Capital Region
National Park Service
1100 Ohio Drive, S.W.
Washington, D.C. 20242

Washington Monument
c/o National Capital Region
National Park Service
1100 Ohio Drive, S.W.
Washington, D.C. 20242

White House
c/o National Capital Region
National Park Service
1100 Ohio Drive, S.W.
Washington, D.C. 20242

FLORIDA

Big Cypress
National Preserve
Star Route, Box 110
Ochopee, FL 33943

Biscayne National Park
P.O. Box 1369
Homestead, FL 33090

Canaveral National Seashore
P.O. Box 6447
Titusville, FL 32782

Castillo de San Marcos
National Monument
1 Castillo Drive
St. Augustine, FL 32084

De Soto National Memorial
75 St. N.W.
Bradenton, FL 33529

Everglades National Park
P.O. Box 279
Homestead, FL 33030

Fort Caroline
National Memorial
12713 Fort Caroline Rd.
Jacksonville, FL 32225

Fort Jefferson
National Monument
c/o Everglades National Park
P.O. Box 279
Homestead, FL 33030

Fort Matanzas
National Monument
c/o Castillo de San Marcos
National Monument
1 Castillo Drive
St. Augustine, FL 32084

Gulf Islands
National Seashore
P.O. Box 100
Gulf Breeze, FL 32561

GEORGIA

Andersonville
National Historic Site
Andersonville, GA   31711

Chattahoochee River
National Recreation Area
1900 Northridge Rd.
Dunwoody, GA   30338

Chickamauga and Chattanooga
National Military Park
P.O. Box 2128
Fort Oglethorpe, GA   30742

Cumberland Island
National Seashore
P.O. Box 806
St. Marys, GA   31558

Fort Frederica
National Monument
Route 4, Box 286-C
St. Simons Island, GA   31522

Fort Pulaski
National Monument
P.O. Box 98
Tybee Island, GA   31328

Kennesaw Mountain
National Battlefield Park
P.O. Box 1167
Marietta, GA   30061

Martin Luther King, Jr.
National Historic Site
522 Auburn Ave., N.E.
Atlanta, GA   30312

Natchez Trace
National Scenic Trail
Southeast Region
National Park Service
Richard B. Russell Building
75 Spring Street, S.W.
Atlanta, GA   30303

Ocmulgee
National Monument
1207 Emery Highway
Macon, GA   31201

Overmountain Victory
National Historic Trail
Southeast Region
National Park Service

75 Spring Street, S.W.
Atlanta, GA   30303

GUAM

War in the Pacific
National Historical Park
P.O. Box FA
Agana, GU   96910

HAWAII

Haleakala National Park
P.O. Box 369
Makawao, HI   96768

Hawaii Volcanoes
National Park
Hawaii National Park, HI   96718

Kalaupapa
National Historical Park
c/o Pacific Area Office
National Park Service
300 Ala Moana Blvd.
Honolulu, HI   96850

Koloko-Honokohau
National Historical Park
c/o Pacific Area Office
National Park Service
300 Ala Moana Blvd.
Honolulu, HI   96850

Pu'uhonua O Honaunau
National Historical Park
P.O. Box 128
Honaunau, Kona, HI   96726

Puukohola Heiau
National Historic Site
P.O. Box 4963
Kawaihae, HI   96743

USS Arizona Memorial
c/o Pacific Area Office
National Park Service
Box 50165
Honolulu, HI   96850

IDAHO

Craters of the Moon Nat'l Monument
P.O. Box 29
Arco, ID   83213

Nez Perce
National Historical Park
P.O. Box 93
Spalding, ID   83551

Fort Scott
National Historic Site
Old Fort Blvd.
Fort Scott, KS   66701

ILLINOIS

Chicago Portage
National Historic Site
c/o Cook County Forest Preserve
Cummings Square
River Forest, IL   60305

Lincoln Home
National Historic Site
426 S. Seventh St.
Springfield, IL   62701

INDIANA

George Rogers Clark
National Historical Park
401 S. Second St.
Vincennes, IN   47591

Indiana Dunes
National Lakeshore
1100 N. Mineral Springs Rd.
Porter, IN   46304

Lincoln Boyhood
National Memorial
Lincoln City, IN   47552

IOWA

Effigy Mounds
National Monument
P.O. Box K
McGregor, IA   52157

Herbert Hoover
National Historic Site
P.O. Box 607
West Branch, IA   52358

KANSAS

Fort Larned
National Historic Site
Route 3
Larned, KS   67550

KENTUCKY

Abraham Lincoln Birthplace
National Historic Site
R.F.D. 1
Hodgenville, KY   42748

Cumberland Gap
National Historical Park
P.O. Box 840
Middlesboro, KY   40965

Mammoth Cave National Park
Mammoth Cave, KY   42259

LOUISIANA

Jean Lafitte
National Historical Park and Preserve
U.S. Customs House
423 Canal St., Room 206
New Orleans, LA   70130

MAINE

Acadia National Park
P.O. Box 177
Bar Harbor, ME   04609

Roosevelt Campobello
International Park
c/o Executive Secretary
Roosevelt Campobello
International Park Commission
P.O. Box 97
Lubec, ME   04652

Saint Croix Island
International Historic Site
c/o Acadia National Park
P.O. Box 177
Bar Harbor, ME   04609

MARIANA ISLANDS

American Memorial Park
P.O. Box 198 CHRB
Saipan, CM   96950

MARYLAND

Antietam National Battlefield
Box 158
Sharpsburg, MD   21782

Assateague Island
National Seashore
Route 2, Box 294
Berlin, MD   21811

Catoctin Mountain Park
Thurmont, MD   21788

Chesapeake and Ohio Canal
National Historical Park
Box 158
Sharpsburg, MD   21782

Clara Barton
National Historic Site
5801 Oxford Rd.
Glen Echo, MD   20812

Fort McHenry
National Monument and
   Historic Shrine
Baltimore, MD   21230

Greenbelt Park
6501 Greenbelt Rd.
Greenbelt, MD   20770

Hampton
National Historic Site
535 Hampton Lane
Towson, MD   21204

Monocacy
National Battlefield
c/o Antietam National Battlefield
Box 158
Sharpsburg, MD   21782

MASSACHUSETTS

Adams National Historic Site
135 Adams St.
Quincy, MA   02269

Boston African American
National Historic Site
Museum of Afro American History
15 State Street
Boston, MA   02109

Boston National Historical Park
Charlestown Navy Yard
Boston, MA   02129

Cape Cod National Seashore
South Wellfleet, MA   02663

Frederick Law Olmsted
National Historic Site
99 Warren St.
Brookline, MA   02146

John Fitzgerald Kennedy
National Historic Site
83 Beals St.
Brookline, MA   02146

Longfellow
National Historic Site
105 Brattle St.
Cambridge, MA   02138

Lowell
National Historical Park
P.O. Box 1098
Lowell, MA   01853

Minute Man
National Historical Park
P.O. Box 160
Concord, MA   01742

Salem Maritime
National Historic Site
Custom House
174 Derby St.
Salem, MA   01970

Saugus Iron Works
National Historic Site
244 Central St.
Saugus, MA   01906

Springfield Armory
National Historic Site
1 Armory Square
Springfield, MA   01105

MICHIGAN

Father Marquette
National Memorial
Parks Division
Michigan Department of Natural
   Resources
P.O. Box 30028
Lansing, MI   48909

Isle Royale National Park
87 North Ripley St.
Houghton, MI   49931

Pictured Rocks
National Lakeshore
P.O. Box 40
Munising, MI   49862

Sleeping Bear Dunes
National Lakeshore
400 Main St.
Frankfort, MI   49635

MINNESOTA

Grand Portage
National Monument
P.O. Box 666
Grand Marais, MN   55604

Pipestone National Monument
P.O. Box 727
Pipestone, MN   56164

Voyageurs National Park
P.O. Box 50
International Falls, MN   56649

MISSISSIPPI

Brices Cross Roads
National Battlefield Site
c/o Natchez Trace Parkway
R.R. I, NT-143
Tupelo, MS   38801

Gulf Islands
National Seashore
3500 Park Rd.
Ocean Springs, MS   39564

Natchez Trace Parkway
R.R. 1, NT-143
Tupelo, MS   38801

Tupelo National Battlefield
c/o Natchez Trace Parkway
R.R. 1, NT-143
Tupelo, MS   38801

Vicksburg
National Military Park
3201 Clay St.
Vicksburg, MS   39180

MISSOURI

George Washington Carver
National Monument
P.O. Box 38
Diamond, MO   64840

Harry S Truman
National Historic Site
P.O. Box 4139
Independence, MO   64075

Jefferson National
Expansion Memorial
National Historic Site
11 North 4th St.
St. Louis, MO   63102

Ozark National
Scenic Riverways
P.O. Box 490
Van Buren, MO   63965

Wilson's Creek
National Battlefield
Postal Drawer C
Republic, MO   65738

MONTANA

Big Hole
National Battlefield
P.O. Box 237
Wisdom, MT   59761

Bighorn Canyon
National Recreation Area
P.O. Box 458
Fort Smith, MT   59035

Custer Battlefield
National Monument
P.O. Box 39
Crow Agency, MT   59022

Glacier National Park
West Glacier, MT   59936

Grant-Kohrs Ranch
National Historic Site
P.O. Box 790
Deer Lodge, MT   59722

NEBRASKA

Agate Fossil Beds
National Monument
P.O. Box 427
Gering, NE 69341

Chimney Rock
National Historic Site
c/o Scotts Bluff National Monument
P.O. Box 427
Gering, NE 69341

Homestead National
Monument of America
Route 3
Beatrice, NE 68310

Ice Age National Scenic Trail
Midwest Region
National Park Service
1709 Jackson Street
Omaha, NE 68102

Illinois and Michigan Canal
National Heritage Corridor
c/o Midwest Region
National Park Service
1709 Jackson Street
Omaha, NE 68102

Lewis and Clark
National Historic Trail
Midwest Region
National Park Service
1709 Jackson Street
Omaha, NE 68102

Missouri National
Recreational River
c/o Midwest Region
1709 Jackson St.
Omaha, NE 68102

North Country
National Scenic Trail
Midwest Region
National Park Service
1709 Jackson Street
Omaha, NE 68102

Scotts Bluff
National Monument
P.O. Box 427
Gering, NE 69341

NEVADA

Lake Mead National Recreation Area
601 Nevada Highway
Boulder City, NV 89005

Lehman Caves
National Monument
Baker, NV 89311

NEW HAMPSHIRE

Saint-Gaudens
National Historic Site
R.R. #2
Cornish, NH 03745

NEW JERSEY

Edison National Historic Site
Main St. and Lakeside Ave.
West Orange, NJ 07052

Morristown National Historical Park
Washington Place
Morristown, NJ 07960

NEW MEXICO

Aztec Ruins
National Monument
P.O. Box U
Aztec, NM 87410

Bandelier
National Monument
Los Alamos, NM 87544

Capulin Mountain
National Monument
Capulin, NM 88414

Carlsbad Caverns
National Park
3225 National Parks Hwy.
Carlsbad, NM 88220

Chaco Culture
National Historical Park
Star Route 4, Box 6500
Bloomfield, NM 87413

El Morro
National Monument
Ramah, NM 87321

Fort Union
National Monument
Watrous, NM 87753

Gila Cliff Dwellings
National Monument
Route 11, Box 100
Silver City, NM 88061

Pecos National Monument
P.O. Drawer 11
Pecos, NM 87552

Salinas National Monument
Box 496
Mountainair, NM 87036

White Sands
National Monument
P.O. Box 458
Alamogordo, NM 88310

NEW YORK

Castle Clinton
National Monument
Manhattan Sites
National Park Service
26 Wall St.
New York, NY 10005

Eleanor Roosevelt
National Historic Site
249 Albany Post Rd.
Bellfield Hq.
Hyde Park, NY 12538

Federal Hall National Memorial
Manhattan Sites
National Park Service
26 Wall St.
New York, NY 10005

Fire Island
National Seashore
120 Laurel St.
Patchogue, NY 11772

Fort Stanwix
National Monument
112 E. Park St.
Rome, NY 13440

Gateway National Recreation Area
Floyd Bennett Field, Bldg. 69
Brooklyn, NY 11234

General Grant National Memorial
Manhattan Sites
National Park Service
26 Wall St.
New York, NY 10005

Hamilton Grange
National Memorial
287 Convent Ave.
New York, NY 10031

Home of Franklin D. Roosevelt
National Historic Site
249 Albany Post Rd.
Bellfield Hq.
Hyde Park, NY 12538

Martin Van Buren
National Historic Site
Route 9H
P.O. Box 545
Kinderhook, NY 12106

Sagamore Hill
National Historic Site
Cove Neck Rd., Box 304
Oyster Bay, NY 11771

Saint Paul's Church
National Historic Site
897 South Columbus Avenue
Mount Vernon, NY 10550

Saratoga National Historical Park
R.D. 2, Box 33
Stillwater, NY 12170

Statue of Liberty
National Monument
Liberty Island
New York, NY 10004

Theodore Roosevelt Birthplace
National Historic Site
28 E. 20th St.
New York, NY 10003

Theodore Roosevelt Inaugural
National Historic Site
641 Delaware Ave.
Buffalo, NY 14202

Vanderbilt Mansion
National Historic Site
249 Albany Post Rd.
Bellfield Hq.
Hyde Park, NY 12538

Women's Rights
National Historical Park
P.O. Box 70
Seneca Falls, NY   13148

NORTH CAROLINA

Blue Ridge Parkway
700 Northwestern Bank Bldg.
Asheville, NC   28801

Cape Hatteras
National Seashore
Route 1, Box 675
Manteo, NC   27954

Cape Lookout
National Seashore
P.O. Box 690
Beaufort, NC   28516

Carl Sandburg Home
National Historic Site
P.O. Box 395
Flat Rock, NC   28731

Fort Raleigh
National Historic Site
c/o Cape Hatteras National Seashore
Route 1, Box 675
Manteo, NC   27954

Guilford Courthouse
National Military Park
P.O. Box 9806
Greensboro, NC   27429

Kings Mountain
National Military Park
P.O. Box 31
Kings Mountain, NC   28086
(Located in South Carolina)

Moores Creek
National Battlefield
P.O. Box 69
Currie, NC   28435

Wright Brothers
National Memorial
c/o Cape Hatteras National Seashore
Route 1, Box 675
Manteo, NC   27954

NORTH DAKOTA

Fort Union Trading Post
National Historic Site
Williston, ND   58801

International Peace Garden
P.O. Box 419
Dunseith, ND   58637

Knife River Indian Villages
National Historic Site
R.R. 1, Box 168
Stanton, ND   58571

Theodore Roosevelt
National Park
Medora, ND   58645

OHIO

Cuyahoga Valley
National Recreation Area
15610 Vaughn Rd.
Brecksville, OH   44141

David Berger
National Memorial
Jewish Community Center
   of Cleveland
3505 Mayfield Road
Cleveland Heights, OH   44118

James A. Garfield
National Historic Site
Lawnfield
8095 Mentor Ave.
Mentor, OH   44060

Mound City Group
National Monument
16062 State Route 104
Chillicothe, OH   45601

Perry's Victory and
International Peace Memorial
P.O. Box 549
Put-in-Bay, OH   43456

William Howard Taft
National Historic Site
2038 Auburn Ave.
Cincinnati, OH   45219

OKLAHOMA

Chicasaw
National Recreation Area
P.O. Box 201
Sulphur, OK   73086

OREGON

Crater Lake
National Park
P.O. Box 7
Crater Lake, OR   97604

Fort Clatsop
National Memorial
Route 3, Box 604-FC
Astoria, OR   97103

John Day Fossil Beds
National Monument
420 W. Main St.
John Day, OR   97845

McLoughlin House
National Historic Site
Oregon City, OR   97045

Oregon Caves
National Monument
19000 Caves Highway
Cave Junction, OR   97523

PENNSYLVANIA

Allegheny Portage Railroad
National Historic Site
P.O. Box 247
Cresson, PA   16630

Benjamin Franklin
National Memorial
The Franklin Institute
20th and Benjamin Franklin Parkway
Philadelphia, PA   19103

Delaware
National Scenic River
c/o Delaware Water Gap
National Recreation Area
Bushkill, PA   18324

Edgar Allan Poe
National Historic Site
c/o Independence National

Historical Park
313 Walnut St.
Philadelphia, PA   19106

Eisenhower
National Historic Site
c/o Gettysburg National Military Park
Gettysburg, PA   17325

Fort Necessity
National Battlefield
R.D. 2, Box 528
Farmington, PA   15437

Friendship Hill
National Historic Site
R.D. 2, Box 528
Farmington, PA   15437

Gettysburg National Military Park
Gettysburg, PA   17325

Gloria Dei (Old Swedes') Church
National Historic Site
Delaware Avenue and Christian Street
Philadelphia, PA   19106

Hopewell Furnace
National Historic Site
R.D. 1, Box 345
Elverson, PA   19520

Independence National Historical Park
313 Walnut St.
Philadelphia, PA   19106

Johnstown Flood
National Memorial
c/o Allegheny Portage
Railroad National Historic Site
P.O. Box 247
Cresson, PA   16630

Pinelands Natural Reserve
c/o Mid-Atlantic Region
National Park Service
143 S. Third Street
Philadelphia, PA   19106

Thaddeus Kosciuszko
National Memorial
c/o Independence National Historical
  Park
313 Walnut St.
Philadelphia, PA   19106

Valley Forge
National Historical Park
Valley Forge, PA   19481

PUERTO RICO

San Juan
National Historic Site
P.O. Box 712
Old San Juan, PR   00902

RHODE ISLAND

Roger Williams National Memorial
P.O. Box 367
Annex Station
Providence, RI   02901

Touro Synagogue
National Historic Site
85 Touro Street
Newport, RI   02840
(Place of Worship)

SOUTH CAROLINA
Congaree Swamp
National Monument
P.O. Box 11938
Columbia, SC   29211

Cowpens National
Battlefield
P.O. Box 308
Chesnee, SC   29323

Fort Sumter
National Monument
1214 Middle St.
Sullivans Island, SC   29482

Historic Camden
Camden District Heritage Foundation
Camden Historical Commission
Box 710
Camden, SC   29020

Kings Mountain
National Military Park
P.O. Box 31
Kings Mountain, NC   28086
(Located in South Carolina)

Ninety Six
National Historic Site

P.O. Box 496
Ninety Six, SC   29666

SOUTH DAKOTA

Badlands National Park
P.O. Box 6
Interior, SD   57750

Jewel Cave
National Monument
P.O. Box 351
Custer, SD   57730

Mount Rushmore
National Memorial
Keystone, SD   57751

Wind Cave National Park
Hot Springs, SD   57747

TENNESSEE

Andrew Johnson
National Historic Site
Depot St.
Greeneville, TN   37744

Big South Fort National River
    and Recreation Area
P.O. Drawer 630
Oneida, TN   37841

Fort Donelson
National Military Park
P.O. Box F
Dover, TN   37058

Great Smokey Mountains
National Park
Gatlinburg, TN   37738

Obed Wild and Scenic River
P.O. Drawer 630
Oneida, TN   37841

Shiloh
National Military Park
Shiloh, TN   38376

Stones River
National Battlefield
Route 10, Box 495
Old Nashville Hwy.
Murfreesboro, TN   37130

TEXAS

Alibates Flint Quarries
National Monument
c/o Lake Meredith
Recreation Area
P.O. Box 1438
Fritch, TX   79036

Amistad
National Recreation Area
P.O. Box 420367
Del Rio, TX   78842

Big Bend National Park
Big Bend National Park, TX   79834

Big Thicket
National Preserve
P.O. Box 7408
Beaumont, TX   77706

Chamizal National Memorial
P.O. Box 722
El Paso, TX   79944

Fort Davis
National Historic Site
P.O. Box 1456
Fort Davis, TX   79734

Guadalupe Mountains
National Park
3225 National Park Hwy.
Carlsbad, NM   88220

Lake Meredith
Recreation Area
P.O. Box 1438
Fritch, TX   79036

Lyndon B. Johnson
National Historical Park
P.O. Box 329
Johnson City, TX   78636

Padre Island
National Seashore
9405 S. Padre Island Dr.
Corpus Christi, TX   78418

Palo Alto Battlefield
National Historic Site
P.O. Box 191
Brownsville, TX   78520

Rio Grande
Wild and Scenic River
c/o Big Bend National Park
Big Bend National Park, TX   79834

San Antonio Missions
National Historical Park
727 E. Durango Blvd.
San Antonio, TX   78206

UTAH

Arches National Park
Moab, UT   84532

Bryce Canyon National Park
Bryce Canyon, UT   84717

Canyonlands National Park
Moab, UT   84532

Capitol Reef National Park
Torrey, UT   84775

Cedar Breaks
National Monument
P.O. Box 749
Cedar City, UT   84720

Golden Spike
National Historic Site
P.O. Box W
Brigham City, UT   84302

Natural Bridges
National Monument
c/o Canyonlands
National Park
Moab, UT   84532

Timpanogos Cave
National Monument
R.R. 3, Box 200
American Fork, UT   84003

Zion National Park
Springdale, UT   84767

VIRGINIA

Appomattox Court House
National Historical Park
P.O. Box 218
Appomattox, VA   24522

Arlington House,
The Robert E. Lee Memorial
c/o George Washington
Memorial Parkway
Turkey Run Park
McLean, VA   22101

Booker T. Washington
National Monument
Route 1, Box 195
Hardy, VA   24101

Colonial National Historical Park
P.O. Box 210
Yorktown, VA   23690

Fredericksburg and Spotsylvania
   County Battlefields Memorial
National Military Park
P.O. Box 679
Fredericksburg, VA   22404

George Washington Birthplace
National Monument
Washington's Birthplace, VA   22575

George Washington
Memorial Parkway
Turkey Run Park
McLean, VA   22101

Green Springs
Historic District
c/o Fredericksburg and
   Spotsylvania County
   Battlefields Memorial
   National Military Park
P.O. Box 679
Fredericksburg, VA   22404

Jamestown
National Historic Site
c/o Association for the
   Preservation of Virginia
   Antiquities
John Marshall House
2705 Park Avenue
Richmond, VA   23220

Maggie L. Walker
National Historic Site
c/o Richmond National Battlefield
   Park
3215 E. Broad St.
Richmond, VA   23223

Manassas National
Battlefield Park
P.O. Box 1830
Manassas, VA   22110

Petersburg
National Battlefield
P.O. Box 549
Petersburg, VA   23803

Prince William Forest Park
P.O. Box 209
Triangle, VA   22172

Richmond National
Battlefield Park
3215 East Broad St.
Richmond, VA   23223

Shenandoah National Park
Route 4, Box 292
Lurray, VA   22835

Thomas Stone
National Historic Site
c/o George Washington Birthplace
National Monument
Washington's Birthplace, VA   22575

Theodore Roosevelt Island
c/o George Washington Memorial
   Parkway
Turkey Run Park
McLean, VA   22101

Wolf Trap Farm Park
   for the Performing Arts
1551 Trap Rd.
Vienna, VA   22180

VIRGIN ISLANDS

Buck Island Reef
National Monument
Box 160
Christiansted
St. Croix, VI   00820

Virgin Islands National Park
P.O. Box 7789
Charlotte Amalie
St. Thomas, VI   00801

WASHINGTON

Coulee Dam
National Recreation Area
P.O. Box 37
Coulee Dam, WA 99116

Ebey's Landing
National Historical Reserve
c/o Pacific Northwest Region
National Park Service
83 South King Street, Suite 211
Seattle, WA 98104

Fort Vancouver
National Historic Site
Vancouver, WA 98661

Klondike Gold Rush
National Historical Park
117 South Main St.
Seattle, WA 98104

Lake Chelan
National Recreation Area
800 State St.
Sedro Wooley, WA 98284

Mount Ranier
National Park
Tahoma Woods
Star Route
Ashford, WA 98304

North Cascades
National Park
800 State St.
Sedro Woolley, WA 98284

Olympic National Park
600 East Park Ave.
Port Angeles, WA 98362

Oregon
National Historic Trail
Pacific Northwest Region
National Park Service
83 South King Street
Suite 211
Seattle, WA 98104

Ross Lake
National Recreation Area
800 State St.
Sedro Woolley, WA 98284

San Juan Island
National Historical Park

P.O. Box 429
Friday Harbor, WA 98250

Whitman Mission
National Historic Site
Route 2, Box 247
Walla Walla, WA 99362

WEST VIRGINIA

Appalachian
National Scenic Trail
P.O. Box 236
Harpers Ferry, WV 25425

Harpers Ferry
National Historical Park
P.O. Box 65
Harpers Ferry, WV 25425

New River Gorge
National River
P.O. Drawer V
Oak Hill, WV 25901

WISCONSIN

Apostle Islands
National Lakeshore
Route 1, Box 4
Bayfield, WI 54814

Ice Age
National Scientific Reserve
Wisconsin Department of
   Natural Resources
Box 7921
Madison, WI 53707

Lower Saint Croix
National Scenic Riverway
c/o Saint Croix National
   Scenic Riverway
P.O. Box 708
St. Croix Falls, WI 54024

Saint Croix
National Scenic Riverway
P.O. Box 708
Saint Croix Falls, WI 54024

WYOMING

Devils Tower
National Monument

Devils Tower, WY   82714

Fort Laramie
National Historic Site
Fort Laramie, WY   82212

Fossil Butte
National Monument
P.O. Box 527
Kemerer, WY   83101

Grand Teton National Park
P.O. Drawer 170
Moose, WY   83012

John D. Rockefeller, Jr.
Memorial Parkway
c/o Grand Teton National Park
P.O. Drawer 170
Moose, WY   83012

Yellowstone National Park
P.O. Box 168
Yellowstone National Park, WY   82190

NATIONAL PARK SYSTEM ARRANGED BY CLASSIFICATION

NATIONAL PARKS

Acadia
Arches
Badlands
Big Bend
Biscayne
Bryce Canyon
Canyonlands
Capitol Reef
Carlsbad Caverns
Channel Islands
Crater Lake
Denali National Park and Preserve
Everglades
Gates of the Arctic National Park
    and Preserve
Glacier
Glacier Bay National Park and
    Preserve
Grand Canyon
Grand Teton
Great Smoky Mountains
Guadalupe Mountains
Haleakala
Hawaii Volcanoes
Hot Springs
Isle Royale
Katmai National Park and Preserve
Kenai Fjords
Kings Canyon
Kobuk Valley
Lake Clark National Park and
    Preserve
Lassen Volcanic
Mammoth Cave
Mesa Verde
Mount Rainier
North Cascades
Olympic
Petrified Forest
Redwood
Rocky Mountain
Sequoia
Shenandoah
Theodore Roosevelt
Virgin Islands
Voyageurs
Wind Cave
Wrangell-St. Elias
Yellowstone
Yosemite
Zion

NATIONAL HISTORICAL PARKS

Appomattox Court House
Boston
Chaco Culture
Chesapeake and Ohio Canal
Colonial
Cumberland Gap
George Rogers Clark
Harpers Ferry
Independence
Jean Lafitte
Kalaupapa
Kaloko-Honokohau
Klondike Gold Rush
Lowell
Lyndon B. Johnson
Minute Man
Morristown
Nez Perce
Pu'uhonua O Honaunau
San Antonio Missions
San Juan Island
Saratoga
Sitka
Valley Forge
War in the Pacific
Women's Rights

NATIONAL BATTLEFIELDS

Antietam
Big Hole
Cowpens
Fort Necessity
Monocacy
Moores Creek

NATIONAL BATTLEFIELDS (cont.)

Petersburg
Stones River
Tupelo
Wilson's Creek

NATIONAL BATTLEFIELD PARKS

Kennesaw Mountain
Manassas
Richmond

NATIONAL BATTLEFIELD SITE

Brices Cross Roads

NATIONAL MILITARY PARKS

Chickamauga and Chattanooga
Fort Donelson
Fredericksburg and Spotsylvania
    County Battlefields Memorial
Gettysburg
Guilford Courthouse
Horseshoe Bend
Kings Mountain
Pea Ridge
Shiloh
Vicksburg

NATIONAL MEMORIALS

Arkansas Post
Arlington House
Chamizal
Coronado
De Soto
Federal Hall
Fort Caroline
Fort Clatsop
General Grant
Hamilton Grange
John F. Kennedy Center
    for the Performing Arts
Johnstown Flood
Lincoln Boyhood
Lincoln Memorial
Lyndon Baines Johnson Grove
    on the Potomac
Mount Rushmore
Roger Williams
Thaddeus Kosciuszko
Theodore Roosevelt Island

Thomas Jefferson
USS Arizona
Washington Monument
Wright Brothers

NATIONAL HISTORIC SITES

Abraham Lincoln Birthplace
Adams
Allegheny Portage Railroad
Andersonville
Andrew Johnson
Bent's Old Fort
Carl Sandburg Home
Christiansted
Clara Barton
Edgar Allan Poe
Edison
Eisenhower
Eleanor Roosevelt
Eugene O'Neill
Ford's Theatre
Fort Bowie
Fort Davis
Fort Laramie
Fort Larned
Fort Point
Fort Raleigh
Fort Scott
Fort Smith
Fort Union Trading Post
Fort Vancouver
Frederick Law Olmsted
Friendship Hill
Golden Spike
Grant-Kohrs Ranch
Hampton
Harry S Truman
Herbert Hoover
Home of Franklin D. Roosevelt
Hopewell Village
Hubbell Trading Post
James A. Garfield
Jefferson National Expansion Memorial
John Fitzgerald Kennedy
John Muir
Knife River Indian Villages
Lincoln Home
Longfellow
Maggie L. Walker
Martin Luther King, Jr.
Martin Van Buren
Ninety Six
Palo Alto Battlefield
Puukohola Heiau
Sagamore Hill

NATIONAL HISTORIC SITES (cont.)

Saint-Gaudens
Salem Maritime
San Juan
Saugus Iron Works
Sewall-Belmont House
Springfield Armory
Theodore Roosevelt Birthplace
Theodore Roosevelt Inaugural
Thomas Stone
Tuskegee Institute
Vanderbilt Mansion
Whitman Mission
William Howard Taft

NATIONAL MONUMENTS

Agate Fossil Beds
Alibates Flint Quarries
Aniakchak
Aztec Ruins
Bandelier
Black Canyon of the Gunnison
Booker T. Washington
Buck Island Reef
Cabrillo
Canyon de Chelly
Cape Krusenstern
Capulin Mountain
Casa Grande Ruins
Castillo de San Marcos
Castle Clinton
Cedar Breaks
Chiricahua
Colorado
Congaree Swamp
Craters of the Moon
Custer Battlefield
Death Valley
Devils Postpile
Devils Tower
Dinosaur
Effigy Mounds
El Morro
Florissant Fossil Beds
Fort Frederica
Fort Jefferson
Fort Matanzas
Fort McHenry National Monument
  and Historic Shrine
Fort Pulaski
Fort Stanwix
Fort Sumter
Fort Union
Fossil Butte

George Washington Birthplace
George Washington Carver
Gila Cliff Dwellings
Grand Portage
Great Sand Dunes
Hohokam Pima
Homestead National Monument
  of America
Hovenweep
Jewel Cave
John Day Fossil Beds
Joshua Tree
Lava Beds
Lehman Caves
Montezuma Castle
Mound City Group
Muir Woods
Natural Bridges
Navajo
Ocmulgee
Oregon Caves
Organ Pipe Cactus
Pecos
Pinnacles
Pipe Spring
Pipestone
Rainbow Bridge
Russell Cave
Saguaro
Salinas
Scotts Bluff
Statue of Liberty
Sunset Crater
Timpanogos Cave
Tonto
Tumacacori
Tuzigoot
Walnut Canyon
White Sands
Wupatki
Yucca House

NATIONAL PRESERVES

Aniakchak
Bering Land Bridge
Big Cypress
Big Thicket
Denali
Gates of the Arctic
Glacier Bay
Katmai
Lake Clark
Noatak
Wrangell-St. Elias
Yukon-Charley Rivers

NATIONAL SEASHORES

Assateague Island
Canaveral
Cape Cod
Cape Hatteras
Cape Lookout
Cumberland Island
Fire Island
Gulf Islands
Padre Island
Point Reyes

NATIONAL PARKWAYS

Blue Ridge
George Washington Memorial
John D. Rockefeller, Jr., Memorial
Natchez Trace

NATIONAL LAKESHORES

Apostle Islands
Indiana Dunes
Pictured Rocks
Sleeping Bear Dunes

NATIONAL RIVERS

Alagnak Wild River
Big South Fork
Buffalo

NATIONAL SCENIC RIVERS AND RIVERWAYS

Delaware
Lower Saint Croix
Missouri
Obed
Ozark
Rio Grande
Saint Croix
Upper Delaware

PARKS

Catoctin Mountain
Constitution Gardens
Fort Washington
Frederick Douglass Home

Greenbelt
Perry's Victory and International
    Peace Memorial
Piscataway
Prince William Forest
Rock Creek
Vietnam Veterans
Wolf Trap Farm for the Performing
    Arts

NATIONAL RECREATION AREAS

Amistad
Bighorn Canyon
Chattahoochee River
Chickasaw
Coulee Dam
Curecanti
Cuyahoga Valley
Delaware Water Gap
Gateway
Glen Canyon
Golden Gate
Lake Chelan
Lake Mead
Lake Meredith
Ross Lake
Santa Monica Mountains
Whiskeytown-Shasta-Trinity

NATIONAL SCENIC TRAILS
(those with National Park addresses)

Appalachian National Scenic Trail
Ice Age National Scenic Trail
Iditarod National Historic Trail
Lewis and Clark National Historic Trail
Mormon Pioneer National Historic Trail
Natchez Trace National Historic Trail
North Country National Scenic Trail
Oregon National Historic Trail
Overmountain Victory National
    Historic Trail
Potomac Heritage National Scenic Trail

AFFILIATED AREAS

American Memorial Park
Benjamin Franklin National Memorial
Boston African American National
    Historic Site
Chicago Portage National Historic Site
Chimney Rock National Historic Site
David Berger National Memorial

AFFILIATED AREAS (cont.)

Ebey's Landing National Historic
  Reserve
Father Marquette National Memorial
Gloria Dei (Old Swedes') Church
  National Historic Site
Green Springs Historic District
Historic Camden
Ice Age National Scientific Reserve
Illinois and Michigan Canal National
  Heritage Corridor
International Peace Garden
Jamestown National Historic Site
Mary McLeod Bethune Council
  House National Historic Site
McLoughlin House National Historic
  Site
Old Post Office Tower
Pennsylvania Avenue National Site
Pinelands National Reserve
Roosevelt Campobello International
  Park
Saint Paul's Church National
  Historic Site
Touro Synagogue National Historic
  Site

INTERNATIONAL HISTORIC SITE

Perry's Victory and International
  Peace Memorial
Saint Croix Island

NATIONAL CAPITAL PARKS

National Mall
White House

FACILITIES NOT INCLUDED
IN THIS GUIDE

NATIONAL SCENIC TRAILS

Continental Divide
Florida
Pacific Crest
[U.S. Forest Service, Box 2417,
  Washington, D.C.   20013]

WILD AND SCENIC RIVERS

Alatna [Gates of the Arctic National
  Park and Preserve, P.O. Box
  74680, Fairbanks, AK   99707]
Allagash Wilderness Waterway [Bureau
  of Parks and Recreation, Augusta,
  ME   04333]
American River, North Fork [Tahoe
  National Forest, Highway 49,
  Nevada City, CA   95959]
Andreafsky River [U.S. Fish and
  Wildlife Service, 1011 East Tudor
  Road, Anchorage, AK   99503]
Aniakchak Wild River [Katmai National
  Park and Preserve, P.O. Box 7,
  King Salmon, AK   99613]
Au Sable River [Huron-Manistee
  National Forest, 421 S. Mitchell,
  Cadillac, MI   49601]
Beaver Creek [U.S. Bureau of Land
  Management, 555 Cordova Street,
  Anchorage, AK   99501]
Birch Creek [U.S. Bureau of Land
  Management, 555 Cordova Street,
  Anchorage, AK   99501]
Charley Wild River [Yukon-Charley
  Rivers, National Preserve, P.O.
  Box 64, Eagle, AK   99738]
Chattooga River [Chattahoochee
  National Forest, P.O. Box 1437,
  Gainesville, GA   30501]
Chilikadrotna Wild River [Lake Clark
  National Park, 701 C Street,
  Box 61, Anchorage, AK   99513]
Clearwater River, Middle Fork
  [Clearwater National Forest,
  Route 4, Orofino, ID   83544]
Delta River [U.S. Bureau of Land
  Management, 555 Cordova Street,
  Anchorage, AK   99501]
Eel River [California Resources
  Agency, 1416 Ninth Street,
  Sacramento, CA   95814; U.S.
  Forest Service, 630 Sansome
  Street, San Francisco, CA   94111;
  U.S. Bureau of Land Management,
  28 Cottage Way, Sacramento, CA
  95825]
Eleven Point River [Mark Twain
  National Forest, 401 Fairgrounds
  Road, Rolla, MO   65401]
Feather River, Middle Fork [Plumas
  National Forest, P.O. Box 1500
  Quincy, CA   95971]
Flathead River [Flathead National
  Forest, P. O. Box 147, Kalispell,

WILD AND SCENIC RIVERS (cont.)

MT 59901]

Fortymile River [U.S. Bureau of Land Management, 555 Cordova Street, Anchorage, AK 99501]

Gulkana River [U.S. Bureau of Land Management, 555 Cordova Street, Anchorage, AK 99501]

Ivishak River [U.S. Fish and Wildlife Service, 1011 East Tudor Road, Anchorage, AK 99503]

John Wild River [Gates of the Arctic, National Park and Preserve, P.O. Box 74680, Fairbanks, AK 99707]

Klamath River [California Resources Agency, 1416 Ninth Street, Sacramento, CA 95814; U.S. Forest Service, 630 Sansome Street, San Francisco, CA 94111]

Kobuk Wild River [Gates of the Arctic, National Park and Preserve, P.O. Box 74680, Fairbanks, AK 99707]

Little Beaver Creek [Ohio Department of Natural Resources, Division of Natural Areas and Preserves, Fountain Square, Columbus, OH 43224]

Little Miami River [Ohio Department of Natural Resources, Division of Natural Areas and Preserves, Fountain Square, Columbus, OH 43224]

Lower American River [California Resources Agency, 1416 Ninth Street, Sacramento, CA 95814]

Lower Saint Croix Riverway [Minnesota Department of Natural Resources Centennial Office Building, St. Paul, MN 55155; Wisconsin Department of Natural Resources, P.O. Box 450, Madison, WI 53701]

Missouri River [U.S. Bureau of Land Management, P.O. Box 30157, Billings, MT 59107]

Mulchatna Wild River [Lake Clark National Park and Preserve, 701 C Street, Box 61, Anchorage, AK 99513]

New River, South Fork [Stone Mountain State Park, Star Route, Box 17, Roaring Gap, NC 28668]

Noatak Wild River [Gates of the Arctic, National Park and Preserve, P.O. Box 74680, Fairbanks, AK 99707; Kobuk Valley National Park, P.O. Box 287, Kotzebue, AK 99752]

North Fork of the Koyukuk Wild River [Gates of the Arctic National Park and Preserve, P.O. Box 74680, Fairbanks, AK 99707]

Nowitna River [U.S. Fish and Wildlife Service, 1011 East Tudor Road, Anchorage, AK 99503]

Owyhee River [U.S. Bureau of Land Management, P.O. Box 2965, Portland, OR 97208]

Pere Marquette River [Huron-Manistee National Forest, 421 S. Mitchell Street, Cadillac, MI 49601]

Rapid River [Hells Canyon National Recreation Area, P.O. Box 907, Baker, OR 97814]

Rio Grande [U.S. Bureau of Land Management, P.O. Box 1449, Santa Fe, NM 87501]

Rogue River [U.S. Bureau of Land Management, P.O. Box 2965, Portland, OR 97208]

Saint Joe River [Idaho Panhandle National Forest, P.O. Box 310, Coeur D'Alene, ID 83814]

Salmon River, Middle Fork [Challis National Forest, Forest Service Building, Challis, ID 83226]

Salmon River [Salmon National Forest, Forest Service Bldg., Salmon, ID 83467]

Salmon Wild River [Kobuk Valley National Park, P.O. Box 287, Kotzebue, AK 99752]

Selawik River [U.S. Fish and Wildlife Service, 1011 East Tudor Road, Anchorage, AK 99503]

Skagit River [Mount Baker-Snoqualmie National Forest, 1601 Second Avenue Building, Seattle, WA 98101]

Smith River [California Resources Agency, 1416 Ninth Street, Sacramento, CA 95814; U.S. Forest Service, 630 Sansome Street, San Francisco, CA 94111]

Snake River [Hells Canyon, National Recreation Area, P.O. Box 907, Baker, OR 97814]

WILD AND SCENIC RIVERS (cont.)

Tinayguk Wild River [Gates of the
    Arctic, National Park and
    Preserve, P.O. Box 74680,
    Fairbanks, AK   99707]
Tikakila Wild River [Lake Clark
    National Park and Preserve,
    701 C Street, Box 61,
    Anchorage, AK   99513]
Trinity River [California Resources
    Agency, 1416 Ninth Street,
    Sacramento, CA   95814; U.S.
    Forest Service, 630 Sansome
    Street, San Francisco, CA   94111]
Tuolumne River [Stanislaus National
    Forest, 19777 Greenley Road,
    Sonora, CA   95370; National
    Park Service, Yosemite National
    Park, P.O. Box 577, Yosemite
    National Park, CA   95389]
Unalakleet River [U.S. Bureau of
    Land Management, 555 Cordova
    Street, Anchorage, AK   99501]
Verde River [Prescott National
    Forest, P.O. Box 2549, Prescott,
    AZ   86302]
Wind River [U.S. Fish and Wildlife
    Service, 1011 East Tudor Road
    Anchorage, AK   99503]
Wolf River [Menominee Restoration
    Committee, P.O. Box 397,
    Keshena, WI   54135]

INDEX OF FACILITIES BY TITLE